Also by Dan Browning

The Cube:
Detailed Design Spec for a 3D Volumetric Solid State Display Device

Project V

A Tour of the Voxel Factory

Vesta Imprints
San Francisco

Project V
A Tour of the Voxel Factory

Published by Vesta Imprints, San Francisco, California, USA
ISBN: 9781734796230

First printing September 2022

This book is an overview of software written by the author in 2014.

Table of Contents

Part One

Project V: A Tour of the Voxel Factory
PART ONE: Voxel and Octree

1.0 *Introduction*

This book is based on voxelization software written in 2014 by the author. A "voxel" is a three-dimensional "volume element", analogous to a two-dimensional "picture element" or "pixel". Every two-dimensional screen is composed of an array of pixels. A 3D display device is composed of a volume of voxels.

During the short history of computing, starting with the first Von Neumann designs of the early 1950s, three-dimensional imaging, that is, true three-dimensional space-filled imaging and not a projection of a three-dimensional model onto a two-dimensional image plane, has remained out of reach because computers have not been fast enough.

It's a two-sided story: hardware and software. On the hardware side, no one has been able to design a volumetric display because the circuitry gets in the way of the display volume. One solution is to blur the circuitry by quickly rotating a display armature, but the viewer still sees a blurry ghost with a post through the middle. My book *The Cube*, available on Amazon, describes a solid state solution with no moving parts. Still, technology has not quite caught up with the design. Nanotechnology and invisibility need to evolve just a bit more.

The software side of the story is just as complex as the display hardware. The hardware is all about speed and parallelism; the software is also very much concerned with speed since hundreds of thousands of voxels are typically computed for a single image. As well, the software brings in algorithms and mathematics. The inherent complexity of the software, combined with the speed requirements of the hardware display, are the main reasons a true 3D display device hasn't yet been developed.

But all of that is changing with the advent of nanotechnology and fast processors. This book is about the software side of the story: not the software that drives the hardware; rather the software that will be needed to generate a voxel image in the first place. Getting those voxels into the display device will be a whole *other* story, some of which is hinted at in *The Cube*.

1.1 *Voxel Pipe*

"Voxel Pipe" is the solution published by NVIDIA in a paper of the same name. It's the inspiration for the software in this book. The open source classes provided by NVIDIA have been used as the starting point for voxel rendering in the special project described in this book, called Project V. "V" stands for *voxel*.

The Voxel Pipe software is concerned with rasterizing an image to a 2D image plane, so is less concerned with voxels as an end-product and more with voxels as a framework for rendering. The rasterization pipeline is divided into two stages: coarse, which divides the whole grid into relatively coarse tiles, performs triangle setup, and emits the list of all triangles overlapping each tile; and fine, which assigns each tile to a single GPU core (Project V does not use parallelism in this fashion), generates all fragments corresponding to the tile's triangles, and performs color-blending in shared memory.

The conversion of a triangle positioned in 3-space to voxels involves plane-projection techniques. There are two main flavors: "conservative" or "thick", and "thin". A thick rasterization can generate up to three times the number of voxels as a thin one. Why not just go for the thin rasterization at all times? Because sometimes a thick rasterization looks smoother than a thin one; and in general a thick rasterization takes less time to compute at lower resolutions even though there are more voxels.

In general a voxel is surrounded by 26 voxel neighbors. This makes 27 voxels total, or 3 cubed. For the voxel in the center, those 26 neighbors can be decomposed as 6 faces, 8 vertices, and 12 edges, adding up to 26. Overlap is considered for all of those geometries, which gives more opportunity for overlap because there's more to match, which means the voxelization is "thick". The full complement of comparisons is called "26-separating" (26-sep for short) or sometimes "26-connecting".

For 26-sep, the voxel is attached to the neighboring 6 voxels attached to each face; to the neighboring 12 voxels that share an edge (note that each edge is shared by 3 other voxels, but 2 of them are the face voxels already considered); and to the 8 vertex neighbors at the extreme corners of the 3 x 3 x 3 neighborhood. That makes 26 voxels plus the center voxel, or 27.

The other flavor is "6-separating" (6-sep for short), corresponding to overlap with the 6 faces only. This is comparable in 2D to the DDA algorithms associated with the Bresenham line algorithm. This results in a "thin" voxelization. There are 6 neighboring voxels and six directions that will be checked by the center voxel. Only "one of six" of those directions will be selected. Since each voxel is considered in turn, the voxelization will eventually include everything in a source-triangle's plane, called an "embedding plane", and finally will be restricted to the triangle's boundaries.

The go-to paper for 26-separating rasterization is "Fast parallel surface and solid voxelization on GPUs" by Schwarz and Seidel. That's also the source for the Voxel Pipe paper. The two papers include all of the math for triangle-voxel intersection and 26-separation rasterization. Neither paper gives an implementation for 6-sep, which turns out to be more complicated. However 6-sep has been implemented by Project V and will be presented in this book.

There are two major components of the Project V software. First, the octree subdivision algorithm; second, the ray tracing through the octree algorithm. Ray tracing is based on Andrew Glassner's ray-tracing paper "Space Subdivision for Fast Ray Tracing" (1984). That paper also presents the major ideas behind octree subdivision.

Octree subdivision is *adaptive*. This means those portions of the octree space where space becomes empty are not further subdivided. To make that decision distance computations are paramount. Project V software follows Voxel Pipe and uses a C++ template approach. The templates are written for the three planes of the Cartesian coordinate system.

Overlap tests between a triangle and a voxel are conducted in the XY, the YZ, and the XZ planes associated with the Cartesian axes. The test result will depend on the triangle normal's "dominant axis". If the normal points mostly in the z direction for example, the dominant overlap tests will be evaluated in the XY plane.

1.2 *Evaluation Algorithm*

Each voxel is associated with a list of triangles specified with pair-values (triangleID, dominantAxis), the latter referring to the triangle's normal. The software does a "gross overlap" test consisting of a bounding box range test. For each triangle of the model, which is decomposed into triangles, if the gross overlap test succeeds, the triangle is added to a compact list of triangles that overlap the voxel under consideration. This list is then used for "fine stage" evaluation.

In the fine stage, the triangles that pass the gross overlap test are then assessed more closely to really determine if overlap truly exists for a voxel. Triangles that don't overlap are not further processed for that voxel. However, in some cases, and this happens with the purely geometric 6-separating algorithm, a non-overlap can actually be a "false negative". With further subdivision it may be found that an overlap actually exists, albeit at a fine-stage of subdivision, usually for a corner of the original parent voxel. Therefore a "look ahead" expedient is used to prevent these false negatives.

Each 2D projection is associated with a voxel plane, which in turn is associated with an orthogonal plane of the Cartesian system. The software creates a permutation (sometimes called a "swizzle") of (x, y, z) coordinates. The end product is a two-dimensional (u, v) plane-projection of the triangle, along with a depth coordinate w. Therefore (x, y, z) coordinates are permuted to 2D projection coordinates in (u, v, w). For thin voxelization, acceptance or rejection of a triangle's overlap is determined in the plane orthogonal to the triangle normal's dominant axis. For conservative or thick voxelization, all 3 planes (XY, YZ, XZ) are considered but evaluation takes place in the dominant-axis plane first.

1.3 *OpenGL*

Once voxels are tagged for a triangle, and the triangle properties such as color are transfered to the voxel data, the voxels are displayed in z-order using OpenGL. Since the octree uses adaptive subdivision, the octree boundary mesh can also be displayed and is also sorted by z. In terms of software architecture, OpenGL is the top-level application class which invokes a comprehensive set of octree, math, and subdivision "worker" classes. All of these worker classes are part of Project V. The software architecture is flat. There are, with the exception of the GLWorker class which inherits OpenGL, no inherited classes or subclasses. Only worker classes.

The reasoning is as follows. Since the octree and the OctreeNode class are central to Project V, and since hundreds of thousands of nodes can be created for a high-resolution voxelization (high resolution is considered 512 cubed and above), then encapsulating worker methods within the octree node structure itself would create a huge memory footprint. Therefore those methods are contained in various worker classes.

Everything is reduced to worker classes and to list and pointer processing. You can think of the voxel software as three-dimensional listmaking software. When you look at the final voxel image in OpenGL, it's actually a collection of lists. This is no accident since all microprocessors are essentially Von Neumann architectures, all of which are list-based.

1.4 *Key Papers*

There are three key papers and three books that were used for creating the software. The three papers are:

Fast Parallel Surface and Solid Voxelization on GPUs, Michael Schwarz and Hans-Peter Seidel, Max Planck Institut Informatik, in Siggraph 2010 Proceedings, 2010
VoxelPipe: A Programmable Pipeline for 3D Voxelization, Jacopo Pantaleoni, NVIDIA Research, 2011

and for ray tracing using voxelization

Space Subdivision for Fast Ray Tracing, Andrew Glassner, UNC Chapel Hill, IEEE CG&A, 1984

The books include a C++ college primer that was consulted for the linked lists, vectors, and other list-type data structures:

Data Structures and Problem Solving Using C++, Second Edition, Mark Allen Weiss, Addison Wesley, 2000

and these graphics books:

Geometric Principles and Procedures for Computer Graphic Applications, Sylvan H. Chasen, Prentice-Hall, 1978
Graphics Gems, ed. Andrew Glassner, Academic Press, 1990

About Andrew Glassner

If anybody can be singled out for their work having a primary influence on Project V it's Andrew Glassner. When he wrote the paper used for this project he was a graduate student at the University of North Carolina at Chapel Hill. Chapel Hill had a reputation for being a top computer graphics school even back then, circa 1984. Andrew had also spent time at the New York Institute of Technology's Computer Graphics Lab, where luminaries like Ed Catmull, one of the founders of Pixar, and Jim Blinn, who pioneered many mathematical solutions for 3D graphics now taken for granted, also plied their trade. Glassner went on to edit the *Graphics Gems* series, several entries in the first volume of which were used for the 6-sep code of Project V. By then he'd gotten his PhD and moved to Palo Alto California to work at Xerox PARC. Never one to rest on his laurels, Andrew became interested in artificial intelligence and started a second career in that field which continues to this day. A remarkable individual, Project V expresses gratitude for everything he's done for the world of computer science.

1.5 *Journey of the Triangle*

The various steps of triangle processing will now be described, with an effort to follow the order of actual processing by Project V. In general each triangle is processed in two steps: a) a pre-level step that creates a "master" triangle; and b) per-level processing which takes into account the adapting resolution at each octree "level".

Triangles that come in from the wild are called *basic triangles.* Basic triangles are constructed from simple models coded inline, or from more complex models read in from a 3DSMax file. Triangle data, when it's first created or read in from a file in the GLWorker class, consists of the vertices and the color. This data is put into the BasicTriangle struct defined in Triangle.h.

```
struct color3 {
    float r, g, b;
};

struct BasicTriangle {
        float3 vert[3];
        color3 color;
};
```

These triangles are then scaled and translated to fit into a universal space, and this makes them into *master triangles.* The basic triangle is copied over to the Triangle class (note no "Basic" qualifier). The geometry is first scaled to the bi-unit bounding box – that is, the bounding box between (-1.0, -1.0, -1.0) and (1.0, 1.0, 1.0). Plane coefficients and the normal are also computed at this stage.

In terms of the Project V execution logic, everything starts with an "evaluation thread" for computing the basic octree. Here's what it looks like:

```
void *OctreeThread::EvalThread(void *arg) {
        Vector<BasicTriangle *> * geom = reinterpret_cast< Vector<BasicTriangle *> * > (arg);

        std::cout << "LAUNCHED!" << std::endl;

        // context for main iteration
        // note start level is 1, i.e., the eval_level
        context_w = new ContextWorker;
        context_w->makeContext(1, g_terminal, false, g_check_false_pos);         // display false for
now
        context_w->setRaster(g_raster);

        // send in basic triangle geometry
        context_w->CopyOverTriangles(*geom);
        int contextID = context_w->getContextID();

        // iterate
        octree_w = new OctreeWorker(contextID);
        octree_w->Top();

        return NULL;
}
```

In Project V there are different Contexts for different types of operations. A different Context is created for each of: a) normal voxel evaluation; b) octree adaptive-mesh display; c) ray-tracing display; or d) on-the-fly false-positive testing.

```
struct Context {
        int start_level, terminal_level, ID;
        bool buffer_display_data, check_false_pos;
        GeomWorker geom_w;
...
}
```

The Context contains its own built-in GeomWorker. The GeomWorker takes a pointer to the triangle data: the triangle data isn't embedded in the GeomWorker class itself, only attached via a pointer. The GeomWorker class has another class, in turn, built into it, being the GeomUtil class. This is where all the templates are, but again it's not heavy on data, so having these two classes embedded in the Context is okay. The Context is a lightweight struct and there are only three Context instantiations at most at any one time.

Here’s the call for copying over the triangle data:

```
void ContextWorker::CopyOverTriangles(Vector<BasicTriangle *> & geom) {
	Context * context = instance[my_count];

	// convert to internal Triangle format
	context->geom_w.TriangleConvert2MasterList(geom);
}
```

And the method in GeomWorker.cpp:

```
/// convert basic triangles to Master list triangles
TriangleList * GeomWorker::TriangleConvert2MasterList(Vector<BasicTriangle *> &geom) {

	if (tri_list != NULL)
		return tri_list;

	tri_list = BiUnitScale(geom);

	// compute edges, normal, dominant axis for each triangle
	MasterEdgesAndNormal();

	return tri_list;
}
```

The actual transfer takes place in the code fragment below (BiUnitScale):

```
/// scale to a bi-unit bounding box and translate to straddle the origin.
TriangleList *GeomWorker::BiUnitScale(Vector<BasicTriangle *> &geom) {
...
	// As we scale, create master triangle list
	// since it's bi-unit, halve the scale factor
	scale = 2.0 / scale;

	// translate first, then scale
	trans_x = -(min_x + dist_x / 2.0);
	trans_y = -(min_y + dist_y / 2.0);
	trans_z = -(min_z + dist_z / 2.0);

	tri_list = new TriangleList;
	tri_list->count = size;
```

```
    Triangle **plist = new Triangle * [size];
    tri_list->list = plist;

    for (i=0; i<size; ++i) {
        Triangle *cur_tri = new Triangle;
        tri_list->list[i] = cur_tri;
        tri_ptr = geom[i];
        cur_tri->color = tri_ptr->color;

        // verts are made explicit for permuting
        cur_tri->v0.x = (tri_ptr->vert[0].x + trans_x) * scale;
        cur_tri->v0.y = (tri_ptr->vert[0].y + trans_y) * scale;
        cur_tri->v0.z = (tri_ptr->vert[0].z + trans_z) * scale;
...
```

Everything is transfered over from the BasicTriangle (tri_ptr) to the Triangle data structure (cur_tri) with scaling and translation. These transformations put the model, e.g. all of the triangles, inside of a "bi-unit" volume, spanning the distance between -1.0 and 1.0 in all dimensions. In other words, the model coordinates, after scaling and translation, span the negative and positive space around the origin and are scaled to the bi-unit cube. A bit of safe space is added so that the entire span is 2.2 units.

A related "master bounding box" is initialized as part of the startup process for the Context.

```
/// called by constructor
void GeomUtil::Init() {
    bbox0 = make_float3( -1.1f, -1.1f, -1.1f );
    bbox1 = make_float3( 1.1f, 1.1f, 1.1f );
}
```

After calling this function the triangle data and the default bounding box have the same scale.

A whole other set of data is computed at this point.

```
void GeomWorker::MasterEdgesAndNormal() {

    if (tri_list == NULL)
        return;

    int count = tri_list->count;
    for (int i = 0; i < count; ++i) {
        Triangle * tri = tri_list->list[i];
```

```
                MasterEdges(tri->v0, tri->v1, tri->v2, tri);
                MasterNormal(tri->edge0, tri->edge2, tri);
                MasterTriAxis(tri->n, tri);
                PlaneEquation(tri);
                g_u.BoundingBox(tri->master_bbox0, tri->master_bbox1,
                                tri->v0, tri->v1, tri->v2);
        }
}
```

The triangle master edges and normals are computed before iterating through the octree levels. Each triangle normal is computed from the associated triangle edges:

```
void GeomWorker::MasterEdges(float3 &v0, float3 &v1, float3 &v2, Triangle *tri) {
        // compute triangle's edges and normal
        // note that the make_float3 goes on the stack,
        // and will be copied over to the heap (edges in tri)
        tri->edge0 = make_float3( v1.x - v0.x, v1.y - v0.y, v1.z - v0.z );
        tri->edge1 = make_float3( v2.x - v1.x, v2.y - v1.y, v2.z - v1.z );
        tri->edge2 = make_float3( v0.x - v2.x, v0.y - v2.y, v0.z - v2.z );
}
```

Let's say the triangle is aligned with the z axis, defined counter-clockwise, and is a right triangle:

v0: (0.0, 0.0, 0.0)
v1: (1.0, 0.0, 0.0)
v2: (0.0, 1.0, 0.0)

The resulting edges are:

edge0 = (1, 0, 0)
edge1 = (-1, 1, 0)
edge2 = (0, -1, 0)

These are lengths, but also cross-product elements stored in triples. The triangle normal is a cross-product as usual:

```
void GeomWorker::MasterNormal(float3 &edge0, float3 &edge2, Triangle *tri) {
        // anti-cross because edge2 order is "triangle order"
        // not "crow's feet" order normally used for normals.
        tri->n = g_u.anti_cross( edge0, edge2 );
}
```

n = (0, 0, 1)

Next, the plane equation is calculated based on the triangle's "dominant axis". The dominant axis is just a magnitude comparison of the normal of each triangle. Here's where the dominant axis is determined:

```
void GeomWorker::MasterTriAxis(float3 &n, Triangle *tri) {
        // compute dominant axis
        const bool byx = fabsf( n.y ) > fabsf( n.x );
        const bool byz = fabsf( n.y ) > fabsf( n.z );
        const bool bzx = fabsf( n.z ) > fabsf( n.x );
        tri->axis = byx ? (byz ? 1 : 2) : (bzx ? 2 : 0);
}
```

This is a bit contorted but is the right logic.

0 = x
1 = y
2 = z

Project V uses C++ templates to simplify the overlap tests. These templates come from the Voxel Pipe open source. The dominant axis of the normal for a triangle has a value as above (0, 1, or 2) and is used to index into the template. At this point all pre-level work has been done. The evaluation context next starts octree iteration for the first level of subdivision.

1.6 *Levels*

The *modus operandum* of Project V is to convert triangle geometry to voxels. As each voxel is tested, two stages of computation take place: *coarse overlap* and *fine overlap* testing. To make the coarse overlap test efficient, the triangle coordinates are scaled and made into integers to match the integer space of the octree. Each level of subdivision is called, naturally, a "level". Subdivision is such that the entire level is processed before moving to the next level. When that move is made, it's called a *level switch*. Every time the octree evaluation switches levels (subdivides and descends a level for new children) it calls this method:

```
/// At every level switch...
void LevelWorker::DoLevelWork() {
        N = context.geom_w.NewN(current_eval_level,
                                context.terminal_level,
                                TerminalLevel());

        context.geom_w.SetBBoxDeltas();
        context.geom_w.DoTriangleWork();
```

```
}
```

At the start of each level a variable N is set:

```
/// First thing to do at every level switch (LevelWorker.cpp)
int GeomUtil::NewN(int level) {
        return N = (int) lroundf(powf(2.0, (float)level));
}
```

This is just a power-of-two computation and is basically a scale factor. When a level switch occurs the triangle coordinates are scaled and packaged for the level as floating-point and integer bounding boxes. These in turn are used for overlap testing. In general, the *volume resolution* is *doubled* at each level as the iteration moves deeper into the octree. At the same time, the *voxel resolution* never departs from the unit cube.

```
/// per level
void GeomWorker::DoTriangleWork() {
        if (tri_list == NULL)
                return;
        int count = tri_list->count;
        for (int i = 0; i<count; ++i) {
                Triangle * tri = tri_list->list[i];
                g_u.ScaleTriangleBBox(tri->bbox0, tri->bbox1, tri);
                g_u.ComputeIntegerBBox(tri->bbox0i, tri->bbox1i,
                                        tri->bbox0, tri->bbox1);
                g_u.InitPlaneTestVars(tri->n, tri->v0, tri);
                TriangleSetup(tri);
        }
}
```

Let's go into detail here to understand what's going on, since triangle processing during a level switch is a critical step. The bounding box of the triangle is used for the "coarse overlap" test. The triangle bounding box is computed by finding the min and max coordinates of the triangle. A master bounding box is computed for each triangle. This is done at the very beginning of the evaluation context along with all of the other master triangle processing.

```
/// Master bbox (to be scaled at all levels)
void GeomUtil::BoundingBox(float3 &tri_bbox0, float3 &tri_bbox1,
                                float3 &v0, float3 &v1, float3 &v2) {
        tri_bbox0.x = v0.x - bbox0.x;
        tri_bbox0.y = v0.y - bbox0.y;
        tri_bbox0.z = v0.z - bbox0.z;
```

```
        tri_bbox0.x = fminf( v1.x - bbox0.x, tri_bbox0.x );
        tri_bbox0.y = fminf( v1.y - bbox0.y, tri_bbox0.y );
        tri_bbox0.z = fminf( v1.z - bbox0.z, tri_bbox0.z );
        tri_bbox0.x = fminf( v2.x - bbox0.x, tri_bbox0.x );
        tri_bbox0.y = fminf( v2.y - bbox0.y, tri_bbox0.y );
        tri_bbox0.z = fminf( v2.z - bbox0.z, tri_bbox0.z );

        tri_bbox1.x = v0.x - bbox0.x;
        tri_bbox1.y = v0.y - bbox0.y;
        tri_bbox1.z = v0.z - bbox0.z;
        tri_bbox1.x = fmaxf( v1.x - bbox0.x, tri_bbox1.x );
        tri_bbox1.y = fmaxf( v1.y - bbox0.y, tri_bbox1.y );
        tri_bbox1.z = fmaxf( v1.z - bbox0.z, tri_bbox1.z );
        tri_bbox1.x = fmaxf( v2.x - bbox0.x, tri_bbox1.x );
        tri_bbox1.y = fmaxf( v2.y - bbox0.y, tri_bbox1.y );
        tri_bbox1.z = fmaxf( v2.z - bbox0.z, tri_bbox1.z );
}
```

For example, given a master triangle: (-1, -1, -1) (0, 0, .5) (-1, .5, .5), the min of the accumulated vertices is computed as:

```
x = (-1 - (-1.1)) = 0.1
y = (-1 - (-1.1)) = 0.1
z = (-1 - (-1.1)) = 0.1
x = min ((0 - (-1.1)) = 1.1, 0.1) = 0.1
y = min ((0 - (-1.1)) = 1.1, 0.1) = 0.1
z = min ((.5 - (-1.1)) = 1.6, 0.1) = 0.1
x = min ((-1 - (-1.1)) = 0.1, 0.1) = 0.1
y = min ((.5 - (-1.1)) = 1.6, 0.1) = 0.1
z = min ((.5 - (-1.1)) = 1.6, 0.1) = 0.1
```

The opposite corner of the bounding box corresponds to the max:

```
x = (-1 - (-1.1)) = 0.1
y = (-1 - (-1.1)) = 0.1
z = (-1 - (-1.1)) = 0.1
x = max ((0 - (-1.1)) = 1.1, 0.1) = 1.1
y = max ((0 - (-1.1)) = 1.1, 0.1) = 1.1
z = max ((.5 - (-1.1)) = 1.6, 0.1) = 1.6
x = max ((-1 - (-1.1)) = 0.1, 1.1) = 1.1
y = max ((.5 - (-1.1)) = 1.6, 1.1) = 1.6
z = max ((.5 - (-1.1)) = 1.6, 1.6) = 1.6
```

These numbers may look foreign compared to the original triangle coordinates. That's because the bounding box is moved into positive space. (This will become clear presently.) The results are stored in the triangle's master bbox, e.g. the caller passes references to those entities which are filled in. The caller arguments are shown below:

```
void GeomWorker::MasterEdgesAndNormal() {
...
                    g_u.BoundingBox(tri->master_bbox0, tri->master_bbox1,
                                    tri->v0, tri->v1, tri->v2);
...
```

These master bounding box values are then transformed at each octree-subdivision level. Let's say subdivision has reached level 7: 2^7 = 128. Therefore N = 128. Anytime the GeomUtil private data member N is used, you know that the method that uses it is being called as part of level processing. First, bounding box deltas (widths) and inverse values (used for scaling) are generated based on N:

```
void GeomUtil::SetBBoxDeltas() {
        MakeBBoxDelta(bbox_delta);
        MakeInvBBoxDelta(inv_bbox_delta);
}

void GeomUtil::MakeBBoxDelta(float3 &delta) {
        delta.x = (bbox1.x - bbox0.x) / float(N);
        delta.y = (bbox1.y - bbox0.y) / float(N);
        delta.z = (bbox1.z - bbox0.z) / float(N);
}

void GeomUtil::MakeInvBBoxDelta(float3 &delta) {
        delta.x = float(N) / (bbox1.x - bbox0.x);
        delta.y = float(N) / (bbox1.y - bbox0.y);
        delta.z = float(N) / (bbox1.z - bbox0.z);
}
```

The data-member inv_bbox_delta, scaled by N = 128, is used to scale the master triangle coordinates by 128:

```
1.1 * (128 / 2.2) = 64 because inv_bbox_delta = (128 / 2.2)
```

Here's the method that scales the master triangle bounding box:

```
void GeomUtil::ScaleTriangleBBox(float3 &tri_bbox0, float3 &tri_bbox1, Triangle *tri) {
```

```
        tri_bbox0.x = tri->master_bbox0.x * inv_bbox_delta.x;
        tri_bbox0.y = tri->master_bbox0.y * inv_bbox_delta.y;
        tri_bbox0.z = tri->master_bbox0.z * inv_bbox_delta.z;

        tri_bbox1.x = tri->master_bbox1.x * inv_bbox_delta.x;
        tri_bbox1.y = tri->master_bbox1.y * inv_bbox_delta.y;
        tri_bbox1.z = tri->master_bbox1.z * inv_bbox_delta.z;
}
```

For example, the min bbox coordinate (0.1, 0.1, 0.1) and the max bbox coordinate (1.1, 1.6, 1.6), are scaled as:

```
x = 0.1 * 58.18 = 5.81          x = 1.1 * 58.18 = 64
y = 0.1 * 58.18 = 5.81          y = 1.6 * 58.18 = 93.09
z = 0.1 * 58.18 = 5.81          z = 1.6 * 58.18 = 93.09
```

This explains why the bounding box coordinates are all positive: the scaling for the current level produces positive coordinates within the positive-coordinate scaled octree. All voxels are contained in positive space. Part of this is a requirement of assigning a unique ID to each voxel, which is based on the voxel's positive coordinates.

The original max coord in x, being 0, generates a bbox max of 1.1, which is the halfway point between 0 and 2.2. This is further scaled to 64, the halfway point between 0 and 128. The integer bounding box for each triangle is then computed from these floating-point coordinates:

```
/// compute integer bbox
void GeomUtil::ComputeIntegerBBox(int3 &tri_bbox0i, int3 &tri_bbox1i,
                    const float3 &tri_bbox0, const float3 &tri_bbox1) {

        tri_bbox0i.x = min( max( int( tri_bbox0.x ), 0 ), N );
        tri_bbox0i.y = min( max( int( tri_bbox0.y ), 0 ), N );
        tri_bbox0i.z = min( max( int( tri_bbox0.z ), 0 ), N );

        tri_bbox1i.x = min( max( int( ceilf( tri_bbox1.x ) ), 0 ), N );
        tri_bbox1i.y = min( max( int( ceilf( tri_bbox1.y ) ), 0 ), N );
        tri_bbox1i.z = min( max( int( ceilf( tri_bbox1.z ) ), 0 ), N );
}
```

or

```
0i.x = 5        1i.x = 64
0i.y = 5        1i.y = 94
```

0i.z = 5 1i.z = 94

This code rounds down on the int conversion for the min corner; and rounds up before taking the int on the max corner. Both clamp to 0 if the bbox goes negative. Finally, both clamp to N = 128 if the bbox exceeds 128. Thus each triangle bbox is between 0 and 128, the boundaries of the voxel universe.

Everything is transformed to positive octant space.

1.7 *On Scaling*

The Voxel Pipe software works at a set resolution of N = 128 x 4 = 512 per side, or 512^3. (The up-tic denotes an exponent in this book.) Unlike Voxel Pipe, the Project V octree changes resolution for each level of the tree. The Voxel Pipe software iterates over 16 subnodes for each of the 128 tiles (being a 4 x 4 2D projection, hence 128 x 4 = 512). The iteration depends on the triangle bounding box in u and v, the (u, v) pair representing the planar projection of the dominant axis. The dominant axis is represented by w. This is efficient because the models typically have small triangles that usually don't exceed the 4-wide, 4-high, or 4-deep grid.

Schwarz and Seidel build their octree from the bottom-up, taking full advantage of the finest resolution of the octree by setting up column-associativity for easy cross-traversal, and parent pointers for up-traversal, and the like. The Project V software compares each triangle via its bounding box to one voxel at a time. A triangle will be completely enclosed by the first level of subdivision, known as "Level 0", since that level covers the entire universe. At the finest levels, the voxel (or really its 2D projection to a quadrant) will be completely enclosed by the triangle – the exact reverse of the level-zero situation. This means that whatever is used to geometrically exclude or include a triangle works both at universal and sub-universal resolutions.

There are two flavors of rasterization: a) rasterize(); and b) rasterize_26sep(). These are called from GeomWorker::FineTest() for some *node group* (to be described shortly), and from GeomUtil.cpp for a specific voxel:

```
/// These top routines deal with the triangle's dominant axis.
bool GeomUtil::RasterizeTop(const ushort3 &coord, Triangle *tri) {
        if (tri->axis == 0)
                return rasterize<X>(coord, tri);
        if (tri->axis == 1)
                return rasterize<Y>(coord, tri);
        return rasterize<Z>(coord, tri);
}

bool GeomUtil::Rasterize_26sepTop(const ushort3 &coord, Triangle *tri) {
```

```
        if (tri->axis == 0)
                return rasterize_26sep<X>(coord, tri);
        if (tri->axis == 1)
                return rasterize_26sep<Y>(coord, tri);
        return rasterize_26sep<Z>(coord, tri);
}
```

The voxel's *base coordinate* (lower lefthand corner) is its *defining* coordinate, sent in as "coord" above. Since the code rasterizes to the current octree level n, overlap tests take place in the following way. Start with a root node at level n = 0, which automatically includes the entire geometry. At each level of the tree, the *voxel resolution* of the subdivision for that level remains at unity, but the *volume resolution* doubles and the geometry expands. The *voxel space* also expands, which is to say, it like the triangle data is doubled. Descend to level n = 1. The geometry is scaled by 2^n = 2, resulting in geometry between 0 and 2 (positive quadrant). Level 1 has (2^n)^3 = 8 octants; (2^n)^2 = 4 quadrants (in 2D); and a span of (2^n)^1 = 2 voxels along any axis.

Descend to level n = 2. Triangle geometry is scaled by 2^n = 4. Indexing in u and v is still over a single unit, although that unit may be offset from the origin depending on the voxel's ID, which is based on the voxel's location in voxel space. Now there are 4^3 = 64 octants, or 4^2 = 16 quadrants in 2D, which means a span of 2^n = 4 voxels along any axis. A single voxel will still have a (u, v) range of unity.

The processing stops at the *terminal level*, specified in Global.cpp with a global variable g_terminal. Choose in advance a maximum level of the octree, say n = L = 9. Descend to level n = 9. Triangle geometry is scaled by 2^n = 512. But at this stage many portions of the octree will be empty, and thus the octree will have become "sparse". For example, for a typical model like the Harrier landing gear, of the 134,217,728 voxels in the voxel space, 256,241 voxels, fewer than 1 percent, will be overlapped by the geometry.

Adaptive subdivision eliminates unnecessary looping in the rasterize functions since only one voxel is considered at a time, not an entire row as in Voxel Pipe. However, the w-range in rasterize_26sep still needs to be calculated: only now the w-value for the current voxel is compared to the range and must be inside that range. The only drawback of adaptive subdivision is that range calculations need to be repeated for each level for this octree; whereas Schwarz and Seidel optimize the octree at lower levels in order to do multiple comparisons against a given range (and likewise Voxel Pipe, but using 4^3 tiles instead of using an optimized octree).

There's no easy way to do any optimization short of Schwarz and Seidel, since the "w" column can be any axis of the volume, depending on the triangle's dominant axis.

1.8 *Templates and Permutations*

The use of templates in C++ simplifies what boils down to permutations of (x, y, z) and (u, v, w) coordinates related to overlap tests. Let's look at the data structures.

The <AXIS> templates are from Voxel Pipe open source and are in utils.h, declared as struct templates:

```
template <int32 axis>
struct uvw {};

template <>
struct uvw<0>
{
static const int32 U = 1;
static const int32 V = 2;
static const int32 W = 0;
...
}
```

and

```
template <>
struct uvw<1>
{
static const int32 U = 0;
static const int32 V = 2;
static const int32 W = 1;
...
}
```

and

```
template <>
struct uvw<2>
{
static const int32 U = 0;
static const int32 V = 1;
static const int32 W = 2;
...
}
```

providing for each dominant axis depending on the index {0, 1, 2}. The dominant axis is always assigned to w. There are three rasterize functions: one for 6-sep and two minor variants for 26-sep. All of these routines in one way or another permute the variables based on the dominant axis, e.g.

```
typedef uvw<AXIS> sel;
```

and then select the resulting (u, v) coordinates as shown in this fragment from "fine" testing:

```
    // the unit voxel is it: no iterating as in voxel-pipe
    int32 u = sel::u(coord);
    int32 v = sel::v(coord);
```

The template functions u(), v(), and w() are in utils.h:

```
template <typename Vec>  static typename base_type<Vec>::value_type u(const Vec a) { return a.y; }
template <typename Vec>  static typename base_type<Vec>::value_type v(const Vec a) { return a.z; }
template <typename Vec>  static typename base_type<Vec>::value_type w(const Vec a) { return a.x; }
```

This is for index AXIS which is passed to the rasterize() function as a template argument:

```
rasterize<X>(coord, tri);
```

for

```
template <int32 AXIS> bool GeomUtil::rasterize()
```

The enum definition in utils.h is:

```
enum XYZ
{
  X = 0,
  Y = 1,
  Z = 2
};
```

So the selection depends on what the current triangle's dominant axis is. All of these permutations are confined to utils.h, GeomUtils.h, and GeomUtils.cpp. It's a very clever use of C++ templates.

1.9 *Tiles in Voxel Pipe*

VoxelPipe uses "tiles" because that's what the GPU understands. Here's how the tiles work.

```
const int32 tile_z = T * (tile_id >> (log_M*2));
const int32 tile_y = T * ((tile_id >> log_M) & (M-1));
const int32 tile_x = T * (tile_id & (M-1));
```

This translates to:

```
tile_z = 16 * (tile_id >> 6);
tile_y = 16 * ((tile_id >> 3) & 7);
tile_x = 16 * (tile_id & 7);
```

The tile_id is 9 bits, 3 bits for each x, y, z coordinate. For example take 011.100.110 for z.y.x. Then:

```
tile_z = 16 * 3 = 48
tile_y = 16 * 4 = 64
tile_x = 16 * 6 = 96
```

Tile_x, tile_y, and tile_z together comprise a scaled tile coordinate.

Each tile has a tile_id and the tile_ids are sorted in sequential order. Voxel Pipe keeps track of triangle/tile pairs. The upshot is that each tile_id will have a set of triangles associated with it. Thus the ranges are discriminated in the rasterize loop: a change of tile_id in the sorted list signifies a new tile. When a new tile is found, the range of triangle/tile pairs for the previous tile ends; and the range for the new tile begins. The range is specified with start and end values that index into the triangle-tile pair arrays.

Thus, each tile has a start and end range of "tile pairs" corresponding to a collection of triangles (starting at index i and ending at index j). This is accomplished with start and end arrays, being a single value for each tile, having a size of M * M * M = 8^3 = 512. There are 512 starts and 512 ends (but there may be considerably more tile pairs). The tile_id serves as an index into either array, and can never be greater-than or equal to M * M * M = 512. This jibes with the bit layout of 111.111.111, i.e. 511.

Project V uses a similar scheme to keep track of triangles, to be explained in Part Two.

1.10 *Levels and Further Triangle Processing*

The Project V code is a little different from Voxel Pipe in that a gridsize of 512 is replaced with adaptive subdivision and levels. Let's move on to the second part of DoTriangleWork(). As explained in section 1.6 the bounding-box processing has already been done. Let's look at what comes next:

```
/// per level
void GeomWorker::DoTriangleWork() {
        if (tri_list == NULL)
                return;
        int count = tri_list->count;
        for (int i = 0; i<count; ++i) {
                Triangle * tri = tri_list->list[i];
                g_u.ScaleTriangleBBox(tri->bbox0, tri->bbox1, tri);
                g_u.ComputeIntegerBBox(tri->bbox0i, tri->bbox1i,
                                tri->bbox0, tri->bbox1);
                g_u.InitPlaneTestVars(tri->n, tri->v0, tri);
                TriangleSetup(tri);
        }
}
```

The triangle list is sitting around in GeomWorker and is accessed for initializing the plane test variables for the current level. The rasterization is either THIN_OV3 or two flavors of conservative: CONSERVATIVE_OV1, this being the name given to the Voxel Pipe rasterization; and CONSERVATIVE_OV3, the Schwarz & Seidel version. "OV" means "overlap". Schwarz & Seidel perform 3 overlap tests on w; compared to Voxel Pipe, which performs one overlap test on the dominant axis only combined with a simple w-clamp.

THIN_OV3 is highly exclusionary and performs overlap tests for all three planes, though the algorithm is quite different otherwise compared to 26-sep. The 6-sep algorithm matches on voxel faces only (the definition of 6-sep) instead of voxel faces, edges, and vertices (the definition of 26-sep), but this limitation can lead to false negatives, e.g. gaps. This will be explained in detail later.

Plane variables are pre-initialized at every level switch. These are for fine testing and the reader can consult the code. Focusing on triangles:

```
/// do this once per level
void GeomWorker::TriangleSetup(Triangle * tri) {
        if (tri->axis == 0) {
                if (raster == CONSERVATIVE_OV1) {
                        g_u.triangle_setup<X>(tri, tri->fine.n_delta_u[0],
                                                tri->fine.n_delta_v[0],
                                                tri->fine.a[0]);
...
```

There are more options in this method: the reader can consult the code. It's important to note that these setup routines are not called once per voxel, but once per *level*. However the rasterize() routine *is* called once per voxel, for all the triangles in that voxel's triangle list.

The triangle_setup methods in the GeomUtil header file differ for THIN and CONSERVATIVE. The conservative setup uses inward pointing edge normals of the projection of the triangle for the dominant axis, to determine half-spaces around the triangle for each edge of the triangle.

The THIN algorithm, being almost purely geometric, simply computes the transformed triangle coordinates for the current level and stores them for easy access during rasterization.

The edge normals are computed from the master triangle edges which in turn are composed from the master triangle coordinates, which recall are scaled to bi-unit space. The 2D normal-values {n} and the 1D bbox distances d are used to compute the overlap magnitudes bundled into the triple (a.x, a.y, a.z) in the code below. The math is explained fully in the paper by Schwarz & Seidel.

For any given (u, v, w) voxel, the 2D overlap test is positive if:

$$\bigwedge_{i=0,1,2} \left(d_i^{xy} + v \cdot n_i^y + u \cdot n_i^x \geq 0\right). \qquad \begin{aligned} n_i^x &= \mathbf{n}_i^{xy}{}_x \cdot \Delta\mathbf{p}_x \\ n_i^y &= \mathbf{n}_i^{xy}{}_y \cdot \Delta\mathbf{p}_y \end{aligned}$$

where d is:

$$d_{\mathbf{e}_i}^{\mathrm{xy}} = -\langle \mathbf{n}_{\mathbf{e}_i}^{\mathrm{xy}}, \mathbf{v}_{i,\mathrm{xy}} \rangle + \max\left\{0, \Delta\mathbf{p}_{\mathrm{x}} \mathbf{n}_{\mathbf{e}_i,\mathrm{x}}^{\mathrm{xy}}\right\} + \max\left\{0, \Delta\mathbf{p}_{\mathrm{y}} \mathbf{n}_{\mathbf{e}_i,\mathrm{y}}^{\mathrm{xy}}\right\}$$

and the p's are the bi-unit extents divided by N, for the current level. The p's are the same as bbox_delta, shown below in the triangle_setup() method in GeomUtil.h. For example, for edge0, n0 and d0 only, with v0 being a triangle vertex:

```
...
      const float2 n0 = make_float2( -sel::v( edge0 ) * sgn_w, sel::u( edge0 ) * sgn_w );
      const float d0 = -(n0.x * sel::u( v0 ) + n0.y * sel::v( v0 )) +
                        fmaxf( 0.0f, sel::u( bbox_delta )*n0.x ) +
                        fmaxf( 0.0f, sel::v( bbox_delta )*n0.y );
...
```

The final values during setup, using {n0, n1, n2}, are stored as part of the Triangle data, in the Schwarz & Seidel CONSERVATIVE_OV3 case, as follows:

```
/// Schwarz & Seidel math for "conservative" (26-sep).
template <int32 AXIS>
void GeomUtil::triangle_setup(Triangle * tri,
                 float3& n_delta_u,
```

```
            float3& n_delta_v,
            float3& a)
{
      typedef uvw<AXIS> sel;
...
      a.x = d0;
      a.y = d1;
      a.z = d2;

      // these are scaling operations for eventual (u,v) application...
      n_delta_u.x = n0.x * sel::u( bbox_delta );
      n_delta_u.y = n1.x * sel::u( bbox_delta );
      n_delta_u.z = n2.x * sel::u( bbox_delta );

      n_delta_v.x = n0.y * sel::v( bbox_delta );
      n_delta_v.y = n1.y * sel::v( bbox_delta );
      n_delta_v.z = n2.y * sel::v( bbox_delta );
...
```

The values n_delta_u and n_delta_v are scaled edge normals. Recall that bbox_delta is divided by N, so the n_delta "fine" variables, when applied to triangle coordinates scaled by N for each level, will have the effect of scaling those coordinates to unit space in the overlap tests.

In summary, values for the triangle's "fine" (processing stage) data variables are calculated in one of the triangle_setup() routines in GeomUtil.h. The use of templates is clever and simplifies the higher-level computations because all of the permutations of (x,y,z) or (u,v,w) are done via the template axis indices, corresponding in turn to the "dominant axis" of the triangle normal and the associated 2D projection plane.

1.11 *Coarse Testing*

Everything has been set up for testing for overlap. Here is the top-level method for that testing:

```
/// top level geometry processing for NodeGroup

/// set the geom_stat bits in the parent NodeGroup (passed in)
/// instantiate new groups for set bits
void GroupWorker::GeomProcess(NodeGroup *group, const Level & level) {

      // mark the parent as "current" during term of child processing
      current = group;
```

```
        if (!CoarseProcess(level))
                return;

        FineProcess(level);
}
```

Here's the key part of the coarse test, which is a bounding-box test:

```
VTList * GeomWorker::CoarseTest(Vector<int> &tri_idx, NodeGroup *group) {
...
x = voxel.coord.x; y = voxel.coord.y; z = voxel.coord.z;
...
                        if ((x >= tri->bbox0i.x && x <= tri->bbox1i.x) &&
                           (y >= tri->bbox0i.y && y <= tri->bbox1i.y) &&
                           (z >= tri->bbox0i.z && z <= tri->bbox1i.z)) {
...
```

Let's run some numbers and see if it works. Start with this triangle:

v0 = (0.2, 0.4, 0)
v1 = (1, 0.2, 0.1)
v2 = (1, 0.9, 0.1)

As explained in section 1.6, the scaled floating point and integer bounding boxes will be:

bbox0.x = 75.63	bbox0i.x = 75
bbox0.y = 75.63	bbox0i.y = 75
bbox0.z = 64	bbox0i.z = 64
bbox1.x = 122.18	bbox1i.x = 123
bbox1.y = 116.36	bbox1i.y = 117
bbox1.z = 69.81	bbox1i.z = 70

Suppose that the scaled base coordinate of the voxel is (100, 80, 64). You can see that this triangle easily passes the coarse test for the voxel. Let's move on.

1.12 *Rasterization and Fine Testing*

The next step is rasterization. Let's compute the setup variables before looking at the first rejection test in (u, v).

The base offset "a" has already been computed for all three triangle edges, as above. The basic "inside" test is called with the current voxel base coordinate (coord) and the current triangle (tri). The voxel coordinate has been scaled by N, and is re-scaled to unit-space via the “scaling normals” n_delta_u or n_delta_v:

```
/// 26-separating raster using basic VoxelPipe code and triangle setup
template <int32 AXIS> bool GeomUtil::rasterize(const ushort3 &coord, Triangle *tri) {

        typedef uvw<AXIS> sel;

        const float4 &plane_eq = tri->fine.plane_eq;

        const float3 &n_delta_u = tri->fine.n_delta_u[0];
        const float3 &n_delta_v = tri->fine.n_delta_v[0];
        const float3 &a = tri->fine.a[0];

        // the unit voxel is it: no iterating as in voxel-pipe
        int32 u = sel::u(coord);
        int32 v = sel::v(coord);

        // translate in voxel space since post-translation in
        // unit space combined with deltas won't work.
        // Don't overwrite original (u, v, w) variables.
        const float u_trans = float(u - (N >> 1));
        const float v_trans = float(v - (N >> 1));

        const float3 b = make_float3(
                                u_trans * n_delta_u.x,
                                u_trans * n_delta_u.y,
                                u_trans * n_delta_u.z );

        const float3 c = make_float3(
                                v_trans * n_delta_v.x,
                                v_trans * n_delta_v.y,
                                v_trans * n_delta_v.z );

        const float c0 = a.x + b.x + c.x;
        const float c1 = a.y + b.y + c.y;
        const float c2 = a.z + b.z + c.z;

        const bool inside =
                (c0 >= 0.0f) &&
                (c1 >= 0.0f) &&
                (c2 >= 0.0f);
```

...

The projection variables and scaling variables are used to test for “inside”. The < 0 test means that there’s no intersection and the next triangle can be tested. Otherwise, further intersection tests for the voxel face are computed.

The 2D “inside” test by itself may not fully determine “inside” status, but it will definitely determine that the triangle is outside. The “w column” is the list of w values that lie within the current projected {u, v} location. You can follow w in depth to determine if the triangle is hovering above or below the voxel face. The w coordinate also has to match the w-value of the current voxel. That is, the projection may be “inside”, but w also needs to be inside for the intersection to be true.

1.13 *Clamping to the Voxel*

In Voxel Pipe the triangle’s bounding box is clamped to the current tile. Another word for “clamped” might be “clipped” although the word “clamp” has a very specific meaning in computer graphics related to signal processing. The (x,y,z) coordinates for a tile range between 0 and 112 at steps of T = 16. (Note that 112 + 16 = 128.) The overlap check is encoded for CUDA tiles as:

```
if (w >= sel::w( tile ) && w < sel::w( tile ) + T)
```

The clamp with example values might be:

```
if (64 >= 64 && 64 < 64 + 16)
  ...inside
```

So this makes sense given the shift-left by 4 bits (or multiply by 16) for each of tile_x, tile_y, and tile_z. But the triangle bounding box can vary over all of those 16 units. The octree code for Project V doesn’t need to worry about skipping on sixteens: it just compares on each voxel base coordinate.

The expression for a row...

```
  if (64 >= 64 && 64 < 64 + 16)
```

... is equivalent to a simple equality for a voxel base coordinate:

```
  if (64 == 64)
```

The first part of the “inside” test goes like this:

```
...
    // next, if inside, see what the w-range is and clip.
    // note: this has been tested and it DOES reject voxels
    if (inside) {
            // compute W depth
            const float min_uf = (u + (plane_eq.x < 0.0f ? 1.0f : 0.0f)) * sel::u( bbox_delta );
            const float min_vf = (v + (plane_eq.y < 0.0f ? 1.0f : 0.0f)) * sel::v( bbox_delta );
            const float min_wf = plane_eq.z - (plane_eq.x*min_uf + plane_eq.y*min_vf);
            int32 min_w = int32( min_wf * sel::w( inv_bbox_delta ) );

            const float max_uf = (u + (plane_eq.x > 0.0f ? 1.0f : 0.0f)) * sel::u( bbox_delta );
            const float max_vf = (v + (plane_eq.y > 0.0f ? 1.0f : 0.0f)) * sel::v( bbox_delta );
            const float max_wf = plane_eq.z - (plane_eq.x*max_uf + plane_eq.y*max_vf);
            int32 max_w = int32( max_wf * sel::w( inv_bbox_delta ) );

            if (max_w < min_w) {
                    int32 tmp = min_w;
                    min_w = max_w;
                    max_w = tmp;
            }
...
```

Variables u and v are derived from the variable "coord" passed in by GeomWorker: it's the base coordinate of the current octant. (See the code fragment in the previous section.) These coordinates are plugged into the plane equation coefficients for the triangle. Depending on the triangle's orientation, the w-coordinate for the current dominant axis will be selected from the octant's (x,y,z) coordinates.

The code above computes the min and max of a triangle edge's extent in w for the given voxel extents, the edge being somewhat orthogonal to the "dominant axis" of the triangle's normal. We're interested in w-extents, not the projection in (u, v). If the min and max are swapped magnitude-wise, they're put in their proper order.

The unit-value wf is then multiplied by inv_bbox_delta, which is scaled by N = 128 for level 7, which means that w will be scaled by 128. In the next part of the "inside" clause the clamp makes its appearance:

```
...
            // note we have a "clamp" here: max of the min, and min of the max,
            // for the "most interior" range : it will bypass loop if voxel w is
            // outside the range; else will enter loop on unit voxel.

            min_w = max( min_w, sel::w( coord ) );
```

```
        max_w = min( max_w, sel::w( coord ) );

        // VoxelPipe doesn't do the remaining two projection tests.
        // It simply accepts the clipped/clamped value.
        for (int32 w = min_w; w <= max_w; ++w) {
            // guaranteed that w == sel::w( coord ) from clip and entry
            return true;
        }
...
```

Notice that the actual clamp is the for-next statement! There are three cases: 1) min and max both less than sel::w(coord); 2) min and max both greater than sel::w(coord); or 3) min and max on either side of sel::w(coord). In the first case, let's say min and max are both less, then the clip or clamp is:

(min, max) = (w, max_w)   (64, 62)

Referring to the code above, since w(coord) > max_w, there can be no iteration in the "for" loop unless w(coord) = max_w. So the triangle doesn't overlap. Now let's say that min and max are both more, the the clip/clamp is:

(min, max) = (min_w, w)   (66, 64)

Since min_w > w(coord), again there can be no iteration unless min_w = w(coord). So the triangle doesn't overlap. Finally, the case where one or the other is on either side gives:

(min, max) = (w, w)   (64, 64)

– because the ordering of min_w, max_w is already such that min_w < max_w. In this case the iteration will succeed and so will the overlap test.

If the triangle is not "inside" the final instruction is to

```
return false;
```

to say that there's no overlap and the voxel can be excluded for the current triangle. As already mentioned, Voxel Pipe looks for a w value in the range of tile_z and tile_z + 16, i.e. somewhere within the region of two successive base locations. But Project V doesn't use tiles, except in the sense of a tile being a voxel face.

The triangle may be inside in the projected dimension, but two additional tests can be performed in the complementary orthogonal dimensions to make sure the triangle is inside from all perspectives. These additional tests are what differentiate the OV3 from the OV1 rasterization procedures.

1.14 *List Ordering and Management*

The Project V class design completely dispenses with the parallel approach because the development computer is an HP desktop without a GPU. The octree is linearly encoded so that each node has a unique ID. Octree traversal is breadth-first, and descend. The only back-traversal is for false-positive testing when parent nodes are zeroed out when all children are found to be false.

Here's the OctreeNode struct from Octree.h:

```
template <class Object>
struct OctreeNode
{
        Object element;
        unsigned char child_bits, child_count;
        OctreeNode *parent;
        // "count" OctreeNode *'s follow, but start with default NULL.
        OctreeNode **child;

        // be strict and require the parent argument
        OctreeNode(Object & theElement, OctreeNode *mparent,
                        unsigned short mcount = 0) : element(theElement),
                        child_count(mcount), parent(mparent) { child = NULL;}
};
```

An OctreeNode represents an octant and is the data element of the octree. In other words, if an octant is empty, there is no corresponding OctreeNode. At level 0 there is one big voxel, so a root OctreeNode must always exist. The first subdivision is represented by what the OctreeNode is classed to, being a NodeGroup of 8 child nodes. But 8 child OctreeNodes aren't created right off the bat. First it must be determined if any elements of the NodeGroup overlap any of the triangles in the parent voxel's triangle list.

This means temporary processing takes place outside of the OctreeNode, and this temporary processing happens in the NodeGroup. The OctreeNode struct is brought into the Octree class for each sub-octant which in fact overlaps one or more triangles. The Octree class is in turn used by the OctreeWorker class.

Each OctreeNode contains a NodeGroup pointer object – that is, a collection of all eight children, being a "group". Here's how the list is instantiated in OctreeWorker.cpp:

```
OctreeNode<NodeGroup *> **o_list = NULL;
```

The indexing used in voxel-pipe is a binary format: 111.111.111 for zzz.yyy.xxx, which covers the spectrum of tiles that cover the 512^3 space. This won't work for octree recursion. We use instead Andrew Glassner's approach whereby the xyz values are concatenated. The nodes are referenced irrespective of (x, y, z) identities by assigning each node a label.

1.15 *Octree Basics*

Each octree level is associated with a series of NodeGroup data structures. (More on this level-based iteration later.) Child octree nodes are only officially created after the children of the current octant subtree have been processed for triangle overlaps. The actual computation of children nodes is initiated by OctreeWorker, then goes to GroupWorker.

Octree node coordinates are integer coordinates in positive space, based on a spatial ID as explained in the Glassner paper. The coordinates are computed in IDWorker.cpp. The basic idea is as follows. Pretend that instead of using an integer ID an arbitrary scale factor is used. Then a rudimentary octree would be built like this:

```
BuildOctree(x, y, z, scale, geomlist) {
   // assign coords to geomlist
   ...

   if (scale == N)
          return;

   // recurse
   scaleq = scale * 2.0;
   for (i = 1; i <= 8; ++i) {
          if (scaleq > minscale) then
             BuildOctree(x * scaleq + ax(i),
                          y * scaleq + ay(i),
                          z * scaleq + az(i), scaleq, geomlist);
   }
}
```

where (indexing from 1) the voxel coordinates are read from the array:

```
ax = (0, 1, 0, 1, 0, 1, 0, 1);
ay = (0, 0, 0, 0, 1, 1, 1, 1);
az = (1, 1, 0, 0, 1, 1, 0, 0);
```

These indices represent the min points or *base coordinates* of each voxel. If scale starts at 1, then the voxel coordinates will be (for x, y, z = 0, 0, 0):

(0, 0, 1) for i = 1
(1, 0, 1) for i = 2
(0, 0, 0) for i = 3
(1, 0, 0) for i = 4
(0, 1, 1) for i = 5
(1, 1, 1) for i = 6
(0, 1, 0) for i = 7
(1, 1, 0) for i = 8

Following the recursion for i = 2 with (x, y, z) = (1, 0, 1) and scale = 2:

(2, 0, 3) for i = 1
(3, 0, 3) for i = 2
(2, 0, 2) for i = 3
(3, 0, 2) for i = 4
(2, 1, 3) for i = 5
(3, 1, 3) for i = 6
(2, 1, 2) for i = 7
(3, 1, 2) for i = 8

This basic approach is extended in IDWorker.cpp to use the Glassner ID technique, from which coordinates can be computed directly. Note that coordinates are computed for all 8 voxels in an octant subdivision.

Layout in the XZ plane is:

```
Z
^
|
.___> X
```

1 2
3 4 (bottom, y = 0)

5 6
7 8 (top, y = 1)

Everything is in positive coordinates. The children are numbered 1 through 8. If the world node or topmost node is labeled 1, then its children become 11 through 18. Let's say that node 13 needs to be subdivided. Then its children become 131 through 138. In general, the parent node passes its ID as a prefix to its children.

Given this naming convention, a point in (x, y, z) can be identified with a node, and likewise the minimum coordinate of a node can be found from its ID. In the first case:

```
/// gets the min coord of the voxel bbox for level
void IDWorker::getXYZ(Glassner ID, ushort3 &coord) {
        Glassner mag, tID;
        int x, y, z, count;

        count = TensMagnitude(ID);          // 412 returns 3
        mag = TensMinusOne(count);          // 3 returns 100

        x = y = z = 0;

        while (mag >= 1) {
                tID = ID / mag;
                x = (x << 1) + ax[tID - 1];
                y = (y << 1) + ay[tID - 1];
                z = (z << 1) + az[tID - 1];

                tID *= mag;
                ID -= tID;
                mag /= 10;
        }
        coord.x = x;
        coord.y = y;
        coord.z = z;
}
```

The reverse transformation is only used in ray tracing, and can be found in the code here:

```
void RayWorker::findNode(const float3 &coord, NodePack &data)
```

There's also a generic version of the reverse transformation in IDWorker. For basic octree traversal there's no need to find an octree node ID from (x,y,z) coordinates. The only place that requires a node ID from (x,y,z) coordinates is ray tracing, in which the ray is being followed in (x,y,z) and a conversion to a node ID helps determine if the ray has entered a node or not. The algorithms and general intention of ray tracing, including the findNode() method, are described in Part Three.

1.16 *Octree versus OpenGL*

The class design allows a routine in the global OpenGL environment to access the octree as follows:

a) to pass geometry to the octree level 0;
b) to start subdivision (launch as a thread)
c) to retrieve final voxels for display

The Project V architecture avoids a second pass through the octree and rather emits the final voxel for display at octree level L. The display task is tied to a Context.

The OpenGL library calls are inherited by the GLWorker class:

```
class GLWorker : public cwc::glutWindow
{
...
}
```

As well, the top-level application inherits glApplication:

```
class myApplication : public cwc::glApplication
{
...
}
```

with a MainLoop() function. Then, in the main function:

```
int main(void)
{
        myApplication*  pApp = new myApplication;
        GLWorker* myWin = new GLWorker();

        pApp->run();    // calls MainLoop()
        delete pApp;
        return 0;
}
```

When the app is run OpenGL knows enough to do everything in myWin. As well, all of the scene setup is done in default GL routine OnRender() in myWin.

The problem is that when the application starts, it falls into glutMainLoop, which would, unless something was done about it, block anything else from running. How are voxels for the octree computed? How does voxel calculation communicate with OpenGL?

The idea is that OnRender launches a separate thread for the octree subdivisions, and then enters a message-passing loop and receives voxels until there's no more data. The data is passed in a message queue. The queue is emptied by the GL code, and filled by the octree thread.

When the octree subdivision code finishes, the OnRender() method finishes the scene, and the scene is displayed.

Here's what the class declaration of the RenderQueue looks like.

// Uses QueueAr and manipulates items in a thread-safe manner. Uses a mutex to lock accesses.

```
// RenderQueue
template <class Object>
class RenderQueue
{
public:
        RenderQueue() : mutex(PTHREAD_MUTEX_INITIALIZER) {}
        ~RenderQueue() {}

        Object enqueue(Object x);

        // dequeuer must call this first!
        bool isEmpty();
        Object dequeue();

private:
        QueueAr<Object> q;
        pthread_mutex_t mutex;
};
```

This in turn is managed by the OctreeThread class. The code uses a mutex on the queue accesses, and lets the octree thread run while myWin processes the queue. When the GLWorker receives a voxel data value of -1, this means the transfer is done, and it can do a thread join to end the octree thread safely (and deallocate thread resources) before exiting OnRender().

The queue has to be a global data structure to be accessed by both classes. The point of all this is to do octree voxel emission on the fly, and keep the octree code completely pure, e.g. divorced from OpenGL. This way, if one day a different graphics driver needs to be used, that driver can be harnessed to the same worker classes without requiring any changes at the worker level.

1.17 *Queues and Contexts*

There are four contexts: a) the normal octree evaluation context; b) the mesh-generation context which uses the octree generated in (a); c) ray-tracing, which also uses the octree from (a); and d) false-positive testing, which spawns a new octree but is otherwise a continuation of the octree from (a). Only one context at a time is active. For example, when false-positive testing is activated normal octree evaluation is suspended until the false-positive context finishes.

The main functionality is normal octree evaluation. Here's how it starts.

```
void *OctreeThread::EvalThread(void *arg) {
	Vector<BasicTriangle *> * geom = reinterpret_cast< Vector<BasicTriangle *> * > (arg);

	std::cout << "LAUNCHED!" << std::endl;

	// context for main iteration
	// note start level is 1, i.e., the eval_level
	context_w = new ContextWorker;
	context_w->makeContext(1, g_terminal, false, g_check_false_pos);		// display false for
now
	context_w->setRaster(g_raster);

	// send in basic triangle geometry
	context_w->CopyOverTriangles(*geom);
	int contextID = context_w->getContextID();

	// iterate
	octree_w = new OctreeWorker(contextID);
	octree_w->Top();

	return NULL;
}
```

The thread code uses a generic void pointer, which is type-cast to a list of triangle pointers. This is the geometry to be processed. The first task is to make a new ContextWorker and then a new Context. The context takes on the global control parameters for when to stop the octree subdivision (g_terminal) and whether or not to check for false positives (g_check_false_pos). It also takes on the global rasterization mode, being g_raster, set in global.cpp. This will be CONSERVATIVE_OV1, CONSERVATIVE_OV3, or THIN_OV3.

The makeContext routine makes the Context, which is a struct managed by the ContextWorker class:

```
class ContextWorker {
public:
	ContextWorker(){}
	~ContextWorker();

	void makeContext(int start_level, int end_level, bool display, bool check_fp);
	void setRaster(const unsigned int raster);
	void setStartAndEndLevels(int start_level, int end_level);
	int getContextID();
	static Context & getContext(int contextID);
	static void CleanUp();
	void CopyOverTriangles(Vector<BasicTriangle *> & geom);
	void CopyOverTriangles(GeomWorker &orig_geom_w);

private:
	static int count;
	static Vector<Context *> instance;
	int my_count;
	Context * context;
};
```

Notice the static elements. This allows a list of Context pointers (called "instance") to be accessed globally, and initialized in Global.cpp:

```
/// this goes with each OctreeWorker instantiation
int ContextWorker::count = 0;
Vector<Context *> ContextWorker::instance;
```

OctreeThread::EvalThread calls makeContext, which looks like this:

```
/// This creates the ID!

/// internal context will be copied when pushed onto instance array
/// the private member then goes out of scope. Hide all this from user.
void ContextWorker::makeContext(int start_level, int end_level, bool display, bool check_fp) {
	context = new Context;

	context->start_level = start_level;
	context->terminal_level = end_level;
	context->buffer_display_data = display;
	context->check_false_pos = check_fp;

	instance.push_back(context);
```

```
        my_count = count++;
        context->ID = my_count;
}
```

This instantiates a Context and adds it to the list, e.g. the global "instance". It also sets the context ID, simply a count starting at 0.

There are really only two different Contexts: a) the normal Octree evaluation; and b) the Ray Tracing context. The Mesh display is a fake context in that it actually reuses the normal Octree context completely. It's just a display function, and all it needs is the completed Octree. There's no fancy processing or modification of the Octree. Here's the entry point, you can see how simple it is.

```
/// tree is already made; iterate through recursively
void OctreeWorker::MeshTop() {
        DrawMesh(tree.getRoot(), 0);
        display.terminateMesh();
}
```

The display class member in OctreeWorker is declared as:

```
        Display display;
```

The Display class uses the RenderQueue as mentioned earlier:

```
        MeshData * md = new MeshData;
        my_stat_thread.EnqueueM(md);
```

where my_stat_thread is the global defined in main.cpp:

```
/// The easiest way to make the queue global.... extern it where used.
OctreeThread my_stat_thread;
```

and where various render queues are declared as part of OctreeThread, along with inline methods:

```
...
        // signatures change unfortunately for different data types
        MeshData * DequeueM() {
                return mesh_queue.dequeue();
        }
        bool IsEmptyM() {
                return mesh_queue.isEmpty();
```

```
        }
        MeshData * EnqueueM(MeshData *mp) {
                return mesh_queue.enqueue(mp);
        }
...
private:
...
        RenderQueue< VoxelData * > render_queue;
        RenderQueue< MeshData * > mesh_queue;
        RenderQueue< ReducedRay * > ray_queue;
...
```

Back to the normal octree evaluation Context. The last thing the OctreeThread does is instantiate an OctreeWorker with the contextID and iterate:

```
        // iterate
        octree_w = new OctreeWorker(contextID);
        octree_w->Top();
```

The OctreeWorker instantiation uses the contextID as follows in its constructor:

```
class OctreeWorker {
public:
        OctreeWorker(int my_contextID) :
                context (ContextWorker::getContext(my_contextID)),
                contextID(my_contextID), fp_context(NULL), fp_contextID(INVALID),
                group_w(context), level_w(context), display(context) {}
        ~OctreeWorker();
...
}
```

where the context members are:

```
private:
        // instantiates in declaration order: start with context
        Context &context;
        int contextID;
        ContextWorker *fp_context;
        int fp_contextID;
```

The Context is created before it's assigned to the OctreeWorker and sits in the global "instance" list of Contexts. Initially the false-positive context (fp_context) is set to NULL and its ID to INVALID.

If false-positive processing is turned on via the global in Global.h/.cpp, g_check_false_pos, then the first thing the normal octree context does is create a second context for false-positive processing. This is only done once for the entire tree, so the triangle list is only copied over once to the second context for false positives. There's only one false-positive context that's reused for all false-positive calls. Here's the code that makes the false-positive context.

```
void OctreeWorker::MakeFPContext() {
        // second context for false positives
        // do this once to avoid copying over triangle list multiple times
        fp_context = new ContextWorker;
        // g_terminal is the eval level to start at
        fp_context->makeContext(g_terminal, g_false_pos_level, false, false);

        // this goes directly to the GeomWorker class:
        fp_context->setRaster(g_raster);

        fp_context->CopyOverTriangles(context.geom_w);
        fp_contextID = fp_context->getContextID();
}
```

The *modus operandum* is to have a nice separation between normal processing up to some terminal level; and a continuance to extra levels for false-positive tests at a finer subdivision level. The false-positive Context is really a "context switch". The context switch is performed if false-positive testing is turned on (via the global) and the octree iteration has reached the terminal level (as specified by the global g_terminal). Here's the routine.

```
/// check for false positive processing
void OctreeWorker::SwitchContext(NodeGroup *group) {
        // first see if this node is a candidate
        if (!isFPCandidate())
                return;

        // iterate
        OctreeWorker octree_w(fp_contextID);
        octree_w.TopFP(group);

        // reset the raster option for next user
        fp_context->setRaster(g_raster);
}
```

This happens in the midst of octree iteration for normal octree evaluation.

1.18 *Level-Order Recursion*

Because the entire geometry must be scaled at each level of recursion, and because the geometry may consist of thousands of triangles, the scaling should only be performed once per level. This means that all nodes on a given level must be processed before moving on to the next level. This is called "breadth-first" or "level-order" iteration.

Level-order iteration insures that the geometry is scaled L times, and no more, with L being the number of levels. Without level-order recursion, the geometry could conceivably be rescaled thousands of times with a huge performance penalty.

The simplest way to achieve level-order recursion is to create children for the next level from the nodes of the current level, and as part of the loop structure, to store those children in a queue, from which the iteration retrieves the "next node". In this way the children are "waiting" in the queue when the current level finishes.

Here's the "Iterate" routine in its entirety:

```
void OctreeWorker::Iterate( TreeIterator<NodeGroup *> & itr) {
        OctreeNode<NodeGroup *> **o_list = NULL;
        int count = 0;

  try {
        // "put" will enqueue children
        for (itr.first(); itr.get(); itr.put(o_list, count) ) {
                NodeGroup *ng_ptr = itr.retrieve();
                if (level_w.LevelSwitch(ng_ptr->ID))
                        level_w.DoLevelWork();

                const Level &level = level_w.getLevel();
                group_w.GeomProcess(ng_ptr, level);

                if (context.check_false_pos && level_w.TerminalLevel())
                  SwitchContext(ng_ptr);

                // check and delete parent VTPairs (after FP processing!)
                group_w.checkVTPairs(level);

                display.displayVoxel(ng_ptr, level);

                if (!level_w.TerminalLevel()) {
                        o_list = MakeChildOctreeNodes(ng_ptr, itr, count);
```

```
                } else {
                        SetChildBitsOnly(ng_ptr, itr);
                        o_list = NULL;
                }
        }
        // terminate the transfer to OpenGL (if active)
        display.terminateTransfer();
    }
    catch(IteratorException & e) {
        std::cout << e.toString();
    }
}
```

A "for" loop advances along the lines of the example method below but with a few differences:

```
template <class Object>
void IterateOctree( TreeIterator<Object> & itr) {
    try {
            for (itr.first(); itr.isValid(); itr.advance() )
              itr.retrieve();
    }
    catch(BadIterator & e) {
            std::cout << e.toString();
    }
}
```

In the actual code from OctreeWorker the isValid() function is replaced with a getter (itr.get()). If there are no more node groups (a node group is the subdivision of a parent voxel into eight sub-voxels) the getter returns false and the iteration ends.

The iteration is "level first" or "breadth first" order, not depth-first. The iteration continues from level to level because the new levels are enqueued while the current level is being dequeued. When the retrieved OctreeNode's node ID belongs to the next level, the LevelWorker class is smart enough to know that a switch to a new level has taken place.

```
/// fetch_level -> from ID of what comes out of the Iterator queue
/// eval_level -> fetch_level + 1
bool LevelWorker::LevelSwitch(Glassner ID) {

        int fetch_level = id_w.Level(ID);
        int eval_level = fetch_level + 1;

        if (eval_level != current_eval_level) {
```

```
                current_eval_level = eval_level;
                current_fetch_level = fetch_level;
                return true;
        }
        return false;     // no level switch
}
```

So all of this is quite efficient since geometry scaling of triangles takes place only once per level.

The call to Iterate() is:

```
void OctreeWorker::IterateTop() {
        // Level Order iteration : enqueues the root
        LevelOrder<NodeGroup *> my_iter(tree);
        Iterate(my_iter);
}
```

A LevelOrder class is instantiated and passed to the Iterate function. The LevelOrder class inherits the TreeIterator class:

```
template <class Object>
class LevelOrder : public TreeIterator<Object>
```

The iterator constructor requires a pointer to the octree to be iterated, and the octree root is copied to the iterator (Iterate.h):

```
template <class Object>
class TreeIterator
{
public:
  TreeIterator(const Octree<Object> & theTree )
        : root( theTree.root ), current( NULL) {}
...
```

Some basic classes are as follows. First an OctreeNode holds the basic information, being a NodeGroup. The typical usage is:

```
OctreeNode<NodeGroup *> *node = itr.currentOctreeNode();
NodeGroup *group = node->element;
```

And here's the OctreeNode struct in its entirety:

```
// Node element to be managed by Octree class

template <class Object>
struct OctreeNode
{
        Object element;
        unsigned char child_bits, child_count;
        OctreeNode *parent;
        // "count" OctreeNode *'s follow, but start with default NULL.
        OctreeNode **child;

        // be strict and require the parent argument
        OctreeNode(Object & theElement, OctreeNode *mparent,
                        unsigned short mcount = 0) : element(theElement),
                        child_count(mcount), parent(mparent) { child = NULL;}
};
```

The OctreeNode is what's known as a variable-length struct. It takes a NodeGroup * template type. For a given iteration step the GroupWorker class instantiates a NodeGroup and evaluates all eight octants for triangle overlap.

However, child OctreeNodes (as opposed to NodeGroups) are created only for child nodes that have been proven to exist. Not all child nodes will be overlapped by triangles. Child creation for an OctreeNode starts with the method:

```
OctreeNode<NodeGroup *> ** OctreeWorker::MakeChildOctreeNodes(NodeGroup *group,
 TreeIterator<NodeGroup *> & itr, int &count)
{
...
```

The heart of the routine is as follows:

```
  // put this on the heap : keep it around for life of octree
  OctreeNode<NodeGroup *> **children =
                        new OctreeNode<NodeGroup *> * [child_count];
  parent->child = children;
```

Notice that the variable-length list can only be allocated when the number of actual children are known (child_count). When this routine is called, triangle-overlap has already been calculated for all possible children, so that when the actual tree data is created, it's known which child octants are empty. This information is written to the parent node, and then as shown above with the "child_count" variable, the appropriate number of child OctreeNodes are created. No children nodes are created for empty octants.

The Octree class (Octree.h/.tpp) references the OctreeNode. The Octree class defines a pointer to the root and the rest is added on the fly. Here's the top part of the class with the various constructors.

```
/// \class Octree
template <class Object>
class Octree
{
public:
        Octree() : root(NULL) {}
        Octree(const Object & rootItem ) : root (new Node(rootItem, NULL)) {}
        Octree(Object & rootItem) : root (new Node(rootItem, NULL)) {}
...
```

This is supported by:

```
...
private:
        typedef OctreeNode<Object> Node;
        Node *root;

        Node *copy_over(Node & orig) const;

        friend class TreeIterator<Object>;
};
```

Notice TreeIterator is given full access by being declared a friend class. The Octree class includes a recursive copy routine. However the octree is never copied since it can be huge and there's no reason to do so. (And in fact the copy method is never used.)

As well there's an operator= routine that includes the critical routine makeEmpty() in case the lefthand side isn't already empty before the copy. makeEmpty() recurses to the terminal nodes and deletes from the bottom up. But like the copy routine, this isn't currently used.

Going higher up in the call stack,

```
void OctreeWorker::Top() {

   // make the NodeGroup FIRST
   NodeGroup *ng_ptr = NodeGroupRoot((Glassner)0);

   // store it to the Octree as root
```

```
  OctreeRoot(ng_ptr, NULL);

  // before iterating, check false pos status
  if (context.check_false_pos)
        MakeFPContext();

  IterateTop();
}
```

Notice that the root node is given a Glassner ID of 0. The Glassner ID of 0 for the root is a special case, after which all indexing starts at 1. Thus the level 1 nodes have IDs of {1, 2, 3, … , 8}, and the children of 1 {11, 12, 13, … , 18}.

Here is where the octree root is stored:

```
/// Takes a parent arg but we set it to NULL.
void OctreeWorker::OctreeRoot(NodeGroup * ng_ptr,
                              OctreeNode<NodeGroup *> * parent) {
        tree.addRoot(ng_ptr, parent);
        // transfer tree pointer so GroupWorker can use tree for cleanup
        group_w.setTreePointer(&tree);
}
```

And at the core (in Octree.tpp):

```
template <class Object>
void Octree<Object>::addRoot(Object & rootItem,
                              OctreeNode<Object> * parent) {
        if (root != NULL)
                return;

        root = new Node(rootItem, parent);
}
```

where Node is an internal typedef for OctreeNode. So that's the C++ scaffolding for the octree.

Obviously if the Octree class only points to the first child, all the other children have to be stored somewhere. They will be stored in a child list, making the octree a "linearly stored" data structure.

Let's return to the iterator. The TreeIterator class is defined as:

```
template <class Object>
class TreeIterator
{
public:
   TreeIterator(const Octree<Object> & theTree )
          : root( theTree.root ), current( NULL) {}

   virtual ~TreeIterator() {}

   virtual void first() = 0;
   virtual bool get() = 0;
   virtual void put(OctreeNode<Object> **list, int count) = 0;
   bool isValid() const { return current != NULL; }
   const Object & retrieve() const;
   OctreeNode<Object> * currentOctreeNode() { return current; }

protected:
   OctreeNode<Object> * root;
   OctreeNode<Object> * current;
};
```

Note the pure virtual declarations for implementation by the derived (inheriting) class, in this case the LevelOrder class. Recall the generic iterating loop:

```
for (itr.first(); itr.isValid(); itr.advance() )
   itr.retrieve();
```

The final form is:

```
for (itr.first(); itr.get(); itr.put(o_list, count) ) {
         NodeGroup *ng_ptr = itr.retrieve();
```

These routines come from the inheriting class:

```
/// \class LevelOrder
template <class Object>
class LevelOrder : public TreeIterator<Object>
{
public:
         LevelOrder( const Octree<Object> & theTree);
         ~LevelOrder() {}
```

```
        void first();
        bool get();
        void put(OctreeNode<Object> **list, int count);

private:
        QueueAr< OctreeNode<Object> * > q;
};
```

The constructor is defined as:

```
/// constructor for LevelOrder iterator
template <class Object>
LevelOrder<Object>::LevelOrder(const Octree<Object> & theTree)
        : TreeIterator<Object>( theTree )
{
        q.makeEmpty();
        if (TreeIterator<Object>::root != NULL)
          q.enqueue( TreeIterator<Object>::root );
}
```

The makeEmpty() method is applied not to the Octree but to the QueueAr, a queue array, which is the very heart of everything in Project V if you think about it. If there was no queue for iteration, there would be no level-ordering, and hence no workable octree traversal. It's strange to think that a beautiful three-dimensional voxelized object which we see in our mind as, for example, a chess pawn, is in fact generated by a queue.

The "first" method is a no-op:

```
template <class Object>
void LevelOrder<Object>::first()
{
        // currently no init ops
}
```

The isValid method in the second position of the "for" signature was changed to a get routine, which basically checks validity in terms of there being something to get. It's the "test" part of the "for" loop, so "get" must return true or false to keep the loop going or to terminate it.

```
template <class Object>
bool LevelOrder<Object>::get()
{
        if (q.isEmpty() ) {
          if (TreeIterator<Object>::current == NULL)
```

```
            throw IteratorException( "Advance past end" );
          TreeIterator<Object>::current = NULL;
          return false;
        }

        TreeIterator<Object>::current = q.getFront();
        q.dequeue();
        return true;
}
```

If the loop continues, then what's dequeued in get() is then retrieved inside the "for" loop. The third station of the "for" loop is the advancer. But itr.put is preferred to itr.advance, and is shown below.

```
/// want to enqueue the OctreeNode<Object> that holds the Object,
/// not the Object itself

template <class Object>
void LevelOrder<Object>::put(OctreeNode<Object> **list, int count)
{
        if (list == NULL)
                return;

        for (int i = 0; i < count; ++i)
                q.enqueue(list[i]);
}
```

These are the critical routines.

Active octants of the NodeGroup are enqueued as a post-operation of the octree iteration "for" loop. And then the loop repeats until all levels have been created and iterated over. Since everything is queued and then dequeued, it all amounts to a "level order" iteration. This explains a great deal of OctreeWorker::Iterate() method, but now there are the tasks inside the "for" loop to understand.

1.19 *Determining Which Children Go Forward*

The "put" method puts children in the queue. This means that the creation of child coordinates from the parent and the ensuing geometry evaluation must take place between the call to get (for the current item), and the enqueueing of the child OctreeNodes. Since the parent NodeGroup and OctreeNode have been created from the previous level, the parent NodeGroup is available via the retrieve() call. Geometry evaluation amounts to the following inside the loop:

```
        const Level &level = level_w.getLevel();
        group_w.GeomProcess(ng_ptr, level);
```

where ng_ptr is the parent NodeGroup. The GroupWorker class is instantiated with a Context:

```
class GroupWorker {
public:
    GroupWorker(Context &mcontext) : current(NULL), context(mcontext) {}
    ~GroupWorker();
...
```

The Context contains its own built-in GeomWorker. So the GroupWorker can be seen as a high-level geometry processing orchestrator. By the time it's all done for the NodeGroup, we know which children are still active, because they contain triangle overlaps, and which have no overlaps and are terminal nodes. Note that the child status is stored in the parent OctreeNode, so that there's no need to actually create an empty terminal OctreeNode. This hints at "false positive" processing in that when all children of a parent OctreeNode are found to be terminal (empty), then that parent OctreeNode is deleted and its empty status promoted to its parent OctreeNode in turn, in a recursive back-traversal called a "deprecation".

Since octree traversal and creation take place in tandem, the octree structure is deterministic, which means there's no need to check the iterator pointers. In fact, there's no need for the Octree class in general except to keep track of the current level during octree construction.

The NodeGroup struct does not need a link to the Octree because no sorting or searching will happen on NodeGroups, which are allocated freely. Rather, all the searching will happen via the Octree. The NodeGroup has a parent pointer to another NodeGroup, not to an OctreeNode.

OctreeWorker builds the octree in tandem with rasterizing the voxels, which is the GeomProcess step, followed by sending those voxels off for display. The traversal and the transfer of voxels back to the GLWorker is ongoing until the entire octree has been traversed. Then a terminator message is sent and GLWorker flips the display to the newly created image.

It's important to realize that the goal of creating voxels isn't image display. The true prize is the voxels themselves. The reason Project V exists is to have a workbench for creating voxel sets that can then be displayed as a three-dimensional image in a solid-state 3D display cube.

The OctreeNode contains a field for child_bits, the same as generated in the main loop of the iterator for the NodeGroup. The child bits won't be set until the NodeGroup is evaluated for level L+1. As well, unlike the NodeGroup which is pre-instantiated at level L (to be evaluated at level L+1), the actual OctreeNodes are created after the fact, when the child overlap status has been computed.

Node status is stored in the NodeGroup in the geom_stat byte:

```
unsigned char geom_stat;        // overlap for nodes 1 - 8 (bit positions 0 - 7)
```

and this is set in GroupWorker::FineProcess() depending on whether there's triangle overlap or not:

```
current->geom_stat |= setbit;
```

For example, the bit at position 7 is set to 1 if node 8 is non-empty, or left at 0 if empty. This byte is then used to make the appropriate children at the iterator level. If false-positive testing is enabled, it may be necessary to delete OctreeNodes that have been created for some parent. OctreeNode children are allocated and enqueued in LSB to MSB order.

When the OctreeNodes are deleted (for example, during false-positive testing in a "deprecate" step) the C++ syntax uses brackets to delete the entire child array:

```
delete [] parent->child;
```

Since the OctreeNode is a variable-length struct the "child" member is really a variable-length list of 1 to 8 children:

```
// "count" OctreeNode *'s follow, but start with default NULL.
OctreeNode **child;
```

1.20 *Unit versus Virtual Coordinates (Mesh Display)*

The xyz coordinates for each voxel are reconstructed from the Glassner ID as follows:

```
/// gets the min coord of the voxel bbox for level
void IDWorker::getXYZ(Glassner ID, ushort3 &coord) {
        Glassner mag, tID;
        int x, y, z, count;

        count = TensMagnitude(ID);          // 412 returns 3
        mag = TensMinusOne(count);          // 3 returns 100

        x = y = z = 0;

        while (mag >= 1) {
```

```
            tID = ID / mag;
            x = (x << 1) + ax[tID - 1];
            y = (y << 1) + ay[tID - 1];
            z = (z << 1) + az[tID - 1];

            tID *= mag;
            ID -= tID;
            mag /= 10;
        }
        coord.x = x;
        coord.y = y;
        coord.z = z;
}
```

with ax, etc., being zero-referenced as:

```
ax = (0, 1, 0, 1, 0, 1, 0, 1);
ay = (0, 0, 0, 0, 1, 1, 1, 1);
az = (1, 1, 0, 0, 1, 1, 0, 0);
```

One can distinguish between an evaluative cell size, being always the unit voxel; and a "virtual" cell size, being the reverse sequence of scale factors applied to the geometry, given level L or 2^n maximum resolution, for example: L = n = 9 => 2^9 = 512. The virtual size is used for drawing terminal cells for mesh visualization.

Level	Eval	Virtual Cell Size	
0	2^0 = 1	512	(overlap assumed for "the universe" at level 0)
1	2^1 = 2	256	
2	2^2 = 4	128	
...			
9	2^9 = 512	1	

Thus, given the (x,y,z) offset and a voxel length, the virtual voxel size is easily computed for a terminal node. For example, if the terminal node is on level 4, and the maximum resolution is 512, then the "display length" of the terminal cell is simply:

2^4 = 16
512 / 16 = 32

Instead of going through the complex level-order iteration, which is only critical when creating new nodes that require geometry evaluation, the mesh generation does a depth-first recursion using the existing octree:

```
/// recursive
void OctreeWorker::DrawMesh(OctreeNode<NodeGroup *> *node, int level) {

	// this is the voxel itself, so draw nothing
	if (node->child_count == 0) {
		if (node->child_bits == 0) {
			std::cout << "FOUND ZERO CHILD COUNT" << std::endl;
			NodeGroup *ng_ptr = node->element;
			std::cout << "ID: " << ng_ptr->ID << std::endl;
		}
		return;
	}

	unsigned char testbit = 0x01;
	int count = 0;

	for (int i = 0; i<OCTANTS; ++i) {
		if (node->child_bits & testbit) {
			// reference node by number of set bits, not by octant
			DrawMesh(node->child[count], level + 1);
			++count;
		} else {
			NodeGroup *ng_ptr = node->element;
			display.MakeMeshData(ng_ptr, i, level);
		}
		testbit <<= 1;
	}
}
```

with the initial call being:

```
/// tree is already made; iterate through recursively
void OctreeWorker::MeshTop() {
	DrawMesh(tree.getRoot(), 0);
	display.terminateMesh();
}
```

As long as the level is known, the virtual cell size can be determined. The mesh display is very useful for precisely locating a bad voxel in the event of a bug. It's also a nice verification that the subdivision is truly adaptive.

Any iterators attached to the Octree class simply use the OctreeNode "child_count" member to index the children node pointers. i.e.:

```
count = my_node.child_count;

for (int i = 0; i < count; ++i) {
  childNode = my_node.child[i];
  etc.
}
```

1.21 *Antialiasing by Supersample*

A cheap trick can be used to accomplish anti-aliasing (AA) of the three-dimensional geometry. Basically the iteration is set up to go an extra level, so that that voxels at the terminal level + 1 become a "supersample" of some parent node. Since the children are processed as a group, at the end of the loop the final voxel value (at the parent level) can be determined from the average of the children and applied to the NodeGroup parent. This value is then displayed in OpenGL.

Here's the averaging code (see Display.cpp, Display::AntiAlias):

```
...
        // we take all octants, even empty ones
        for (i = 0; i < OCTANTS; ++i) {
                if (group->geom_stat & testbit) {
                        Blend(group, i, tri_list, color);
                        colors[i].r = color.x;
                        colors[i].g = color.y;
                        colors[i].b = color.z;
                } else {
                        // make aa go to black background.
                        // for 3D display this is a voltage
                        colors[i].r = 0.0;
                        colors[i].g = 0.0;
                        colors[i].b = 0.0;
                }
                testbit <<= 1;
        }
        color.x = color.y = color.z = 0.0;
        for (i = 0; i < 8; ++i) {
                color.x += colors[i].r;
                color.y += colors[i].g;
                color.z += colors[i].b;
        }
        color.x /= 8.0;
```

```
        color.y /= 8.0;
        color.z /= 8.0;
...
```

The Blend() function takes each color for each triangle associated with the voxel, and averages those colors together. Most voxels only have one triangle overlap, so the color is the triangle's color.

Of course, really doing anti-aliasing on a 3D display is a whole area of research because the added dimension, plus the translucency of the voxels, plus being able to change perspective instantly and thus see a part of a model against a different set of background voxels, makes anti-aliasing a whole new problem. Part of this has been addressed in hardware with the *sous-bande*. (See my book *The Cube* for details.)

END OF PART ONE

Part Two

2.0 *Triangle Processing, Review*

Triangle processing was introduced in Part One in terms of general scaling and basic overlap tests. Triangle processing will now be presented in more detail. As well, the list data structures and methods that associate individual triangles with voxels will be explained.

To review, each triangle has an associated bounding box, specified as a min and max point; and an integerized version of that bounding box. This bounding box is scaled at each level switch from the triangle's master coordinates.

The scale factor for the geometry, i.e., {1, 2, 4, ... , 2^n} is the same as constant N. The value of N depends on the level of the octree subdivision. The master triangle geometry is bounded by -1 and 1 in each dimension and the "master list" of triangles never changes from its "bi-unit" scaling. A "level list" of triangles is scaled from the master for each level but never changes during processing for that level.

Since each triangle may be evaluated for many different voxels for some level, the bounding box information is attached to the triangle, not the voxel. As well, the Triangle struct contains three edge specifiers, a normal, the dominant axis specifier, and a sub-struct for variables associated with the fine rasterization stage, called FineVars.

The scaling happens at every change in level, which is called a *level switch.* Because the octree is processed in Level order, there are only n level switches. For example, if n = 8 then the voxel resolution is 2^n = 256 and there are 8 level switches. The code that handles the operations that occur during a level switch is in LevelWorker.cpp:

```
/// At every level switch...
void LevelWorker::DoLevelWork() {
        N = context.geom_w.NewN(current_eval_level,
                                context.terminal_level,
                                TerminalLevel());
        context.geom_w.SetBBoxDeltas();
        context.geom_w.DoTriangleWork();
}
```

The LevelWorker is embedded in the OctreeWorker, so is instantly accessible during octree iteration. One level down, the GeomWorker does the scaling as follows:

```
/// per level
void GeomWorker::DoTriangleWork() {
        if (tri_list == NULL)
```

```
            return;

        int count = tri_list->count;
        for (int i = 0; i<count; ++i) {
            Triangle * tri = tri_list->list[i];
            g_u.ScaleTriangleBBox(tri->bbox0, tri->bbox1, tri);
            g_u.ComputeIntegerBBox(tri->bbox0i, tri->bbox1i,
                                   tri->bbox0, tri->bbox1);
            g_u.InitPlaneTestVars(tri->n, tri->v0, tri);
            TriangleSetup(tri);
        }
}
```

The triangle bounding boxes are rescaled even though the master Triangle list remains the same, so tri_list pointers referenced by the GeomWorker class don't need to be touched once they're assigned. The trick of using master coordinates for the rescale instead of sequentially reusing the last level's coordinates prevents roundoff error as the iteration goes deeper into the octree subdivision.

Order counts, since the master coordinates are applied in ScaleTriangleBBox(), and then those freshly scaled coordinates are used by ComputeIntegerBBox(). The GeomUtil class has private data for bbox_delta and inv_bbox_delta vectors, both scaled by N, the current scale factor, once per level. These are used for scaling in the rasterize() code. When GeomUtil assigns those values for the level, it also computes various spherical boundaries for the 6-sep rasterization for that level. (See Part Five.)

The triangle setup code uses no voxel position information, only the bbox_deltas which are position independent. Thus at the bottom level:

```
void GeomUtil::SetBBoxDeltas() {
        MakeBBoxDelta(bbox_delta);
        MakeInvBBoxDelta(inv_bbox_delta);
}

void GeomUtil::MakeBBoxDelta(float3 &delta) {
        delta.x = (bbox1.x - bbox0.x) / float(N);
        delta.y = (bbox1.y - bbox0.y) / float(N);
        delta.z = (bbox1.z - bbox0.z) / float(N);
}

void GeomUtil::MakeInvBBoxDelta(float3 &delta) {
        delta.x = float(N) / (bbox1.x - bbox0.x);
        delta.y = float(N) / (bbox1.y - bbox0.y);
```

```
        delta.z = float(N) / (bbox1.z - bbox0.z);
}
```

Here's the code to scale the master bounding box:

```
void GeomUtil::ScaleTriangleBBox(float3 &tri_bbox0, float3 &tri_bbox1, Triangle *tri) {
        tri_bbox0.x = tri->master_bbox0.x * inv_bbox_delta.x;
        tri_bbox0.y = tri->master_bbox0.y * inv_bbox_delta.y;
        tri_bbox0.z = tri->master_bbox0.z * inv_bbox_delta.z;

        tri_bbox1.x = tri->master_bbox1.x * inv_bbox_delta.x;
        tri_bbox1.y = tri->master_bbox1.y * inv_bbox_delta.y;
        tri_bbox1.z = tri->master_bbox1.z * inv_bbox_delta.z;
}
```

This scales the triangle bounding box up, since voxel resolution remains at unit size from level to level, while the universe expands around each unit voxel. At each level there are more voxels which fill more space.

As always the GeomWorker is embedded in the Context, which is passed to the GroupWorker and LevelWorker. The Context is instantiated outside of the octree iterator main loop and persists for the entire iteration. The Context is associated with the Octree as well as the GroupWorker and LevelWorker classes.

The Triangle and FineVars structs are found in Triangle.h:

```
/// The indices are swizzles for (u,v) pairs per triangle dominant axis
struct FineVars {
        // master fields
   float4 plane_eq;

   // level fields
   float3 a[3];
   float3 n_delta_u[3], n_delta_v[3];
   float2 c0[3], c1[3], c2[3];              // xformed
   float2 h0[3], h1[3], h2[3];              // halo from xformed
   float3 cw[3];
   unsigned char planebits;                 // valid halo planes
};

/// uses same names as voxel-pipe
struct Triangle {
        // master fields
```

```
    float3 v0, v1, v2;
    float3 edge0, edge1, edge2;
    float3 n;
    float3 master_bbox0, master_bbox1;
    color3 color;
    int axis; // dominant axis (based on normal n)

    // level fields
    int3 bbox0i, bbox1i;
    float3 bbox0, bbox1;
    float3 big_center, little_center;
    float big_radius, little_radius;

    // for plane test...
    float r1, r2;
    float d;
    // for fine test....
    FineVars fine;
};
```

Some of these entries are used for thin rasterization, such as the cx and hx values in FineVars, and some are used for conservative or thick rasterization. The thin rasterization process will be explained in Part Five.

2.1 *Triangles vs. Octree Hierarchy*

Each triangle's bounding box defines a volume in (x,y,z) which may overlap one or more tile or voxel locations. In Voxel Pipe there's a tile_id array and a triangle-index array associated with the complete span of these (x,y,z) values. These tile_ids are sorted and a pair-relationship with the triangle-index is maintained.

One big difference between Voxel Pipe and the octree approach is that Voxel Pipe analyzes triangles over a fixed resolution of N = 128 * 4. However, the triangles in the octree approach will start with a resolution of 2 x 2 x 2, and go from there. There are many fewer overlap possibilities in the first stages of adaptive subdivision than in later stages, although potentially many triangles; and in the later stages many octree nodes will have become terminal, thus reducing the voxel load due to empty spaces in the adaptive subdivision.

A master triangle's bounding box will always have the same maxima and minima, so the basic unit-space calculation only needs to be done once. The change will come with the scale by successive inv_bbox_deltas, which are applied to the "master" bbox to create each "level" bbox. Then the integer bbox is computed. These things only need to be done once at each level.

The octree descent is such that it becomes difficult to fill in voxels "all in a row" as with Voxel Pipe. When the scale gets large a triangle will have a bbox range that may span many voxels. For Voxel Pipe this is all right since it uses a scanline approach with a fixed resolution. But for adaptive subdivision it doesn't make sense to loop over the triangle bbox coords (each integer unit-step representing a unit voxel) since we're focused on an individual voxel or NodeGroup octant which is somewhere in the middle of that iteration.

For adaptive subdivision it makes sense to reverse the approach: to go from a voxel to the triangle bbox. This is where the triangle-tile pairs come in. The pairs are sorted by voxel; in Voxel Pipe the tile_id is 111.111.111 for z.y.x. An ascending sort will be by x, then by y, then by z. Again, this doesn't work for an octree encoding, which is subdivided into groups of 8, e.g. a NodeGroup.

Instead the iteration proceeds in octant order, {1, 2, 3, … , 8}, and furthermore in level-octant order:

{11, 12, 13, … , 18}
{21, 22, 23, … , 28}
…
{81, 82, 83, … , 88}

In general it seems like a good idea to follow the Voxel Pipe procedure as much as possible, if only because the rasterization process is so complex. In Voxel Pipe the two-stage idea takes the form of coarse and fine overlap tests.

2.2 *Coarse Testing Stage*

In Voxel Pipe a method called coarse_raster_kernel() in coarse.h loops on triangles and for each triangle does the following:

setup_triangle ::
makes the scaled triangle bbox
makes the integer triangle bbox
calculates edges
uses edges 0 and 2 to make normal n
calculates the dominant axis

The tiles are processed in the following loop:

```
for (all triangles) {
   int3 tri_bbox0i;
   int3 tri_bbox1i;
```

```
    tri_idx = ...
    if (tri_idx is valid) {
        setup_triangle(... tri_bbox0i, tri_bbox1i);
        store tri_bbox0i;
        store tri_bbox1i;

        for (x...) {
            for (y...) {
                for (z...) {
                    output pair
                }
            }
        } // x
    } // triangle valid
} // triangle loop
```

The tile counts, that is, the number of tiles overlapped by a given triangle, are based on the triangle bbox. The loop on {x,y,z} is a loop on tile counts. It outputs a series of tiles for the triangle in the form of a series of triangle-tile pairs, each pair being called in computer science lingo a "tuple".

The coarse overlap stage therefore combines the mathematical overlap check with this loop on the triangle bbox.

In the Project V approach, setup_triangle() is called once per level rather than for every triangle at a fixed resolution. If Project V was to follow the Voxel Pipe formula, the ensuing bbox iteration to make the pair list would be done for an *entire level.* This would require special processing on the Octree queue, by indexing through the queue array twice, in two passes, and requeueing the level after the first pass. This requires keeping flags around to tell when the first pass is being repeated; and when the second pass is finished. It also requires new data structures to store all of the triangles processed during the first pass. This is a very inefficient way to go since at deeper levels there will be many overlaps in many different voxel groups. At the very least a binary search has to be implemented to speed up the listmaking chores. All of this has been tried and in fact NodeGroup.h still contains some of the data structures for this reverse approach, since they're complementary to the data structures actually used and so may come in handy some day.

In the octree approach the triangle bbox in integer space is compared to a candidate voxel's base coordinates and its unit extents. This happens in the coarse stage. There are two choices for the order of looping. The triangle loop can be outside of the octant/voxel loop, or the voxel/octant loop can be outside of the triangle loop. The two-stage approach is to have *coarse* exclusion proceed in triangle loop outside of voxel loop order, whereby a *pair list* is made.

Only one NodeGroup is processed at a time because each OctreeNode contains a NodeGroup data element, so there are only 8 voxels processed in the voxel loop for a given NodeGroup. In an intermediate step the pair list is sorted for the NodeGroup by octant. Then the *fine* stage proceeds as a voxel loop outside of the triangle loop, and uses the the pair list created in the previous stage for the triangle loop. A triangle may be marked INVALID for an octant in the NodeGroup if it falls outside of that octant (a NodeGroup contains eight octants or subdivisions) during fine processing. In other words, a triangle's overlap status for a parent is not always guaranteed to be the same for a child. A child at the subdivided corner of a parent may be outside of the triangle, even though the triangle is inside of the parent.

Therefore the final coarse loop is:

```
/// Outer loop: triangles ; inner loop: voxels per octant
VTList * GeomWorker::CoarseTest(Vector<int> &tri_idx, NodeGroup *group) {
        int i, j, size;
        unsigned short x, y, z;
        Vector<VTPair *> pairs;

        size = tri_idx.size();
        for (i = 0; i < size; ++i) {
                Triangle *tri = tri_list->list[ tri_idx[i] ];

                for (j=0; j<OCTANTS; ++j) {
                        NodeData voxel = group->node[j];
                        x = voxel.coord.x; y = voxel.coord.y; z = voxel.coord.z;
                        if ((x >= tri->bbox0i.x && x <= tri->bbox1i.x) &&
                           (y >= tri->bbox0i.y && y <= tri->bbox1i.y) &&
                           (z >= tri->bbox0i.z && z <= tri->bbox1i.z)) {
                                // tri bbox volume includes (x,y,z)
                                // make the voxel-triangle pair
                                VTPair *pair = new VTPair;
                                pair->tri_idx = tri_idx[i];
                                pair->vox_idx = j;              // reference from zero
                                pairs.push_back(pair);
                        }
                } // octants
        } // triangles
...
}
```

The new VTList is assigned to the NodeGroup, and hence becomes, through the OctreeNode that contains the NodeGroup, accessible to the next level of iteration as the "parent list". For the root node of the octree the list includes all triangles. As the octree iteration proceeds, the parent triangle list for some NodeGroup will become smaller as the voxel resolution becomes progressively finer.

Let's say at L = 1 a triangle is in {1, 2, 3, 4} but not in {5, 6, 7, 8} for some NodeGroup. The voxel-triangle pair list becomes:

(1,1)
(2,1)
(3,1)
(4,1) (m,n) : m = voxel, n = triangle

This information is calculated when level L = 1 is evaluated. The NodeGroup and its NodeData have been pre-instantiated at level L = 0 but aren't evaluated until L = 1. Note that the triangle bboxes have not yet been scaled for L = 1 at L = 0, so bounding box inclusion tests can't proceed until after the level switch, when the triangle bboxes are recalculated for the new N.

New OctreeNodes for L = 2 aren't created until a voxel at L = 1 has passed all overlap tests, both coarse and fine. The NodeGroup is the working data structure that provides the bridge from parent to child. The coarse bbox overlap test will prevent a voxel from producing children; as will the plane test; and finally the fine test will determine which children are intersected by the triangle.

In the example above the children for each of {1, 2, 3, 4} are created for level L = 2. These children have a Glassner ID of {1x, 2x, 3x, 4x}, the x representing 8 potential children for each node.

Let's say for 1x that the returned bit setting at L = 2 is:

10000011
87654321

The entries 18, 12, and 11 are added to the queue; the parent passes its ID as a prefix to its children. Geometrically, this tells us that 18, 12, and 11 are not empty locations for the triangle. Conceptually the sorted pair list for the child is:

(11,1)
(12,1)
(18,1)

At level L = 3, the triangle bbox is scaled by inv_bbox_delta, integerized, and these new extents are used for overlap testing. For example, if at level L = 2 the entry 11 is stored, standing for 11x, then what's been established is that the triangle intersects voxel 11 at the parent level, but what hasn't been determined yet is which elements of 11x the triangle overlaps. The first step of determining this is to match the triangle extents to voxels {111, 112, 113, ... , 118}.

However, this can't be done by iterating over the entire spatial extents of the triangle bbox, because many iterations on empty nodes outside of the immediate cluster of 8 would take place, especially as subdivision gets deeper into the octree and the relative scale of the triangle to unit voxels causes the number of voxels to increase.

But there is another problem. There may be more than one triangle that overlaps a child octant. One wants to avoid looping over the entire master triangle list for each NodeGroup!

Because of level-order octree traversal, it's known in advance which triangles need to be tested at level L = 3. These are the triangles evaluated at the parent level: say triangles (1, 2, 3). In which case at the parent level L = 2 the NodeGroup evaluation would have already produced the following pair list:

(11,1)
(11,2)
(11,3)

This is enough information to create a triangle list for the child. The child, when its turn comes for evaluation, uses its NodeGroup parent pointer to retrieve the pairs. Only triangle indices in the pair list will be passed on to level L + 1 for testing. The processing stays local to the octant group, and iterates through all triangles contained in the parent. This results in a new list of pairs, which can then be sorted on the octant ID. In the fine test, the looping is on octants first, then triangles. Each triangle is retrieved for the current voxel from the pair-list for the current octant group. This then eliminates any expensive ranging over the entire triangle list at higher resolutions and deeper levels.

Note that 100,000 triangles require an "int" data type, 4 bytes, the same as a pointer. Therefore an integer index is used for the triangle element of the VTPair. This will become clearer presently. The pair-list is sorted by node (vox_idx), an index between 0 and 7. Therefore the basic element is called a voxel-triangle pair or VTPair (NodeGroup.h):

```
struct VTPair {
    unsigned short vox_idx;     // voxel index, 0 - 7, reference from zero
    int tri_idx;                // instead of Triangle *
};
```

Each pair in the pair list must be accessible to the GroupWorker via the NodeGroup; and accessible for the iteration during the fine step, as well as for transfer to the children nodes if the voxel passes all the intersection tests. Thus the NodeGroup is the logical place for the pair list. The VTList looks like this:

```
/// for sorting, want to put VTPairs in a Vector, then
/// reference vox_id directly in the sort routine.
/// Alternately, can reference list[i] below.

struct VTList {
    int count;
    VTPair **list;
};
```

This is a variable-length struct similar to the OctreeNode struct elsewhere in the code. The same type of list is used for the TriangleList (see Triangle.h). VTPairs are allocated and managed on the heap. A historical note is that the first Solid Modeling software offered by Autodesk, called AutoSolid, was written in C++ in 1988; it was almost completely designed around this kind of struct. In 1988 the existence of this variable-length construct was a closely guarded secret. Thankfully programmers are a gregarious lot, and word spread quickly.

Note that the VTList is allocated in a chunk. This means it can't be allocated until its final size is known. To avoid resizing outside of a Vector, a Vector is used to accumulate results for a given NodeGroup, and once the results are known, and the final size of the VTList is known, then the VTList is allocated and the VTPairs transferred from the Vector to the allocated array in one fell swoop.

Here's the pertinent part of the coarse test which fills the pairs Vector:

```
VTList * GeomWorker::CoarseTest(Vector<int> &tri_idx, NodeGroup *group) {
        int i, j, size;
        unsigned short x, y, z;
        Vector<VTPair *> pairs;
...
... inside the loop ...
                        // make the voxel-triangle pair
                        VTPair *pair = new VTPair;
                        pair->tri_idx = tri_idx[i];
                        pair->vox_idx = j;              // reference from zero
                        pairs.push_back(pair);
...
```

When the loop is done, the new pair pointers are copied into a new VTList allocated on the heap. This VTList belongs to the NodeGroup "group". More specifically, a list of VTPair pointers is allocated based on the Vector size, and the pointers copied from the "pairs" Vector to the allocated list:

```
...
        size = pairs.size();
        VTList * vt_list = new VTList;
        vt_list->count = size;
        VTPair **plist = new VTPair * [size];
        vt_list->list = plist;

        // copy pointers
        for (i = 0; i < size; ++i) {
                vt_list->list[i] = pairs[i];
        }
        // go ahead and attach to group
        group->pairs = vt_list;

        // pairs about to go out of scope, but not what the pointers point to
        return vt_list;
}
```

Since the Vector is instantiated on the stack it's automatically freed when the method exits. No excess memory is used from NodeGroup to NodeGroup. The Vector, which is automatically resized, is freed, along with its excess allocation.

The triangles themselves are *not* copied to the children. Rather, when L goes to L + 1 the children reach up to the parent NodeGroup through the available parent pointer, and get the parent triangles via the parent's begin-end list for octant[i]. Each triangle is retrieved by index. A begin-end list is a collection of "triangle spans" – to be explained next.

2.3 *Fine Testing Stage*

The second stage of rasterization in the Voxel Pipe implementation is in fine.h. At this stage, the pairs have been sorted by tile ID.

fine_raster => fine_raster_kernel:

```
for (...) {
   tile_idx = ...
   if (tile_idx < N_tiles) {
      fine_raster_block<>::process( ... , tile_start[tile_idx], tile_end[tile_idx], ...)
   }
```

```
}
```

The process() method is given the tile_start and tile_end values for the current tile. These are indices into the sorted triangle-tile pairs: the start index accesses the current tile's first triangle; the end index accesses the current tile's final triangle.

The process() method first performs a plane test with r1, r2, c, and np. If this fails, the current triangle for the tile fails. Then the triangle bbox is fetched and is clamped/clipped to the current tile. The integer bounding box is computed in setup_triangle() and stored in coarse.h.

Finally, the triangle's vertices and edges are passed to the rasterize() routine along with the triangle bbox and the triangle's dominant axis (via the appropriate template argument).

The method plane_setup() in utils.h is called from the rasterize functions, with a triangle vertex, normal, and the geometry bbox0. This is triangle-centric (level independent) and can be done once at initialization. Also, triangle_setup() in utils.h is called for the passed triangle. This computes n0, n1, n2, d0, d1, d2, &a, &n_delta_u, &n_delta_v, e.g. the fine variables.

For Project V, the fine test is pretty much the same as for Voxel Pipe, but with minor modifications for octree iteration and levels. For example, since triangle_setup() uses bbox_delta that makes the method level-dependent in the Project V world, and so the method must be called when the level transition takes place for a new N.

For fine processing the inner loop is over triangles, as shown below.

```
/// if at least one triangle overlaps the current octant,
/// then return true: the octant will spawn children.
bool GeomWorker::FineTest(NodeGroup *group, int octant, int begin, int end) {
	int i;
	VTPair **pair = group->pairs->list;
	Vector<int> compact_list;
	bool valid, tvalid;
	const ushort3 &coord = group->node[octant].coord;

	// for all triangles of current octant
	valid = false;
	for (i = begin; i <= end; ++i) {
		int tri_idx = pair[i]->tri_idx;
		Triangle *tri = tri_list->list[tri_idx];

		//
		if (!g_u.PlaneTest(coord, tri->n, tri)) {
			compact_list.push_back(i);
```

```
                continue;           // try another triangle
            }

            // next, call rasterize or rasterize_26sep
            if (raster & CONSERVATIVE_MASK)
                tvalid = g_u.Rasterize_26sepTop(coord, tri);
            else
                tvalid = g_u.RasterizeTop(coord, tri);

            if (!tvalid) {
                compact_list.push_back(i);
                continue;
            }
            // one triangle overlap is enough to validate voxel
            if (!valid)
                valid = true;
        }
        // whether valid or not, may need to compact pair list
        compactPairList(pair, compact_list);

        return valid;
}
```

This routine is called with begin and end indices from an outer loop over octants,

```
/// follow voxel-pipe example and loop by voxel in the fine stage
void GroupWorker::FineProcess(const Level & level) {
        int i, count, begin, end;
        unsigned char setbit = 0x01;

        current->geom_stat = 0x00;

        for (i=0, count = 0; i<OCTANTS; ++i) {
            // get the begin-end indices
            begin = current->span[i].begin;
            end = current->span[i].end;
            if (begin != -1) {
                if (context.geom_w.FineTest(current, i, begin, end)) {
                    current->geom_stat |= setbit;
                    ++count;
                }
            }
            setbit <<= 1;
```

```
        }
...
```

where "current" is a GroupWorker class variable for the current NodeGroup:

```
private:
        NodeGroup *current;
```

The looping is first by octants, and then for each octant, by triangles via FineTest(). At the beginning levels, the fine stage will be processing voxels that encompass potentially many triangles, since the geometry only spans two voxels in each dimension. But at deeper levels there will be more voxels and fewer triangles per voxel. Along those lines, at the beginning levels most triangle extents will be interior to the voxel extents. But at deeper levels most voxel extents will be interior to triangle extents.

The VTList is stored in memory that's referenced by a second array in the NodeGroup, being the "spans". Each span is defined as:

```
/// initialize the array to -1, since some voxels will have no overlap.
struct TSpan {
    int begin;    // many overlap possibilities
    int end;
};
```

TSpan stands for "Triangle Span". The NodeGroup includes it as follows:

```
struct NodeGroup {
...
    TSpan span[OCTANTS];
...
};
```

where

```
static const int OCTANTS = 8;
```

There are 8 spans, one for each octant, and each span has a beginning and ending index into the parent NodeGroup's VTList. The VTList is sorted by voxel ID and the begin-end list is constructed the same way as in Voxel Pipe. Starting with voxel index 1, and ending with 8, the transitions in the VTList mark the begin and end indices into the VTList for each octant. In other words, this is a segmentation scheme by voxel index. There can be arbitrarily many triangles for a given voxel index: the span marks the beginning and end of the entire segment for each octant in sorted VTPair memory.

```
bool GroupWorker::CoarseProcess(const Level & level) {
...
        // sort the VTPairs for current node
        sort.quicksort(vt_list);

        // now make the Triangle spans for each octant
        MakeTriangleSpans();
...
}
```

Let's look at the method MakeTriangleSpans(). Before anything happens, the spans are initialized to -1:

```
/// -1 means empty
void GroupWorker::SetDefaultTSpan(NodeGroup *ng) {
        for (int i = 0; i < OCTANTS; ++i) {
                ng->span[i].begin = -1;
                ng->span[i].end = -1;
        }
}
```

Then they're filled in for each octant, that is each active octant that has one or more triangle overlaps. Not all octants will be represented in the VTList for the current NodeGroup unless every single octant has been overlapped by one or more triangles. (This is simple but tricky.)

```
/// vt_list has already been checked and sorted by caller
void GroupWorker::MakeTriangleSpans() {
        unsigned short vox_id, prev_id;
        int i, count;

        VTList *vt_list = current->pairs;
        count = vt_list->count;

        // init the first pair...
        VTPair *pair = vt_list->list[0];
        vox_id = pair->vox_idx;
        current->span[vox_id].begin = 0;
        current->span[vox_id].end = 0;

        prev_id = vox_id;

        // and succeeding pairs...
```

```
        for (i = 1; i< count; ++i) {
                VTPair *pair = vt_list->list[i];
                vox_id = pair->vox_idx;
                if (vox_id != prev_id) {
                        current->span[vox_id].begin = i;
                        current->span[prev_id].end = i - 1;
                        prev_id = vox_id;
                }
        }
        // final end value
        current->span[vox_id].end = i - 1;
}
```

If the processing gets to MakeTriangleSpans() then *something* has been added to the VTList. In other words, there's at least one overlap. For example, triangle 0 in octants 1, 4, and 7; and triangle 2 in octants 1, 3, 7. Triangle 1 has not passed the coarse test.

In this example there are six pairs in the pair list. The pairs are sorted by node (vox_idx):

```
(1, 0)
(1, 2)
(3, 2)
(4, 0)
(7, 0)
(7, 2) (m = node, n = tri_idx)
```

The first part of MakeTriangleSpans() initializes the first span to pair-list entry 0. The relevant voxel index value is fetched from the first item in the pair list.

```
count = 6

span[1].begin = 0
span[1].end = 0

prev_id = 1
```

Then the next pairs are evaluated in the loop:

```
i = 1
vox_id = 1
[no action]

i = 2
```

```
vox_id = 3
span[3].begin = 2
span[1].end = 1

prev_id = 3
i = 3
vox_id = 4
span[4].begin = 3
span[3].end = 2

prev_id = 4
i = 4
vox_id = 7
span[7].begin = 4
span[4].end = 3

prev_id = 7
i = 5
vox_id = 7
[no action]

span[7].end = 5
```

The end result is:

```
span[1].begin = 0
span[1].end = 1
span[3].begin = 2
span[3].end = 2
span[4].begin = 3
span[4].end = 3
span[7].begin = 4
span[7].end = 5
```

The span index is the voxel ID, and the begin/end values are the indices into the pair-list. There can be many many entries between those begin and end markers, each entry a different triangle for the voxel index. So for voxel ID 1, its "span" is 0 to 1, meaning these two entries:

```
(1, 0)
(1, 2)
```

In other words, triangles 0 and 2. Likewise, for voxel ID 3, it begins and ends with this entry:

(3, 2)

In other words, triangle 2 exclusively. This might seem kind of dumb, but in programming what looks obvious to the programmer needs to be spelled out for the program. This is a simple example and in practice the triangle indices can be large, and there can be many indices for a voxel.

The fine stage then uses those triangle spans for the fine tests. Remember, the fine stage first loops on octants, and then triangles, e.g.:

```
bool GeomWorker::FineTest(NodeGroup *group, int octant, int begin, int end) {
        int i;
        VTPair **pair = group->pairs->list;
...
        // for all triangles of current octant
        valid = false;
        for (i = begin; i <= end; ++i) {
                int tri_idx = pair[i]->tri_idx;
                Triangle *tri = tri_list->list[tri_idx];
...
```

This is a very efficient double dereferencing for the relevant triangles. At this point certain triangles may fail the fine (expensive) tests. The VTPair entry for that triangle is marked INVALID. INVALID or -1 entries are then "compacted" after the last triangle has been evaluated in the fine test for the current voxel.

The way this is done is to keep a running compaction list, defined as follows:

```
bool
 GeomWorker::FineTest(NodeGroup *group, int octant, int begin, int end) {
        int i;
        VTPair **pair = group->pairs->list;
        Vector<int> compact_list;
...
```

The pair list contains all the parent Triangle indices, but not all of those indices are guaranteed to overlap the current NodeGroup octant. If the rasterize method of choice returns false, the compact_list is filled with the VTPair index (retrieved from the span) for the failed triangle.

```
...
        for (i = begin; i <= end; ++i) {
                int tri_idx = pair[i]->tri_idx;
```

```
        Triangle *tri = tri_list->list[tri_idx];
...
        compact_list.push_back(i);
...
```

At the end of the fine test, the compaction routine is called with the pair list and compaction list:

```
    // whether valid or not, may need to compact pair list
    compactPairList(pair, compact_list);
```

The method of interest is:

```
/// do this the easy way by overwriting -1 for invalid triangles
/// This preserves the TSpan indexing.
void GeomWorker::compactPairList(VTPair **pair, Vector<int> &compact_list) {
    int i, size, index;

    size = compact_list.size();
    for (i = 0; i< size; ++i) {
        index = compact_list[i];
        pair[index]->tri_idx = INVALID; // = -1
    }
}
```

In the example, let's say tri_idx 2 fails for VTList index 1. Then compact_list[0] = 1, and the list is now:

(1, 0)
(1, -1)
(3, 2)
etc.

2.4 *Voxel Display*

After the fine stage there are some other things that can happen, including a stage of false-positive processing if the octree recursion has reached the terminal level. But assuming that there's no false-positive processing, and the terminal level has been reached, the span list finally goes to the Display class, where all the triangles for the voxel are pre-processed for final transfer to OpenGL. A check for INVALID preempts any triangles that have been rejected in the fine testing stage.

Here's an example display function for blending together the colors of all overlapping triangles for a voxel before sending the voxel to OpenGL.

```
/// Blend colors for all triangles
void Display::Blend(NodeGroup *group, int octant, TriangleList * tri_list, float3 &color) {
	int i, begin, end, tri_idx, count;

	// these will be valid for passed octant
	begin = group->span[octant].begin;
	end = group->span[octant].end;
	count = 0;
	color.x = color.y = color.z = 0.0;

	for (i = begin; i <= end; ++i) {
		tri_idx = group->pairs->list[i]->tri_idx;
		if (tri_idx == INVALID)
			continue;
		Triangle * tri = tri_list->list[tri_idx];
		color.x += tri->color.r;
		color.y += tri->color.g;
		color.z += tri->color.b;
		++count;
	}
	if (count > 1) {
		color.x /= (float)count;
		color.y /= (float)count;
		color.z /= (float)count;
	}
}
```

For anti-aliasing (AA) processing, the average color for n triangles is found for a voxel; and then an average color for all 8 voxels which form the supersample. This will be the anti-aliased value for the parent NodeData. The average consists adding all the children colors together and then dividing by 8. Empty voxels are set to some low threshhold value: for example, 0 for a black background. As mentioned in Part One, anti-aliasing in 3D is another problem altogether.

At the AA level, there's no need to backtrack to the parent level, since the parent level will have written nothing, only created nodes for voxels with triangle overlap. In AA mode the child level at max L + 1 will write the average value for the entire octant to the (x, y, z) of the parent. The parent NodeGroup and node_idx are used to get the (x,y,z) value directly from the parent NodeData:

```
void Display::AntiAlias(NodeGroup *group) {
...
        // use the coord for this node group which is stored with the parent
        int idx = group->node_idx - 1;
        ushort3 &coord = group->parent->node[idx].coord;
        queueVoxel(color, coord);
...
```

The decrement on the node_idx is simply because the NodeData ("node") is referenced from 0 to 7 rather than the Glassner-ready range of 1 to 8. NodeData is kept around in the NodeGroup and looks like this,

```
struct NodeGroup {
    NodeData node[OCTANTS];
    unsigned char node_idx;      // index of parent NodeData (1 - 8): 0 for root
...
```

and is declared as:

```
/// can be a wrapper for any simulation data
struct NodeData {
        ushort3 coord;
        uchar3 color;
};
```

2.5 *Deriving Fine Stage Variables from Triangle Data*

The conservative rasterize methods rasterize() and rasterize_26sep() are called with a template argument of the triangle's dominant axis. Before rasterize() is called, the plane_setup() method is called once with the triangle's dominant axis. The method triangle_setup() is also called once for the triangle's dominant axis. This is because there's only one overlap test, hence the name CONSERVATIVE_OV1.

In rasterize_26sep(), the plane_setup is called once with sel::W for the current dominant axis. However triangle_setup() is called three times with all three axes. This is because there are three overlap tests for the different principal planes, hence the name CONSERVATIVE_OV3.

For each call to triangle_setup() the return variables are stored in:

```
u_n_delta_u, u_n_delta_v, u_a
v_n_delta_u, v_n_delta_v, v_a
w_n_delta_u, w_n_delta_v, w_a
```

These are references to the FineVars struct that are passed in:

```
...
        if (raster == CONSERVATIVE_OV1) {
            g_u.triangle_setup<X>(tri, tri->fine.n_delta_u[0],
                                        tri->fine.n_delta_v[0],
                                        tri->fine.a[0]);
        } else {
            g_u.triangle_setup<uvw<X>::U>(tri, tri->fine.n_delta_u[0],
                                        tri->fine.n_delta_v[0],
                                        tri->fine.a[0]);
            g_u.triangle_setup<uvw<X>::V>(tri, tri->fine.n_delta_u[1],
                                        tri->fine.n_delta_v[1],
                                        tri->fine.a[1]);
            g_u.triangle_setup<uvw<X>::W>(tri, tri->fine.n_delta_u[2],
                                        tri->fine.n_delta_v[2],
                                        tri->fine.a[2]);
        }
...
```

The arrays are then dereferenced in the rasterize methods as follows.

```
/// 26-separating raster using basic VoxelPipe code and triangle setup
template <int32 AXIS> bool GeomUtil::rasterize(const ushort3 &coord, Triangle *tri) {

    typedef uvw<AXIS> sel;

    const float4 &plane_eq = tri->fine.plane_eq;

    const float3 &n_delta_u = tri->fine.n_delta_u[0];
    const float3 &n_delta_v = tri->fine.n_delta_v[0];
    const float3 &a = tri->fine.a[0];
...
```

and

```
/// 26-separating raster (Schwarz & Seidel 3 overlap tests)
template <int32 AXIS> bool GeomUtil::rasterize_26sep(const ushort3 &coord, Triangle *tri) {

    typedef uvw<AXIS> sel;

    const float4 &plane_eq = tri->fine.plane_eq;
```

```
        const float3 &u_n_delta_u = tri->fine.n_delta_u[0];
        const float3 &v_n_delta_u = tri->fine.n_delta_u[1];
        const float3 &w_n_delta_u = tri->fine.n_delta_u[2];

        const float3 &u_n_delta_v = tri->fine.n_delta_v[0];
        const float3 &v_n_delta_v = tri->fine.n_delta_v[1];
        const float3 &w_n_delta_v = tri->fine.n_delta_v[2];

        const float3 &u_a = tri->fine.a[0];
        const float3 &v_a = tri->fine.a[1];
        const float3 &w_a = tri->fine.a[2];
...
```

These values are stored in the FineVars struct for convenience (Triangle.h). To summarize, the rasterization setup either accesses one index or all three, for rasterize() and rasterize_26sep() respectively. The setup for 6-sep rasterization is quite different: refer to Part Five and also the class listing for GeomUtil.

2.6 *False Positives Due to Roundoff*

A natural consequence of increasing resolution at each level is that roundoff error may cause voxels that shouldn't be included to be included. The octree naturally becomes finer and so at finer levels these false positives should be trimmed. This is simply done by descending an extra level or two for some NodeGroup and seeing if all descendants are without children. If so, the parent node is trimmed. As false positives get trimmed, their zero status is cascaded up the tree in what's called a "deprecation" and this may lead to parents of parents also having a zero status, and so on.

The trimming won't climb very far since these roundoff cases are all on the edges of the polygon, not its interior. This solves the false positive problem and as well the octree subdivision is halted for a branch. That said, there are very few false positives generated either for 26-sep or for 6-sep. For example, for a high-resolution 6-sep rendering at L = 9, N = 512, with false-positive checking going an additional level for candidate nodes, to L = 10 and N = 1024, only 30 false positives were found among the total voxel count of 256,241. While this number is being considered, consider further that the total voxel count of the rasterization is itself a miniscule percentage of the 512-cubed total voxel universe: 0.19 percent. That's one-fifth of one percent.

As the deprecation goes up the octree, OctreeNodes that have no more children because of false-positive checking are deleted. NodeGroup pointers are kept in a separate list that gets deleted by the GroupWorker class at destruction time.

An octant with only one or two geom_stat bits set is a good candidate for forward-checking for the disappearance of the octant. This is done by spawning a new context for a parallel OctreeWorker instantiation that goes to work on the candidate node.

If the node is a false positive it will be cleared in the DeprecateOnUp() procedure. The expensive part of false-positive checking is the descent for each candidate node. The clearing of parents once a false-positive is found takes no time at all considering the paucity of false positives. This means that checking for false positives will become a critical speed issue only at very high resolutions. Most people can't even tell where a false positive is showing up when looking at a final image; but in some cases the false positives are obvious. So checking or not checking is really up to the designer.

Specifically, the False Positive Context runs exactly the same as the Evaluation Context except it only works on an isolated node and its children, starting at some terminal level of the main iteration. The LevelWorker constructor is initialized for the false-positive evaluation level, instead of defaulting to L = N = 0. These level arguments are passed from the OctreeWorker constructor, which gets the same arguments.

Since the child iteration is spawned in the middle of the currently evaluating terminal level of the main iteration, and to avoid copying master triangle data for each terminal candidate, the master triangle data is copied (once) when the Context for false-positive testing is created. Since the triangle list is stored as a member of the GeomWorker class, the triangle data will be preserved as long as the Context is preserved, since the GeomWorker in turn is declared as a member of the Context. The Context is allocated once for the entire process. The triangles are only deleted when the Context is deleted, by the class destructor for GeomWorker.

The general procedure is as follows. Nodes with <= 2 geom_stat bits set are selected as candidates for false-positive processing. The processing continues until: a) the geom_stat bit is zero for some NodeGroup; or b) the false-positive terminal level is reached. The false-positive terminal level is specified in global.h. DeprecateOnUp() reaches up through the sub-tree until it possibly reaches the root, which has the same GlassnerID as the terminal node from the main sequence.

When proceeding to false positive processing, here's what happens:

1. Spawn a new OctreeWorker object, which has its own GroupWorker as a class member.
2. Make a root NodeGroup that has the same GlassnerID as the original candidate NodeGroup.
3. Copy the original NodeGroup's parent pointer to the new NodeGroup's parent pointer.

Step three attaches the original NodeGroup's parent to the new NodeGroup for the express purpose of reusing the parent's VTList to retrieve the parent triangles, e.g. a subset of triangles for the NodeGroup. The triangle indices will be valid for the False Positive Context just as for the Evaluation Context. However this is for reference only, since the original

NodeGroup isn't stored in the NodeGroup list of the new GroupWorker.

The new NodeGroup is then evaluated with the referenced parent triangle data in the spawned OctreeWorker as the root. As the new Octree is evaluated for false positives, it will be DeprecatedOnUp() from either a mid-level or from the false-positive terminal level.

A global variable called g_false_pos_level (global.h) allows the user to select how deeply the iteration should go to check for false positives.

```
const int g_false_pos_level = 9;
```

Usually two sub-levels is enough. In summary, each candidate node at L = g_terminal becomes the "root" node of an entirely new octree iteration. The iteration starts at g_terminal, and ends at g_false_pos_level.

At the end of the false-positive processing, the geom_stat of the spawned NodeGroup is copied back to the original since the candidate node will continue to be evaluated in the master loop, whether or not a false positive is found. If the root becomes deprecated, it will be deleted from the master iteration before the display step of the iteration is reached. The spawned NodeGroups are made using instantiateGroup() and so will be destroyed when the spawned OctreeWorker goes away. OctreeWorker is instantiated once per candidate NodeGroup, and then discarded.

This fragment from the main iteration loop shows how the context switch happens before the call to displayVoxel():

```
...
for (itr.first(); itr.get(); itr.put(o_list, count) ) {
        NodeGroup *ng_ptr = itr.retrieve();
        if (level_w.LevelSwitch(ng_ptr->ID))
                level_w.DoLevelWork();

        const Level &level = level_w.getLevel();
        group_w.GeomProcess(ng_ptr, level);

        if (context.check_false_pos && level_w.TerminalLevel())
          SwitchContext(ng_ptr);
 ...
        display.displayVoxel(ng_ptr, level);
 ...
}
...
```

Triangles are copied up front into separate Contexts – one for the main iteration, and one for all false-positive processing. The triangle list is copied over once, when the one and only FP Context is created at the start of normal octree iteration. Then that list and its Context are reused by all sub-iterations on false-positive nodes. Each instantiation of an OctreeWorker uses the same false-positive Context, so that triangles don't have to be copied over each time.

Context.check_false_pos belongs to the False Positive Context and is *not* a global variable (otherwise the spawned OctreeWorker will spawn yet another OctreeWorker, *ad infinitum*).

The False Positive Context has its own GeomWorker class that holds the master triangle data. When spawning a new OctreeWorker, the False Positive Context with the GeomWorker is used over and over again. Thus, at the top level:

```
/// check for false positive processing
void OctreeWorker::SwitchContext(NodeGroup *group) {
        // first see if this node is a candidate
        if (!isFPCandidate())
                return;

        // iterate
        OctreeWorker octree_w(fp_contextID);
        octree_w.TopFP(group);

        // reset the raster option for next user
        fp_context->setRaster(g_raster);
}
```

The new OctreeWorker is instantiated within the scope of SwitchContext. Since it's already deep in the tree and only goes a few levels down for false-positive processing, this doesn't stress the stack.

The creation of the false-positive Context is shown below.

```
/// will reuse this
void OctreeWorker::MakeFPContext() {
        // second context for false positives
        // do this once to avoid copying over triangle list multiple times
        fp_context = new ContextWorker;
        // g_terminal is the eval level to start at
        fp_context->makeContext(g_terminal, g_false_pos_level, false, false);
```

```
        // this goes directly to the GeomWorker class:
        fp_context->setRaster(g_raster);

        fp_context->CopyOverTriangles(context.geom_w);
        fp_contextID = fp_context->getContextID();
}
```

Each call to spawn an OctreeWorker happens sequentially, and the entire subtree goes out of scope and is discarded when each FP candidate voxel is done. When spawning the new OctreeWorker the original octree iteration has reached its terminal level, and the VTList for the parent will reflect that. At deeper levels the number of triangles should be small.

The next method in the FP call stack is shown below. The OctreeWorker is the new one – not the original one, which is waiting in its own Context, or really waiting higher in the call stack. The spawned OctreeWorker contains its own GroupWorker and node-group list (ng_list):

```
/// for spawn call (for false positive processing)
void OctreeWorker::TopFP(NodeGroup *orig_ptr) {
        // copy the node via instantiateGroup, so it will be destroyed
        NodeGroup * ng_ptr = NodeGroupRoot(orig_ptr->ID);

        // for getting the parent tris need to assign the parent ptr;
        // will allow sub-tree deprecate to enter the main tree, and
        // meanwhile there's no danger of parent-node deletion since
        // the parent isn't in the ng_list in GroupWorker class.
        ng_ptr->parent = orig_ptr->parent;

        // store it in the (loosely attached) Octree as root;
        // make a new root node with NULL parent pointer to
        // stop deprecateOctreeNodesOnUp in its tracks.
        OctreeRoot(ng_ptr, NULL);

        IterateTop();

        // over-copy the original geom_stat
        if (ng_ptr->geom_stat == 0x00) {
                // for diagnostics, display FP in RED
                /*
                const Level &level = level_w.getLevel();
                display.displayVoxelFP(orig_ptr, level);
                */
```

```
                orig_ptr->geom_stat = ng_ptr->geom_stat;

                // Note that the entire spawned octree will have
                // been deleted if this is true. The original
                // octree node and its parents will be processed
                // through main iteration to follow.

                std::cout << "FALSE POS!" << std::endl;
        }
}
```

In the Project V world the word "spawn" is used in two different ways: a) to mean the spawning of a child NodeGroup; and b) to mean the spawning a new OctreeWorker for false-positive checking.

The g_check_false_pos global is "localized" as part of the Context data that's associated with the ContextWorker. This avoids infinite recursion, as mentioned already. start_level and terminal_level are also localized. In the FP Context, the start_level is set to g_terminal and the terminal_level is set to g_false_pos_level:

```
fp_context->makeContext(g_terminal, g_false_pos_level, false, false);
```

GroupWorker, LevelWorker, and Display all take a Context in their constructors, and so can access terminal levels and false-positive status. All of them are declared as OctreeWorker members. It should also be mentioned that the spawned OctreeWorkers have NULL ContextWorkers. There is only one False Positive Context (and ContextWorker) in the master OctreeWorker which spawns all the other OctreeWorkers. When that master OctreeWorker is destroyed, the False Positive ContextWorker is freed.

This is how it looks in the OctreeWorker class:

```
class OctreeWorker {
public:
        OctreeWorker(int my_contextID) :
                context (ContextWorker::getContext(my_contextID)),
                contextID(my_contextID), fp_context(NULL), fp_contextID(INVALID),
                group_w(context), level_w(context), display(context) {}
        ~OctreeWorker();
...
private:
        // instantiates in declaration order: start with context
        Context &context;
        int contextID;
```

```
        ContextWorker *fp_context;
        int fp_contextID;
...
```

And here's the destructor:

```
OctreeWorker::~OctreeWorker() {
        if (fp_context != NULL)
                delete fp_context;
}
```

2.7 *False Negatives*

It turns out that false negatives can be created in the case of 6-sep rasterization.

The scanline approach of Voxel Pipe avoids this problem because it's not hierarchical. In Project V 6-sep rasterization at lower resolutions can exclude entire octants from the final rasterization at the terminal level; these exclusions show up as holes, e.g. false negatives. These false negatives are due to the geometric nature of the 6-sep algorithm. Remember that 6-sep doesn't want the company of all 26 neighbors in the 3 x 3 x 3 neighborhood. 6-sep just cares about immediate face-centered neighbors, and limits interaction to the 6 voxels attached to its 6 faces. It's not a "good neighbor" policy but nobody asked to be born into the 6-sep family!

The reader may consult Part Five for details of the 6-sep algorithm as well as for the solution to false negatives, which involves "looking ahead" into the iteration – not looking for false positives but for false negatives.

END OF PART TWO

Part Three

Project V: A Tour of the Voxel Factory
PART THREE: Ray Tracing 1

3.0 *Ray Tracing*

The main idea of ray tracing is as follows. In normal ray tracing a light ray emitted from a light source is projected into the model, and bounced around just as a natural light ray would bounce between objects.

The Project V implementation is very specific, you might say a subset of general ray tracing. The main interest is intersections with voxel planes, not light and shading equations. Ray tracing in Project V is purely geometric.

Before going farther, it also has to be said that ray tracing is used as a tool to simulate a rotating armature-type display device, such as the one patented by Ed Berlin. Since the final display device envisioned as part of the Project V experience is a solid-state block without any moving parts whatsoever, the use of ray tracing isn't really relevant to the envisioned display device at all. So this feature is more an experiment than anything else.

To see if the rotational armature can really work, it seemed like a fun project to implement ray tracing and to trace out the octree geometry with each arm represented by a ray. In this application, the normal evaluation of the octree for some model made of triangles is completed; then a new Context is created for ray tracing, which is a second pass over the already computed octree. Therefore the rays are being intersected with voxels, not triangles.

But what are the rays? The rays are not coming from a light source in this application. They are the arms of the rotating armature itself. Each arm acts as a "ray" which is traced through the octree hierarchy. The armature can be envisioned as a tree with arms sticking out at right angles to the tree trunk.

Each arm is studded with LEDs, light emitting diodes. These diodes are turned on when they overlap some voxel. Since the armature is rotating very quickly, each arm will be in a different part of the model depending on how far the armature has rotated over some time period. So the entire armature "persists" the geometry, as seen by an outside observer, by intersecting the same part of the model (perhaps with different arms) at, say, 60 times per second.

This scheme, as one can see from the explanation so far, is very complex. Originally the intent in Project V was to see the persistance of an image in a real-time simulation using OpenGL. However, it soon became apparent that the sheer volume of data would overload the computer. So, the final implementation just shows a freeze-frame, or snapshot, of the entire scanned model, for a rotation of 360 degrees.

The looping structure of the code is therefore:

```
void RayWorker::Top() {
...
        for (interleave = 0; interleave < 2; ++interleave) {
                for (course = 0; course < MAX_COURSE; ++course) {
                        offset = 0;
                        for (level = 0; level < max_level; level += skipper[offset%4]) {
                                ++offset;
                                for (angle = 0; angle < DEGREES_360; ++angle) {
#ifdef DIAGNOSTIC_MSG
                                        std::cout << "ANGLE: " << angle << ", LEVEL: " << level
                                                << ", COURSE: " << course << std::endl;
#endif
                                        DoRayWork(interleave, course, level, angle);
                                }
                                display.terminateLevel();
                        }
                }
        }
...
```

The innermost loop is a rotation over one-degree increments of 360 degrees, a full circle. The next outer loop is on levels (ignore the skipper for now, it's just a tool for skipping levels to "look inside" of the model). There are four "courses" representing the division of the armature into four processing units in hardware. Finally there are two interleaves, an idea similar to the interleaving of an NTSC television signal.

The variables are set up as follows:

```
        Nt = r_u.NewN(context.terminal_level);
        spindle_diam = Nt / 16;            // spindle ratio
        max_level = (Nt - spindle_diam) / MAX_COURSE;
        helical_index = DEGREES_360 / max_level;
```

Let's say the terminal level (being g_terminal) is 7. Then Nt = 2^7 = 128. (N is the same N used in normal octree iteration. N is applied to t, a value which is the heart of ray tracing, to be explained shortly.) The center of the armature is called the "spindle" and, like a tree trunk, it has a diameter, being 128 / 16 = 8. Since voxels are always unit-voxels, this amounts to 8 voxels.

The armature was envisioned to be run by 4 processors running in parallel. Each processor runs a "course", so MAX_COURSE = 4. This is a "hardware constant". A course is a vertical partitioning of the arms. You can think of the tree trunk divided in 4 sections vertically.

The number of levels per course is (128 - 8) / 4 = 30. So max_level = 30. Meanwhile, the arms are positioned around the trunk, for each of those 30 levels, in a helix. For example, if the first arm is positioned at 12 o'clock, then the next arm up will be positioned at the next helical index, which is 360 degrees / 30 = 12 degrees. Say 12 o'clock is 0 degrees, then, going clockwise, the next arm is at 12 degrees, then the next at 24, and so on, all the way around. The helix keeps winding up into the next course, and then the next, until all 4 courses have been covered.

3.1 *Interleaving*

The sample rate on 1 degree increments radially isn't quite enough to cover all voxels. At any resolution the smallest voxel has a size of unity in each dimension. The rotation of the radial arm is such that given a one-degree increment, towards the outer regions of the arm, a "sample gap" can occur.

The diagnostics from RayWorker.cpp, a portion of which is shown below, illustrate how a sample gap occurs when the ray crosses a corner of a voxel, for which the ray-voxel intersections fall between the LED positions on the radial arm.

```
ANGLE: 301, LEVEL: 7, COURSE: 3
no gap, count: 6
no gap, count: 5
no gap, count: 4
no gap, count: 1
no gap, count: 8
no gap, count: 1
no gap, count: 1
no gap, count: 0
no gap, count: 2
SAMPLE GAP! 59.2998, 45, 108.758, T:27.0529 (x,y,z,t)
SAMPLE GAP! 59, 44.3738, 108.968, T:27.7783 (x,y,z,t)
no gap, count: 1
no gap, count: 4
no gap, count: 3
no gap, count: 3
no gap, count: 4
no gap, count: 17
```

The LED count typically falls to 1 near a sample gap, as the distance between intersections becomes smaller, thus leading to an "in" status for some voxel, which, however, falls between the sample distance for LEDs.

The solution to this problem is to "interleave." This means that the samples are effectively doubled in the rotational plane. The alpha pass is on whole degrees, while the beta pass is offset in angle by 0.5 degrees. But further, the LED positions are also offset by 0.5 along the length of the arm – which isn't something that can be physically managed in hardware, unless the LEDs are doubled.

This has the effect of "filling in the gaps." It's not at all intuitive that gaps could even occur in the first place. In fact, it was only after the original algorithm was run on a collection of models that the missing samples were revealed, leading to the interleave solution.

Interleave has been implemented and tested visually. To test it actually the diagnostics such as shown above would need to be kept in a list of some kind. This is complicated, since the "in" voxels may differ for the whole angle and the angle +/- 0.5 degrees. A test would need to keep track of all voxels that are "in" for a center angle and its two side angles at +/- 0.5 degrees, and then make sure that voxels that fall between the LED cracks for the alpha pass (the middle angle) are caught by either one of the beta passes to either side; and vice versa – that is, that the sample gaps for the beta pass(es) are caught by the alpha pass.

No doubt there are voxels that are sampled twice, for example by adjacent arms close to the armature axis, but this is not an error, since they will be sampled only once per radial arm, which is correct for the display device. In any case an analytic validation requires that for each radial arm a list of sample gaps is maintained, and then checked against a second list of "in" voxels for the wing arms. Something like that. All of this remains a project for the future; put on hold since the whole radial approach is problematic.

Visually, at least, the interleave approach leaves no sample gaps and the entire model is captured by LEDs that are inside of voxels in the octree hierarchy.

That's a lot to take in, but let's keep going. Exactly how much data is being collected? Each arm has 60 LED positions. If you think of the height of 120 levels, then 60 LEDs projecting from either side of the spindle makes a rough cube, though the corners of the actual octree world will be cut off, because the armature traces out a cylinder inscribed in a cube, basically.

For a single arm, that's 60 LED positions x 360 degrees = 21,600 data samples. The real memory criteria is:

120 (vertical resolution) x 360 (radial resolution) = 43,200 rays.

Many LED elements will be zero, so there will be no display, or a diagnostic display of a blue dot instead of a voxel.

The armature arms are being intersected with voxels, but the actual display comes from the LED in the real world. Therefore the normal octree display and the ray-traced LED display are different. Instead of cubes that touch each other, all orthogonal to the Cartesian axes, the LED positions are simulated by displaying half-voxels on LED centers, and oriented with the ray direction. The critical thing here isn't the size of the voxel-as-displayed, but that all voxels in the octree have been properly sampled by the armature. Once the proper voxel is sampled, it can be displayed in whatever way makes sense.

To show the whole image, without interleave, it would take:

21,600 data samples x 120 rays = 2.592 million data samples!

For interleave, double it. That's too much work for a real-time simulation with OpenGL on most desktops – it can probably be done in real time (that is, in 1/60 of a second, 60 times a second) on a GPU machine. Therefore the model is displayed as a single frame computed for 1/60 of a second, which precludes animation. Depending on the complexity of the model (how many triangles) the computation takes two to four seconds on a dual-core HP desktop.

3.2 *Ray Casting*

The next order of business, now that the mechanics of the armature are out of the way, is the casting of the ray itself. Here the presentation moves into mathematics. This is where things get tricky. The basic idea is to start the ray close to the tree trunk, to the armature spindle, and then work outwards along the arm. Recall that each arm is a "ray". Unlike shading simulations, no ray bounces need be computed.

As the computation works its way out along the arm, it looks for intersections with voxels. Since the code is dealing with the final voxel hierarchy as computed for some model in the "Evaluation Context", it doesn't have to do any triangle calculations – that's already been done in the first pass. It only has to find the voxels and compute intersections with the voxel faces.

What's more, only the LED position is considered along the arm – remember there are 60 LEDs on each arm for L = 7. The arrangement is supposed to work so that each LED corresponds to a voxel position at the finest resolution. In fact, the inner LEDs, because of the rotation at the smaller radius, over-sample the octree; and it was found that the outermost LEDs, because of the larger radius, under-sample. So "interleave" was added, nudging the angle by 0.5 degrees to get the "in-between" spots. Also, the LED position itself, for interleave, is offset by 0.5 (moving the LEDs outward to cover the gaps in the XZ plane, if the plane of rotation is orthogonal to the Y-axis in 3-space).

So each LED position must be considered. Whether or not an LED is found to be inside of a voxel, the ray must be "pushed" into the next voxel position. And this brings us to the parameter "t".

A ray r is defined as follows.

For a unique 3D base point q, sometimes called the ray "origin", there is a unique direction vector u, a unit-length vector in 3D, such that all points p in 3 dimensions can be calculated if there exists a t, belonging to positive numbers in 3D, such that p = q + tu; i.e., point p is equal to the base point plus a positive t scalar on the unit-length vector.

When a ray and a graphical object intersect, the distance from the origin to the nearest common point (the point of intersection) will be a positive real value (based on t). Otherwise, the distance (and t) is theoretically infinite.

Obviously, an octree's empty cells, or the terminal cells, will form boundaries so that the intersection can never be infinite. But the intersections on those boundaries will not necessarily fall within the voxel volume currently being considered. So how to proceed?

For an implicit surface f(x, y, z) = 0, use the parametric representation for the ray:

$$R(t) = O + tD$$

where O is the origin as usual, t is the positive scalar as usual, and D is the unit-length direction vector as usual. Then:

$$Rx(t) = Ox + tDx$$
$$Ry(t) = Oy + tDy$$
$$Rz(t) = Oz + tDz$$

i.e., we have the components of the 3D vectorization. Note that a ray that starts at the origin (0, 0, 0), and goes through point (x, y, 1), will have parametric components (equations):

$$(xt, yt, t)$$

These can be substituted into the implicit equation (for a plane, for example):

$$f(Ox + tDx, Oy + tDy, Oz + tDz) = 0$$

The equation is then solved (for the plane) to find the intersection. Here's how.

Again, define a ray as:

$$P = P0 + P1t$$

with P0 the origin, and P1 the unit-length direction vector; t as usual.

Then, given a triangle A, B, C (being three points of an octant plane), define the plane unit-normal as:

$$n = [(C - A) \text{ x } (B - A)] / \text{length}[(C - A) \text{ x } (B - A)]$$

where 'x' is the cross product,

$$(v1y\ v2z - v1z\ v2y) - (v1x\ v2z - v1z\ v2x) + (v1x\ v2y - v1y\ v2x) \text{ or}$$
$$(v1y\ v2z - v1z\ v2y) + (v1z\ v2x - v1x\ v2z) + (v1x\ v2y - v1y\ v2x)$$

and the length is

$$\text{sqrt}(vx\hat{\ }2 + vy\hat{\ }2 + vz\hat{\ }2)$$

The plane equation is equivalent to

$$P.n - A.n = 0$$

where A is the vector representation of point A on the voxel face, and ' . ' is the dot product, i.e.:

$$v1x * v2x + v1y * v2y + v1z * v2z$$

Now, since

$$P = P0 + P1t$$

then by substitution

$$(P0 + P1t).n = A.n$$

and

$$t = (A.n - P0.n) / (P1.n)$$

This is substituted into the original ray equation

$$P = P0 + P1t$$

to give the vector position of the plane intersection.

Next, it has to be determined if the intersection is inside of the bounding rectangle associated with the octant face. This is a simple bounds check since all planes of the octree are parallel to the principal axes.

Note that we're not interested in min t (the first intersected surface relative to the origin) but in the t-values for all six bounding planes, since this is a 3D device and the ray travels in three dimensions.

3.3 *Setting Up the Ray*

Let's look at how a ray is set up. There are two reference origins: a) the armature_origin; and b) the zero origin.

```
void RayWorker::DoRayWork(int interleave, int course, int level, int angle) {
    ...
    center_coord = float(Nt / 2);
    armature_origin = make_float3(center_coord, center_coord, center_coord);
    zero_origin = make_float3(0.0, 0.0, 0.0);
    ...
```

The armature origin is exactly (128 / 2) = 64, for all three coordinates: (64.0, 64.0, 64.0), which puts it exactly at the center of the octree voxel volume. The zero origin is the minimum coordinate of the voxel volume: (0.0, 0.0, 0.0).

Next, the ray's yoffset or height is calculated:

```
    ...
    // center Nt - spindle_diam on Nt / 2, i.e. add in spindle_diam / 2.
    y_offset = float(course * max_level + level + spindle_diam / 2 );
    ...
```

Since "course" in the high-level loop goes from 0 to 3, then the height or level will go from (0) to (3 * 30 + 29 = 119) – which covers all 120 levels for N = 7, and also the height of each ray. Recall that spindle_diam is 8, and 4 units are added in since the *actual* height of the 0-level octree is, in geometry-units, 128. So the rays are being centered in height.

Next, the arm angles are computed as:

```
    ...
    if (interleave == T_ALPHA) {
        arm_angle = float(level * helical_index + angle);
        point5_radius = float(spindle_diam + 1) / 2.0 - 0.25;
    } else {
        arm_angle = float(level * helical_index + angle) + 179.5;
        point5_radius = float(spindle_diam + 1) / 2.0 + 0.25;
    }
```

...

The arm angles repeat for all four courses, so “course” isn’t needed here. Angle goes from 0 to 359, which is added to the default arm angle, dependent on the arm’s level (0 to 29) * 12 degrees.

Meanwhile, some tricky math is used for the “interleave”. If the interleave is the first pass (T_ALPHA = 0) the radius (the distance out along the arm to start LED placement) is

(8 + 1) = 9.0 / 2.0 = 4.5 - 0.25 = 4.25

and if on the second pass:

(8 + 1) = 9.0 / 2.0 = 4.5 + 0.25 = 4.75

This explains why the LED “voxel” differs from the canonical voxel and is displayed as a “half voxel”. Essentially the LED voxels in this example go from 4 to 4.5 in the first case; and from 4.5 to 5.0 in the second. The next interleave would be {5.25, 5.75} with extents 5.0 to 5.5, and 5.5. to 6.0 – and so on.

Next, 12 o’clock is defined as a vector in the positive Z direction:

```
...
        // 12 o'clock in positive Z-axis direction
        twelveoclock = make_float3(center_coord + HALF_INDEX,
                                   y_offset + HALF_INDEX,
                                   center_coord + point5_radius);
...
```

In other words, for the first pass interleave, and say a height of (30 + 4 = 34) this is:

(64.0 + 0.5, the ray height + 0.5, and 64.0 + 4.25) = (64.5, 34.5, 68.25)

It might be hard to visualize this, but it’s the ray starting at z = 68.25 (4.25 units beyond z = 64.0), at the given height + 0.5, and at the centerline in x + 0.5. Why add 0.5 to x and y? The reason is to have the ray at 12 o’clock go through the centers of the voxels, or at least not have a default position parallel to and touching a voxel face, which would complicate intersections when the ray is at orthogonal positions relative to the voxel grid.

Doesn’t this make the 12 o’clock position off-center? No, because of rotational symmetry. Visualize the 12 o’clock position being rotated a full 360 degrees. At 90 degrees, or at the 3 o’clock position, it will be in the middle of the row of voxels in X; at 180 degrees it will likewise travel through the middle of the column of voxels in Z (though on the other side of the centerline in Z); and at 270 degrees the ray will travel through the middle of the row in -X (on the other side of the centerline in X).

The last thing to do is to actually make the vector components from this information. Recall that each ray has an origin or base point, and then a direction component. Thus,

```
...
        // rotate by arm_angle in XZ (positive angle = ccw)
        xform.rotateYAxis(ray.base_origin, twelveoclock, arm_angle, armature_origin);

        // make the direction vector and rotate that too.
        // (Could use NT instead of zero origin argument.)
        direction = make_float3(0.0, 0.0, 1.0);
        xform.rotateYAxis(ray.base_direction, direction, arm_angle, zero_origin);
...
```

The rotations are around the Y-axis in our *left-handed coordinate system* (Z going into the page, e.g. the middle finger of the left hand; and X and Y the forefinger and thumb, respectively, of the left hand, indicating positive directions of those axes). If you think of the mechanical armature rotating around the spindle axis, and the spindle oriented with the Y-axis, it becomes clearer.

So, the first transformation is for the base point of the ray. Our 12 o'clock position is rotated by the arm angle, which is the helical angle (depending on the level) plus the 0 to 359 angle passed from the main loop. The armature_origin is used for translating the 12 o'clock position to the origin before applying the rotation. The armature is translated to the global origin, rotated, then translated back by the armature_origin (64.0, 64.0, 64.0).

```
/// angle is in degrees
void Transform::rotateYAxis(float3 & rp, const float3 & p, const float angle,
                                        const float3 & origin) {
        double theta = angle * M_PI / 180.0;
        float3 translated;

        translated.x = p.x - origin.x;
        translated.z = p.z - origin.z;

        rp.x = translated.x * cos(theta) - translated.z * sin(theta) + origin.x;
        rp.y = p.y;
        rp.z = translated.x * sin(theta) + translated.z * cos(theta) + origin.z;
}
```

The second transformation is for the direction component, which simply points to Z = 1 for the 12 o'clock position. Again, the arm_angle is used as the rotation angle, but this time no translation (NT) is needed; one way of doing this is just sending in a zero-origin, which gives a virtual translation of zero.

One other thing can be done, which is a *virtual rotation* of the armature (of the current arm or ray) to simulate the rotation of the model. Remember, the model has already been rasterized to voxels, and the octree is fixed in space, so the octree itself certainly can't be rotated. But the armature can be rotated as a unit to simulate the rotation of the model. For example, the armature can be rotated 90 degrees around the Z-axis. If the model, say of a chess pawn sitting on its base, is oriented with its axis of revolution along the Y-axis, then the armature rotation will make the chess pawn look like it's laying on its side. This works for any arbitrary rotation in three dimensions.

This works because when a list of intersections for this "relative" base and direction are computed, and this relative intersection data is sent to the display code, the armature is turned "rightside up" before display, but the list of LED intersections still reflects the arbitrary rotation. To restore the base orientation the display code is provided with the original arm rotation and orientation (e.g. the untransformed "base" coordinates).

Note that the t parameters for the LED positions never change: only the direction vector and the origin need to be transformed; the t values are invariant under rotation and translation. (Scaling is not allowed since everything depends on sample frequency.)

Here's where the base_origin is transformed, and put into ray.origin. Same for the base_direction vector.

```
...
// otherwise use virtual rotation (set up in Top())
xform.rotateByMatrix(ray.origin, ray.base_origin, armature_origin);
xform.rotateByMatrixNT(ray.direction, ray.base_direction);
...
```

At this point the ray is ready for processing. Note that the base point of the ray, even after rotation, will always be inside of the voxel space. That's important, because testing for intersections with voxel planes starts with that base point and moves outwards until reaching the end of the arm, or "exiting the universe", whichever comes first. (More on this later.)

3.4 *Finding a Voxel*

Recall that the voxel nodes are referenced irrespective of (x, y, z) identities by assigning each node a special label called a Glassner ID, consistent with the ordering in the IDWorker class.

The voxel layout in the XZ plane is:

```
z
^
|
.___> x

1 2
3 4 (bottom, lesser y)

5 6
7 8 (top, greater y)
```

This is just a transposition of Glassner's scheme. The children of node 1 are: {11, 12, 13, ... , 18}. The children of node 13 are: {131, 132, 133, ... , 138}, and so on.

Thus we can find a node based on (x, y, z) coordinates (with the layout above) with almost the same logic as used for the octree, with just a few additions. Here's the setup part of the routine.

```
/// See the octant numbering this follows in IDWorker.cpp

/// The coord is the "pushed" ray coordinate that we
/// want to find the octree octant for.

void RayWorker::findNode(const float3 &coord, NodePack &data) {
        OctreeNode<NodeGroup *> *curnode;
        NodeGroup *ng_ptr;
        float x, y, z;
        float3 center;
        ushort3 voxcoord;
        Glassner ID = 0; // root
        int level, scale, N, Nt;
        bool empty;

        OctreeNode<NodeGroup *> *nextnode = tree.getRoot();
        x = coord.x; y = coord.y; z = coord.z;

        // get N for terminal level
        Nt = r_u.NewN(context.terminal_level);
        level = 0;
```

```
do {
        curnode = nextnode;

        // get the center coordinates scaled for this level
        N = r_u.NewN(++level);

        // if terminal level is 4, and current level is 1, we have:
        // level 1 = 2 ; level 4 = 16, so: 16 / 2 = 8.
        // 0 * 8 = 0 ; 1 * 8 = 8; [0 - 1] = 0 to 8; [1 - 2] = 8 to 16.

        scale = Nt / N;

        // get the (1,1,1) (relative) position (= center point)
        ng_ptr = curnode->element;
        voxcoord.x = ng_ptr->node[OCTANT_EIGHT].coord.x;
        voxcoord.y = ng_ptr->node[OCTANT_EIGHT].coord.y;
        voxcoord.z = ng_ptr->node[OCTANT_EIGHT].coord.z;

        center.x = float(voxcoord.x * scale);
        center.y = float(voxcoord.y * scale);
        center.z = float(voxcoord.z * scale);
...
```

In this code fragment "tree" is a reference to the Octree already computed in the Evaluation Context; the reference is stored as a RayWorker class variable when the ray tracing Context is created in the thread code:

```
/// use existing octree (from Eval)
void *OctreeThread::RayThread(void *unused) {

    // context for ray work, seems easier than somehow
    // reusing the octree context.
    // note start level is 1, i.e., the eval_level
    context_w = new ContextWorker;
    // we just care about g_terminal and display, since everything
    // else applies to what's already been done in Eval stage.
    context_w->makeContext(1, g_terminal, true, g_check_false_pos);
    context_w->setRaster(g_raster);

    int contextID = context_w->getContextID();

    // instantiate RayWorker
    ray_w = new RayWorker(contextID, octree_w->getTree());
```

```
        ray_w->Top();

        return NULL;
}
```

getTree() is a public getter in the OctreeWorker class:

```
Octree<NodeGroup *> & getTree() {return tree;}
```

The RayWorker object is equipped with the ray tracing Context so it knows about things like the terminal level.

Returning to findNode(), the find code starts with ID = 0 to determine some octant in level 1. Since level 0 is the whole undivided octree space, it's starting with the broadest subdivision of space. It then computes a scale factor, being

```
        scale = Nt / N;
```

where N for level 1 is 2^1 = 2, so the scale factor is 64. The scale factor is applied to the (1, 1, 1) coordinate, which is the geometric "center" of the NodeGroup given the full extent of (2, 2, 2). The scale factor for level 1 applied to (1, 1, 1) results in (64.0, 64.0, 64.0).

Recall the array ordering:

1 2
3 4 (bottom, lesser y)

5 6
7 8 (top, greater y)

The numbers are an index + 1 into the array of coordinates shown below (IDWorker.cpp):

```
static int ax[] = {0, 1, 0, 1, 0, 1, 0, 1};
static int ay[] = {0, 0, 0, 0, 1, 1, 1, 1};
static int az[] = {1, 1, 0, 0, 1, 1, 0, 0};
```

OCTANT_EIGHT = 5, but since the GLASSNER ID goes from 1 to 8, this corresponds to "6" in the numbering scheme, e.g. the (1, 1, 1) position. "EIGHT" refers to the bit value of (7 + 1). This is a little confusing since the bit value isn't the same as the array index, but the convention has been set.

Let's forge on with the next section of the findNode() method:

```
...
            if (x > center.x) {
                if (y > center.y) {
                    if (z > center.z)
                        ID = (ID * 10) + 6;
                    else
                        ID = (ID * 10) + 8;
                } else {
                    if (z > center.z)
                        ID = (ID * 10) + 2;
                    else
                        ID = (ID * 10) + 4;
                }
            } else { // x < center.x
                if (y > center.y) {
                    if (z > center.z)
                        ID = (ID * 10) + 5;
                    else
                        ID = (ID * 10) + 7;
                } else {
                    if (z > center.z)
                        ID = (ID * 10) + 1;
                    else
                        ID = (ID * 10) + 3;
                }
            }
            // get child n
            nextnode = ChildNodeForID(curnode, (unsigned char)(ID % 10L), empty);
    } while (curnode->child_count != 0 && nextnode != NULL);
...
```

This shows how the center of the NodeGroup is used to "home in" on the ray's "pushed" position. The word "pushed" refers to the progressive journey of the ray vector from one voxel to the next. Since the find code is descending the Octree, and since an early-level OctreeNode may overlap geometry, but some of its children may not, it could be that the ray is in a huge mostly empty voxel with no children in the region of the pushed ray coordinate. Or it could be that the voxel has been subdivided and the loop finds a child node that, relative to the centerpoint, brackets the ray's position, and continues to contract around that position until: a) the current node has no children; and b) the next node is a terminal node in the octree (nextnode == NULL).

Let's say the coordinates of the ray position are all greater than the centerpoint. The routine starts with ID = 0, so the next ID is (0 * 10) + 6 = 6. This is the Glassner ID, not the array index.

It's this thing:

5 6
7 8 (top, greater y)

The loop continues in this fashion, extending the Glassner ID until the stop conditions are met, as above. The third and final section of the findNode() routine is:

```
...
        // get the (0,0,0) (relative) position (= base point)
        voxcoord.x = ng_ptr->node[OCTANT_ZERO].coord.x;
        voxcoord.y = ng_ptr->node[OCTANT_ZERO].coord.y;
        voxcoord.z = ng_ptr->node[OCTANT_ZERO].coord.z;

        // return voxel ID, offset, length, Octree Node, and empty status
        data.ID = ID;
        id_w.addScaledUnitOffset(data.coord, voxcoord, scale, (unsigned char)(ID % 10L));
        data.length = scale;
        data.empty = empty;
        data.node = curnode;

        // get the voxel color (set in Display.cpp)
        if (!empty) {
                int index = (int)(ID % 10L) - 1;
                data.color.x = ng_ptr->node[index].color.x;
                data.color.y = ng_ptr->node[index].color.y;
                data.color.z = ng_ptr->node[index].color.z;
        }
}
```

This section follows the main loop. The NodeGroup pointer ng_ptr is still pointing to curnode because the loop has exited:

```
  ng_ptr = curnode->element;
```

The voxel coordinate is stored in a structure called a NodePack:

```
/// stuff that gets returned from findNode
struct NodePack {
        Glassner ID;            // not currently used
        ushort3 coord;          // min coord of voxel
        uchar3 color;           // color of terminal non-empty
        int length;             // size of voxel (at terminal N)
```

```
        bool empty;                 // empty voxel?
        OctreeNode<NodeGroup *> *node;
};
```

The whole point of findNode() is to find the ID and base coordinate of the voxel that contains the current position on the ray. For example, if on exiting the loop, level = 3 and scale = 128 / (2^3 = 8) = 16, the base coordinate is extracted with OCTANT_ZERO = 2, e.g. Glassner ID 3, which is the lower-lefthand coordinate of the NodeGroup:

```
1 2
3 4 (bottom, lesser y)
```

OCTANT_ZERO is the index into the NodeGroup/NodeData ordering, and even though the node is “referenced” as (0, 0, 0), it comes back as a real coordinate:

```
        // get the (0,0,0) (relative) position (= base point)
        voxcoord.x = ng_ptr->node[OCTANT_ZERO].coord.x;
        voxcoord.y = ng_ptr->node[OCTANT_ZERO].coord.y;
        voxcoord.z = ng_ptr->node[OCTANT_ZERO].coord.z;
```

Then the following routine is called to add in a scaled unit offset of the actual containing voxel, since the coordinates from the loop are all OCTANT_EIGHT. The ID passed in is the *actual* voxel id in the least significant (tens) place. For example, an ID of 412 would be parsed as (412 mod 10) = 2. This is the most resolved level of the GlassnerID since parent levels become prefixes, e.g. everything to the left of 2 is parent levels. Therefore idx = 2 would be passed to the method shown below:

```
void IDWorker::addScaledUnitOffset(ushort3 &r_coord, const ushort3 &coord,
                int scale, unsigned char idx) {
        r_coord.x = coord.x * scale + ax[idx - 1] * scale;
        r_coord.y = coord.y * scale + ay[idx - 1] * scale;
        r_coord.z = coord.z * scale + az[idx - 1] * scale;
}
```

To fully understand this, let’s see how node coordinates are made in the first place, during the normal evaluation of the octree. Here’s the xyz routine:

```
/// gets the min coord of the voxel bbox for level
void IDWorker::getXYZ(Glassner ID, ushort3 &coord) {
        Glassner mag, tID;
        int x, y, z, count;

        count = TensMagnitude(ID);              // 412 returns 3
```

```
        mag = TensMinusOne(count);              // 3 returns 100

        x = y = z = 0;

        while (mag >= 1) {
                tID = ID / mag;
                x = (x << 1) + ax[tID - 1];
                y = (y << 1) + ay[tID - 1];
                z = (z << 1) + az[tID - 1];

                tID *= mag;
                ID -= tID;
                mag /= 10;
        }
        coord.x = x;
        coord.y = y;
        coord.z = z;
}
```

Let's say the ID is 412. Then mag = 100. tID = 412 / 100 = 4 (this is integer arithmetic). The {ax, ay, az} arrays are indexed by (tID - 1) = (4 - 1) = 3, giving {1, 0, 0}.

```
x = 1
y = 0
z = 0
```

Then: tID = 400, ID = 12, and mag = 10. In the next iteration, tID = 12 / 10 = 1. The index (tID - 1) points to {0, 0, 1}.

```
x = 2 + 0 = 2
y = 0 + 0 = 0
z = 0 + 1 = 1
```

Then: tID = 10, ID = 2, mag = 1. In the next iteration, tID = 2 / 1 = 2. The index (tID - 1) gives {1, 0, 1}.

```
x = 4 + 1 = 5
y = 0
z = 2 + 1 = 3
```

Then: tID = 2, ID = 0, mag = 0. So the final coordinates are:

```
x = 5
```

```
y = 0
z = 3
```

These are scaled coordinates; the values are shifted left with each iteration. Since the NodeGroup contains 8 octants the following method is called to find the base coordinates for all 8 of them:

```
void GroupWorker::FillXYZ(NodeGroup *ng) {
        int i;
        Glassner base;

        base = ng->ID * 10;

        for (i=0; i<OCTANTS; ++i) {
                id_w.getXYZ((Glassner)(base + i + 1), ng->node[i].coord);
        }
}
```

Given a parent ID of 41, base = 410 (not a legal Glassner ID), and coordinates are retrieved for

{411, 412, 413, 414, 415, 416, 417, 418}

The base coordinate at the end of findNode() corresponds to 413, but let's say that the ray origin is actually inside of 412 (it won't be at first, but findNode will home in on it). Then, from the code above, scale will be Nt / N where N = 2^3 = 8, so scale = 128 / 8 = 16. The coordinate "voxcoord" is the voxel base coordinate (4, 0, 2), and the idx passed to addScaledUnitOffset() is 2. The method addScaledUnitOffset() gives

```
r_coord.x = coord.x * scale + ax[2 - 1] * scale;
r_coord.y = coord.y * scale + ay[2 - 1] * scale;
r_coord.z = coord.z * scale + az[2 - 1] * scale;
```

or (and forgive the double multiply, only need one: compiler hopefully optimized!)

```
r_coord.x = 4 * 16 + 1 * 16 = 80;
r_coord.y = 0 * 16 + 0 * 16 = 0;
r_coord.z = 2 * 16 + 1 * 16 = 48;
```

Notice that (80, 0, 48) = (5, 0, 3) * 16.

3.5 *Calls to findNode()*

The ray's initial position is the ray origin:

```
/// pass in the TData pointer for the ray origin
/// Note: Use the relative origin and direction, not base.
void RayWorker::RayLoop(Ray & ray, SortedLList<TData *, TData> & td_list) {
...
        // start with the ray origin
        r_u.copy_float3(ray.origin, coord);
...
        do {
                // find the voxel node of current td_ptr
                findNode(coord, data);
...
}
```

This is the "relative" coordinate, not the untransformed "base" coordinate – although they can be the same if the armature is in its default position without a virtual rotation. This is an important point because the ray can be pointing in any direction relative to the cardinal voxel grid.

The meaning of the td_list and td_ptr are now briefly explained. "td" stands for "TData", referring to the ray-vector "t" scalar. This is the scalar that's extended bit by bit as the ray "pushes" through the voxel hierarchy. A td_list is simply a list of TData pointers.

The first step is to find the voxel at the current relative position along the ray. The first position, the ray's origin, is guaranteed to be inside of the voxel hierarchy.

Here's the full inner loop from RayWorker::RayLoop():

```
...
        do {
                // find the voxel node of current td_ptr
                findNode(coord, data);
                current->in = !data.empty;
                if (current->in) {
                        current->color[T_RED] = data.color.x;
                        current->color[T_GREEN] = data.color.y;
                        current->color[T_BLUE] = data.color.z;
                }
                // get the intersections for this voxel
                r_u.TIntersect(ray, data.coord, data.length);

                // push the coords to the next voxel node
                PushRay(ray, coord, tpack);
```

```
            // transfer intersect to a TData record
            current = tdata_w.AddTDataRecord(tpack.t, tpack.i);
            // progressive insert (fast)
            td_list.insertNext(current);
      } while (!RayExitsUniverse(tpack.i));
...
```

Suppose the node has been found and it's not empty. In this case the color returned from findNode() is transfered to "current", which is the current entry in the TData list. Here's what comes next:

```
            // get the intersections for this voxel
            r_u.TIntersect(ray, data.coord, data.length);
```

This is the second most important part of ray tracing. It takes the scaled coordinate just computed, and also the voxel "length" which, in the example, is set to scale = 16 = 128 / 2^3 for level 3. If level was equal to 1, the length would be 128 / 2 = 64, being the first subdivision of space with 8 octants. TIntersect uses this data to compute intersections of the ray against all six voxel face-planes.

3.6 *T Intersection*

An explanation of T-intersection is complicated, but doesn't involve the TData infrastructure so let's continue to put the latter off and dig into the intersection math.

Andrew Glassner takes two intersections per bounding box principal plane, one for each parallel face of the voxel. In C++ these principal plane orientations are managed with a template index attached to the method at hand. Caller methods simply rotate the template index so that the called method only has to be written once instead of three times. This same praxis is used in the voxel evaluation code for rasterizing triangles to a dominant axis.

The code looks at some voxel: for example, the one found in the previous section for the current ray position. The voxel itself has a base or lower-lefthand position (x,y,z) and a length, not necessarily unity since many voxels will be terminal at higher levels.

The template argument is simply one of the 3 plane orientations: XY, YZ, or XZ. The template methods in utils.h are oriented towards a dominant axis that fill the w position. For example, dominant axis X gives a mapping of (u, v, w) to (y, z, x).

These template methods can be used for ray tracing with the knowledge that the plane components returned are the members not equal to the dominant axis. In other words:

The XY plane corresponds to uvw<2>, which is dominant axis Z.
The XZ plane corresponds to uvw<1>, which is dominant axis Y.
The YZ plane corresponds to uvw<0>, which is dominant axis X.

Therefore an intersection call takes the form:

t_intersect<X> (for YZ)

and so on.

The t_intersect() method is called for each of the three orientations, resulting in six intersection points. Here's the first part of the code.

```
template <int32 AXIS>
void RayUtil::t_intersect(Ray &ray, Intersect **data, float3 &voxel_base, int len) {
        float3 tD, t1, t2;

    typedef uvw<AXIS> sel;
    typedef uvw_p<AXIS> put;

    uvw_float3 base;

    // everything in XY by default
    // octant planes
    base.u = sel::u(voxel_base);
    base.v = sel::v(voxel_base);
    base.w = sel::w(voxel_base);

    float3 A1, B1, C1, A2, B2, C2;

    // plane 1
    put::u(A1, base.u);
    put::v(A1, base.v + len);
    put::w(A1, base.w);

    put::u(B1, base.u);
    put::v(B1, base.v);
    put::w(B1, base.w);

    put::u(C1, base.u + len);
    put::v(C1, base.v);
    put::w(C1, base.w);
```

```
  // plane 2
  put::u(A2, sel::u(A1));
  put::v(A2, sel::v(A1));
  put::w(A2, base.w + len);

  put::u(B2, sel::u(B1));
  put::v(B2, sel::v(B1));
  put::w(B2, base.w + len);

  put::u(C2, sel::u(C1));
  put::v(C2, sel::v(C1));
  put::w(C2, base.w + len);

  // subtract for u, v
  float3 v1, v2;

  put::u(v1, sel::u(C1) - sel::u(A1));
  put::v(v1, sel::v(C1) - sel::v(A1));
  put::u(v2, sel::u(B1) - sel::u(A1));
  put::v(v2, sel::v(B1) - sel::v(A1));

  // compute normal (un-normalized) to voxel plane
  float3 n;
  n.x = n.y = n.z = 0.0;
...
```

This method is called with template indices as follows:

```
void RayUtil::TIntersect(Ray & ray, ushort3 & base, int voxlen) {
        float3 basef;
        Intersect **pair_ptr;

        // re-use the Intersect Records
        clearIntData();

        // transfer base to float coords
        basef.x = float(base.x);
        basef.y = float(base.y);
        basef.z = float(base.z);

        // XY
        pair_ptr = &int_list->list[T_XY<<1];
        t_intersect<Z>(ray, pair_ptr, basef, voxlen);
```

```
		// YZ
		pair_ptr = &int_list->list[T_YZ<<1];
		t_intersect<X>(ray, pair_ptr, basef, voxlen);
		// XZ
		pair_ptr = &int_list->list[T_XZ<<1];
		t_intersect<Y>(ray, pair_ptr, basef, voxlen);
}
```

When RayUtil is instantiated the first thing it does is make an "intersection list":

```
void RayUtil::makeIntList() {
	int_list = new IntersectList;
	int_list->count = T_MAX;

	Intersect **plist = new Intersect * [T_MAX];
	int_list->list = plist;

	for (int i = 0; i < T_MAX; ++i) {
		Intersect *cur_int = new Intersect;
		cur_int->plane = i;
		int_list->list[i] = cur_int;
	}
}
```

T_MAX is 6, for a maximum of 6 intersections for the 6 bounding planes of the current voxel. The Intersect struct holds both a t-value along the ray and the associated intersection point:

```
struct Intersect {
		int t_flag, plane;
		float t;
		unsigned short i_bits;
		float3 i;
		Intersect() : t_flag(0), t(0.0), i_bits(0) {
				i.x = i.y = i.z = 0.0;
		}
		// we're using < as a > test
		bool operator<(const Intersect & rhs) {
				if (this != &rhs) {
						// greater than
						return (rhs.t < t);
				}
				return false;		// equal
		}
```

```
};
```

The struct is sortable. Six of these data structures are put in a list. Each has a plane identifier, being 0 to 5, and the rest is filled in later.

The intersection bits or i_bits are just on/off bits, 6 of them, corresponding to t-intersects. Consider the following intersection results:

```
XZ:
t1:000001    infinite        none
t2:000000    infinite (0)    none (line)

YZ:
t1:000000    3.3541      (0,2,1.5)
t2:100000    1.11803     (2,2,0.5)   "in front"

XY:
t1:000000    2.236068     (1,2,1)
t2:001000    6.708205     (-3,2,3)  "left"
```

The first column shows the i_bits; the second shows the t-value; and the third shows the intersection point on the plane. There are two valid intersections, and in terms of increasing t, they are:

```
t1:XY to t1:YZ
```

The t-value can be infinite when the ray is parallel to the voxel plane. Going from the top row to bottom, the ray is parallel to the XZ planes (both of them obviously), so the t-values are infinite. The ray-vector resides at y = 2.

Next, the first intersection in YZ is at (x, z) = (0, 1.5) and is within the voxel boundaries. The second YZ intersection at (x, z) = (2, 0.5), when looking down the Z-axis in the positive direction, is "in front" of the voxel on the YZ plane.

Next, the first intersection in XY at (x, z) = (1, 1) is within the voxel boundaries, and the second XY intersection at (x, z) = (-3, 3) is "left" of the voxel on the XY plane. Notice how the ordering of t indicates the order of intersections along the ray. It's YZ(t2), XY(t1), YZ(t1), and XY(t2).

3.7 *Example Intersect Cases*

The i_bits are what's called an "out-code" in clipping algorithms. The out-code is six bits, with a bit being true (1) when the appropriate condition is satisfied:

bit 1 – point is above voxel volume: y > 1
bit 2 – point is below voxel volume: y < 0

Note that the only way a point can be above or below the voxel is if it's been computed in the YZ plane or the XY plane (y being the common coordinate).

bit 3 – point is right of voxel volume: x > 1
bit 4 – point is left of voxel volume: x < 0

Here, either XY or XZ applies.

bit 5 – point is behind voxel volume: z > 1
bit 6 – point is in front of voxel volume: z < 0

Here, either XZ or YZ applies.

The voxel can be thought of as a *canonical view volume* against which the ray is clipped. The extents are arbitrarily set to (0, 1) for all dimensions in the list above but the logic applies to an arbitrarily-sized voxel.

Thinking in terms of clipping, each pair of intersections for a plane orientation describes a line. So, as with line clipping, there are two codes: one for t1, and one for t2.

If the logical "and" of the codes != 0, the pair is outside of the volume and the voxel is rejected. The "ands" just say: both endpoints are above/below; to left/right; or in front of/behind the volume. Remember there's a 6-bit code for each intersection. A rejection for one orientation is enough to reject the voxel.

However a valid intersection requires that the logical "and" of the codes should be zero for all three pairs for all three orientations (and all three clipping line segments). If not, an error is thrown because the "push" went wrong. It's always wise to enforce the intended logic because something could go wrong with a future code change and then this error condition will be caught.

The first part of t_intersect() constructs a triangle, which is all you need for the plane equation; then a second triangle parallel to the first, "length" units away; in the example (Glassner ID = 412) the length is 16.

Let's look at the final part of t_intersect():

```
...
   float sign = 1;
```

```
if (AXIS == Y)
  sign = -1;

put::w(n, sign * (sel::u(v1) * sel::v(v2) - sel::v(v1) * sel::u(v2)) );

// Dot(A1, n)
float dot_a1 = sel::w(A1) * sel::w(n);
// Dot(A2, n)
float dot_a2 = sel::w(A2) * sel::w(n);

// Dot(ray.origin, n)
float dot_o = sel::w(ray.origin) * sel::w(n);

// Dot(ray.direction, n)
float dot_d = sel::w(ray.direction) * sel::w(n);

if (fp_u.equalBoundsf(dot_d, 0.0, PRECISIONf)) {
	// infinity
	if (fp_u.equalBoundsf(dot_a1 - dot_o, 0.0, PRECISIONf))
		data[0]->t_flag = T_INFINITE_ZERO;
	else
		data[0]->t_flag = T_INFINITE;

	if (fp_u.equalBoundsf(dot_a2 - dot_o, 0.0, PRECISIONf))
		data[1]->t_flag = T_INFINITE_ZERO;
	else
		data[1]->t_flag = T_INFINITE;

	GetInfiniteBits<AXIS>(ray.origin, A1, data[0]->i_bits);
	GetInfiniteBits<AXIS>(ray.origin, A2, data[1]->i_bits);

	// no intersection: caller must check t_flag
	// but make a t stand-in for the sort
	data[0]->t = data[1]->t = T_BIG_NEG;
	return;
}

// no parallelism
data[0]->t = (dot_a1 - dot_o) / dot_d;
data[1]->t = (dot_a2 - dot_o) / dot_d;
for (int i = 0; i < T_PAIR; ++i) {
	VectorScale(tD, ray.direction, data[i]->t);
	VectorAdd(data[i]->i, ray.origin, tD);
```

```
        data[i]->t_flag = T_OKAY;
        GetBits<AXIS>(data[i]->i, base, len, data[i]->i_bits);
    }
}
```

The cross product determines the plane normal. The orthogonal orientation of the voxels simplifies things since one of the terms is always zero.

In XY, Z is zero.

Say that the voxel length is 4, and base.x,y,z = 1. Referring to first part of t_intersect() above,

```
A1 = (1,5,1)
B1 = (1,1,1)
C1 = (5,1,1)
```

Then:

```
C1 - A1 = (4,-4,0) = V1
B1 - A1 = (0,-4,0) = V2
```

The second part of t_intersect first zeros out the normal. The orthogonal nature of each plane leads to a cross-product of the two 3D vectors as follows:

```
cross = -4 * (V2.z = 0) - (V1.z = 0) * - 4
          + (V1.z = 0) * 0 - 4 * (V2.z = 0)
          + (4 * - 4) - (0 * - 4)
```

Since Z is always zero, the reduced cross product is:

```
cross = (0, 0, v1x v2y - v1y v2x)
```

In other words, the significant portion omits the sel::w position. For example, for selection/swizzle axis = Z, the components (x, y) of V1 and V2 are used and z is ignored. That's the portion that this instruction handles:

```
put::w(n, sign * (sel::u(v1) * sel::v(v2) - sel::v(v1) * sel::u(v2)) );
```

The cross-product is the definition of the plane normal by linear algebra. The normal is not unit-normalized, but in any case the vector length is simply:

```
sqrt(vz^2) ~= abs(vz)
```

so no square root is needed. Using the values above, n = (0, 0, -16/16 = -1). The value remains un-normalized at -16. Next the two plane terms come into play: A1 and A2. Notice what happens when taking the dot product with the normal:

```
Dot(A1, n) = (1,5,1)(0,0,-16) = 0 + 0 - 16 = -16
```

So only the third term needs to be multiplied, i.e.:

```
sel::w(A1) * sel::w(n)
```

Same for A2, which is the parallel plane "length" units away.

Likewise, dot_o (origin) and dot_d (direction) are also single multiplies. Let's say the ray has an origin of (0.5, 1.5, 2) and a direction vector that passes through (3,3,3). This isn't a realistic setup because the armature would be closer to the center of the universe and so would the ray origin. In any case, the direction vector is thus:

```
(3,3,3) - (0.5,1.5,2) = (2.5, 1.5, 1)
```

Dot(ray.origin, n) is:

```
sel::w(ray.origin) * sel::w(n) = 2 * -16 = -32
```

Dot(ray.direction, n) is:

```
sel::w(ray.direction) * sel::w(n) = -16
```

The t-value can now be computed for A1:

```
t = (dot_a1 - dot_o) / dot_d = (-16 - (-32)) / -16 = -1
```

The call to VectorScale produces

```
tD = ray.direction * t = (-2.5, -1.5, -1)
```

and VectorAdd gives the final intersection:

```
t1 = ray.origin + tD = (-2, 0, 1)
```

Remember that t is a distance or scalar, and t1 is the actual intersection in 3D. The values above are calculated in the final loop for the intersection pair in t_intersect() as shown above. Since the ray origin is beyond the voxel front plane at z = 1, specifically at z = 2, the intersection is behind the ray origin, but relative to the voxel it's "left" and "below".

To compute the second intersection point "t2", the plane coefficients labeled "2" {A2, B2, C2} are calculated. The voxel "length" determines the depth of the voxel in Z (assuming that the pair for the XY plane is being evaluated). In the example the length is 4, and base.x,y,z = 1. So {A2, B2, C2} is just a copy of {A1, B1, C1} with Z = 1 + 4 = 5.

```
A2 = (1,5,5)
B2 = (1,1,5)
C2 = (5,1,5)

dot_a2 = sel::w(A2) * sel::w(n) = 5 * -16 = -80
```

The t-value for A2 is:

```
t = (dot_a2 - dot_o) / dot_d = (-80 - (-32)) / -16 = 3
```

and

```
tD = ray.direction * t = (7.5, 4.5, 3)
t2 = ray.origin + tD = (8, 6, 5)
```

The ray origin at (0.5, 1.5, 2) is shooting towards (3, 3, 3) and continues on to intersect the voxel rear plane (XY) way out at (8, 6, 5). Relative to the voxel, the intersection is both "right" and "above". Since neither intersection is within the voxel bounds, one might think the ray doesn't intersect the voxel. But by inspection we know that (3, 3, 3) is inside of the voxel, and here's where the clipping algorithm comes to the rescue. The i_bits are:

```
t1:001010   "left" "below"
t2:000101   "right" "above"
```

The voxel can't be rejected because the logical "and" of the two codes is zero. The voxel can only be rejected if the logical "and" for the pair is != 0.

Before getting to clipping for this particular line segment, let's look at the complicated conditional near the end of t_intersect() involving T_INFINITE.

If dot_d is zero, the t-values will be infinite, or undefined. Another word for this is "singular". None of this qualifies as an intersection. It means the line segment or ray is parallel to one or more planes. A ray can be parallel to two planes and perpendicular to the third. Or parallel to one plane only.

What's more, though the armature is set up to avoid this, a ray can be parallel to and touching a plane. For example a ray will cross a voxel on the voxel's upper XZ plane if the ray.origin is (3,2,0) and goes through (-1,2,2); and the voxel base is (0,0,1) and the length = 2. The rule is that if the ray is parallel to and coincident with a voxel plane, it's not an intersection.

In this difficult case dot_d is zero, but t is also zero. The intersection is said to be "infinitely zero" which is a different status than "infinite". The intersection, a line, is rejected and the difference between "infinite" and "infinitely zero" is taken into account for the "push" of the ray into the next voxel.

The first thing the infinity logic at the end does is check, within some epsilon, for dot_d == 0. The final clause of t_insersect computes the t-values:

```
data[0]->t = (dot_a1 - dot_o) / dot_d;
data[1]->t = (dot_a2 - dot_o) / dot_d;
```

If dot_d == 0 then the numerator is checked. If (dot_a1 - dot_o) == 0, then the t-intersection is flagged as INFINITE_ZERO. Otherwise it's flagged as INFINITE. The same check is made for (dot_a2 - dot_o) and the same flags applied. The t-values, for sorting purposes, are set to T_BIG_NEG = -1.0e+10, a big negative number.

In general, if a t-value is negative, the resulting intersection is automatically rejected. t must be greater than or equal to 0. But it's still necessary to determine which planes these values come from, so that the "push" can be conducted in the relevant orientations. The key here is that t is increased, not reduced. Its direction is maintained.

Let's look at the "bits" routines. The normal (non-infinite) routine is:

```
template <int32 AXIS>
void RayUtil::GetBits(const float3 &intersect, const uvw_float3 &base,
                        int len, unsigned short &bits) {
    typedef uvw<AXIS> sel;

        // note that the lookups cycle with the template argument
        // use an epsilon!
        bits = 0;
        if (fp_u.lessThanBoundsf(sel::u(intersect), base.u, PRECISIONf))
                bits |= sel::u(lt_set);
        else if (fp_u.greaterBoundsf(sel::u(intersect), base.u + len, PRECISIONf))
                bits |= sel::u(gt_set);

        if (fp_u.lessThanBoundsf(sel::v(intersect), base.v, PRECISIONf))
                bits |= sel::v(lt_set);
```

```
        else if (fp_u.greaterBoundsf(sel::v(intersect), base.v + len, PRECISIONf))
                bits |= sel::v(gt_set);

        // w intersect is always equal to base: don't need this
}
```

and is called like this from t_intersect():

```
        GetBits<AXIS>(data[i]->i, base, len, data[i]->i_bits);
```

where i is {0, 1} for {t1, t2}. The last argument is the return value. "base" is the voxel base coordinate. GetBits() is a template function so will swizzle coordinates depending on the axis. For example, uvw<Z> selects u = x and v = y per the template definitions in utils.h. GetBits() is just a bounds check, but don't be deceived: the bounds check is actually the clipping.

The lt_set and gt_set variables are initialized when the RayUtil class is instantiated:

```
void RayUtil::Init() {
        lt_set.x = 0b001000;
        lt_set.y = 0b000010;
        lt_set.z = 0b100000;

        gt_set.x = 0b000100;
        gt_set.y = 0b000001;
        gt_set.z = 0b010000;
...
}
```

The selection of these bits is a template sel::{u, v} of unsigned shorts, where the two "sets" are:

```
LESS THAN (lt_set):
(001000,  000010,  100000)
left      below    in front

GREATER THAN (gt_set):
(000100,  000001,  010000)
right     above    behind
```

The logic for assignment is shown in the GetBits() function above. Keep in mind that the same AXIS index is used for the i_bit position and the intersection coordinate, because they have to match. A selection of v = y for the intersection coordinate can't be assigned with a selection for i_bits of v = z, for example. They both have to be v = y. In this case the selection of v = y corresponds to "below" or "above". But if the AXIS is X, then u = y; whereas if the AXIS is Z, then v = y. The coordinates have to be ordered in some fashion, and given the constraints, there's going to be at least one position change for one of the elements in the mapping of {x,y,z} to {u,v,w} for two different AXIS indices; for example, y going from the v position for axis-Z to the u position for axis-X. Despite the brain calisthenics, it all works out.

The infinite version of GetBits() is:

```
/// which side is the infinite parallelism on?
template <int32 AXIS>
void RayUtil::GetInfiniteBits(const float3 &ray_origin, const float3 &A,
                               unsigned short &bits) {
  typedef uvw<AXIS> sel;

  bits = 0;        // default parallel and "on" plane; equal
  // otherwise, infinitely to one side:
  if (fp_u.greaterBoundsf(sel::w(ray_origin), sel::w(A), PRECISIONf))
        bits = sel::w(gt_set);
  else if (fp_u.lessThanBoundsf(sel::w(ray_origin), sel::w(A), PRECISIONf))
        bits = sel::w(lt_set);
}
```

and is called with:

```
        GetInfiniteBits<AXIS>(ray.origin, A1, data[0]->i_bits);
        GetInfiniteBits<AXIS>(ray.origin, A2, data[1]->i_bits);
```

The logic for GetInfiniteBits() in pseudocode is:

```
  if sel::w(ray.origin) == sel::w(A1), bits = 0
  else if sel::w(ray.origin) > sel::w(A1), bits = sel::w(gt_set)
  else bits = sel::w(lt_set)
```

The axis selection is going to be infinitely to one side or the other of the current voxel plane depending on the template index: it's only a selection on w. Therefore "infinitely left/right" means w = x ({u,v}={y,z} for AXIS X); "infinitely above/below" means w = y ({u,v}={x,z} for AXIS Y); and "infinitely in front/behind" means w = z ({u,v}={x,y} for AXIS Z). Since the ray is known to be parallel to the current voxel plane, instead of an intersection point the ray origin serves just as well. Likewise, a single point on the voxel plane is fine. GetInfiniteBits() is called for the voxel's parallel faces, and no matter what the orientation of the ray is it's still known to be parallel and thus infinite, so all that matters is the distance in w to one side or the other of (or on) the current face.

3.8 *Post Clipping*

The ray is almost clipped to the voxel, but there are a few more steps. Let's back up a bit and look at RayLoop() in the RayWorker class. First it calls findNode() to find the voxel the ray is inside of; then calls TIntersect, which computes intersections for all three plane pairs; and then it clips – only the clipping is encapsulated in the ray's "push" to the next voxel.

```
...
        do {
                // find the voxel node of current td_ptr
                findNode(coord, data);
                current->in = !data.empty;
                if (current->in) {
                        current->color[T_RED] = data.color.x;
                        current->color[T_GREEN] = data.color.y;
                        current->color[T_BLUE] = data.color.z;
                }
                // get the intersections for this voxel
                r_u.TIntersect(ray, data.coord, data.length);

                // push the coords to the next voxel node
                PushRay(ray, coord, tpack);
...
```

Notice that even if the voxel is empty, the ray must go on! So intersections are still calculated, and the ray is pushed through. The idea is to "push" the ray just beyond the border of the current voxel into the next voxel space. The next voxel may be at a different level than the current voxel, so findNode() is called all over again for the new ray position. The code loops until the ray has been "pushed" out of the universe. (The extents of the voxel space are called "the universe".)

PushRay() simply calls Push() in RayUtil:

```
/// push into the next voxel : put coords in coord
void RayUtil::Push(Ray & ray, float3 &coord, TPack & tpack) {
        int i, size, plane;
        float max_t;
        Intersect * current;
        Vector<Intersect *> my_list;
        Vector<Intersect *> top_list;
        SortByRef<Intersect *, Intersect> my_sort;

        // fill a vector with the Intersect data
```

```
	for (i = 0; i < T_MAX; ++i) {
		// check infinite-zero and throw exception
		if (int_list->list[i]->t_flag == T_INFINITE_ZERO)
			throw RayException("Infinite Zero");
		my_list.push_back(int_list->list[i]);
	}

	// sort the list
	my_sort.quicksort(my_list);

	// get the top t's (with zero ibits)
	for (i = 0; i < T_MAX; ++i) {
		if (my_list[i]->i_bits == 0x00)
			top_list.push_back(my_list[i]);
	}
	// get the max t that has ibits == 0, and the intersect
	max_t = top_list[0]->t;
	copy_float3(top_list[0]->i, coord);
	// return data
	tpack.t = max_t;
	copy_float3(coord, tpack.i);

	// go through list, look at plane vals, and push
	size = top_list.size();
	for (i=0; i<size; ++i) {
		if (!fp_u.equalBoundsf(top_list[i]->t, max_t, PRECISIONf))
			break;
		current = top_list[i];
		plane = current->plane >> 1;
		if (plane == T_XY) {
			coord.z += HALF_INDEX * Sign(ray.direction.z);
		} else if (plane == T_YZ) {
			coord.x += HALF_INDEX * Sign(ray.direction.x);
		} else { // XZ
			coord.y += HALF_INDEX * Sign(ray.direction.y);
		}
	}
}
```

Notice the check for T_INFINITE_ZERO in the assignment loop. In the infinite-zero case the ray is straddling two voxels: right on the boundary of them. The ray and the boundary faces are "coplanar". This shouldn't happen because the base orientation is set up so that rays are, by default, traveling through the centers of voxels.

The whole idea of ray casting is that the ray will only intersect a single voxel at a time. So a "policy" decision is needed here: if T_INFINITE_ZERO is anywhere in the list of T_MAX = 6 intersections, throw an error. This should never happen.

Recall that the int_list is a class variable which holds a list of 6 intersections. The first loop of Push() stores the 6 pointers to the 6 Intersect structs in a Vector. The Intersect struct has a comparator so that it can be sorted.

The list is then sorted by t-value. As the comment says, the greatest t's are then copied to a second list called the "top list". An i_bits "and"-value equal to 0 means there's a valid point-intersection within the boundaries of the voxel. In the parallel case a ray cannot be both above and below, left and right, or front and behind: it has to be one or the other, so a parallel ray will also have an i_bits "and"-value of 0. But remember parallel rays have a t-value that's T_BIG_NEG. They're at the bottom of the list after it's sorted.

A parallel ray can be "pushed" because the non-parallel AXES *do* have valid intersections. Remember that a parallel ray has already been determined to be "in" the current voxel, whether through the initial ray setup, or via the previous "push". So the i_bits will be zero for at least one of the non-parallel axes.

Still, it's not quite so simple. Basically you want to count up all the valid intersections at the max t value for the set, and use all those elements in terms of pushing the voxel via the direction vector signs. That's what the top_list Vector is for.

If the ray exits on a vertex, there will be three valid intersections for that vertex, on three planes, and three directions to be pushed with the appropriate sign.

If the departing ray hits an edge, there will be two valid intersections for two planes. And if the ray exits on a single face (the usual case), there's just one exiting intersection for one plane.

The max zero-bit t-value and its intersection are stored as return data in the passed tpack reference. This is critical because the calculated intersection and not the pushed coordinate is going to be the next reference coordinate for the next push.

Finally, the Push() routine does the push, which is the final loop that iterates on the top_list. It cycles through all the intersections that are valid, and pushes. Notice that the t-value for a vertex (3 planes) or an edge (2 planes) has to be the same value for each iteration. If it's outside of the epsilon check, it's not truly on a vertex or edge, and the loop exits.

The ray is pushed a "half index" into the next voxel. HALF_INDEX = 0.5, based on an unscaled voxel being a unit voxel. For a unit voxel the ray is pushed to its center. But if the next voxel is scaled, 0.5 will get the ray minimally inside of the voxel, no matter how big it is. As will be explained next, this pushed coordinate is only used for the next call to findNode(). It's not an actual position on the ray. The actual position is the intersection already computed – and this valid ray position will be transferred from TPack to TData before the next iteration of RayLoop().

Here's why the pushed coordinate isn't on the ray. For a line segment defined by its two endpoints, P0 and P1, the direction vector is defined as:

```
d = P1 - P0
```

For example:

```
(5,5,5) - (1,1,1) = (4,4,4)
```

Let's say the ray exits the voxel at top_t all equal to (3,3,3). Suppose it exits on a vertex: the "pushed" ray becomes (3.5, 3.5, 3.5). However, the "push" in most cases won't follow the original ray-vector.

Take this example:

```
(6,2,2) - (2,1,1) = (4, 1, 1)
```

Let's say the ray exits at (6, 2, 2). Suppose that the only intersection is in YZ, at x = 6. Only the x-coordinate will be "pushed", and the ray goes to (6.5, 2, 2). But wait, the pushed coordinate isn't on the ray anymore! It's been nudged from the true direction. It turns out the pushed coordinate is only used for the next call to findNode(). Once that's accomplished, the ray origin, the original direction, and the valid intersection point are used to compute the correct intersections for the next voxel.

The idea for the "push" comes from the Glassner paper; Andrew Glassner calls it a "minlen move". He writes: "These movement operations are trivial to compute and perform because each is perpendicular to a coordinate axis."

To review, the call to findNode is

```
findNode(coord, data);
```

where "coord" is the pushed coordinate for which an octree node is to be found. Before entering the ray loop, that coordinate is initialized to the ray's origin:

```
r_u.copy_float3(ray.origin, coord);
```

In fact that coordinate is completely local to RayLoop(), which defines it on the stack:

```
float3 coord;
```

For each iteration of the ray loop, that same coord is overwritten from push to push. Each call to findNode() returns a NodePack with the found voxel's coordinates, but the "pushed" coordinate is only used for the findNode() "inside" test. The coord is then completely rewritten in the call to Push(). It starts out as the top intersection, retrieved from the top_list:

```
copy_float3(top_list[0]->i, coord);
```

and is then "pushed", but the push (usually) doesn't represent an actual point on the ray. It just represents a point inside of the next voxel. Meanwhile, the actual intersection point is stored in TPack, which is transferred to a TData record in RayLoop.

Note that a ray going in the negative X direction will enter a voxel on the high-X side. The entry won't be at the base position of the voxel, but at the base+length position. Does this matter? No. The (x,y,z) position of the pushed coordinate will still return the correct voxel, with the correct base, even though the voxel has been entered from a non-positive direction, because the direction vector has a negative component and the sign of that component is used for the "push" offset.

END OF PART THREE

Part Four

Project V: A Tour of the Voxel Factory
PART FOUR: Ray Tracing 2

4.0 *Ray Tracing Recap*

To summarize so far, ray tracing in Project V, unlike Glassner's scheme which keeps track of nodes with a hash table, descends the octree directly to find the node with the pointer to the NodeGroup data. But the NodeGroup isn't really needed except if using the triangle list for some reason. Still, the code needs to determine when to stop, i.e., when a terminal node for some input coordinate has been reached.

During the evaluation stage, in the Evaluation Context, the octree is built on the fly and the size of the voxel at each level is always unity, with the model geometry and the voxel universe expanding around it. But for ray tracing, traversal of the octree takes place after the fact, which means terminal nodes can range from unit-sized to an eighth the size of the entire universe.

Therefore, for ray tracing the terminal node gives the extent of the voxel in three dimensions. Glassner's scheme of pushing the ray-vector into the next voxel via the face/edge/vertex status (one, two, or three dimensions) and by minlen / 2, e.g. the "minlen move" scheme, is used for the Project V. In the ray-tracing scheme minlen is always unity to reflect the smallest-sized voxel, being the unit voxel. Therefore the "minlen move" is 1/2 or 0.5. Unlike the voxel coords which are scaled for the center point comparison, minlen remains unity: a huge empty octant can abut the most finely subdivided octant, so minlen pushes the vector by the minimum distance, giving a new (x,y,z), leading to a new lookup in the findNode() routine. That new lookup finds the the next voxel that the ray has been pushed into.

So far we've traced through only the first voxel. But the ray must go on! If everything works, the ray casting will result in a sequence of voxels along the ray that the ray intersects. The voxels may be face-connected, edge-connected, or rarely, vertex-connected. It doesn't matter: the sequence comes from the extension of the ray into the next space, and the next, and so on.

The push stops when the ray reaches one of the boundaries of the voxel universe. When that happens intersection t+ will be on a face, edge, or vertex with coordinates equal to 0 in x, y, or z; or on the other side of the universe with coordinates equal to 2^N.

Since the origin of the ray is near the "center" of the universe the push is always working out towards the boundaries. If the armature is given a virtual rotation before ray tracing, the boundary may be reached quite quickly for the lower or upper "courses" of the armature.

Rotation of the model itself is relative. To rotate the model, the octree remains untouched; the octree has already been computed, so voxel offsets and sizes can't change. Instead, the rays are rotated relative to the base orientation of the model. The model remains untransformed: only the rays are rotated. This can be called a "virtual rotation." This works because the final display flips the armature back to its default position, but the intersections are for the rotated or "virtual" orientation. Therefore the model appears rotated.

The virtual rotation scheme is very slick because the base model stays invariant while the samples along the rays change – and this reduces "crawling" and roundoff artifacts that would otherwise occur when rotating the model and redoing all the voxel rasterization. Of course the model *can* be rotated if desired before rasterizing in the normal evaluation stage, but this hasn't been pursued for ray tracing. As far as viewing angles, OpenGL provides a viewing transformation so that the model, though not changing its orientation, can be viewed from different angles.

Ray tracing is only used to simulate the sampling of a model by the positions of LEDs on armature "arms" (which are the rays) of the rotating display device. Ray tracing isn't used for generic voxelization, which is the workhorse of the solid-state display device which is a completely different piece of hardware. Though ray tracing through a voxelization could eventually be used for lighting calculations, for now ray tracing is only a way to explore and assess a rotational device such as the one patented by Ed Berlin, who, by the way, was my old boss when I worked for Cubicomp, the company he founded with Steve Crane.

This brings us to LEDs.

4.1 *Determining "in" and "out" Status of LED Sample Positions*

The LED positions along a ray are interspersed between ray-casting voxel intersections. Thus each pair {t, t+} describing the voxel extents and the ray's extent through the voxel in parameter space t, will have either an "on" or "off" status depending on whether the voxel is active or empty, and if "on" a color; and the LED sample positions that reside between any of these t-values will inherit that status and color. A very small percentage of the voxels in the octree overlap the master triangle data that describes the model geometry in three dimensions. Those that do are "on" in this language.

This is the same kind of list structure that's used for begin/end pairs for VTList indices (voxel-triangle entries).

The LED positions are specified with constant offsets. The main loop for ray tracing sweeps out a full rotation of the armature by rotating each arm one degree for each of 360 degrees of the circle. A second pass offsets the angles by half a degree, and also offsets the LEDs along the arm by 0.5 units, to fill in "sample gaps".

Here again is the loop of the RayWorker::RayLoop() routine:

```
...
        do {
```

```
            // find the voxel node of current td_ptr
            findNode(coord, data);
            current->in = !data.empty;
            if (current->in) {
                    current->color[T_RED] = data.color.x;
                    current->color[T_GREEN] = data.color.y;
                    current->color[T_BLUE] = data.color.z;
            }
            // get the intersections for this voxel
            r_u.TIntersect(ray, data.coord, data.length);

            // push the coords to the next voxel node
            PushRay(ray, coord, tpack);

            // transfer intersect to a TData record
            current = tdata_w.AddTDataRecord(tpack.t, tpack.i);
            // progressive insert (fast)
            td_list.insertNext(current);
    } while (!RayExitsUniverse(tpack.i));
...
```

Part Three discussed the findNode procedure; the TIntersect and clipping code; and PushRay which uses the Glassner "minlen move" to push into the next voxel. Recall that the last thing the push did was to store the maximum valid t-value and the corresponding voxel-plane intersection in the temporary tpack transfer record (TPack) passed to the Push routine. In RayLoop() that tpack data is then transfered to a TData record via the TDataWorker class:

```
TData * TDataWorker::AddTDataRecord(float tval, const float3 &pos) {
        TData *td = new TData(tval, pos);
        td_list.push_back(td);
        current = td;
        return td;
}
```

The TDataWorker class declares as a private data member a Vector of TData pointers called td_list. TData is a sortable class:

```
class TData {
public:
        // make all of this public to emulate a struct

        float t;
        // either the intersect coord, or the LED position
```

```
        float3 position;
        // count of LED entries that follow
        short count;
        // universe boundary? ; is LED? ; leads into non-empty voxel?
        bool boundary, LED, in;
        // color of t if it's in (LED inherits this in run)
        unsigned char color[3];

        TData(float tval, const float3 &pos) {
                t = tval;
                position.x = pos.x;
                position.y = pos.y;
                position.z = pos.z;
                count = 0;
                boundary = LED = in = false;
                color[0] = color[1] = color[2] = 0;
        }

        bool operator<(const TData & rhs);

private:
        FPUtil fp_u;
};
```

Since any interval {t, t+} can bracket more than one LED, the count of LEDs from one intersection to the next is similar to keeping a sorted list of runlengths – in this case it would be "t-runlengths". The t-intersection can possibly be at the same position as an LED for an arbitrary rotation of the armature. The main thing we want to know is whether the voxel that the ray has just been "pushed into" is non-empty. If so, the LEDs are active for the "run". Notice an operator overload for the '<' operator for the sort on t.

The signature of RayLoop is:

```
void RayWorker::RayLoop(Ray & ray, SortedLList<TData *, TData> & td_list) {
...
```

and it's called like this:

```
/// Here's where the linked list comes in.
void RayWorker::CastRay(Ray & ray, const float3 &zero_origin) {
        // make a dummy TData element for the header
        TData * td_ptr = tdata_w.AddTDataRecord(-1.0, zero_origin);
```

```
        // Instantiate the sorted linked list
        SortedLList<TData *, TData> td_list(td_ptr);

        // Since the ray origins will all be in some
        // voxel (either empty or filled), the linked
        // list should start out officially with a
        // t = 0 entry.
        td_ptr = tdata_w.AddTDataRecord(0.0, ray.base_origin);
        // but we don't know the intersect status yet. Insert it
        // anyway, we can pass the base pointer to the next step.
        td_list.insert(td_ptr);

        RayLoop(ray, td_list);
        ProcessLEDs(ray, td_list);
        MakeRunLengths(ray, td_list);

        // clean up TData for finished ray
        tdata_w.DeleteTDataRecords();
}
```

Notice that the td_list is instantiated in this routine. However the data that fills it is instantiated in TDataWorker. As was just pointed out, TDataWorker has a member with the same name – "td_list" – but the TDataWorker td_list is a Vector. It's not the same as the RayWorker td_list, which is a SortedLList type, a sorted linked list. However, the same data is stored in both. The SortedLList type has a fast progressive insert, and also it can be snipped and relinked. We're about to get into some fancy pre-processing for runlengths.

4.2 *Boundaries of the Universe*

Unless the voxel resolution is arbitrarily increased from the default N, so that the original cubical space becomes a subspace, then the cubical region will be cut off in the corner-regions of the XZ plane: the effect of inscribing a circle in a square. This will only be noticeable if the model extends beyond the cylinder traced out by the armature. The ray casting therefore looks for two conditions:

1) The ray has reached a universe boundary in voxel space.
2) The ray has passed the last LED position t-value on the ray.

Here's the code for item 1:

```
/// looks at current intersection data from Push routine, above.
bool RayUtil::ExitsUniverse(float3 & intersect, const float Nt) {
        if (fp_u.equalBoundsf(intersect.x, 0.0, PRECISIONf) ||
```

```
            fp_u.equalBoundsf(intersect.y, 0.0, PRECISIONf) ||
            fp_u.equalBoundsf(intersect.z, 0.0, PRECISIONf))
            return true;

    if (fp_u.equalBoundsf(intersect.x, Nt, PRECISIONf) ||
            fp_u.equalBoundsf(intersect.y, Nt, PRECISIONf) ||
            fp_u.equalBoundsf(intersect.z, Nt, PRECISIONf))
            return true;

    return false;
}
```

The armature spindle is stuffed with routing wires and since there's nothing to display within the valuable real estate taken up by the spindle, everything within the spindle-radius is given a value of "off". In fact t-parameterization of LEDs begins at the first voxel outside of the spindle-radius so there's nothing to turn off.

Rays can partially rotate out of the universe if the armature has been virtually rotated. So the code must always look for the universe boundary because an LED or LED group may be outside of that boundary. The TData class therefore keeps a "boundary" flag for each LED in the ray's linked list.

Once the basic Vector is filled with t-values and intersection coordinates all along the ray from the ray origin to the end of the universe, the next step in the CastRay() method is ProcessLEDs().

In preparation, the final display of the LEDs is based on a simplified data structure for a ray called a ReducedRay. It includes a simple list of runlengths that can be processed quickly by the GLWorker class. Thus the Linked List needs to facilitate a couple of things:

a. Counting up run-lengths and bytes for the ReducedRay.
b. Quick find and insertion for building the ray.
c. Setting a "boundary" flag on the TData element.

4.3 *LED Positioning and Merging*

The sorted LinkedList (td_list) used in RayWorker::CastRay is sorted on the t parameter. The td_list has already been filled with t-values and intersections from the RayLoop pass. LEDs are inserted into this list at the correct t position in the ProcessLEDs method, which is a merge operation. The TData record for an LED will have its LED flag set. Then for each LED position, the "in" or "out" status is determined according to the t-span the LED resides in, which reflects in turn the "empty" status of the voxel the t-values span.

For this to work some listmaking tasks are required, with the understanding that TData records can correspond to a t-intersection position or an LED position:

a) find the first of the ensuing TData entries != LED
b) find the previous TData entry != LED
c) increment the count for the previous entry (count of LEDs that follow)
d) get the color if the previous entry is "in", and transfer to LED entry

This will be explained in detail as we go along. The initial TData entry is set to zero, e.g. t = 0, which is the ray origin. The first real t is the intersection of the ray with the voxel that contains the ray origin. Thus the initial LED position will probably be outside of this t, unless the voxel spans more than the canonical unit distance.

If the ray origin is inside of a voxel, and t_plus is the boundary of the universe, then all the LED positions are placed between the first t and t_plus, in order; and all take on the voxel's "empty" status whatever that is.

```
/// Use transformed or untransformed t values which are invariant.
/// However, make untransformed (base) positions for LEDs.
void RayWorker::ProcessLEDs(Ray & ray, SortedLList<TData *, TData> & td_list) {
	int t, max_LED;
	float tf;
	float3 tD, LED_pos;
	TData * td_ptr;

	// Take advantage of the fact that inserts are progressive
	// by starting insert search at previously inserted item.
	td_list.setStartNode();

	max_LED = (Nt - Nt / 16) / 2;
	for (t = 0; t < max_LED; ++t) {
		// use base coordinates
		tf = float(t);
		r_u.VectorScale(tD, ray.base_direction, tf);
		r_u.VectorAdd(LED_pos, ray.base_origin, tD);
		td_ptr = tdata_w.AddTDataRecord(tf, LED_pos);
		td_ptr->LED = true;
		// use insertNext for speedy insertion
		td_list.insertNext(td_ptr);
	}
	ScanThroughLinks(ray, td_list);
}
```

The sorted linked list uses progressive insertion, with the first insertion preceded by a call to setStartNode():

```
/// For quick insert when caller KNOWS that inserts are progressive.
template <class Object, class ConstObj>
void SortedLList<Object, ConstObj>::setStartNode() {
        startNode = LList<Object>::zeroth( );
}
```

Then there's some active management for each insertion. The "prev" and "curr" pointers are set to startNode, and then startNode is updated after the insertion. So this is very quick for a large number of elements:

```
template <class Object, class ConstObj>
LListNode<Object> * SortedLList<Object, ConstObj>::insertNext( const Object x )
{
  LListItr<Object> prev = LListItr<Object>(startNode);
  LListItr<Object> curr = LListItr<Object>(startNode->next);

  while( !curr.isPastEnd( ) && get(curr.retrieve( )) < get(x) )
  {
    prev.advance( );
    curr.advance( );
  }

  return startNode = LList<Object>::insertNext( x, prev );
}
```

There are max_LED = 60 LEDs added in t-order. Notice the flag setting in the ProcessLEDs loop for LED = true.

All t math is floating point. To understand the t-ordering consider the "twelve o'clock" position parallel to the Z axis. Before virtual rotation the ray is centered in the row of voxels traveling down the Z axis. This is the orthogonal non-transformed position. The "twelve o'clock" ray origin is (64.5, y, 68.5). The start LED will be at the Z-value starting at 68.5, and will increment by 1 along the length, i.e., {68.5, 69.5, ..., 127.5} for 60 entries. Thus the first LED will also be the Ray origin with t = 0. Then, each LED will, in the twelve-o'clock position, be added at t = {1, 2, 3, ... , 59}.

Given a direction vector of (0,0,1) for the default ray, then:

(64.5, y, 68.5) + t (0,0,1) = LED, or in numbers:

(64.5, y, 68.5) + 1 (0,0,1) = (64.5, y, 69.5) and so on.

If the armature has been virtually rotated, t will still be parameterized in units, but the direction vector and origin will be more complicated. The same rule holds, though. For example:

(88.2, y, 76.43) + 2 (.882, 0, .445) = (89.96, y, 77.32) and so on.

T values remain the same under any rotation, but the direction vectors change. And really, the scale and the add are the extent of the transformation. Scale the direction by t, then add the resulting direction to the ray origin. That's the final LED position. This same procedure holds not just for the "twelve o'clock" position, but for arms given a counter-clockwise (ccw) rotation with a positive rotation angle.

The t-region of one voxel will always connect to the t-region of the next voxel along the ray, so that a boundary-pair describing a voxel adjacency is specified as: t_plus (n) = t (n + 1). However pairing is redundant so the unpaired sequence is: origin -> t_plus(m) -> t_plus(n), and when the list is processed duplicate t-values are omitted. The origin takes on the initial voxel status; and each t_plus is "leading" because it takes on the next voxel's status, unless t_plus is terminal, at the universe boundary, in which case it's simply a terminal indicator and the "boundary" flag is set accordingly.

The linked list's initial entries are the t_plus entries; subsequent insertions are made in the appropriate places for the LED entries (which are parameterized to t).

When an LED is inserted into the sorted linked list, it's placed at the correct t-position in the list automatically. But the code still has to iterate through the list to get the in-out status which is stored in leading t entries. Several LEDs can reside in the same large, empty voxel, so the previous or next entry in the linked list isn't necessarily a t-entry. It may be another LED.

When inserting LED groups, the LED itself counts as an element and so LEDs are inserted in low-to-high order: the lowest is referenced for the next insertion, unless existing t-boundaries come into play. The insert code checks for all of this.

The overload for the '<' operator, to check t, is a little tricky because of a preferred ordering:

```
bool TData::operator<(const TData & rhs) {
        if (this != &rhs) {
                if (fp_u.equalBoundsf(t, rhs.t, PRECISIONf) &&
                                (LED == false && rhs.LED == true)) {
                        return true;  // put LED AFTER voxel t
                }
                return (t < rhs.t);
```

```
        }
        return false;     // equal
}
```

Since the LED insertion comes after the "t-bounds" insertion, the voxel t-boundary is already in the list. In insertNext(), since "curr" is startNode->next, the first check is against a t-boundary. If an LED has the same t-value, it's placed *after* the t-boundary. In other words, prev is advanced (to curr), curr is advanced (to curr->next), and the LED is placed *after* prev (which points to the t-boundary node). The startNode then becomes the just-inserted LED.

On the next round, prev is the last LED, and curr is the next *after that*, being the next t-boundary. Most likely the next t-boundary will not be < the new LED, so nothing is advanced, and the new LED is inserted *after* prev, being the last inserted LED. And so on. This style of coding and the main ideas come out of the Weiss textbook (*Data Structures and Problem Solving Using C++*, 2nd Edition, Mark Allen Weiss). This type of code is very powerful but it can also be extremely opaque in terms of readability.

4.4 *Making Runlengths*

The third method call of the CastRay() method is MakeRunLengths(). The objective of this exercise is to get the data into a form that can then be repackaged as a list of ReducedRay data.

The linked list structure will be too big to keep around, so once a ray is computed, the data needs to be put in a heap-based runlength structure, that can then be passed back to OpenGL. This runlength structure will be memory efficient (as opposed to the linked list).

The runlengths can be set up as:

```
1.xxxxxxx
```

where 1 means that color values follow. The runlength "count" is in the 'xxx' position. If the runlength is in a non-empty voxel, the RGB encodings for that voxel are stored directly into the dataset as 3 bytes:

```
R (8bits) G (8 bits) B (8 bits)
```

They are then scanned out over "count" LEDs. This count is for one voxel only, with one color, so there's only one RGB for that voxel.

```
0.xxxxxxx
```

means the voxel is empty. The run-length for LEDs is in the 'xxx' position, and there's no data that follows (it being all zero). Empty voxels are not subdivided all the way to g_terminal and so can contain several LEDs, even though the LEDs are all “off”.

The ReducedRay package is shown next:

```
/// Compact data structure for returning voxels on a ray
/// back to OpenGL for display. (See RayWorker.)
struct ReducedRay {
	float3 base_origin, base_direction;
	// accumulated level; (level % max_level) * helical_index
	// + (angle = 0) determines helical offset, where max_level
	// and helical index are known.
	short level, angle, interleave;
	short count; // bytes
	unsigned char *list;
};
```

Everything needed for OpenGL display is included in this package. The list is allocated on the heap simply as an array of unsigned chars. The size is counted up from the Linked List environment. The transformed coordinates for a ray (that are evaluated in the Linked List environment) don’t extend to OpenGL because once the LED positions are “forged” the direction vector or the origin of the ray in their “virtual” positions don’t matter.

All that matters is a “base” origin (in base position). The armature is turned “rightside up” again for display, and the virtual rotation persists only in the LED “in” status. The end result is that the geometry will appear rotated. One can think of the orthogonal original voxel space as having been copied and transformed into LED space.

Thus the ray needs a base origin. The ray’s armature orientation requires the default helical offset (in 12 degree increments, clockwise when looking down on the base) to be on hand as well. The base origin/direction comprise the “start” position of the 360-degree arc rotation for a given arm. Notice that in OpenGL the language is back to “arms” and “LEDs” and not “rays”.

As already mentioned, the helical offset starts along the Z axis, at 12 o’clock when looking down at the base. Unlike the canonical voxel display in OpenGL, which is based on integer coordinates, the radial display uses floating point coordinates.

For counting runs, the first step is to find a t-boundary in the linked list, say the first one; say it’s in a voxel. Then it starts out as “in”. The code proceeds to the next t, it may be “out”. Everything after an “in” t gets the status of that t – until the next t is reached.

The first section of MakeRunLengths() is shown below.

```
/// This does not merge adjacent empty voxels.
void RayWorker::MakeRunLengths(Ray & ray, SortedLList<TData *, TData> & td_list) {
	unsigned char write_byte;
	int i, byte_count, offset, max_led, led_count;
	TData * current;

	LListItr<TData *> itr = LListItr<TData *>(td_list.first());

	// first count up the bytes for the run-length storage:
	// a) empty voxel is one byte (for count)
	// b) non-empty voxel is one byte (for count)
	//    plus 3 bytes for the color
	byte_count = 0;
	while (itr.isValid()) {
		// don't count terminator
		if (!itr.peekNextValid())
			break;

		++byte_count;
		current = itr.retrieve();
		if (current->in)
			byte_count += 3;			// RGB
		for (i = 0; i < current->count; ++i) {
			itr.advance();
		}
		// now advance to next voxel
		itr.advance();
	} // for all entries
...
```

There's no merging of adjacent empty voxels, not a terrible thing, but possibly an optimization for the future. As the comment says, the first step is to compute the byte count for the runlength data to be stored on the heap.

But here a mystery presents itself. Notice that the TData record has a "count" element. Where did that get assigned? At the end of ProcessLEDs there's a call to ScanThroughLinks(). Let's take a look. Here's the first section:

```
/// set "in" status for LEDs
void RayWorker::ScanThroughLinks(Ray & ray, SortedLList<TData *, TData> & td_list) {
	bool found_LED;
	TData *current, *t, *t_plus;
```

```
LListItr<TData *> itr = LListItr<TData *>(td_list.first());
current = itr.retrieve();
if (current->LED == true)
        throw RayException("LList Does Not Start with Voxel T");

// get successive pairs
while (itr.isValid()) {
        t = current;
        t_plus = NULL; found_LED = false;
        while (itr.advance() && itr.isValid()) {
                current = itr.retrieve();
                if (current->LED == false) {
                        t_plus = current;
                        break;
                }
                found_LED = true;
        }
...
```

First note the insurance check, to make sure that the list starts with a voxel t-boundary entry. The first t (in the base orientation) is the distance from the armature axis centerline to the first voxel outside of the armature spindle radius. In practice the ray origin will always be inside of a voxel. But the scanning should always start with a t = 0 boundary entry, and this has been inserted before the RayLoop() call in CastRay():

```
// Since the ray origins will all be in some
// voxel (either empty or filled), the linked
// list should start out officially with a
// t = 0 entry.
td_ptr = tdata_w.AddTDataRecord(0.0, ray.base_origin);
// but we don't know the intersect status yet. Insert it
// anyway, we can pass the base pointer to the next step.
td_list.insert(td_ptr);
```

No matter how many LEDs are floundering in the first voxel, they'll be placed (as explained in the previous section) *after* this initial voxel t-boundary. After getting past the insurance check, the first part of the linking happens. Two things are ascertained: first, that there is a pair of successive t-boundaries: t and t_plus; and second, whether or not any LED entries have been found in-between.

The next section is as follows:

...

```
            // Note that LEDs can extend out of the universe.
            // They're all zero, but we need this info anyway.
            if (t_plus == NULL && t->boundary) {
                    if (!found_LED)
                            return;
                    // add a dummy terminator : will go at end of list
                    TData *td_ptr = tdata_w.AddTDataRecord(T_BIG_POS, ray.base_origin);
                    td_list.insert(td_ptr);
                    itr.advance();                  // point at dummy
            } else if (t_plus == NULL) {
                    throw RayException("Unpaired Voxel T in LList");
            }
            // get first LED after t
            LListItr<TData *> LED_itr = LListItr<TData *>(td_list.findNext(t));
            TData *cur_LED = LED_itr.retrieve();
            // always valid because framed by voxel T
            while (cur_LED->LED) {
                    t->count++;
                    cur_LED->in = t->in;
                    LED_itr.advance();
                    cur_LED = LED_itr.retrieve();
            }
    }
}
```

The section of the code before this will have found t and t_plus, the pair of t-boundary values. But if t_plus is NULL, no pair was found. A valid case is when t is a voxel boundary (on exit) and the voxel abuts the universal boundary. There may be LEDs hanging outside of the universe, in which case a dummy terminator is added. An invalid case is if t is somehow not a boundary, in which case an exception is thrown. Otherwise, a valid pair has been found.

Remember that t_plus is the next voxel-boundary t, but there may be other t-values before it that are LED t-values. A check on the LED flag serves as the condition for counting LEDs, and the count is attached to the TData record for the previous boundary-t. The "in" flag status, indicating whether the voxel is active (1) or empty (0) is copied to each LED entry.

So that explains "count", which is used in the first part of MakeRunLengths(). Returning to that method, here's the next section.

```
...
    // allocate ReducedRay (caller will free)
    ReducedRay *my_ray = new ReducedRay;
```

```
        r_u.copy_float3(ray.base_origin, my_ray->base_origin);
        r_u.copy_float3(ray.base_direction, my_ray->base_direction);
        my_ray->level = ray.level;
        my_ray->angle = ray.angle;
        my_ray->interleave = ray.interleave;

        my_ray->count = byte_count;

        // allocate byte list (caller will free)
        unsigned char *plist = new unsigned char[byte_count];
        my_ray->list = plist;

        // now scan through again for pertinent data
        itr.reset(td_list.first());
        offset = 0;

        // for diagnostic:
        led_count = 0;
        max_led = (Nt - spindle_diam) / 2;
...
```

First, the information that will allow an arm's position and orientation to be calculated from scratch is copied to the ReducedRay struct. As well, the interleave status is copied over. Also, the heap-allocation byte count that was calculated in the first section of the method is copied over – this is the byte count of all the runlengths for the entire length of the arm, for all LEDs in other words. The memory for the runlengths is then allocated on the heap and the pointer is copied to the ReducedRay.

Then some counters are reset and max_led is set to (128 - 8) / 2 = 60. Here's the last section of the MakeRunLengths() method:

```
...
        while (itr.isValid()) {
                // don't count terminator
                if (!itr.peekNextValid())
                        break;

                current = itr.retrieve();
                // a diagnostic only:
                // this says: the current voxel is non-zero ("in"), but:
                // the LED count is zero. In other words, we've missed
                // a voxel because there's no LED in it. This happens when
```

```
			// the ray intersects close to a voxel corner, with a small
			// distance to the next voxel face (less than 1, the voxel
			// size).
			if (current->count == 0 && current->in && led_count < max_led) {
#ifdef DIAGNOSTIC_MSG
				std::cout << "SAMPLE GAP!" << current->position.x << ", "
								<< current->position.y << ", "
								<< current->position.z << ", T:"
								<< current->t << std::endl;
#endif
			} else {
#ifdef DIAGNOSTIC_MSG
				std::cout << "no gap, count: " << current->count << std::endl;
#endif
				led_count += current->count;
			}

			write_byte = current->count;
			if (current->in)
				write_byte |= IN_BIT;

			// write count byte
			plist[offset++] = write_byte;
			if (current->in) {
				// write color bytes
				for (i = 0; i < T_COLORS; ++i) {
					write_byte = current->color[i];
					plist[offset++] = write_byte;
				}
			}
			// skip
			for (i = 0; i < current->count; ++i) {
				itr.advance();
			}
			// now advance to next voxel
			itr.advance();
		} // for all entries

		// queue it for OpenGL display
		display.MakeRayData(my_ray);
}
```

The first part of the iteration checks for a "sample gap" – the diagnostic will still fire if enabled but the sample gap is filled in with interleave. Diagnostic message or not, if there's a "sample gap" the led_count is not incremented. If there's no sample gap the led_count is incremented. Usually the current->count will be at least 1, but it's not illegal for the LED count to be 0, which might happen near the ray origin.

The led_count variable is an "int" datatype, which provides plenty of room for larger resolution armatures. By comparison, the LED count between t-boundaries is a "short" datatype in the TData record, which still allows for a long run of LEDs within a large voxel. Meanwhile, the ReducedRay "count" variable is a count of bytes of runlengths and color data stored for the entire arm. It's not a direct count of LEDs.

Since a runlength is stored for an empty cell or voxel, even though nothing is displayed, this means that at higher resolutions the number of LEDs between t-boundaries is limited to 127 since the count byte's high-order bit is reserved for an "in" status, e.g. IN_BIT = 0x80 (ReducedRay.h). For N = 7, which results in 60 LEDs per arm, even if half the voxel space is "empty" the runlength can accommodate the full LED count. But for higher resolutions the individual runlengths would have to be coded as a word instead of an unsigned byte. This is something that will have to be refactored. (Note to the author!)

In any case, the write_bytes are stored on the heap. As already mentioned, if the count byte is "in", the color bytes for RGB (T_COLORS = 3, RayUtil.h) will follow. Since the color is pulled from the TData record, a TData "current" pointer is being used and the next part of the code skips over the TData LED entries for the runlength, to advance to the next voxel boundary. Finally, the ReducedRay, which includes a pointer to the runlength data, is passed to the Display class, to be transfered to OpenGL.

4.5 *Queues and Threads*

The architecture of Project V is such that the Contexts are associated with threads. For ray work, runlength data is queued into the RenderQueue for each of the 120 levels of the armature. The arm for each level is displayed at the correct height and rotation along the armature spindle. The queued data is then displayed all at once. The original idea was to display the imagery in real time (60 Hz) but compute-power nixed that idea. If this was a Siggraph paper there would be a big table inserted here of model sizes versus processor cores, but let's skip that. In a nutshell: more triangles, more time!

Each ReducedRay record is enqueued as follows:

```
void Display::MakeRayData(ReducedRay *ray) {
        if (!context.buffer_display_data)
                return;
        my_stat_thread.EnqueueR(ray);
}
```

buffer_display_data is set to "true" when the Ray Tracing Context is created. For now the value is hardcoded in RayThread() (OctreeThread.cpp):

```
    context_w->makeContext(1, g_terminal, true, g_check_false_pos);
```

Obviously the normal octree shouldn't be displayed on top of the ray tracing, so normal evaluation gets a "false" argument as hardcoded in EvalThread() (OctreeThread.cpp):

```
    // display false for now
    context_w->makeContext(1, g_terminal, false, g_check_false_pos);
```

Here's EnqueueR (short for Enqueue Ray), an inline method in OctreeThread.h:

```
    ReducedRay * EnqueueR(ReducedRay *ray) {
        return ray_queue.enqueue(ray);
    }
```

Each ReducedRay then gets dequeued in GLWorker. Since there's so much data, each "pack" of queued data is limited to a single level. That explains the inner loops from the Top routine:

```
void RayWorker::Top() {
    int interleave, course, level, angle, offset;
...
    for (interleave = 0; interleave < 2; ++interleave) {
        for (course = 0; course < MAX_COURSE; ++course) {
            offset = 0;
            for (level = 0; level < max_level; level += skipper[offset%4]) {
                ++offset;
                for (angle = 0; angle < DEGREES_360; ++angle) {
#ifdef DIAGNOSTIC_MSG
                    std::cout << "ANGLE: " << angle << ", LEVEL: " << level
                              << ", COURSE: " << course << std::endl;
#endif
                    DoRayWork(interleave, course, level, angle);
                }
                display.terminateLevel();
            }
        }
    }
...
```

The important thing is that a "level" includes all 360 degrees of rotation. This corresponds to all 360 rotation increments of the arm: there's one arm per level. After the inner loop for the rotations finishes, the data for the level is terminated with a -1 byte.

```
/// caller knows enough to write n levels
void Display::terminateLevel() {
	if (!context.buffer_display_data)
		return;

	ReducedRay *ray = new ReducedRay;
	ray->level = -1;
	// no count, no list
	my_stat_thread.EnqueueR(ray);
}
```

In the ongoing example N = 7, Nt = 128, and each arm has (128 - 8) / 2 = 60 LEDs on it. In the Top() code, max_level = (120 / 4) = 30, which is the number of levels in a "course"; there are 4 courses. The rationale is that each course is assigned to a separate microprocessor in the hardware design, and the 4 courses are computed in parallel. Levels are counted from 0 to 29, over 4 courses and 2 interleaves.

Let's look at the transfer function. The word "transfer" is used because the function launches the RayWorker which does all the work, and then quietly receives packets in parallel with that work. There are two threads running at the same time. This same thread architecture is used for normal octree evaluation, which launches the OctreeWorker and then quietly receives voxel data in the background.

Here's the first half of the transfer function for Ray Tracing:

```
void GLWorker::CastRays() {
	int i, size, level, x;
	ReducedRay *my_ptr;
	Vector<ReducedRay *> ptr_list;
	extern OctreeThread my_stat_thread;

	// compute key variables
	DevicePack device;
	device.Nt = (int)lroundf(powf(2.0, (float)g_terminal));
	device.spindle_diam = device.Nt / 16;			// spindle ratio
	device.max_level = (device.Nt - device.spindle_diam) / MAX_COURSE;
	device.helical_index = DEGREES_360 / device.max_level;
	device.total_levels = device.max_level * MAX_COURSE * T_ALPHABETA *
LEVEL_SHOW / LEVEL_BAND;
```

```
        TranslateScaleCube();

        // launch a thread for computing & displaying radial mapping
        my_stat_thread.RayStart();
...
```

The critical function call is RayStart() because it launches the RayWorker thread. After doing that the GLWorker just sits back, rakes in the data, and transfers it to OpenGL at intervals. Here's the second half of CastRays:

```
...
        // loop over queue and get entries
        for (level = 0, x = 0; level < device.total_levels; ++level, x = 0) {
                while (x != -1) {  // -1 terminates the level
                        if (!my_stat_thread.IsEmptyR()) {
                                my_ptr = my_stat_thread.DequeueR();
                                if ((x = my_ptr->level) != -1) {
                                        // add it to a list
                                        ptr_list.push_back(my_ptr);
                                }
                        }
                }
                // delete level terminator (no embedded list)
                delete my_ptr;

                size = ptr_list.size();
                for (i = 0; i < size; ++i) {
                        my_ptr = ptr_list[i];
                        DrawRay(my_ptr, device);
                }
                // free the original pointers on the heap
                for (i = 0; i < size; ++i) {
                        my_ptr = ptr_list[i];
                        delete [] my_ptr->list;
                        delete my_ptr;
                }
                // going to reuse this so clear it
                ptr_list.clear();
        }

        my_stat_thread.RayEnd();
}
```

The outer loop iterates on device.total_levels:

```
device.total_levels = device.max_level * MAX_COURSE * T_ALPHABETA *
                        LEVEL_SHOW / LEVEL_BAND;
```

Total levels is equal to: 30 * 4 (courses) * 2 (interleaves) * LEVEL_SHOW / LEVEL_BAND. The LEVEL_SHOW and LEVEL_BAND constants are for skipping levels as a visual diagnostic for "seeing into" the model. The interested reader can look at Hardware.cpp for an explanation. When the see-through option isn't used LEVEL_SHOW = LEVEL_BAND = 1.

After dequeueing a complete level of 360 rotations of an arm, the code then creates the "rotated" voxels, one per LED position, for those arm positions. Unlike the normal voxel display in OpenGL, which is based on integer coordinates, the radial display uses floating point coordinates. Instead of displaying cubes in an orthogonal grid, LEDs are half-voxels at interleave positions, oriented with the ray direction. The half-voxels for interleave 0 meet up with the half-voxels for interleave 1.

Backing up a little bit, CastRays() is called from the default OpenGL routine, OnRender():

```
void GLWorker::OnRender(void) {
...
        if (shader) shader->begin();

        PaintVoxels();
        //ShowMesh();
        CastRays();
        cleanupThread();

        if (shader) shader->end();
...
```

The call to PaintVoxels() launches the thread for the OctreeWorker:

```
        // this will spawn the Octree thread
        my_stat_thread.EvalStart(my_geom);
```

Likewise, the call to CastRays() launches the thread for the RayWorker:

```
        // launch a thread for computing & displaying radial mapping
        my_stat_thread.RayStart();
```

Since the octree is computed first, no triangle geometry needs to be passed into the ray tracing thread. When ray tracing, nothing is queued for display in PaintVoxels(), since the display is turned off via the Eval Context. All data is queued and displayed in the Ray Context. As soon as each ReducedRay is put on the RenderQueue, it's dequeued by the GLWorker. Once all of the data for the level is received, OpenGL geometry is created in the GLWorker thread, while the next level is simultaneously computed in the worker thread.

Here's the DrawRay() routine:

```
/// Only show filled entries here
void GLWorker::DrawRay(ReducedRay *ray, DevicePack &device) {
	float3 color;
	float angle;
	unsigned char read_byte;
	int i, j, count, runlength, t;
	bool in;

	// rotate the default cube (and normals) by the ray angle
	if (ray->interleave == T_ALPHA)
		angle = float((ray->level % device.max_level) * device.helical_index + ray->angle);
	else
		angle = float((ray->level % device.max_level) * device.helical_index + ray->angle) +
179.5;

	RotateAngle(angle);

	// draw arm: always positioned at angle == 0
/*
	if (ray->angle == 0)
		DrawArm(ray, device);
*/
/*
	else if (ray->angle % 10 == 0)
		DrawDots(ray, device);
*/

	// For LEDs on ray
	count = ray->count;
	for (i = 0, t = 0; i < count; ++i) {
		read_byte = ray->list[i];
		runlength = read_byte & (~IN_BIT);
		in = read_byte & IN_BIT;
		if (in) {
```

```
                    read_byte = ray->list[++i];
                    color.x = (float)read_byte / 255.0;
                    read_byte = ray->list[++i];
                    color.y = (float)read_byte / 255.0;
                    read_byte = ray->list[++i];
                    color.z = (float)read_byte / 255.0;
                    glBegin(GL_QUADS);

#ifdef TWO_COLOR_INTERLEAVE
                    if (ray->interleave == T_ALPHA)
                         glColor4f(color.x, color.y, color.z, 1.0);
                    else
                         glColor4f(1.0, color.y, color.z, 1.0);
#else
                    glColor4f(color.x, color.y, color.z, 1.0);
#endif
                    for (j = 0; j < runlength; ++j, ++t)
                         MakeLED(ray, t, in);

                    glEnd();

               } else {
                    for (j = 0; j < runlength; ++j, ++t)
                         ; // count zero runlength
               }
          }
}
```

The interesting part is the looping on runlengths:

```
...
               if (in) {
                    ...
                    for (j = 0; j < runlength; ++j, ++t)
                         MakeLED(ray, t, in);
                    ...
               } else {
                    for (j = 0; j < runlength; ++j, ++t)
                         ; // count zero runlength
               }
...
```

The runlength is dictates how many LEDs are displayed if the voxel has “in” status. It’s important to realize that adaptive subdivision continues to subdivide the voxel space to ever-narrower tolerances relative to the “skin” of the model geometry. This means the only voxels that are actually being displayed are unit voxels at the terminal level. These are the finest voxels and the voxels closest to the model “skin”.

The reason terminal voxels at a higher level are an issue for ray tracing is because a ray has no choice but to traverse that empty voxel space to get to (or not to get to as the case may be) the final “active” voxel(s). In general, then, the runlengths for “in” voxels will be very small, whereas the intervening empty voxel spaces will generally have longer runlengths.

The looping in the fragment shown above reflects this, in that both “in” and “not in” status is associated with a runlength, and t-values and the overall runlength counter are both incremented in both cases.

A neat feature is that t in the DrawRay() routine above is an integer, and is simply incremented. Recall that LED positions along an arm are separated from each other by one unit. And recall also that no matter what the orientation of the ray is, the t-scalar is rotation-invariant. This means that no matter how the arm has been virtually rotated, or rotated relative to the armature’s “twelve o’clock” position, those t-offsets will always be unit distances from each other!

Therefore t is passed into MakeLED() and it’s just an integer counter value, incremented by one for each LED. Here’s the math that makes that t-value into an LED position.

```
/// only call if voxel isn't empty
void GLWorker::MakeLED(ReducedRay *ray, int t, bool in_flag) {
        float3 tD, position;

        xform.VectorScale(tD, ray->base_direction, (float)t);
        xform.VectorAdd(position, ray->base_origin, tD);

        DrawLED(position);
}
```

Once the t-scalar is applied to the direction vector, t has done its job and the only thing sent to the DrawLED routine is the LED position in 3-space. Simple. So ends the ray tracing journey. The reader can consult the GLWorker code in the class listing for further details.

The ray tracing feature was prototyped in June 2014 and finished in October 2014.

END OF PART FOUR

Part Five

5.0 *Thin Rasterization, Introduction*

The previous parts of this book have explained all the details of Project V except for thin rasterization. There's a myth abounding that 6-sep rasterization is a simple version of 26-sep. That's because most people who've implemented 26-sep, and who haven't implemented 6-sep, automatically assume that because fewer voxels are associated with 6-sep that must mean that 6-sep is "simpler".

That's far from the truth. In fact, just the reverse is true: 26-sep is the easy one. 6-sep is difficult. It turns out that the 6-sep equations presented by Schwarz & Seidel could not be made to work in any form by this author. The Voxel Pipe authors don't even mention 6-sep. And most papers available online gloss over 6-sep or provide a half-attempted but otherwise untested implementation.

Still, Schwarz & Seidel's timing tables give a useful metric for the difference in the number of voxels generated by either method. In their tests, with various curvy models, 6-sep generates about 60% of the voxels generated by 26-sep. But even this is misleading, since the difference depends on two factors: a) the final resolution, since the higher the resolution the more savings; and b) how many flat planes orthogonal to the Cartesian axes the model includes, because on these flat planes 26-sep and 6-sep perform identically.

Project V found that the biggest savings came with polygons that were oriented at 45 degrees relative to two of the principal planes, that is, a kitty-corner ramp. This is where the conservative approach stumbles badly. The DDA-style rasterization of 6-sep produces a thin, 6-connected plane that's 33% the number of voxels generated by 26-sep!

Given that 6-sep produces almost identical results but contains possibly many thousands fewer voxels, every voxel implementation should include it as an option.

The key to 26-sep is this following bit of C++ code (GeomUtil.cpp, GeomUtil::rasterize_26sep):

```
...
        // Offset is 1 or 0 depending on plane equation signs:
        // compute W depth range
        const float min_uf = (u + (plane_eq.x < 0.0f ? 1.0f : 0.0f)) * sel::u( bbox_delta );
        const float min_vf = (v + (plane_eq.y < 0.0f ? 1.0f : 0.0f)) * sel::v( bbox_delta );
        const float min_wf = plane_eq.z - (plane_eq.x*min_uf + plane_eq.y*min_vf);
        int32 min_w = int32( min_wf * sel::w( inv_bbox_delta ) );

        const float max_uf = (u + (plane_eq.x > 0.0f ? 1.0f : 0.0f)) * sel::u( bbox_delta );
        const float max_vf = (v + (plane_eq.y > 0.0f ? 1.0f : 0.0f)) * sel::v( bbox_delta );
```

```
    const float max_wf = plane_eq.z - (plane_eq.x*max_uf + plane_eq.y*max_vf);
    int32 max_w = int32( max_wf * sel::w( inv_bbox_delta ) );
...
```

The conditionals embedded in the min and max assignments translate to diagonals, sides, and the origin of the voxel's currently projected face. Remember that a voxel is always unit-scaled, so choosing from {0, 1} amounts to choosing a corner of the voxel face. You'd never guess that all 26 neighbors are accounted for with such a simple conditional, but that's what's happening, as shown in the following diagram.

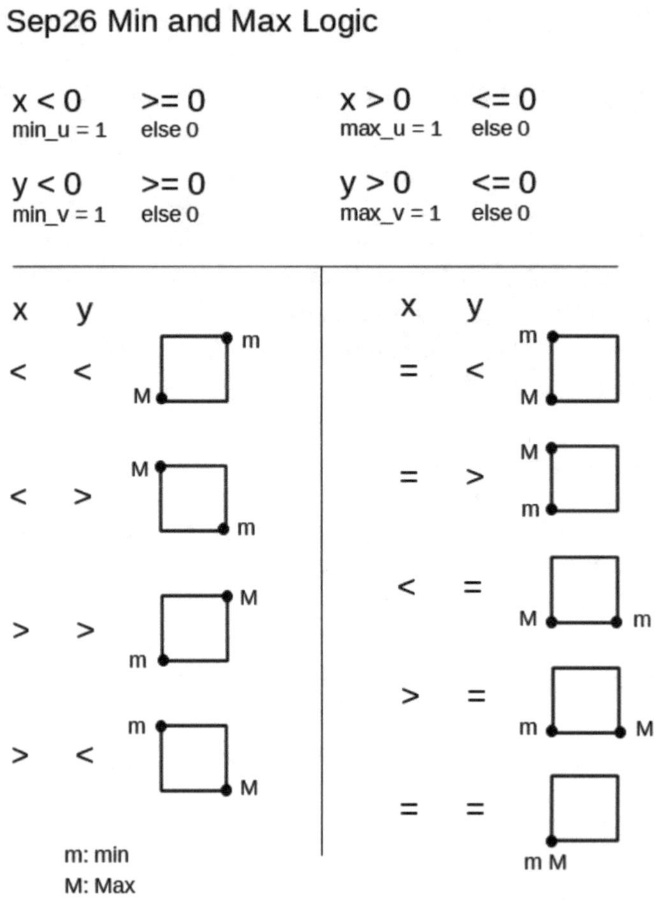

Notice how cleverly the logic omits the righthand and upper voxel edges. This is desirable because the next voxel over and the next voxel up will test those edges as part of their lefthand and lower conditions. Likewise, a full equality reduces to the lower lefthand corner, so that neighboring voxels in all directions will uniquely test the other corners as part of their lower lefthand corner conditions. Brilliant.

That's a lot of punch packed into a few lines of code. This author tried to adapt the *modus operandum* of these min/max statements to 6-sep, but nothing worked: in fact, the skin that was produced ended up having *more* voxels that 26-sep!

Instead, a geometric approach was taken. The question became: is there a three-dimensional implementation of the Bresenham DDA algorithm? Imagine that instead of a line being etched out with differences, an entire bounded plane in any orientation.

It turns out 6-sep isn't called 6-sep for nothing. The key is to treat the *center* of the voxel as the voxel's canonical coordinate, and extend a ray from that center location to each of the six planes that bound the voxel. This then becomes a "one of six" intersection test. At least one of those six rays will intersect the triangle plane at a distance of less than 0.5 units from the voxel center. The ray in the dominant-axis direction is always tested first, and in any case the first intersection that meets the distance criterion is accepted.

Sounds easy but there are some other considerations that need to be taken into account for the entire algorithm to work.

5.1 *Boundaries*

The "DDA" in Bresenham DDA stands for Digital Differential Analyzer. This algorithm generates lines from their differential equations. But basically it's a matter of simple differences. The differences add up until a threshold requires a move in the orthogonal direction as well as a move in the principal direction. Bresenham figured out how to set up deltas and use those as a check for when to add or subtract 1 to or from the orthogonal coordinate.

A DDA algorithm can also be used to draw circles and curves, working off of their first derivatives just as with lines. The cleverness in the DDA is less in the basic math, and more in how many different people have implemented it.

What about rendering a plane? It's interesting to note that the CUDA library that runs on GPUs has a built-in voxel-rendering routine to render polygons down to pixel resolution. This is very much what happened to line-drawing algorithms: they were implemented in hardware after their utility was proven in software. CUDA routines that take advantage of GPU parallelism and that run "natively" are almost as good as hardware in this day and age.

So it would seem that a voxel approach is a good way to render planes if Voxel Pipe and the CUDA library is any indication. That said, Voxel Pipe does not offer a 6-sep solution, and Schwarz & Seidel write out their 6-sep implementation without giving full details, making it impossible to decipher what they did.

So Project V had to start from scratch. One drawing that was referred to again and again during the design stages is shown below.

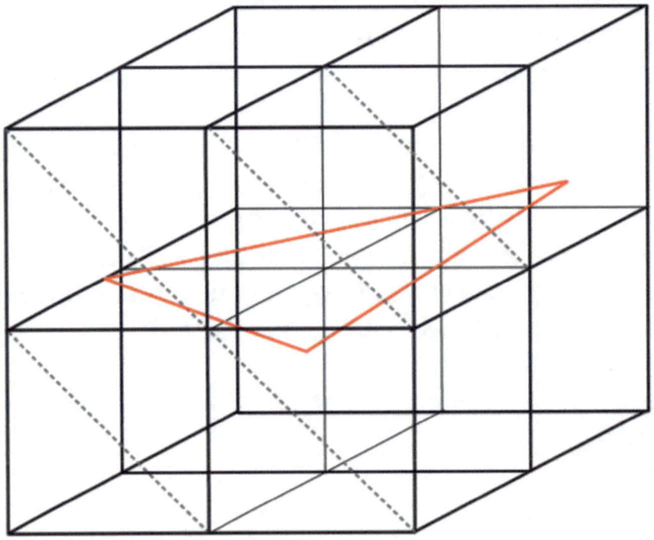

The triangle to be rendered is shown in red. The subdivision is at level 1 with 1 set of octants forming a node group. The voxels with a dashed diagonal across their front faces are the ones which should pick up an intersection with the triangle. There are a few take-aways from this drawing.

First, a triangle can fill the entire space, as shown in the drawing; or there can be many small triangles that are located in one of these high-level voxels only. So there needs to be a way to determine where these triangles are located relative to the voxels. This can be done with a triangle bounding box – and in fact this is what's done at the coarse stage for both 6-sep and 26-sep rasterization.

However a bounding box, though fine for testing extents, is harder to test for an actual intersection – say for a ray extending from the center of the voxel to some face of the bounding box. A much easier sort of intersecting surface is that of a sphere. So the first element of the 6-sep algorithm is to compute the bounding sphere for each triangle. This "big sphere" is computed for each triangle once per level.

The bounding sphere is useful for testing whether a voxel is outside of a triangle entirely, but we also need a sure test for when the voxel is inside of the triangle. To render a plane at fine resolution there will be hundreds or even thousands of voxels inside a triangle. The quickest way to determine this is with another sphere – but this one inscribed inside the triangle's 3D position and orientation. This "little sphere" is also computed once per level for each triangle.

So far so good. But that leaves the spaces outside of the little sphere to worry about. In this case a test is needed to determine of one of the six orthogonal rays shooting out from the center of the voxel intersects the triangle inside the triangle. The "little sphere" inside test is very quick and accounts for most interior voxels. But a lengthier test is required for the corners of the triangle outside of the little sphere but inside of the triangle boundaries.

This calculation is very similar to what's being done in the 26-sep algorithm. It seems that Snyder and Barr in their 1987 paper, "Ray Tracing Complex Models Containing Surface Tesselations" (ACM Computer Graphics) were the first to make use of the "dominant axis" approach to project a triangle to a 2D plane and then compute intersections based on that 2D projection. They were the first also to popularize the idea of an "embedding plane" – being the plane that the triangle resides in. In essence, the first test in 26-sep rasterization is an embedding plane calculation.

6-sep also uses an embedding plane calculation in non-terminal levels. The difference is that the distances to those embedding planes are measured from the voxel's center, rather than using the almost cellular-automata min/max logic shown in the last section. Embedding plane calculations are tricky because, at least when measuring from the voxel center to the embedding plane in the six orthogonal (face-oriented) directions, all six of those rays can be "outside" of the distance of 0.5 units, and yet a portion of that plane may be represented by a corner of the original voxel – a corner that will result in a hole in the plane rasterization if the parent voxel isn't accepted.

Therefore, a very simple "look ahead" is performed, based on a simple heuristic. The failed intersection will occur with a distance of 0.5. This because the "last range". The child of the parent is scaled by half. This is the only time, in fact, when the "voxel unit" rule is ignored. This means the range to be checked in 0.25. But the last range is kept on hand because if one of the rays that is shot out fails at 0.25, but succeeds at twice that distance, at 0.5, then the next level of recursion is taken.

There's some max number of recursions (dynamically set) or if the terminal level is reached the recursion will also end. If at any of those levels the ray is within the current range, the recursion ends with a "true" status and travels up the recursion stack to the parent voxel, which is then accepted. Obviously it would be expensive to perform this recursion for every voxel, so some preconditions must be met. The main precondition is that the voxel is inside of the "big sphere". Secondarily, if the voxel is way outside of the previous range that's kept around for the double-check, the recursion will end immediately and so the time taken is minimal.

That's almost the entirety of the 6-sep algorithm. But there are few more things having to do with that 0.5 distance. Remember that the 26-sep algorithm isn't really geometric because it uses unit distances from the voxel "base coordinate" – not a half-distance of 0.5 in an orthogonal direction from the voxel center. And because of the min/max logic, the 26-sep algorithm doesn't have to worry about voxels whose orthogonal rays intersect the triangle's embedding plane but are technically outside of the triangle.

This was a big problem with the 6-sep algorithm. It caused the boundaries of the triangle to look ragged. Voxels were being missed because the projection of the voxel center onto the triangle plane was technically outside of the triangle, and the triangle "inside" test was failing. This precluded any subsequent test for the voxel on the range of 0.5.

This border problem turned out to be the hardest problem to solve for 6-sep. Finally, it was decided to compute a "halo" around each orthogonal projection of the triangle. (Actually, the dominant-axis projection turns out to be the only one that's needed.) The halo extends the maximum orthogonal distance corresponding to 0.5 units from each triangle edge. This is basically a line-intersection problem. In any case, the coordinates of the triangle halo are used instead of the native triangle coordinates for the "inside triangle" test. The halo, like the triangle's "big sphere" and "little sphere", is computed once for each level.

Then, a further test is employed to see if one of the six rays extending orthogonally from the voxel center is within the 0.5 range of the triangle's embedding plane. The ragged edges cease to be a problem.

There's one other subtle aspect to the 0.5 range. It amounts to which voxel gets the triangle if the distance is exactly equal to 0.5 rather than less-than-or-equal to 0.5. If two voxels are both at the same distance from the triangle, this leads to a non-simple DDA of the plane rasterization which further results in two voxels instead of one for a single triangle location.

The problem can be clarified with the following diagram.

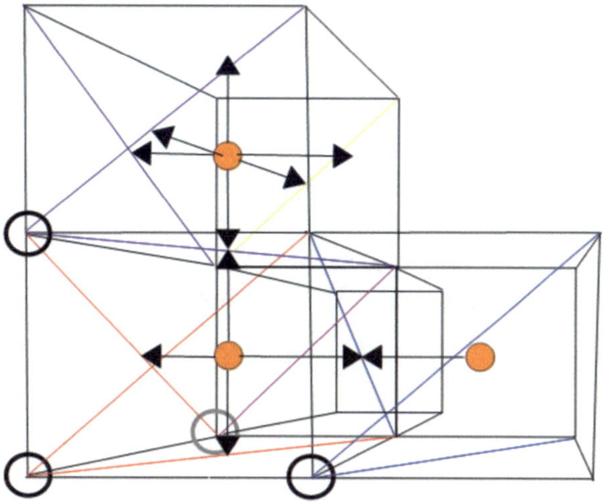

Here are shown four voxels, the one in the lower lefthand corner, and three of its neighbors. The black circles show the base coordinates of each voxel; and the orange filled circles show the voxel centers. Extending from the center are various orthogonal rays.

The faces of importance for each voxel are attached to the base point of the voxel. This means there are three faces of importance. Therefore, when the range to a triangle plane is exactly 0.5, the faces of importance take priority. The two front-row lower voxels might both have a distance of 0.5 in the horizontal orthogonal direction (shown with arrows) to the triangle that intersects both voxels on their common face. However, even though the two voxels share a face, the triangle will only be assigned to the rightmost voxel because the rightmost voxel's face of importance corresponds to the intersection. The lefthand voxel's intersection is not in the direction of a face of importance, so even though the voxel is within range, it will be skipped for that voxel.

The way this is implemented is by checking signs. All faces of importance are at a negative distance from the voxel center. For a given dominant axis there are two directions to check for: positive and negative. If, for example, the positive axis generates an intersection point which is "behind" it, then the axis has to be flipped. These are minor details that ensure that the scheme works properly. With the basics explained, let's look at some code.

5.2 *Top Level Algorithm*

The previous section serves as a nice introduction to the top-level routine for 6-sep, shown next. The various methods should look familiar. Besides the technical details, the basis of the algorithm is a combination of exclusion and inclusion.

```
/// 6-separating "thin" raster
template <int32 AXIS> bool GeomUtil::rasterize_6sep(const ushort3 &coord,
            Triangle *tri) {
      typedef uvw<AXIS> sel;

      // you need to think in three dimensions to do this.
      // but not only that, you need to think upstream and
      // downstream, e.g. what happens at each level as
      // subdivision progresses -- you could call this the
      // "time" dimension. So really this is a 4D algorithm.

      float3 vox_center, ranges;
      int dom_axis = AXIS;
      short facecount;
      float dist;

      vox_center.x = coord.x + 0.5f;
      vox_center.y = coord.y + 0.5f;
      vox_center.z = coord.z + 0.5f;

      // first test if inside the big sphere
      if (!centerTest(vox_center, tri->big_center, tri->big_radius)) {
            // outside: do the center-to-center ray test
            if (!StraightToSphere(vox_center,
                        tri->big_center, tri->big_radius, dist)) {
                  // not in or within 0.5 of big sphere, but may
                  // be close. This next test is to catch the single
                  // voxels at a triangle vertex, when resolution gets
                  // higher. dist comes back squared: 1^2 = 1.0f
                  if (dist <= 1.0f) {
                        if (!TrivertSpheres(tri, vox_center))
                              return false;
                  }
            }
            // else fall through if close enough : more tests
      } else if (terminal) {
            // inside the big sphere, now is it inside the little?
            if (centerTest(vox_center, tri->little_center, tri->little_radius)) {
                  // the little sphere entirely encompasses the triangle surface,
                  // so just need to do the easy embedding plane test: guaranteed
                  // triangle surface!
                  return OneOfSixToEmbeddingPlane(vox_center, tri, dom_axis,
                                                                              0.5f,
```

```
ranges);
                }
                // else fall through to other tests; part of the
                // triangle will be outside of the little sphere
        }
        // we are inside of the big sphere, possibly terminal level
        // or: the big sphere is close, within 0.5 of vox center.

        if (!terminal) {
                // Only run the edge tests on non-terminal levels as it's "liberal"
                // and will otherwise introduce unwanted voxels.
                EdgeTests(coord, tri, facecount);
                if (facecount == 3)
                        return true;
                // don't reject if facecount == 0 because there can be a
                // big "projection hole" at finer resolutions when a voxel
                // is in the middle of a triangle.

                if (OneOfSixToEmbeddingPlane(vox_center, tri, dom_axis,
                                                        0.5f, ranges))
                        return true;

                // last_range for 0.5 is 1.0f, and 1 + sqrt(1) = 2
                if (checkRange(ranges, 2.0f)) {
                        // As a last resort (because of speed issues), look ahead.
                        // Args: 0.5f last; 0.25f max
                        return LookAheadChildrenToEmbedding(vox_center, tri, dom_axis,
                                        0.5f, 0.25f, g_level, 0);
                }
                return false;
        }

        // terminal and very close to acceptance: final test
        return OneOfSixToTriIntersect(vox_center, tri, dom_axis);
}
```

Since each application of a template function acts like a C macro in that a separate copy of the code is created for each instance, the decision was made to pass the selector to the sub-functions not as a template argument, but as a normal argument:

```
int dom_axis = AXIS;
```

The pertinent coordinate rotations are then accessed with an index based on that argument.

In general the algorithm makes a distinction right from the start between the terminal level and all levels leading up to the terminal level. All inclusion testing leading up to the terminal level amounts to: a) being inside of the big sphere; and b) as a condition of a), being within a distance of 0.5 of the triangle's embedding plane.

Looking at item a), the voxel is given three chances with three slightly different tests to be within range of the big sphere. The main test is simply a Pythagorean test, center of voxel to center of sphere:

```
// is passed coord inside the sphere?
bool GeomUtil::centerTest(const float3 vox_center,
                    const float3 center, float radius) {
        float dx, dy, dz, dist;

        dx = vox_center.x - center.x;
        dy = vox_center.y - center.y;
        dz = vox_center.z - center.z;

        dist = dx * dx + dy * dy + dz * dz;
        return (dist <= radius * radius);
}
```

A convention for distance testing is not to take the square root since all that matters is magnitude, not the actual distance. If this test fails, it may be that the voxel is close to the big sphere's surface, e.g. 0.5 units or less from the sphere boundary. This second test is more expensive, but will admit many voxels at the sphere boundary.

```
// see of the voxel center is <= 0.5 from the sphere surface
// in one of the six orthogonal ray directions.
bool GeomUtil::StraightToSphere(const float3 vox_center,
                    const float3 center, float radius, float &dist) {
        float3 V, P;
        float eox, eoy, eoz, tri_v, scale;
        float norm, norm2, vsx, vsy, vsz, range;

        // tri_v = EO . V
        // get ray direction V
        // it will be a vector from voxel center to sphere center

        // O is sphere center (origin)
        // E is voxel center (passed in)
```

```
    // store this since it's used twice
    eox = center.x - vox_center.x;
    eoy = center.y - vox_center.y;
    eoz = center.z - vox_center.z;

    norm2 = eox * eox + eoy * eoy + eoz * eoz;
    norm = 1.0f / sqrt(norm2);

    // this is what we want for straight to center
    V.x = eox * norm;
    V.y = eoy * norm;
    V.z = eoz * norm;

    // tri_v = triangle side
    tri_v = eox * V.x +
            eoy * V.y +
            eoz * V.z;

    // P = E + (tri_v - radius)V
    scale = tri_v  - radius;
    vsx = scale * V.x;
    vsy = scale * V.y;
    vsz = scale * V.z;

    // here's the intersection point on the sphere:
    P.x = vox_center.x + vsx;
    P.y = vox_center.y + vsy;
    P.z = vox_center.z + vsz;

    // how far?
    range = (P.x - vox_center.x) * (P.x - vox_center.x) +
            (P.y - vox_center.y) * (P.y - vox_center.y) +
            (P.z - vox_center.z) * (P.z - vox_center.z);
    dist = range;

    // if == to boundary, next voxel over will be "inside"
    // and will capture it. Voxel is sphere with r = 0.5.
    if (range < (0.5 * 0.5))
            return true;

    return false;
}
```

This sphere test is an invention of Jeff Hultquist who wrote it while at NASA Ames Research Center. (See *Graphics Gems*, p. 388.) There's a square root in this test, but in this age of fast processors it can be tolerated. If the voxel is still outside of the sphere, there's one more test: a special case at the triangle corners.

The third test is only applied if the voxel distance from the big sphere's surface, as computed in Test Two and returned in the "dist" variable, is less than or equal to unity. This means very few voxels will qualify for the third test at higher resolutions. The problem being addressed is related to our old friend 0.5. Remember that the boundary of the triangle has to be extended with a halo for the "inside triangle" test for a voxel to accurately reflect the voxel's 0.5 distance constraint. That halo testing only takes place at the terminal level when it's already been determined that a voxel is inside of the big sphere. But there's a problem: since the triangle is inscribed by the sphere, this means that each triangle vertex is coincident with the sphere's surface. Since there's no 0.5 extension of the triangle boundary (being the vertex in this case) during big-sphere testing a voxel can miss both the big sphere and the vertex. This causes the triangle corners to be rounded because of the missing voxel.

The solution is simply to surround each triangle vertex with a unit sphere (radius 0.5). The distance is then computed from the voxel center to the surface of that unit sphere. This is shown in the diagram below.

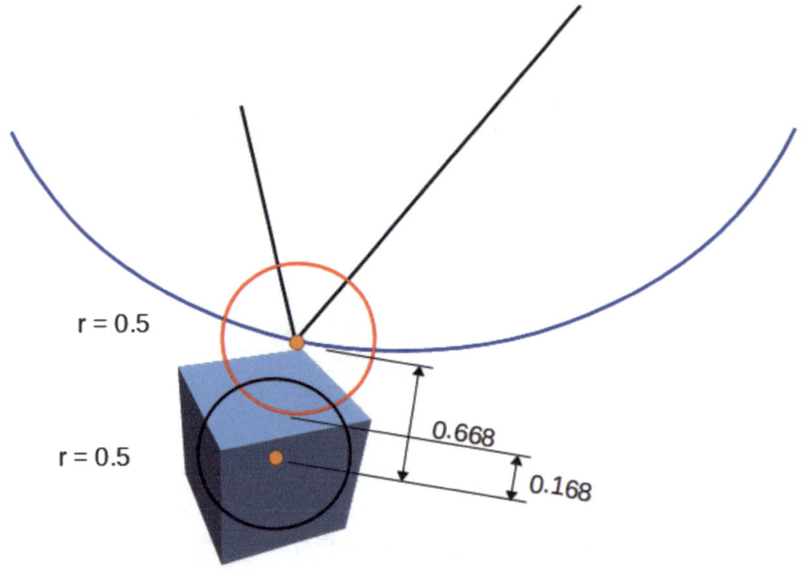

But wait, if the voxel is 0.668 units from the big sphere's surface, isn't it legally outside also of the triangle? Here's where the time element of the 6-sep 4D algorithm comes in. Yes, legally it's outside, but a small corner of the voxel will be inside at the terminal level. Since subdivision is adaptive, if the parent isn't included at a higher level, the actually intersecting voxel at a lower level (higher resolution) will be lost. So this third test is really a preventive measure in a "sequence of time" sense.

```
// this seems the simplest way to get the voxels that
// are excluded right around the triangle vertices, which
// are right on the surface of the big sphere (just barely
// in it). Voxels that sample that vertex can be outside
// of the sphere, even beyond the 0.5 range. (Geometry!)
bool GeomUtil::TrivertSpheres(Triangle *tri, const float3 vox_center) {
	float3 center;
	float radius, dist;

	radius = 0.5f;	// triangle-vertex sphere radius

	// for each triangle vertex and its virtual sphere r = 0.5
	for (short i = 0; i < 3; ++i) {
		// use axis Z which goes uvw = xyz
		switch (i) {
		case 0:
			center.x = tri->fine.c0[2].x;
			center.y = tri->fine.c0[2].y;
			center.z = tri->fine.cw[2].x; // v0
			break;
		case 1:
			center.x = tri->fine.c1[2].x;
			center.y = tri->fine.c1[2].y;
			center.z = tri->fine.cw[2].y; // v1
			break;
		case 2:
			center.x = tri->fine.c2[2].x;
			center.y = tri->fine.c2[2].y;
			center.z = tri->fine.cw[2].z; // v2
			break;
		}

		if (StraightToSphere(vox_center, center, radius, dist))
			return true;
		// try next triangle vertex
	}
	return false;
}
```

The third test encompasses three calls to the NASA sphere test, one for each triangle vertex. The routine exits on the first intersection that qualifies. Keep in mind that the algorithm doesn't know where the voxel is – it could be anywhere on the border of the big sphere. So it has to check all triangle vertices to make sure the voxel, if it *is* near a vertex, is included.

There's one important thing about this method that shows up again in other methods, which is the way it retrieves the coordinates of the triangle. At each level, the triangle's transformed coordinates for all three dominant axes, with the appropriate coordinate swizzling, are computed upfront. In other words, the master triangle is scaled to the current level. The coordinates are stored in the FineVars struct as a tuple for (u, v). Each vertex gets transformed, so there are three tuples: c0, c1, and c2. Tuples are used for plane projections, but sometimes the w-value is useful as well, such as in the routine above. The w-values are stored in a triple: (x, y, z) ⟶ (v0, v1, v2). The final detail in the unmapping of the switch statement is that the unswizzled transformed coordinates will always be stored in the Z-axis mapping, because in this case (u, v, w) maps to (x, y, z), e.g. to the canonical Cartesian coordinate ordering.

The same scheme is used for the triangle's halo coordinates, which are stored in h0, h1, and h2. In this case the halos are only evaluated in plane projections, so there's no need for the additional w coordinates.

At this point the big sphere tests are all done. If the level is the terminal level, and the terminal voxel has passed the big sphere test, meaning it's inside of the big sphere (if it's within range or near a vertex as in tests two and three, this next step doesn't apply), then the algorithm checks if the terminal voxel is inside of the little sphere – e.g. the sphere that's inscribed inside the triangle.

The little sphere is only used for this terminal test. If the voxel is inside of the little sphere, the final "inside" test is whether one of the orthogonal rays extending from the voxel's center intersects the triangle's embedding plane. This is a simpler test than determining if the intersection point is actually inside of the triangle. Though the little sphere doesn't cover all of the interior of the triangle, it covers a good portion and this expedient is a time savings.

However, if the terminal voxel is outside of the little sphere but inside of the big sphere, the chain of execution drops into the second main clause of the algorithm.

At this point, the voxel may be terminal or non-terminal. If terminal, the more expensive test to see if one of the voxel's six rays intersects the triangle proper (not just its embedding plane) is performed. This is a two-step process: a) determine if the ray intersection is inside the "halo triangle" – which is a slightly expanded triangle that takes into account the 0.5 extension near the triangle's boundary; and if it is inside the halo triangle, calculate the distance to the embedding plane, since it's known that the ray's intersection is inside the halo triangle and there's no reason to do a second "inside" test using the triangle's actual (non-halo) coordinates.

Part if the problem is the rigidity of the triangle "inside" testing. The conditions for acceptance for the original triangle coordinates make no allowance for that 0.5 distance that extends beyond the triangle borders. Hence the halo. The follow-up testing was originally written so that the conditions are relaxed in a second test that computes the intersection relative to the *original* triangle coordinates, but with the relaxed condition of being able to compute a point *outside* of the triangle – to determine if the point is within 0.5 of the *actual* triangle interior (not the halo).

It became clear that if the voxel is inside of the halo, then all that really needs to be done is to determine the distance to the embedding plane – because the ray-triangle intersection is already known to be inside of the "halo". A comparison of the second-pass "inside" approach and the second-pass "embedding" approach show that the numerical results are identical. So the simpler approach is taken in this case. Here's the code.

```
bool GeomUtil::OneOfSixToTriIntersect(const float3 vox_center, Triangle * tri,
                    int dom_axis) {
        int i, j;
        int order[6];
        float3 D, P;
        float2 selcoord, direction, alpha_beta;
        float num, range;
        bool use_halo;
        unsigned char checks;

        getOrder(order, dom_axis);  // this is a pointer

        // Graphics Gems, p.390
        // Since the intersection formula doesn't care about
        // parallel planes (the resulting projection will be
        // the same for either), then we don't need to iterate
        // on 6 ray directions: instead just iterate on the 3
        // principal planes.

        // tri->d is the same as d0 etc. for the conservative
        // rasterization: see triangle_setup_6sep in GeomUtil.h
        num = tri->d + (
                        tri->n.x * vox_center.x +
                        tri->n.y * vox_center.y +
                        tri->n.z * vox_center.z);
```

```
// no visible difference when enabling non-dominant axes
// so just loop over first (dominant) pair.
for (i = 0; i < 1; ++i) {
        // get ray direction D (but only use u and v);
        // only change between i & i+1 is dom axis dir,
        // which is being assumed and ignored.
        D.x = ray6[order[i<<1]][0];
        D.y = ray6[order[i<<1]][1];
        D.z = ray6[order[i<<1]][2];

        // it's possible to match the selected (u,v)
        // dimensions with the plane-face that ends
        // up having edge overlaps in UV. That can be
        // done by checking the planetest returns as
        // in EdgeTests(). But generally you start
        // with the dominant axis plane and go from
        // there: e.g. the ordering of this loop.

        unsigned short select;
        j = (order[i<<1])>>1;  // 4 -> 2; 2 -> 1; 0 -> 0
        switch (j) {
        case X:
                selcoord.x = vox_center.y;
                selcoord.y = vox_center.z;
                direction.x = D.y;
                direction.y = D.z;
                select = X;
                break;
        case Y:
                selcoord.x = vox_center.x;
                selcoord.y = vox_center.z;
                direction.x = D.x;
                direction.y = D.z;
                select = Y;
                break;
        case Z:
                selcoord.x = vox_center.x;
                selcoord.y = vox_center.y;
                direction.x = D.x;
                direction.y = D.y;
                select = Z;
                break;
        }
```

```
				// first compute with threshold perimeter, to see
				// if the extended voxel distance of 0.5 is "in".
				// will also fail if principal plane is "edge on" in
				// non-dominant axis and no halo was made for that orientation.
				if (!Inside(tri, selcoord, direction, select, alpha_beta,
								use_halo = true, checks))
					continue;

				// if it passes the threshold, use the threshold checks
				// to compute the actual intersection (alpha and beta)
				// ** Since we're not using alpha:beta can skip this second
				// call.
/*
				Inside(tri, selcoord, direction, select, alpha_beta,
								use_halo = false, checks);
*/
				// Use status as signal that voxel position may be within
				// range. Can use an embedding plane calc, or an alpha:beta
				// calc. They both give same results, so use the faster one:
				if (!EmbeddingPlaneIntersection(vox_center, tri, D, num, P))
					continue;

//				AlphaBetaIntersection(tri, select, alpha_beta, P);

				// we've got the intersection point on the triangle
				// but we don't know which side of vox center it's on.
				// this matters for the equality test at the end.
				for (j = 0; j < 2; ++j) {
					// look at ray direction coord as coord of interest
					// Important Note: for select = 0, P.z is X (e.g. w);
					// for select = 1, P.z is Y; for select = 2, P.z = Z.
					// Secondary Note: we are not using alpha:beta, which
					// has a (u,v) mapping associated with it and thus the
					// the (w) coord (P.z) is the critical intersection.
					// Instead, using generic Embedding which has no (u,v)
					// association and so we use P.x, P.y, and P.z accordingly.
					if (order[i<<1] < 2) {
						// 0: negative direction
						if (j == 0)
							range = (vox_center.x - P.x);
						else  // 1: positive
							range = (P.x - vox_center.x);
						if (range < 0.0f)
```

```
                        continue;
            } else if (order[i<<1] < 4) {
                if (j == 0)
                        range = (vox_center.y - P.y);
                else
                        range = (P.y - vox_center.y);
                if (range < 0.0f)
                        continue;
            } else {
                if (j == 0)
                        range = (vox_center.z - P.z);
                else
                        range = (P.z - vox_center.z);
                if (range < 0.0f)
                        continue;
            }
            // if == will be picked up by next voxel over.
            // but need to do some association to make this work:
            // if even, is a negative direction: use <=
            // if odd, is positive direction: use <
            if (j == 0) {
                if (range <= 0.5f)
                        return true;
                // skip redundant calc
                break;
            } else {
                if (range < 0.5f)
                        return true;
            }
        } // j
    } // i

    return false;
}
```

The original approach of relaxing the triangle intersection for a second "inside" test has been commented out. The comments are retained as a reminder of all the decisions that went into this routine. Before showing the "Inside" method, a remark about the last part shown above is in order. This is the implementation of the 0.5 equality test discussed in section 5.1. The determination of whether the current voxel or a neighboring voxel gets the intersection in the case of equality all comes down to how the rays are ordered.

Therefore the rays are ordered by dominant axis first, followed by the other two axes. It doesn't matter which of the other two axes comes first. For each axis there are two rays. The negative-pointing ray comes first in the ordering, and then the positive.

Here's the ordering routine:

```
void GeomUtil::getOrder(int *order, int dom_axis) {
	switch (dom_axis) {
	case 0:
		order[0] = 0;
		order[1] = 1;
		order[2] = 2;  // xx...
		order[3] = 3;
		order[4] = 4;
		order[5] = 5;
		break;
	case 1:
		order[0] = 2;
		order[1] = 3;
		order[2] = 4;      // xx...
		order[3] = 5;
		order[4] = 0;
		order[5] = 1;
		break;
	case 2:
		order[0] = 4;
		order[1] = 5;
		order[2] = 0;      // xx...
		order[3] = 1;
		order[4] = 2;
		order[5] = 3;
		break;
	}
}
```

The ordering list is then iterated through as shown in the main routine. One related detail is that it was found that no further testing beyond the two rays associated with the dominant axis was needed! These extra tests just resulted in the generation of false positives. Therefore the iteration was limited to the dominant axis only.

Given all of that explanation, the direction of the ray determines how the equality is evaluated. The range is calculated always to be positive. The ordering in the j-loop is 0 = negative direction and 1 = positive direction. The range is computed accordingly. But it's unknown which side of the voxel the triangle is on: and the range can come out negative. If j is 0, this means the intersection is on the positive side, not the negative, so the next iteration of j, which is the positive ray, is taken. Otherwise the intersection is in the negative direction as desired.

The final test for equality only happens when a valid positive range has been calculated for the associated ordering of j. In the direction of the "face of importance", being the negative direction, an equality is accepted. Otherwise the equality is rejected and left for a neighboring voxel.

Moving on, here's the Inside() test. This test was written by Didier Badouel of IRISA, France. (*Graphics Gems*, p. 390.) It uses determinants to compute ratios along two of the triangle edges, these ratios being alpha and beta. These ratios would then normally be applied to the triangle's edge vectors to get the actual intersection point, but in this application alpha and beta are simply used for determining the "inside" status.

```
// vox_center and direction are pre-selected for (u, v)
bool GeomUtil::Inside(Triangle *tri, const float2 vox_center,
                      const float2 direction, unsigned short select,
                      float2 &alpha_beta, bool use_halo, unsigned char &checks) {

    // this is just the transformed triangle v0
    // always use w direction as defined by select
    // f.e: w for 0 (X axis) gives uv for YZ plane.
    // f.e: w for 2 (Z axis) gives uv for XY plane.
    // w_c0 really means c0.x = c0.u; c0.y = c0.v
    float2 *c0;
    float2 *c1;
    float2 *c2;

    if (use_halo) {
        // is polygon orthogonal to principal plane?
        unsigned char selbit = 0x01 << select;
        if (!(tri->fine.planebits & selbit))
            return false;

        c0 = &(tri->fine.h0[select]);
        c1 = &(tri->fine.h1[select]);
        c2 = &(tri->fine.h2[select]);
        checks = 0x00; // initialize
    } else {
        c0 = &(tri->fine.c0[select]);
        c1 = &(tri->fine.c1[select]);
```

```
		c2 = &(tri->fine.c2[select]);
	}
	const float2 &w_c0 = *c0;
	const float2 &w_c1 = *c1;
	const float2 &w_c2 = *c2;

	float2 w_uv1, w_uv2;
	w_uv1.x = w_c1.x - w_c0.x;
	w_uv1.y = w_c1.y - w_c0.y;
	w_uv2.x = w_c2.x - w_c0.x;
	w_uv2.y = w_c2.y - w_c0.y;

	// ray direction is along the AXIS of dominant axis
	// always work from voxel origin (as the ray origin)
	// O = (u + 0.5f, v + 0.5f, w + 0.5f)
	// D = (0.0, 0.0. 1.0) [for example]
	// P = O + Dt
	// P = (u + 0.5f, v + 0.5f, w + 0.5f + 1)
	float2 P = make_float2(
			vox_center.x + direction.x,
			vox_center.y + direction.y);
	// P.z would be the dominant axis: the projection can
	// be on the origin plane face or on origin + 1 face,
	// doesn't matter. But actual intersection point +
	// direction.z *will* matter for range test.

	// in (uvw) coordinates, ray direction = w = 1.0f.
	// Ray magnitude (t) doesn't matter, leave it at implicit 1.0.
	float2 w_uv0 = make_float2(
				P.x - w_c0.x,
				P.y - w_c0.y);

	float alpha, beta;
	alpha = beta = -1.0f;  // neg means default out of bounds
	if (fp_math.equalBoundsf(w_uv1.x, 0.0f, PRECISIONf)) {
		beta = w_uv0.x / w_uv2.x;
		if (use_halo && beta >= 0.0f && beta <= 1.0f)
			checks |= BETA_IN_01;

		if (checks & BETA_IN_01)
			alpha = (w_uv0.y - beta * w_uv2.y) / w_uv1.y;
	} else {
		// compute the determinant as in Graphics Gems,
```

```
            // Glassner, Vol 1, p. 393
            beta = (w_uv0.y * w_uv1.x - w_uv0.x * w_uv1.y) /
                    (w_uv2.y * w_uv1.x - w_uv2.x * w_uv1.y);
            if (use_halo && beta >= 0.0f && beta <= 1.0f)
                    checks |= BETA_IN_01;

            if (checks & BETA_IN_01)
                    alpha = (w_uv0.x - beta * w_uv2.x) / w_uv1.x;
        }
        alpha_beta.x = alpha;
        alpha_beta.y = beta;

        // beta conditions determine alpha, don't need to retest beta
        // only care about this for halo; status for original triangle
        // as calculated below (on second call) is ignored.
        bool inside = (alpha >= 0.0f) && ((alpha + beta) <= 1.0f);

        // here we put an indiscriminate return for "just
        // being inside" without any range tests. The caller
        // is responsible for using alpha and beta to check
        // the range.
        return inside;
}
```

Like the calling routine, the original two-pass logic has been retained even though the method is only called once in the final tally. The relaxation is accomplished by retaining the conditional “checks” from the first pass, and using those same conditions for the second pass. Otherwise the logic jumps out prematurely because the alpha-beta logic is so restrictive. However the second pass is omitted, so the Inside() test is only performed for the threshold polygon, being the expanded “halo” triangle.

If the voxel fails the halo test, it’s rejected. Otherwise, the embedding test determines if the voxel is really within 0.5 units of the triangle’s embedding plane. This brings us to the other part of the main algorithm, being the tests performed for voxels which are not terminal.

5.3 *Embedding Plane Tests*

Non-terminal voxels and, as mentioned in the previous section, terminal voxels both make use of equations that determine a ray distance to the plane of a triangle, called an “embedding plane” since there are no triangle boundaries to worry about. The embedding plane formula is very similar to the 2D half-space calculations used for 26-sep rasterization.

The last part of the 6-sep algorithm is the code that handles everything between the first level up to but not including the terminal level. Here again is the specific conditional clause from the main routine:

```
if (!terminal) {
        // Only run the edge tests on non-terminal levels as it's "liberal"
        // and will otherwise introduce unwanted voxels.
        EdgeTests(coord, tri, facecount);
        if (facecount == 3)
                return true;
        // don't reject if facecount == 0 because there can be a
        // big "projection hole" at finer resolutions when a voxel
        // is in the middle of a triangle.

        if (OneOfSixToEmbeddingPlane(vox_center, tri, dom_axis,
                                                0.5f, ranges))
                return true;

        // last_range for 0.5 is 1.0f, and 1 + sqrt(1) = 2
        if (checkRange(ranges, 2.0f)) {
                // As a last resort (because of speed issues), look ahead.
                // Args: 0.5f last; 0.25f max
                return LookAheadChildrenToEmbedding(vox_center, tri, dom_axis,
                                0.5f, 0.25f, g_level, 0);
        }
        return false;
}
```

The first call is to EdgeTests(). The idea here is to take the three "faces of importance" connected to the voxel's base coordinate, and basically clip each triangle edge in turn against each of these faces, with each face acting as a "viewport". Of course the goal isn't to subdivide and clip the triangle to the viewport: the goal is to determine if the 2D projection of the triangle edge has intersected the 2D projection of the voxel's face. Moreover, it would be nice to know how many of the voxel's faces end up with one or more triangle edges that intersect some part of each face.

The code for doing this isn't re-entrant Sutherland and Hodgman clipping, which has been used for other graphics applications and is very elegant. The code comes from, once again, *Graphics Gems* p. 121. Spoelder and Ullings of Vrije University, Amsterdam (at the time of the writing in 1990) give a clipping algorithm that covers every case under the Sun it seems, some of which are not relevant if the line that intersects the viewport is not subsequently subdivided and reconnected to form sub-polygons. Again, the goal isn't actual clipping: just intersection.

Here's the top-level routine:

```
void GeomUtil::EdgeTests(const ushort3 &coord, Triangle *tri, short &facecount) {
        bool planetest[3];
        short i;

        planetest[0] = IntersectsTop<X>(coord, tri);
        planetest[1] = IntersectsTop<Y>(coord, tri);
        planetest[2] = IntersectsTop<Z>(coord, tri);

        facecount = 0;
        for (i = 0; i < 3; ++i) {
                if (planetest[i])
                        ++facecount;
        }
}
```

In this case the second-level routine, IntersectsTop(), is a template method because the voxel and the triangle will be evaluated for all three principal axes. This routine performs the tests and simply returns how many of the voxel's base-faces (e.g. the faces attached to the base coordinate, or "faces of importance") are overlapped by the triangle.

Here's the second-level routine:

```
// Use template selection to simplify readability
template <int32 AXIS> bool GeomUtil::IntersectsTop(
                                        const ushort3 &coord, Triangle *tri) {

        bool plane_status;
        float2 v_p0, v_p1;   // voxel points
        unsigned short p0_off, p1_off, edge, select;

        // X:0=YZ; Y:1=XZ; Z:2=XY
        typedef uvw<AXIS> sel;
        select = AXIS;

        for (edge = 0; edge < 4; ++edge) {
                p0_off = (select << 2) + edge;
                p1_off = (select << 2) + (edge + 1)%4;
                float3 p0 = make_float3(
                                faces[p0_off][0],
                                faces[p0_off][1],
                                faces[p0_off][2]);
```

```
                float3 p1 = make_float3(
                                faces[p1_off][0],
                                faces[p1_off][1],
                                faces[p1_off][2]);
                v_p0.x = sel::u(coord) + sel::u(p0);
                v_p0.y = sel::v(coord) + sel::v(p0);
                v_p1.x = sel::u(coord) + sel::u(p1);
                v_p1.y = sel::v(coord) + sel::v(p1);

                plane_status = Intersects(tri, v_p0, v_p1, select);
                // any intersection counts as TRUE for voxel face.
                if (plane_status)
                        return true;
        }
        return false;
}
```

Since the EdgeTests() procedure doesn't determine the final acceptance of a terminal voxel, it can be regarded as a complicated heuristic. Notice that only one edge of the voxel face is analyzed at a time, underscoring the fact that this is not a full clip against a full viewport. In the original code some edge can be tested against an arbitrary polygon, not just a voxel face with four edges, and to make that work the authors use a linked list for the polygon edges. However, a linked list isn't needed for this simple application. Notice also that the loop exits on the first intersection: one intersection is enough for this heuristic.

Here's the Intersects() routine:

```
// for true 6sep processing, no getting around edge intersection
// select: plane projection select: YZ (0/X); XZ (1/Y); XY (2/Z)
// they are implied for the current AXIS, as sub-tests, they are
// direct indices.
bool GeomUtil::Intersects(Triangle *tri, float2 &v_p0,
                float2 &v_p1, unsigned short select) {

        float2 t_p0, t_p1; // t = triangle, v = voxel

        // transformed triangle vertices, 2D
        const float2 &c0 = tri->fine.c0[select];
        const float2 &c1 = tri->fine.c1[select];
        const float2 &c2 = tri->fine.c2[select];
        const short COINCIDE = 1;
        const short PARALLEL = 2;
        const short CROSS = 3;
```

```
const short NO_CROSS = 4;
short type;
float a, b, c, s, x, y;

// for triangle edges
for (int i = 0; i < 3; ++i) {
	switch (i) {
	case 0:
		t_p0.x = c0.x; t_p0.y = c0.y;
		t_p1.x = c1.x; t_p1.y = c1.y;
		break;
	case 1:
		t_p0.x = c1.x; t_p0.y = c1.y;
		t_p1.x = c2.x; t_p1.y = c2.y;
		break;
	case 2:
		t_p0.x = c2.x; t_p0.y = c2.y;
		t_p1.x = c0.x; t_p1.y = c0.y;
		break;
	}
	a = (t_p1.y - t_p0.y) * (v_p1.x - v_p0.x) -
		(t_p1.x - t_p0.x) * (v_p1.y - v_p0.y);
	b = (t_p0.x - v_p0.x) * (v_p1.y - v_p0.y) -
		(t_p0.y - v_p0.y) * (v_p1.x - v_p0.x);
	c = (t_p0.x - v_p0.x) * (t_p1.y - t_p0.y) -
		(t_p0.y - v_p0.y) * (t_p1.x - t_p0.x);

	if (fp_math.equalBoundsf(a, 0.0f, PRECISIONf)) {
		if (fp_math.equalBoundsf(b, 0.0f, PRECISIONf))
			type = COINCIDE;
		else
			type = PARALLEL;
	} else {
		if (a > 0.0f) {
			if ((b >= 0.0f && b <= a) &&
				(c >= 0.0f && c <= a))
				type = CROSS;
			else
				type = NO_CROSS;
		} else {
			if ((b <= 0.0f && b >= a) &&
				(c <= 0.0f && c >= a))
```

```
                        type = CROSS;
                    else
                        type = NO_CROSS;
                }
            }
            // determine if there's a crossing
            switch (type) {
            case NO_CROSS:
            case PARALLEL:
            case COINCIDE:
                break;
            case CROSS:
                // c == 0 is intersect of tri edge with vox endpoint: reject
                // b == 0 is tri endpoint on vox faceline: accept
                if (fp_math.equalBoundsf(b, a, PRECISIONf) ||
                    fp_math.equalBoundsf(c, a, PRECISIONf) ||
                    fp_math.equalBoundsf(c, 0.0f, PRECISIONf))
                    break;
/*
                s = b / a;
                if (fp_math.equalBoundsf(v_p0.x, v_p1.x, PRECISIONf))
                    x = v_p0.x;
                else
                    x = t_p0.x + s * (t_p1.x - t_p0.x);
                if (fp_math.equalBoundsf(v_p0.y, v_p1.y, PRECISIONf))
                    y = v_p0.y;
                else
                    y = t_p0.y + s * (t_p1.y - t_p0.y);
*/
                return true;
            }
            // try next edge
        }
        return false;
}
```

The commented out part at the end computes the actual intersection point, which can be handy for debugging, so the comment-block is retained. Notice the extensive use of the floating-point methods to determine equality within some precision. As with the ray-tracing code, these equality tests are critical and so to avoid roundoff error, the floating-point methods are used. The general rule is to use the floating-point methods for all equality tests, but to use regular precision for all other magnitude comparisons. This approach seems to work well.

Otherwise the only complicated thing, besides the quadrant tests, is the computation of a, b, and c. These quantities are simply linear combinations.

When the 6-sep algorithm was being developed combinations of 1, 2, and 3 face intersections were considered for further processing. However it quickly became clear that only 3 face intersections qualify for acceptance of a non-terminal voxel. In other words, if the triangle projects onto all three faces of importance, the voxel is guaranteed to somehow overlap that triangle. One face-overlap doesn't really mean anything; and two face-overlaps is a can of worms that quickly becomes untenable when trying to formalize a strategy.

The next test in the sequence, which for most voxels will be the first important test, especially at finer resolutions when the three-face overlap only applies to voxels that overlap the triangle border-edges directly, is the embedding plane test. Thinking in terms of levels, and the transitions between levels, as the subdivision becomes progressively finer, voxels will fall into an interior "hole" where there are likely to be no edge overlaps as in the edge tests. So the embedding plane test is critical.

Here's the main routine:

```
// test orthogonal rays to triangle embedding plane
// rangelist is a return list of the discovered ranges.
// send in an unused float3 for regular calls...
bool GeomUtil::OneOfSixToEmbeddingPlane(const float3 vox_center, Triangle * tri,
                    int dom_axis, float range_max, float3 &rangelist) {
        int i, j;
        int order[6];
        float3 D, V;
        float num, range;
        unsigned short axis;

        getOrder(order, dom_axis); // this is a pointer

        // tri->d is the same as d0 etc. for the conservative
        // rasterization: see triangle_setup_6sep in GeomUtil.h
        num = tri->d + (
                        tri->n.x * vox_center.x +
                        tri->n.y * vox_center.y +
                        tri->n.z * vox_center.z);

        // Graphics Gems, p.390
        for (i = 0; i < 6; ++i) {
                // tri_v = EO . V
                // get ray direction V
```

```
D.x = ray6[order[i]][0];
D.y = ray6[order[i]][1];
D.z = ray6[order[i]][2];

if (!EmbeddingPlaneIntersection(vox_center, tri, D, num, V))
        continue;

// look at ray direction coord as coord of interest
j = order[i] & 0x01;
if (order[i] < 2) {
        // 0: negative direction
        if (j == 0)
                range = (vox_center.x - V.x);
        else  // 1: positive
                range = (V.x - vox_center.x);
        if (range < 0.0f)
                continue;
} else if (order[i] < 4) {
        if (j == 0)
                range = (vox_center.y - V.y);
        else
                range = (V.y - vox_center.y);
        if (range < 0.0f)
                continue;
} else {
        if (j == 0)
                range = (vox_center.z - V.z);
        else
                range = (V.z - vox_center.z);
        if (range < 0.0f)
                continue;
}
axis = (order[i])>>1;

// if == will be picked up by next voxel over.
// but need to do some association to make this work:
// if even, is a negative direction: use <=
// if odd, is positive direction: use <
if (j == 0) {
        if (range <= range_max)
                return true;
        // skip redundant calc
        ++i;
```

```
            } else {
                    if (range < range_max)
                            return true;
            }
            // store for look ahead check
            if (axis == 0)
                    rangelist.x = range;
            else if (axis == 1)
                    rangelist.y = range;
            else
                    rangelist.z = range;

            // try next direction
    }
    return false;
}
```

The last part of this routine may look familiar: it uses the same equality logic as OneOfSixToTriIntersect() at the terminal level. This is because this embedding method is also applied to the terminal level and the neighbor logic is mandatory. The neighbor logic also works for non-terminal voxels. The goal for non-terminal voxels is to both accept overlapping voxels and to thin out the field by making appropriate exclusions.

Like the TriIntersect implementation, the ordering of rays is retrieved at the top of the routine, with the dominant axis taking priority and being evaluated first. Both methods use the exact same ordering, and the negative ray direction comes before the positive as a matter of convention. One difference is that the embedding checks are performed for all six ray directions; whereas the tri-intersect routine was limited to the negative and positive rays of the dominant axis only. This isn't set in stone. Even though almost all intersections will be found in the first two iterations for the dominant axis, there are some tricky spatial cases where the dominant axis fails, and one of the other orthogonal directions succeeds. In any case, the first success breaks the loop and returns "true".

Like the TriIntersect routine, this routine also calls EmbeddingPlaneIntersection(), shown next.

```
bool GeomUtil::EmbeddingPlaneIntersection(const float3 vox_center, Triangle *tri,
            const float3 D, float num, float3 &V) {
    float t, denom;

    // get magnitude ray scalar t
    denom = tri->n.x * D.x +
                    tri->n.y * D.y +
                    tri->n.z * D.z;
```

```
    if (fp_math.equalBoundsf(denom, 0.0f, PRECISIONf))
            return false; // parallel
    t = -num / denom;

    // intersect to plane
    V.x = vox_center.x + D.x * t;
    V.y = vox_center.y + D.y * t;
    V.z = vox_center.z + D.z * t;
    return true;
}
```

This is just a scalar applied to the ray extending from the ray's origin, being the voxel center. The direction vector D is passed in, and the intersection V is returned.

However, this may not be the end of the story for our voxel. If the overlap test fails, there's the business of "holes" to attend to. The upshot is that Project V uses adaptive subdivision. However Voxel Pipe and most CUDA implementations use arrays at a set final resolution. The problem with adaptive subdivision is that a very small corner of a parent voxel can "fill a hole" in the plane of the triangle's interior, but it will be outside of the orthogonal testing range because orthogonal rays go straight to the center of the associated voxel faces. That is to say, the hole will be outside of the voxel's range until the voxel is subdivided to a fine enough level at which a valid intersection can be computed. Unlike 26-sep, voxel corners are not evaluated in 6-sep. That's the whole point of 6-sep. This isn't a problem at a set array resolution, say 512, but it becomes a problem when parent voxels cover large volumes compared to the final resolution, which is a "given" with adaptive subdivision.

The holes manifest as a regular grid of black voids, the spacing of which is entirely dependent on the slope of the plane. Here's a particularly pretty example:

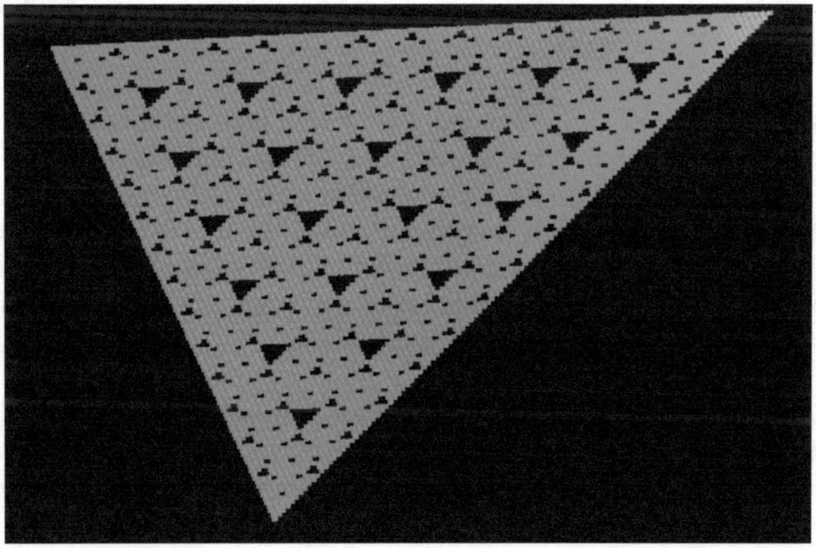

Cellular Automata and Voxels

You might think that the game of Life has nothing to do with voxels. In fact a rasterization is a type of cellular growth based on rules. Cells are a big part of voxel algorithms, since a voxel itself is a cell in three dimensions. In 2D a neighborhood consists of 8 cells around the center, making a total of 3 squared = 9 cells. In 3D the expansion of that is: 26 cells around the center voxel, making a total of 3 cubed = 27 voxels in the volumetric neighborhood.

The Project V software includes two algorithms: 6-sep and 26-sep. These names indicate how many directions a covering or rasterization can go. Mathematically, the thing being rasterized is a pure planar entity without any thickness. The aim is to approximate that plane of zero thickness in the volume of voxels. If you go in 26 directions the rasterization is "thick" because there are more opportunities for filling in cells – almost exactly like a rule in the game of Life.

If you limit the choices to 6, the rasterization in "thin" because it's just looking in 6 directions. At first glance the results of the two flavors look very similar; but are actually very different when you look closely.

At Autodesk when I worked there in 1989 the company released software called Rudy Rucker's Cellular Automata, which included examples of the game of Life. I first saw Life in action when I worked at the Exploratorium, which had an exhibit that kids could play with, an Apple II locked away running a Basic program, which included the famous glider. It was actually not a very popular exhibit because kids got bored with the actual output and ignored all the explanation behind it.

The grid is sparse because most of the voxel testing within the 0.5 distance-constraint covers most of the plane. But a parent voxel can be rejected even though one of its children does in fact cover the plane.

The solution is to "look ahead". Just as octree subdivision is adaptive from level to level, so too is the look-ahead adaptive in that it keeps track of a "virtual resolution" that is halved with each recursive iteration deeper into the hierarchy. The embedding test uses a plane coefficient that's scaled at each level to one of the scaled vertices of the triangle. The look ahead takes place within a level. This means that, unlike the default behavior of the geometry expanding around the voxel, so that the voxel always remains a unit voxel, now the voxel is scaled down from the scaled triangle geometry, which stays constant.

The virtual resolution of the voxel children isn't stored anywhere except the call stack, so no fancy structs or classes are needed. After some experimentation, it was found that the number of recursion levels should track the terminal level, whatever that is. The solution that works is to halve the global terminal level, g_terminal, and add one. For example, if g_terminal is 8, the *continued*

The world of cellular automata includes fractals. A fractal called "Pascal's Triangle" is very similar to a voxel rasterization that's buggy – a triangle with holes – where gaps in the rasterization at one level replicate at increasingly finer levels. The voxel software is a subdivision algorithm – just like fractals – but subdivision in three dimensions instead of two, aimed at approximating the surface of a model made up of triangles. Both fractals in 2D and voxel rasterization in 3D are visual outputs, that is, something that the eye can judge very minutely.

A snowflake is similar to a cellular automaton except that its growth is based on the rules of Nature. A water droplet forms a hexagonal base due to hydrogen valencies, and then grows from there. The ordering and growth of a snowflake is a kind of *self assembly* and this idea is a major research area of nanotechnology. There's a lot of research around self assembly for so called metamaterials, materials that have strange physical properties. For example, metamaterials that bend light can be used as invisibility cloaks. The challenge is to create order and repeating patterns at the nanometer scale. For example, researchers have created a surface layer of nanospheres in a hexagonal pattern using self assembly. Self assembly can be done chemically, electrically, and with heat, or with a combination of these. But self assembly under tension isn't enough: the metamaterial has to be durable and stand up to shocks and general use.

A 3D display is a tough nut to crack because the LEDs that light up within the volume are fed by conduits. Those conduits get in the way of the image. The LEDs are embedded in transparent color planes, one stacked on top of the other. When invisibility becomes a reality it probably won't make headlines because the first cloaks will be millimeters in size – but that's just the right size to hide the conduits of a display volume.

number of recursions will be 8 / 2 + 1 = 5. Of course 5 levels at terminal-level minus 2 will exceed the terminal level, so the terminal level is used as a "hard barrier" to stop the recursion in that case.

Both the geometry and the ray-distance range are halved at each level of recursion. In almost all 6-sep routines the ray distance is tested against 0.5. This is now halved to 0.25, 0.125, and so on. Meanwhile, the previous range is kept on hand; for example, the previous range for the 0.25 recursion will be 0.5. This previous range is used as a "safety margin" to determine whether to keep going with the recursion or to bail out. Remember that the only reason recursion is being done is because the regular distance test has failed. If the first level of recursion results in embedding plane intersections that are all outside of the safety margin, the recursion ends. And no matter what, the recursion ends after going MAX_DEEP levels.

Before showing the listing, it might be mentioned that the recursion calls OneOfSixToEmbeddingPlane, the core method, and this explains the "rangelist" array that's sent in as a reference argument. This argument is also used for the default call in the non-terminal clause of the main routine that precedes the look-ahead call. Because the look ahead is recursive, and because all 8 children of the parent voxel have to be evaluated, the method is bulky. Here it is:

```
// check ahead to see if any subdivisions of current voxel
// qualify (to fill holes)
bool GeomUtil::LookAheadChildrenToEmbedding(const float3 vox_center, Triangle *tri,
                int dom_axis, float last_range, float max_range, short cur_level, short deep) {

        // do a local subdivision without scaling, and pass
        // to OneOfSixToEmbeddingPlane
        float3 coord, child_center, ranges;
        float last_off = last_range;
        float cur_off = max_range;
        float next_range = max_range / 2.0f;
        bool in_range;

        // recursion terminal condition is terminal level!
        if (cur_level == g_terminal_level || deep == MAX_DEEP)
                return false;

        // reassign last_range to reflect max-45 ray distance
        last_range = ray_dist[deep];

        coord.x = vox_center.x - last_off;
        coord.y = vox_center.y - last_off;
        coord.z = vox_center.z - last_off;

        child_center.x = coord.x + cur_off;
        child_center.y = coord.y + cur_off;
        child_center.z = coord.z + cur_off;
        if (OneOfSixToEmbeddingPlane(child_center, tri, dom_axis, max_range, ranges))
                return true;

        if (checkRange(ranges, last_range)) {
                in_range = LookAheadChildrenToEmbedding(child_center, tri, dom_axis,
                                max_range, next_range, cur_level + 1, deep + 1);
                if (in_range)
                        return true;
        }

        child_center.x = coord.x + cur_off;
```

```
child_center.y = coord.y + cur_off;
child_center.z = coord.z + last_off + cur_off;
if (OneOfSixToEmbeddingPlane(child_center, tri, dom_axis, max_range, ranges))
        return true;

if (checkRange(ranges, last_range)) {
        in_range = LookAheadChildrenToEmbedding(child_center, tri, dom_axis,
                        max_range, next_range, cur_level + 1, deep + 1);
        if (in_range)
                return true;
}

child_center.x = coord.x + last_off + cur_off;
child_center.y = coord.y + cur_off;
child_center.z = coord.z + last_off + cur_off;
if (OneOfSixToEmbeddingPlane(child_center, tri, dom_axis, max_range, ranges))
        return true;

if (checkRange(ranges, last_range)) {
        in_range = LookAheadChildrenToEmbedding(child_center, tri, dom_axis,
                        max_range, next_range, cur_level + 1, deep + 1);
        if (in_range)
                return true;
}

child_center.x = coord.x + last_off + cur_off;
child_center.y = coord.y + cur_off;
child_center.z = coord.z + cur_off;
if (OneOfSixToEmbeddingPlane(child_center, tri, dom_axis, max_range, ranges))
        return true;

if (checkRange(ranges, last_range)) {
        in_range = LookAheadChildrenToEmbedding(child_center, tri, dom_axis,
                        max_range, next_range, cur_level + 1, deep + 1);
        if (in_range)
                return true;
}

//
child_center.x = coord.x + cur_off;
child_center.y = coord.y + last_off + cur_off;
child_center.z = coord.z + cur_off;
if (OneOfSixToEmbeddingPlane(child_center, tri, dom_axis, max_range, ranges))
```

```
        return true;

    if (checkRange(ranges, last_range)) {
        in_range = LookAheadChildrenToEmbedding(child_center, tri, dom_axis,
                        max_range, next_range, cur_level + 1, deep + 1);
        if (in_range)
            return true;
    }

    child_center.x = coord.x + cur_off;
    child_center.y = coord.y + last_off + cur_off;
    child_center.z = coord.z + last_off + cur_off;
    if (OneOfSixToEmbeddingPlane(child_center, tri, dom_axis, max_range, ranges))
        return true;

    if (checkRange(ranges, last_range)) {
        in_range = LookAheadChildrenToEmbedding(child_center, tri, dom_axis,
                        max_range, next_range, cur_level + 1, deep + 1);
        if (in_range)
            return true;
    }

    child_center.x = coord.x + last_off + cur_off;
    child_center.y = coord.y + last_off + cur_off;
    child_center.z = coord.z + last_off + cur_off;
    if (OneOfSixToEmbeddingPlane(child_center, tri, dom_axis, max_range, ranges))
        return true;

    if (checkRange(ranges, last_range)) {
        in_range = LookAheadChildrenToEmbedding(child_center, tri, dom_axis,
                        max_range, next_range, cur_level + 1, deep + 1);
        if (in_range)
            return true;
    }

    child_center.x = coord.x + last_off + cur_off;
    child_center.y = coord.y + last_off + cur_off;
    child_center.z = coord.z + cur_off;
    if (OneOfSixToEmbeddingPlane(child_center, tri, dom_axis, max_range, ranges))
        return true;

    if (checkRange(ranges, last_range)) {
        in_range = LookAheadChildrenToEmbedding(child_center, tri, dom_axis,
```

```
                        max_range, next_range, cur_level + 1, deep + 1);
            if (in_range)
                return true;
        }

        return false;
}
```

Notice that any one of the 8 children can recurse an arbitrary number of levels before finding an overlap or being completely out of range and failing. Though consolidating the 8 clauses into a single routine is possible, it's less clear than a single function because in the consolidated approach the entry point isn't from the recursive function itself, but from the subfunction, so there are two methods on the call stack instead of one. The main function would still need 8 calls to the subfunction, and the subfunction would need all the arguments that go to the main function to be able to *call* the main function – hopefully the reader will appreciate that sometimes "more is less".

The checkRange method is as follows:

```
bool GeomUtil::checkRange(const float3 rangelist, float last_range) {
        // These are axes, not a coordinates
        if (rangelist.x <= last_range)
                return true;
        if (rangelist.y <= last_range)
                return true;
        if (rangelist.z <= last_range)
                return true;
        return false;
}
```

Only one of the dimensions needs to be within the safety margin to qualify for promotion to the next level of recursion. But what exactly is that safety margin?

It turns out that a single particular orientation of an embedding plane, being a plane that's kitty-corner at 45 degrees relative to two principal axes, and therefore relative to the voxel faces, will generate an intersection with the ray along the dominant axis from the voxel center, and this intersection is the maximum distance for considering an overlap. Anything beyond this distance is rejected. This distance is called the "max-45 ray distance". This makes sense when considering that the "dominant axis" will change if the 45-degree orientation shifts in any way, and the resulting dominant axis distance will always be less than the maximum distance at 45 degrees.

The following diagram shows the setup for computing the “max-45 ray distance” for a voxel.

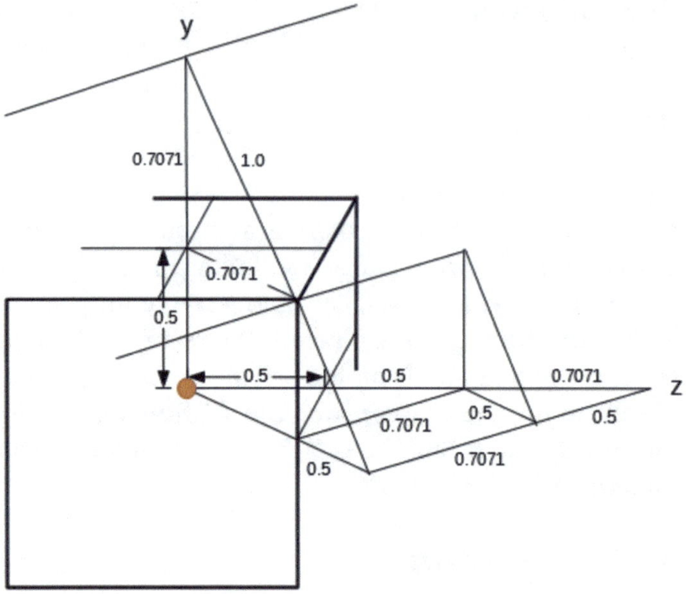

The kitty-corner 45-degree plane is touching the top right corner of the voxel. The ray distance in the Y direction is shorter than the ray distance in the X or Z directions. So the larger distance is used, because any one of the cardinal directions could be selected as the dominant axis, and in fact the dominant axis for this plane is X because the dominant-axis logic orders X first for same values.

The formula is simply 2 * 0.5 + sqrt(0.5). This distance is the maximum distance for which an intersection may be valid for further recursion. Roundoff isn’t an issue because this distance is on a diagonal; that is, the plane of the triangle is touching a vertex of the voxel. For 6-sep rasterization such an intersection is automatically out of bounds. So there’s no reason not to use this.

However the decision was made to provide a safety margin by using the value of the “last range”, being the range from the preceding level (that failed). But instead of using the X or Z distance, the Y distance, which is shorter, is applied, and the net effect is a “padding” of the range value that guarantees that voxels close to the surface will be passed from level to level of the recursion; and at the same time will reject voxels outside of the safety margin.

The following table shows how the 45-max-ray-distance proceeds from level to level; the values used are on the right; the actual max values for the current range (as opposed to the “last range”) are shown on the left. The safety margin, if there was a roundoff danger, nicely pads the value so that no roundoff error nor false exclusion of a voxel could occur based on the max-45-ray-dist criterion.

current: 2x + sqrt(x)		last: x + sqrt(x)	
0.5	1.7071	1	2
0.25	1	0.5	1.2071
0.125	0.6035	0.25	0.75
0.0625	0.375	0.125	0.4785
0.03125	0.2392	0.0625	0.3125
etc.			

Keep in mind that the measures derived from the 45-degree construction plane are applied to and properly admit or exclude all other plane orientations. This list resets itself at every level of the octree subdivision, that is at every "level switch", because the voxel is always a unit voxel. "Look ahead" recursion is the only task in the entire pipeline that halves the voxel geometry, but it does so locally, away from the "eyes" of OctreeWorker, and always starts testing for the default ray distance of 0.5 for each voxel.

The GeomUtil Init() routine takes care of initializing the numbers shown above. The numbers are stored in a lookup table to avoid using a square root for the hundreds of thousands of voxel comparisons that come through the loop.

```
// to eliminate false negatives, look ahead this many levels
// into the octree for the current voxel.
static short MAX_DEEP;
// allocate a lookup make it 12 entries for 12 max recursion
// levels which is beyond overkill...
static const short MAX_RECURSION = 12;
// lookup for 45-degree max dominant ray distance
static float ray_dist[MAX_RECURSION];

/// called by constructor
void GeomUtil::Init() {
        bbox0 = make_float3( -1.1f, -1.1f, -1.1f );
        bbox1 = make_float3( 1.1f, 1.1f, 1.1f );

        // MAX_DEEP heuristic tracks g_terminal to make
        // sure recursion for look ahead is adequate
        MAX_DEEP = g_terminal / 2 + 1;

        double start = 0.5f;
        float entry;
```

```
        for (short i = 0; i < MAX_DEEP; ++i) {
                entry = start + sqrt(start); // ortho dist to max-45 plane
                ray_dist[i] = entry;
        }
}
```

5.4 *Parametric Line Routines*

There are a few operations such as the halo construction and the little sphere calculation which use line intersections and line constructions based on parametric line equations. Two line representations are used: a) the *slope-intercept* form; and b) the *standard* or *normal* form. The standard form is usually what all the hard work is done with; and the slope-intercept form is usually transformed (easily) into the standard form. The slope-intercept form is used when the line is being first specified from two points.

The little sphere code is an implementation from Chasen, in two parts. First, the 3D transformed triangle is "snapped" to 2D using a simple transformation given by Chasen. Below is a diagram of the 3D working variables.

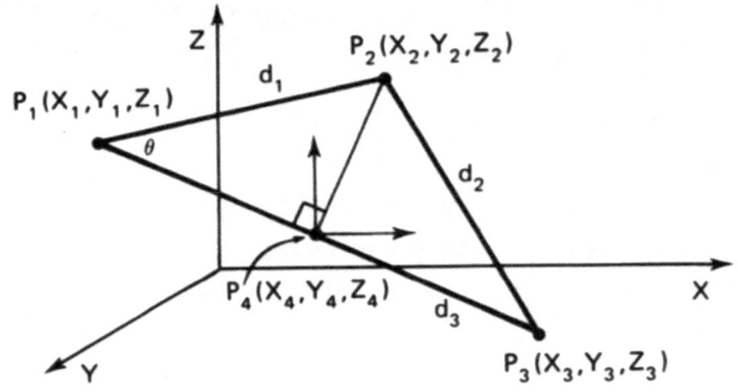

This arbitrary 3D triangle is snapped to a (u, v) coordinate system in 2D that looks like this:

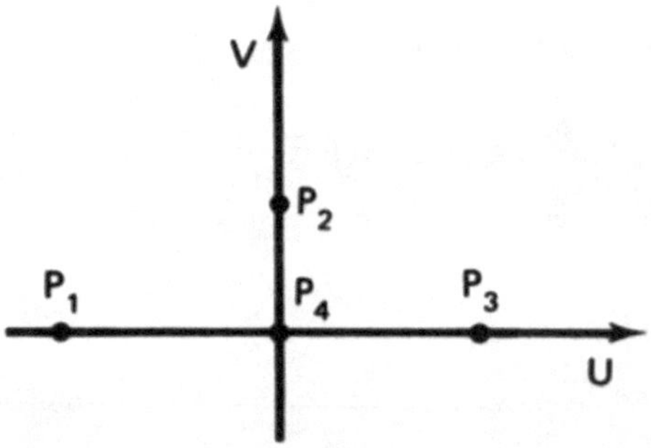

In this 2D coordinate system a construction is made for a circle inscribed in a 2D triangle. Here are the working variables for a 2D circle tangent to three lines, as given by Chasen.

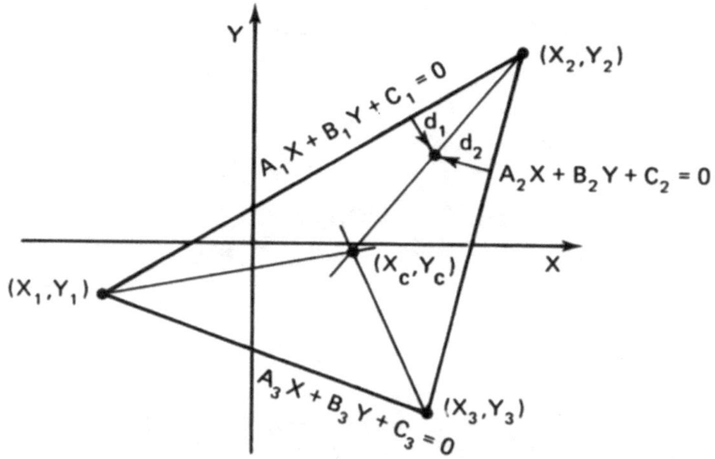

Once this is done, and with the simple understanding that the center of the circle in 2D is the center of the sphere in 3D, the circle center is transformed back to 3D. The 3D center is now the sphere center, and the end result is a sphere inscribed in an arbitrary 3D triangle.

The line construction in this case is for making angle bisector lines for two of the triangle's three corners, and then taking the intersection for the barycentric centerpoint of the circle. Therefore a line intersection routine is required.

Many line intersections are also computed for the triangle halo. Each triangle has 3 orthogonal plane projections, one of which corresponds to the triangle's dominant axis. The halo constructions are made in these 2D projection planes. As shown in the diagram below, there are two possible vectors that can be attached to each edge midpoint, corresponding to the orthogonal ray directions associated with some voxel center residing outside of the triangle boundaries, but within the default distance of 0.5.

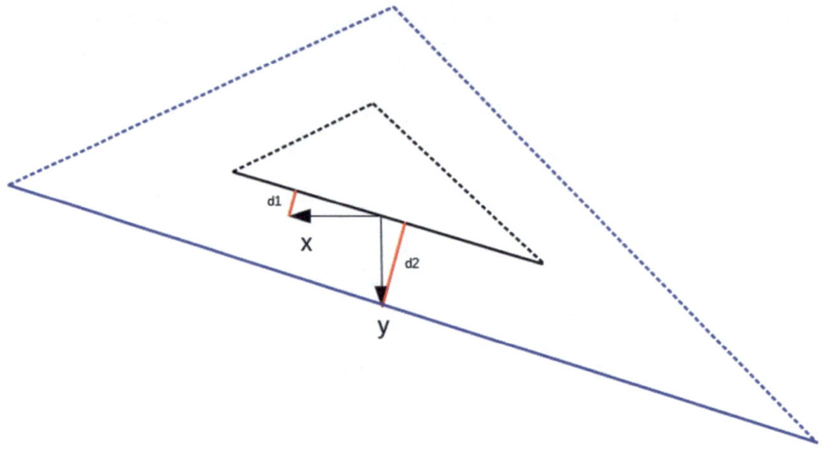

After determining that the edge vectors (the arrows) are pointing away from the interior of the triangle, a vertical line is dropped from the end of each vector to the triangle edge, perpendicular to the edge, which is a simple line formula slope reciprocal. The greater of distances {d1, d2} is taken, to give the widest halo for a given triangle edge.

Then a line parallel to the triangle edge is constructed through the winning vector's endpoint, as shown in blue. This is done for all three triangle edges, and finally the intersections of pairs of lines are taken to get the new halo-triangle endpoints.

The reader can refer to the class listing for GeomUtil.cpp for the implementation of the halo and little sphere features. This section aims to present the core line utilities upon which the higher level routines are based.

The slope-intercept form is simply y = mx + b, where x and y are variables, m is the slope, and b is the y-intercept, the y-axis intersection point of the line. The standard form is Ax + By + C = 0, where the slope is -A/B, and C is -b, the negation of the y-intercept.

In almost all cases, the line will be specified with two points. Theoretically the points are on a line of infinite length, even though the "line" is the segment between the two points. Here's the routine for making the line from two points.

```
// Return the line coefficients (xyz = ABC) in standard form
bool GeomUtil::getSlopeIntercept(float2 p1, float2 p2, float &m, float &b,
                float3 &coeff) {
        if (fp_math.equalBoundsf(p2.x, p1.x, PRECISIONf)) {
                m = 1.0f;  // undefined but set to anything, unused
                coeff.x = 1.0f;
```

```
            coeff.y = 0.0f;  // y term will vanish
            b = p1.x;
            coeff.z = -b;
            return true;
        }
        // Note that slope-intercept form, y = mx + b, has m = A/B
        // But the conversion to "standard form" has -A/B in front of X,
        // so a negative sign is added below for "standard" use.
        // However, this reflects the actual slope of A/B on the RHS.
        coeff.x = (p2.y - p1.y);
        coeff.y = (p2.x - p1.x);
        m = coeff.x / coeff.y;
        // and correct for Lefthand Side
        coeff.x = -coeff.x;

        // b in standard form gets multiplied by B after being
        // shifted to the LHS (negated).
        b = (p1.y - m * p1.x);
        coeff.z = -b * coeff.y;
        return false;
}
```

A horizontal line has a slope of zero; but a vertical line is undefined. This routine returns "true" is the line is vertical, false otherwise. Even though the vertical line is undefined, various terms must be set but especially the x coefficient (A). Notice now that b has become the x-intercept! Otherwise, if the line isn't vertical, the slope is computed from the two points; notice that the coefficients A (.x) and B (.y) are simply delta values for the given coordinate elements.

The reader might see this as high-school algebra but things get tricky quickly so the two line forms (slope-intercept and standard) have to be understood perfectly before proceeding. One of the most important things you can do with two lines is take their intersection. Here's the code used by the halo code for calculating the intersection between: a) the perpendicular line dropped from the orthogonal outward-pointing vector and the triangle edge; and b) the pair of halo lines to get the new halo-vertex of the triangle.

```
// fills in reference to new "halo point" (hp)
void GeomUtil::intersectPair(const float3 coeff1, const float3 coeff2,
            float2 &hp) {
        float lla1, llc1, lla2, llc2, diffla, difflc;

        // solve simultaneously : A = x, B = y, C = z
        if (fp_math.equalBoundsf(coeff1.y, 0.0f, PRECISIONf)) {
```

```
            // solve first equation for y
            hp.x = -coeff1.z / coeff1.x; // may be 0 if vertical
            hp.y = (-coeff2.z - hp.x * coeff2.x) / coeff2.y;
        } else if (fp_math.equalBoundsf(coeff2.y, 0.0f, PRECISIONf)) {
            // solve second equation for y
            hp.x = -coeff2.z / coeff2.x;
            hp.y = (-coeff1.z - hp.x * coeff1.x) / coeff1.y;
        } else {
            lla1 = coeff1.x * coeff2.y;
            llc1 = coeff1.z * coeff2.y;
            lla2 = coeff2.x * coeff1.y;
            llc2 = coeff2.z * coeff1.y;

            diffla = lla1 - lla2;
            difflc = llc1 - llc2;
            // diffla should never be 0.0f?
            // get new point:
            hp.x = -difflc / diffla;
            // solve for y
            hp.y = ((coeff1.x * hp.x) + coeff1.z) / (-coeff1.y);
        }
}
```

This formalizes very similar code used by the little sphere code for finding the intersection of the two angle bisector lines. It finds the simultaneous solution to the two line equations, which, by definition ("line" = "linear") are linear equations. Notice the special-case conditions for vertical lines appearing in one linear equation or the other.

The beautiful thing about all of this mathematical code is that bugs will show up in the displayed results of the rasterization process. Usually the procedure is to notice something amiss, then to turn on the adaptive grid display to more easily locate suspect voxels by coordinate, and then to put a breakpoint in the code for the suspect coordinate, and step through the code after the breakpoint is reached. Almost always, stepping through the code very quickly shows where the math went wrong. This code was developed using the Eclipse development environment on Linux, which includes a visual debugger.

Another useful thing to do with lines is to find a line parallel to another line through a given point in the 2D plane. For the halo application, the point is the maximum-distance orthogonal vector endpoint. Here's the parallel-line code.

```
// return the coefficients in standard form of
// the new lines that form the triangle halo
void GeomUtil::findParallel(const float2 ortho, const float2 v0,
```

```
			const float2 v1, float3 &coeff) {
	float m, b, newb;
	float3 coeffb; // baseline
	bool vertical;

	// get line coeffs for original triangle edge
	vertical = getSlopeIntercept(v0, v1, m, b, coeffb);
	if (vertical) {
			newb = ortho.x;
			coeff.x = coeffb.x;		// 1
			coeff.y = coeffb.y;		// 0
			coeff.z = -newb; // standard form
			return;
	}

	// slope is -A / B, can reform standard into
	// mx - y + b = 0; plug in point for new b, use m
	newb = -(m * ortho.x - ortho.y);
	// rearranging gives:
	newb = newb * -coeffb.y; // e.g. C * -B
	// so the new line is:
	coeff.x = coeffb.x;
	coeff.y = coeffb.y;
	coeff.z = newb;
}
```

{v0, v1} are the original triangle's edge endpoints, "ortho" is the 2D orthogonal vector endpoint, and the parallel line is returned in standard form in "coeff". Notice how these routines tend to stack up on each, as shown here with the call to getSlopeIntercept() for the triangle edge.

Another useful thing is to find a line perpendicular to a given line through a point. Both the intersection and parallel line computations were made into utility routines, but the perpendicular code is only used in the distance test of the halo code, and so was left within the context of the distance test. Here's that particular test:

```
// choose the outward orthogonal farthest
// from the triangle edge
void GeomUtil::maxAwayFromEdge(const float2 reach,
			const float2 v0, const float2 v1, const float2 midp,
			float2 &ortho) {
	double dx, dy, distx, disty;
	float m, b, perpm, perpb;
```

```
float3 coeff, pcoeff;
float2 x_perp_on_edge, y_perp_on_edge;

// vertical and horizontal are simply points on
// the original edge (and will always have shorter
// chords than their orthogonal counterpart)
if (fp_math.equalBoundsf(reach.x, midp.x, PRECISIONf)) {
        ortho.x = midp.x;
        ortho.y = reach.y;
        return;
}
if (fp_math.equalBoundsf(reach.y, midp.y, PRECISIONf)) {
        ortho.x = reach.x;
        ortho.y = midp.y;
        return;
}

// drop a perpendicular: only way to do it.
// get line equation of original edge
// checks above guarantee line isn't vertical
getSlopeIntercept(v0, v1, m, b, coeff);

// first outward point: reach.x
// perpendicular slope is B/A eg .y/.x
perpm = coeff.y / coeff.x;
perpb = -(perpm * reach.x - midp.y);
pcoeff.x = perpm;
pcoeff.y = -1.0f;
pcoeff.z = perpb;
intersectPair(coeff, pcoeff, x_perp_on_edge);

// second outward point: reach.y
perpb = -(perpm * midp.x - reach.y);
pcoeff.z = perpb;
intersectPair(coeff, pcoeff, y_perp_on_edge);

// get perp distance to reach.x
dx = reach.x - x_perp_on_edge.x;
dy = midp.y - x_perp_on_edge.y;
distx = dx * dx + dy * dy;

// get perp distance to reach.y
dx = midp.x - y_perp_on_edge.x;
```

```
        dy = reach.y - y_perp_on_edge.y;
        disty = dx * dx + dy * dy;

        if (disty > distx) {
                ortho.x = midp.x;
                ortho.y = reach.y;  // this pair is higher
        } else {
                ortho.x = reach.x;
                ortho.y = midp.y;   // else this one is
        }
}
```

In this routine the only tricky part is when both the triangle edge and the orthogonal vector (by definition) are aligned with the principal axes. In this case, a vertical vector would be colinear with the vertical triangle edge; or likewise a horizontal vector would be colinear with the horizontal triangle edge. Luckily an edge can't be both horizontal and vertical! In either case, the other vector will by default be the "higher" distance from the triangle edge, because the colinear vector has a distance of zero. Here's a quick sketch of the situation.

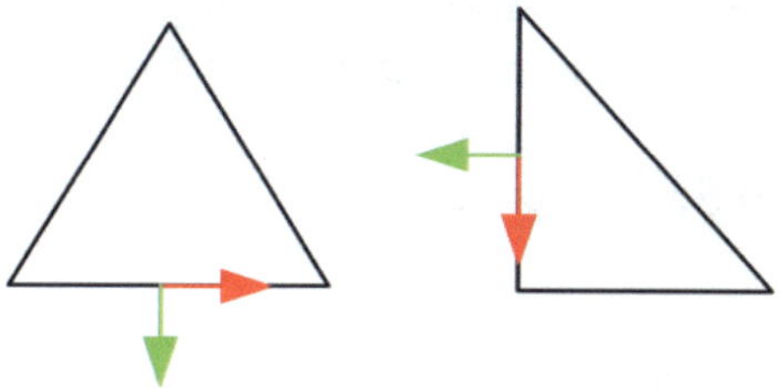

The red vectors are the colinear vectors with a zero distance. The other orthogonal direction is shown in green.

As mentioned, line math is used to construct triangle angle bisectors for the little sphere construction. That operation involves many steps and is given by Chasen. The user may consult the GeomUtil class listing for the implementation. Here's where the sphere code is called:

```
// for 6sep bounds testing
void GeomUtil::makeSpheres(Triangle *tri) {
        // Get the transformed coordinates of the triangle
        // irrespective of uv specialization

        const float3 v0 = make_float3(
                                (tri->v0.x - bbox0.x) * inv_bbox_delta.x,
                                (tri->v0.y - bbox0.y) * inv_bbox_delta.y,
```

```
                    (tri->v0.z - bbox0.z) * inv_bbox_delta.z);
    const float3 v1 = make_float3(
                    (tri->v1.x - bbox0.x) * inv_bbox_delta.x,
                    (tri->v1.y - bbox0.y) * inv_bbox_delta.y,
                    (tri->v1.z - bbox0.z) * inv_bbox_delta.z);
    const float3 v2 = make_float3(
                    (tri->v2.x - bbox0.x) * inv_bbox_delta.x,
                    (tri->v2.y - bbox0.y) * inv_bbox_delta.y,
                    (tri->v2.z - bbox0.z) * inv_bbox_delta.z);

    makeBigSphere(v0, v1, v2, tri->big_center, tri->big_radius);
    makeLittleSphere(v0, v1, v2, tri->little_center, tri->little_radius);
}
```

This routine is called once per level for each triangle.

There is one last note having to do with certain components of the "direction cosines" which are used for the transformation from (u, v) to (x, y, z) for the little sphere construction. The formula calls for both cosine theta and a sine theta values. There are several ways to differentiate these two values, but the easiest way is interpret sine theta as a simple translation and reflection of cosine theta. This solution is an insight from vector geometry.

Consider the points of the triangle as shown below.

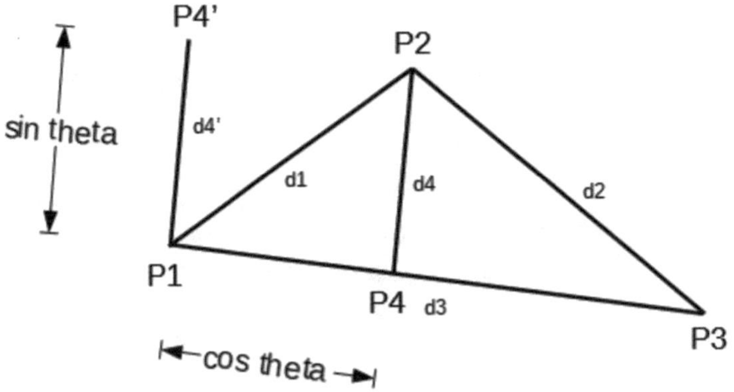

The (u, v) coordinate system is such that the cardinal axes go right through the points of the triangle in two dimensions. However the diagram shown above can be imagined to be in three dimensions. The side associated with cosine theta is shown with the dimension line and the "cosine theta" label. The side associated with sine theta is a simple translation of the v axis, that is, segment P4 P2, to form an opposite side of a parallelogram. The two related vectors are said to be “orthogonal” to each other. Distance d4’ = distance d4. And that’s all there is to it.

The code below computes the various distances shown in the diagram from the given triangle points; and as well computes cosine theta and sine theta geometrically, without actually using the cosine or sine functions. Note that this transformation geometry is computed in double precision since the distances are used to make P4, which is the origin of the 2D (u, v) system; and the values are also components of the direction cosines used to bring the circle center in 2D back to 3D. That’s a long sequence of transformations, so minimizing roundoff error is essential. length3() just computes the distance between the two given points in 3D.

```
// the distances and origin for the (u,v) system
void GeomUtil::makeOrigin(UVPack &uvpack) {
        double d1, d3, d4, cos_theta, sin_theta;
        double3 p1, p2, p3, p4, t, pp4;

        p1.x = (double)uvpack.p1.x;
        p1.y = (double)uvpack.p1.y;
        p1.z = (double)uvpack.p1.z;
        p2.x = (double)uvpack.p2.x;
        p2.y = (double)uvpack.p2.y;
        p2.z = (double)uvpack.p2.z;
        p3.x = (double)uvpack.p3.x;
        p3.y = (double)uvpack.p3.y;
        p3.z = (double)uvpack.p3.z;

        // first find P4 (according to Chasen, p. 142)
        length3(p1, p2, d1);
        length3(p1, p3, d3);

        cos_theta = (
                        (p2.x - p1.x) * (p3.x - p1.x) +
                        (p2.y - p1.y) * (p3.y - p1.y) +
                        (p2.z - p1.z) * (p3.z - p1.z)) / (d1 * d3);

        // origin : d4 is dist ratio between p1/p4
        d4 = ((d1 * cos_theta) / d3);
        p4.x = p1.x + d4 * (p3.x - p1.x);
        p4.y = p1.y + d4 * (p3.y - p1.y);
        p4.z = p1.z + d4 * (p3.z - p1.z);

        // sine theta is orthogonal to cos in the vector world.
        // t is translation vector
        t.x = p4.x - p1.x;
```

```
        t.y = p4.y - p1.y;
        t.z = p4.z - p1.z;

        // translated p4/p2 to p1: call it p4' (prime)
        pp4.x = p2.x - t.x;
        pp4.y = p2.y - t.y;
        pp4.z = p2.z - t.z;

        length3(p4, p2, d4);  // p2 to p4 (same as len pp4)
        sin_theta = (
                        (pp4.x - p1.x) * (p2.x - p1.x) +
                        (pp4.y - p1.y) * (p2.y - p1.y) +
                        (pp4.z - p1.z) * (p2.z - p1.z)) / (d1 * d4);

        uvpack.p1p3 = d3;
        uvpack.p1p2 = d1;
        uvpack.p1p4 = d1 * cos_theta;
        uvpack.p4p2 = d4;
        uvpack.cos_theta = cos_theta;
        uvpack.sin_theta = sin_theta;
        uvpack.p4.x = p4.x;
        uvpack.p4.y = p4.y;
        uvpack.p4.z = p4.z;
}
```

There's more to the actual transformation – for example the computation of the "direction cosines" used to transform arbitrary points in (u, v) back to (x, y, z). The reader may refer to GeomUtil::makeLittleSphere() for details.

END OF PART FIVE

About the Author

Dan Browning is a programmer, systems engineer, and writer living in the San Francisco Bay Area. When an undergraduate at UC Berkeley he studied computer architecture with David Patterson, inventor of the RISC chip. An erstwhile member of SIGARCH, he has retained his love of hardware design while putting his software engineering talents to work in Silicon Valley.

Dan wrote the Project V software during the summer and autumn of 2014. The rotating 3D display device patented by Ed Berlin, cofounder of Cubicomp, was in mind when writing the ray tracing code. A nod also goes to Andrew Glassner for the seminal ray tracing paper which became such a core part of Project V, and for *Graphics Gems*, the textbook which Glassner edited.

Gallery

1. (Right) The Harrier landing gear model. Rendered 26-sep overlap-3, 9 levels = 512 cubed resolution, with 1 additional level for false-positive checking. 337,366 voxels. Sep-26 is generally very fast: this took 1 min 5 sec to compute and render. Here are the voxel counts for 26-sep and 6-sep for this model.

	Level 9	Level 8	Level 7
6-sep	256,241	63,533	15,666
26-sep	337,366	82,540	19,929
%	0.7595	0.7697	0.7861

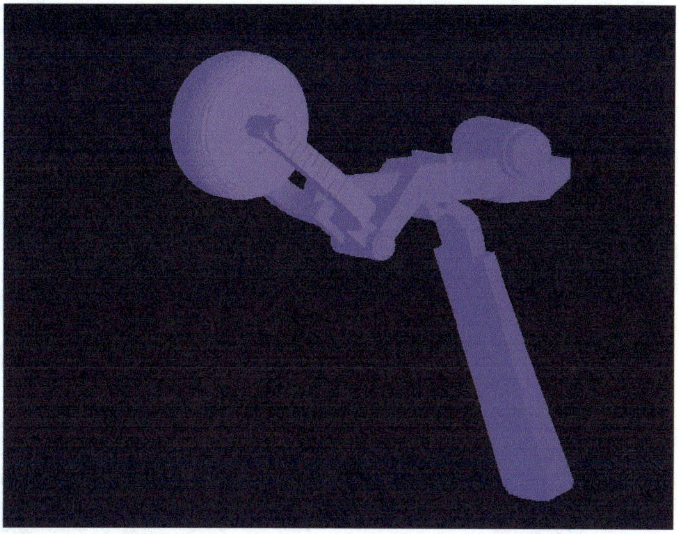

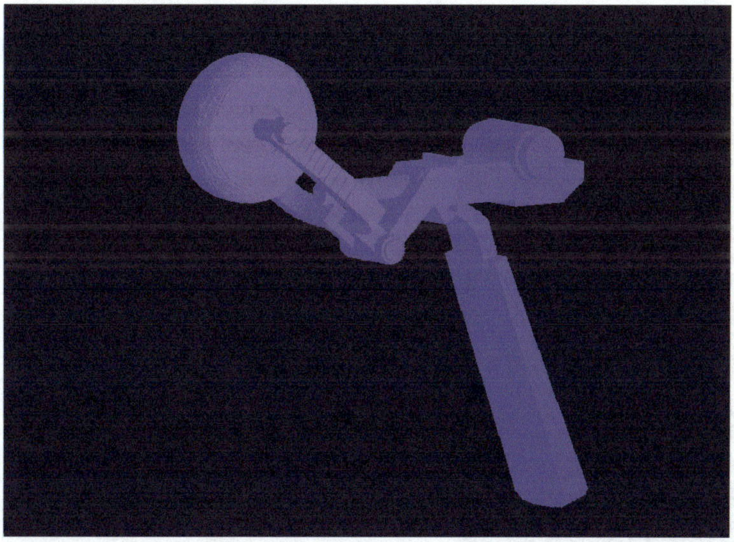

2. (Left) Landing gear rendered 6-sep, 9 levels = 512 cubed resolution, with 1 additional level for false-positive checking, and recursion of max 5 levels on the lookahead to check for false negatives. 256,241 voxels. This took 6 minutes to compute and render on an HP Pavilion s5-1014: dual core Pentium E5800 @ 3.2GHz w/ 2MB cache; 4GB DDR3 memory, 3.8 GB available; 11.7 GB swap space. This is a vanilla HP desktop running Linux, purchased in 2013.

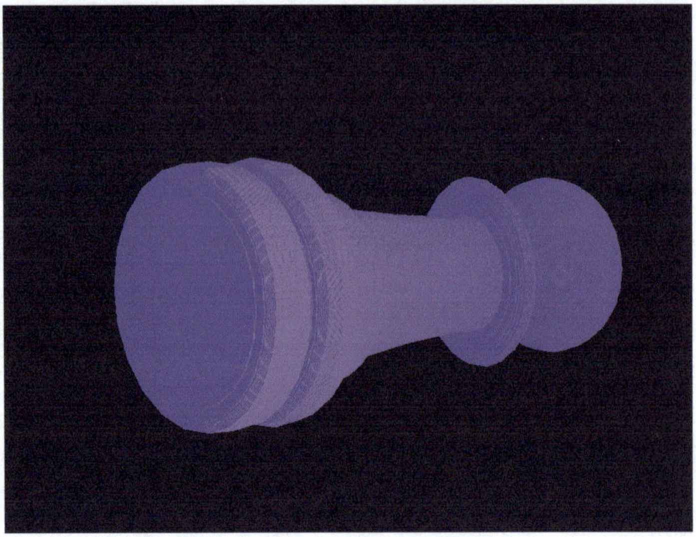

3. (Right) The pawn model. Rendered 6-sep, 9 levels = 512 cubed resolution, with 1 additional level for false-positive checking. 309,445 voxels. This took 9 min 20 sec to compute and render. Compared to the landing gear (see above), this model has fewer planes orthogonal to the cardinal axes. 26-sep and 6-sep render planes orthogonal to the cardinal axes exactly the same: one voxel thick. So orthogonal planar models offer less savings when using 6-sep. The pawn model does very well in 6-sep.

	Level 9	Level 7
6-sep	309,445	19,667
26-sep	491,624	30,825
%	0.6294	0.6380

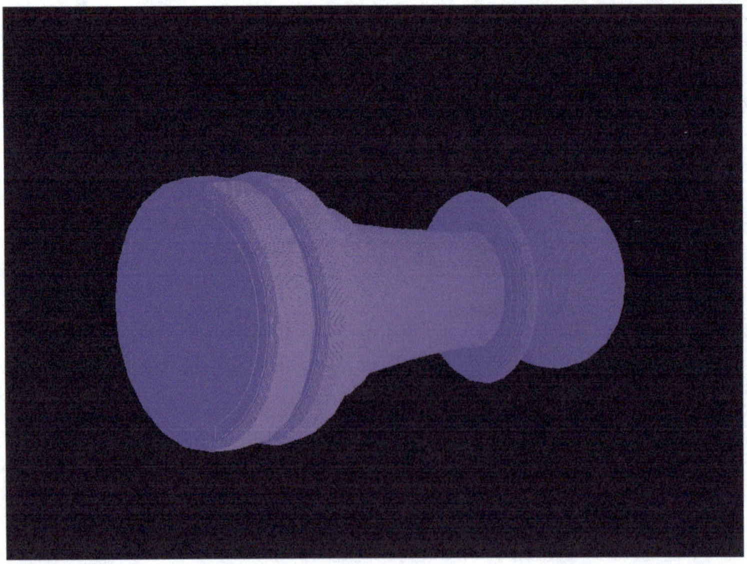

4. (Left) Pawn rendered 26-sep, 9 levels = 512 cubed resolution, with 1 additional level for false-positive checking. 491,624 voxels. This took 1 min 30 sec to compute and render. The regularity of the rasterization can be seen clearly here. 26-sep is very fast and because of its symmetry, extremely nice looking. The only drawback is the number of voxels it generates. That's why 6-sep became a second category.

5. (Right) The stellated dodecahedron unit test model. Rendered 6-sep, 7 levels = 128 cubed resolution. 38,561 voxels. Compare to the 26-sep rendering, 7 levels, at 68,339 voxels (see next item). The percentage is 0.5642, a very good savings. The reason for the large percentage difference is that 26-sep does very badly when rasterizing planes that are tilted away from the cardinal axes.

6. (Left) Stellated dodecahedron rendered 26-sep, 7 levels = 128 cubed resoliution. 68,339 voxels. The maximum savings when comparing 26-sep to 6-sep comes with a 45-degree tilt relative to one cardinal axis, combined with an additional 45-degree tilt relative to a second cardinal axis. The tetrahedron model (not shown) fulfills this condition. With that model at level 7, 6-sep generates 27,380 voxels; 26-sep generates 81,450 voxels. The percentage is 0.3361. A single face of the tetrahedron at level 9 generates 108,811 voxels in 6-sep; and 326,059 voxels in 26-sep, giving a percentage of 0.33371, suggesting that the limit of comparative efficiencies is one-third.

7. (Above) Harrier model ray traced at level 7 = 4 courses of 30 arms each. Recall that the idea is to have a dedicated microprocessor for each course. The output looks pretty ragged because of the virtual rotations. Ray tracing uses the base voxel rasterization as a reference for voxel intersections; the beautiful symmetry of the rasterization then gets lost in the ray traced output oriented towards LEDs. Things look a little better at higher resolutions, but in general this is very much a raw output. One future direction is to ray trace the original polygons instead of the voxel rasterization, but this makes ray intersections more difficult.

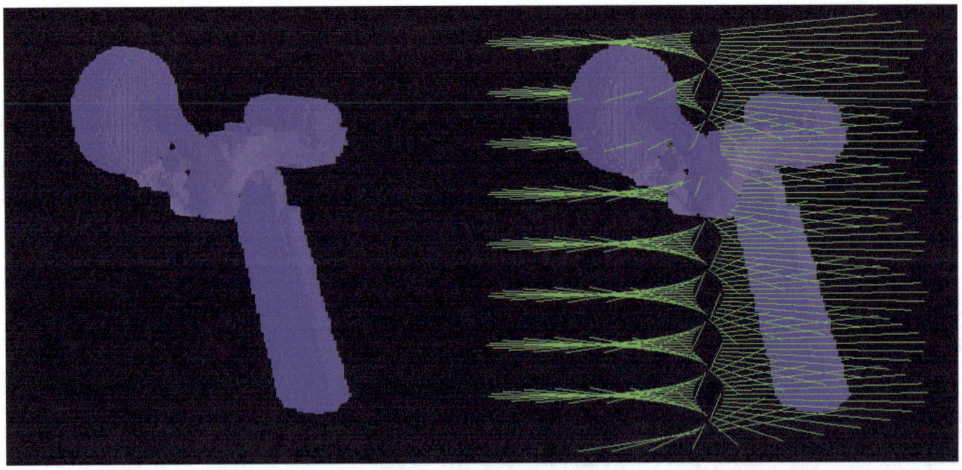

8. (Above) Harrier model ray traced at level 7 in the default position, with no virtual rotations. This looks somewhat better because at least the y-direction matches the default underlying voxel reference space, even though voxels are still slightly shifted in the XZ plane to be oriented in the direction of each armature arm – to try to simulate LED placements. The armature is shown on the right with green lines as a diagnostic. To properly sample the surfaces an interleave approach is used; both interleave passes are shown in the arm display. The ALPHA pass is offset from the BETA pass by 180 degrees. All arms are shown in their 0-degree positions.

9. (Above) Stellated dodecahedron ray traced at level 7. On the left the sample frequency is too low, leaving holes in some of the surfaces. On the right the interleave approach is used and the holes are mostly filled. You can see that part of the model is cut off on the right, on the apex of the stellation between the purple and blue. The arms are circular and cylindrical but the voxel space is rectanguloid, so proper scaling and centering of the model is required to avoid the cut off. The extreme left and right are also cut off (compare to item 6).

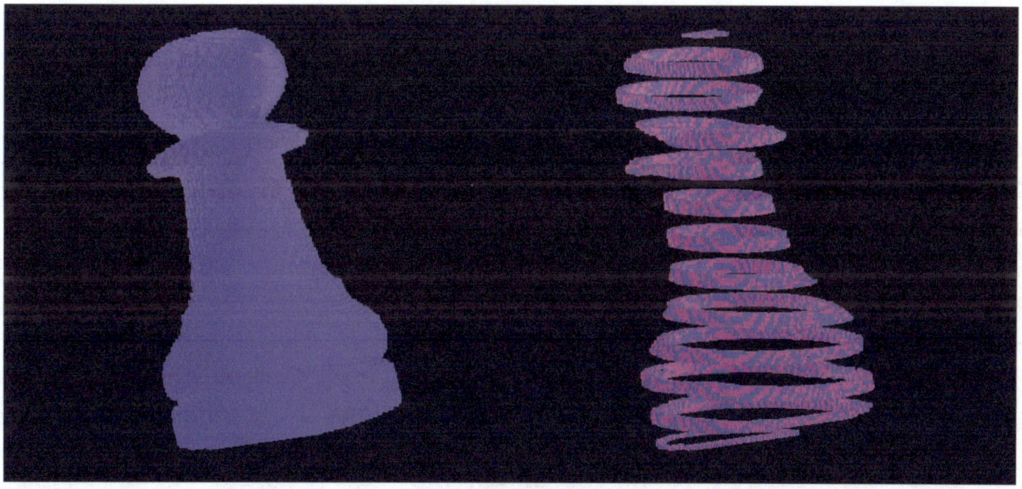

10. (Above) Pawn model ray traced at level 7. On the left all levels are shown – note the hole through the crown of the pawn. There's no way to avoid the gap which is in fact the armature axis in a rotating display device. On the right the diagnostic skipper is applied, with a setting of display 4, skip 6. The thickness of the rendering is a direct consequence of the thickness of the underlying rasterization which is used as a reference for ray intersection. The two interleave passes are shown in different colors, showing that neither pass is redundant.

11. (Right) The house model, ray traced at level 7. There are no virtual rotations and so the cardinally-oriented planes of the house look acceptable, even though this is a ray tracing and not the original voxel representation. Note the hole through the roof due to the central armature axis. Also, like the stellated dodecahedron model which has no special scaling and positioning for an armature, the edges of the walls are cut off. It's very clear how the arms simply stop where the wall rendering stops.

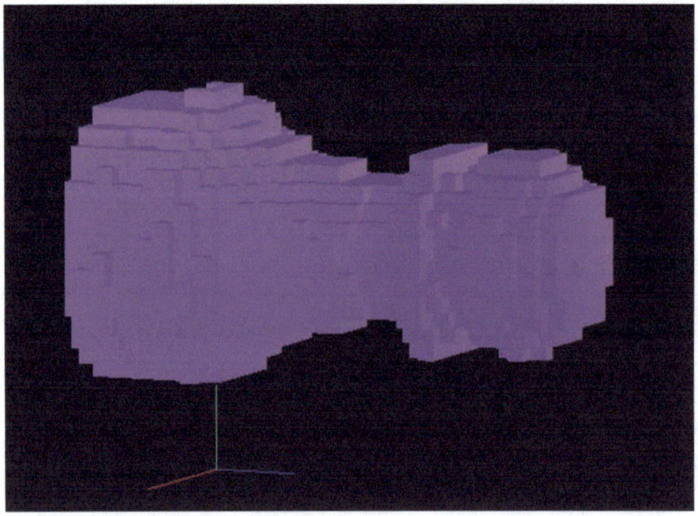

12. (Left) Pawn model rendered 26-sep at level 5 = 32 cubed resolution. All level 7 and below voxel renderings are essentially realtime on the host computer (see item 2 for specs). There are many other low resolution renderings that are sitting around, but after a while you realize that "a low resolution rendering is a low resolution rendering" and the initial fascination wears off. It's enough to know that these middle levels are middle stages of the finer, higher resolution renderings.

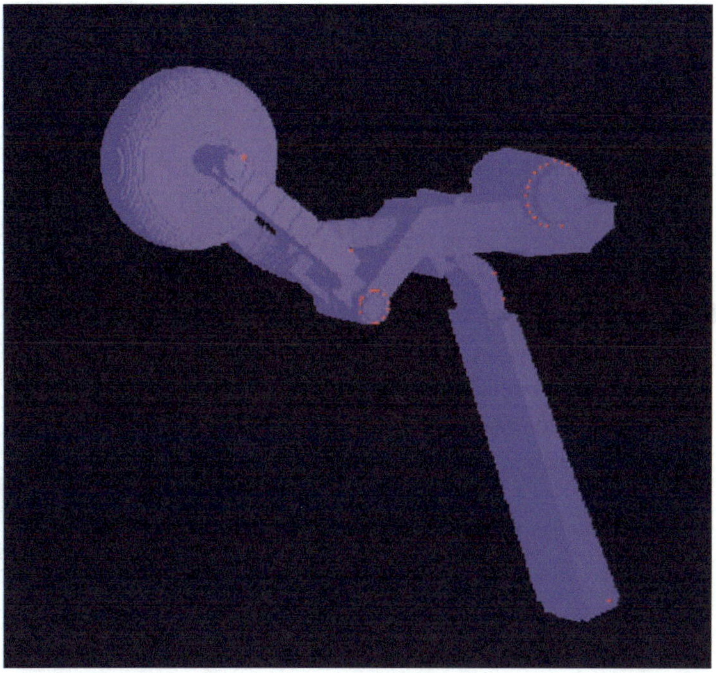

13. (Right) Harrier model rendered 26-sep at level 8 = 256 cubed resolution. False positives are checked on two additional levels (going to level 10) and shown in red. Normally the red voxels would not be displayed with false positive checking turned on. Showing the false positives can be useful as validation that the checks are really working. The 26-sep and 6-sep algorithms generate very few false positives. For example, the level 9 renderings shown in items 1 and 2 generate only generate 52 and 30 false positives for 26-sep and 6-sep respectively. For the pawn at level 9, 26-sep and 6-sep generate 13 and 51 false positives respectively. This means the voxels accepted by either algorithm are in fact actual overlaps of the triangle geometry and not mathematical errors except in a few cases.

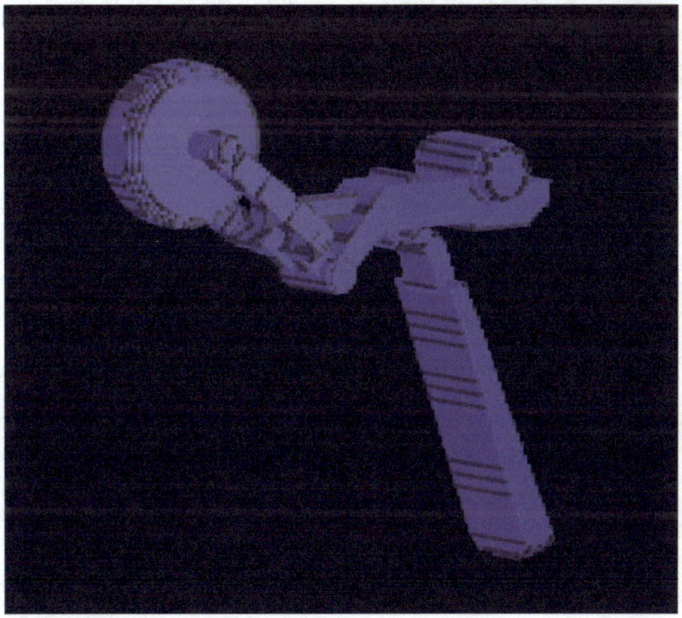

14. (Left) Harrier model rendered 26-sep at level 8 = 256 cubed resolution. This image has anti-aliasing turned on. The anti-aliasing solution simply descends an extra level and treats the 8 voxels of the extra level as a supersample of the parent voxel. But then things become complicated, as this image shows. The darker the color, the greater the transparency relative to the background – but transparency isn't turned on in OpenGL, so the darkest voxels are opaque. Note that many planes which occupy integer offsets at level 8, reside at half-integer offsets at level 9, and the entire plane is dimmed as a result. Unlike anti-aliasing in 2D, which deals with edges, anti-aliasing in 3D must deal with planes. It's an open area for research.

15. (Right) Harrier model rendered 26-sep at level 5 = 32 cubed resolution, with diagnostic mesh display turned on. The mesh display is a rendering of the entire octree, not just the terminal level. It represents the state of the octree subdivision from level to level, as the octree adaptively approaches the surface of the model, up to the maximum resolution. The mesh display is very useful for debugging, to determine the position of an individual voxel.

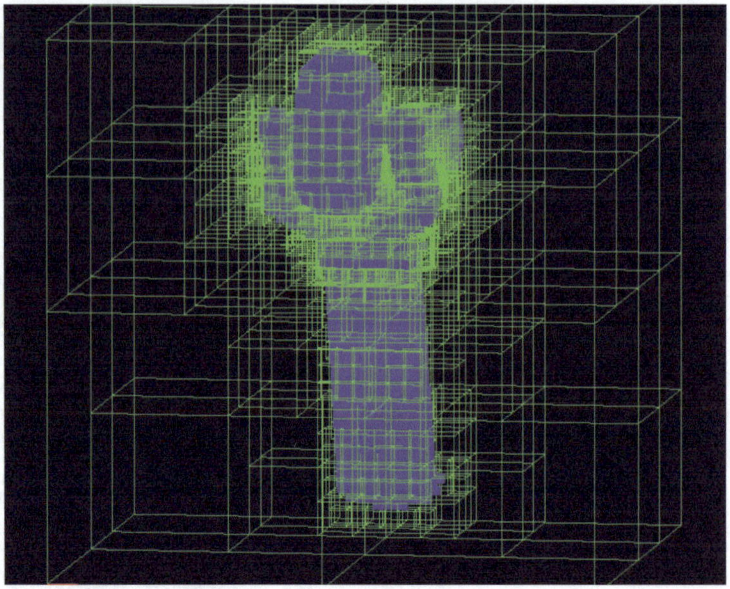

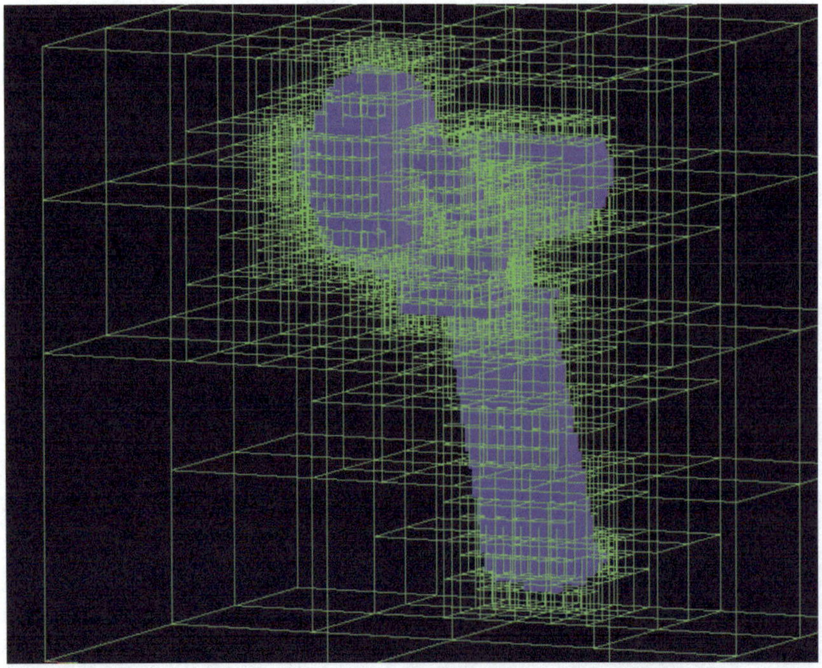

16. (Left) Harrier model rendered 26-sep at level 5 = 32 cubed resolution, with diagnostic mesh display turned on, from another angle relative to item 15.

17. (Above) An early visualization of the solid state device. Things became more refined later on, but for a quick visual this does the job. The uniformed figure mocked up in the solid state display is Jessica Alba, in a scene from the television series *Dark Angel.* A complete description of the hardware can be found in *The Cube*, available on Amazon.

Class Listing

Class Listing

Independent Modules

Exception Classes

main.cpp and Compiler Settings

ContextWorker Class Reference

Public Member Functions

ContextWorker ()
~ContextWorker ()

:: This creates the ID!
void makeContext (int start_level, int end_level, bool display, bool check_fp)

void setRaster (const unsigned int raster)
void setStartAndEndLevels(int start_level, int end_level)
int getContextID ()
void CopyOverTriangles (Vector<BasicTriangle * > &geom)

:: force the user to pass in an existing GeomWorker instance
void CopyOverTriangles (GeomWorker &orig_geom_w)

Static Public Member Functions

static Context& getContext (int contextID)

:: OctreeThread does this to get rid of stale pointers for next round.
static voidCleanUp ()

Private Attributes

int my_count
Context *context

Static Private Attributes

static int count = 0

:: this goes with each OctreeWorker instantiation
static Vector<Context * > instance

Detailed Description

Manages the current “context,” e.g. use, of the octree for iteration and processing.

Constructor & Destructor Documentation

ContextWorker::ContextWorker () [inline]
{}

```
ContextWorker::~ContextWorker ()
{
    if (context != NULL)
       delete context;
}
```

Member Function Documentation

```
// OctreeThread does this to get rid of stale pointers for next round.
void ContextWorker::CleanUp () [static]
{
    instance.clear();
    count = 0;
}

// force the user to pass in an existing GeomWorker instance
void ContextWorker::CopyOverTriangles (GeomWorker &orig_geom_w)
{
    Context * context = instance[my_count];

    // alias test
     if (&orig_geom_w == &context->geom_w)
       return;

    // transfer existing triangles to this instantiation
    context->geom_w.transferTriangles(orig_geom_w.getTriangleList());
}

void ContextWorker::CopyOverTriangles (Vector<BasicTriangle * > &geom)
{
    Context * context = instance[my_count];

    // convert to internal Triangle format
    context->geom_w.TriangleConvert2MasterList(geom);
}

Context& ContextWorker::getContext (int contextID) [static]
{

    if (contextID < 0 || contextID > instance.size() - 1)
       throw IndexOutOfBoundsException("Context ID error.");

    return *(instance[contextID]);
}

int ContextWorker::getContextID ()
{
```

```
    return   my_count;
}

// This creates the ID!
// internal context will be copied when pushed onto instance array
// the private member then goes out of scope. Hide all this from user.
void ContextWorker::makeContext (int start_level, int end_level, bool display, bool check_fp)
{
    context  =  new   Context;

    context->start_level  = start_level;
    context->terminal_level  = end_level;
    context->buffer_display_data  = display;
    context->check_false_pos  = check_fp;

    instance.push_back(context);
    my_count  =  count++;
    context->ID  =  my_count;
}

void ContextWorker::setRaster (const unsigned int raster)
{
    Context  *  context  =  instance[my_count];

   context->geom_w.setRaster(raster);
}

void ContextWorker::setStartAndEndLevels(int start_level, int end_level)
{
   context->start_level = start_level;
   context->terminal_level = end_level;
}
```

Associated Data Holders

```
// since triangle scaling will be different with different
// instances of OctreeWorker, need to copy the triangle list
// to each instance. For the current configuration there are
// two instances: 1) the main iteration; 2) false positives.
// False positives reuse the triangles stored in context 2.

/// Flags and control data for a "context"

struct Context {
    int start_level, terminal_level, ID;
    bool buffer_display_data, check_false_pos;
    GeomWorker geom_w;
```

```
    Context(int start = 0, int terminal = 0,
            bool buffer = true, bool check_fp = false) :
        start_level(start),
        terminal_level(terminal),
        buffer_display_data(buffer),
        check_false_pos(check_fp){}

    Context operator=( Context rhs)
    {
        if (this != &rhs)        // alias test
        {
            start_level = rhs.start_level;
            terminal_level = rhs.terminal_level;
            ID = rhs.ID;
            buffer_display_data = rhs.buffer_display_data;
            check_false_pos = rhs.check_false_pos;
            geom_w = rhs.geom_w;
        }
        return *this;            // return pointer to self
    }
};
```

The documentation for this class was generated from the following files:
- ContextWorker.h
- ContextWorker.cpp
- Global.cpp

Display Class Reference

Public Member Functions

Display (Context&mcontext)
~Display ()
void displayVoxel (NodeGroup *group, const Level&level)

:: quick and dirty way to display false positives
:: takes the original group, not the copy.
void displayVoxelFP (NodeGroup *group, const Level&level)

:: do this even if display is off, to release the caller!
void terminateTransfer ()

:: Note that level comes in as 0, but eval level is level + 1 = 1,
:: so we get the first subdivision of the unit cube.
void MakeMeshData (NodeGroup *ng_ptr, int octant, int level)

void terminateMesh ()
void MakeRayData (ReducedRay *ray)

:: caller knows enough to write n levels
void terminateLevel ()

Private Member Functions

void AntiAlias (NodeGroup *group)
void BlendTop (NodeGroup *group)

:: Blend colors for all triangles.
void Blend (NodeGroup *group, int octant, TriangleList *tri_list, float3& color)

:: put the context check here: allows color to be computed.
void queueVoxel (const float3& color, const ushort3& coord)

void StoreColor (float3& color, uchar3& ncolor)

Private Attributes

Context& context

Detailed Description

Set up the display data for each voxel
to be transfered back to OpenGL via thread.

Constructor & Destructor Documentation

```
Display::Display (Context&mcontext) [inline]
: context(mcontext) {}

Display::~Display () [inline]
{}
```

Member Function Documentation

```
void Display::AntiAlias (NodeGroup *group) [private]
{
    unsigned char testbit = 0x01;
    int i;
    float3 color;
    Vector<color3> colors(OCTANTS);

    if (group->geom_stat == 0x00)
        return;

    TriangleList *tri_list = context.geom_w.getTriangleList();

    // we take all octants, even empty ones
    for (i = 0; i < OCTANTS; ++i) {
        if (group->geom_stat & testbit) {
            Blend(group, i, tri_list, color);
            colors[i].r = color.x;
            colors[i].g = color.y;
            colors[i].b = color.z;
        } else {
            // make aa go to black background.
            // for 3D display this is a voltage
            colors[i].r = 0.0;
            colors[i].g = 0.0;
            colors[i].b = 0.0;
        }
        testbit <<= 1;
    }
    color.x = color.y = color.z = 0.0;
    for (i = 0; i < 8; ++i) {
        color.x += colors[i].r;
        color.y += colors[i].g;
        color.z += colors[i].b;
    }
```

```
    color.x  /= 8.0;
    color.y  /= 8.0;
    color.z  /= 8.0;

    // use the coord for this node group which is stored with the parent
    int  idx = group->node_idx  - 1;
    ushort3   &coord  = group->parent->node[idx].coord;
    queueVoxel(color, coord);
    StoreColor(color, group->parent->node[i].color);
}

// Blend colors for all triangles.
void Display::Blend (NodeGroup *group, intoctant, TriangleList *tri_list, float3 &color) [private]
{
    int  i, begin,  end, tri_idx,  count;

    // these will be valid for passed octant
    begin = group->span[octant].begin;
    end = group->span[octant].end;
    count = 0;
    color.x  = color.y  = color.z  = 0.0;

    for  (i = begin; i  <=  end; ++i) {
      tri_idx = group->pairs->list[i]->tri_idx;
      if  (tri_idx ==  INVALID)
          continue;
      Triangle  * tri = tri_list->list[tri_idx];
      color.x  += tri->color.r;
      color.y  += tri->color.g;
      color.z  += tri->color.b;
      ++count;
    }
    if  (count  >  1) {
      color.x  /= (float)count;
      color.y  /= (float)count;
      color.z  /= (float)count;
   }
}

void Display::BlendTop (NodeGroup *group) [private]
{
    unsigned   char  testbit = 0x01;
    int  i;
    float3   color;

    if  (group->geom_stat  == 0x00)
       return;

    // get the triangle list pointer
```

```
    TriangleList  * tri_list =  context.geom_w.getTriangleList();

    // look at all the octants for this level
    for  (i=0; i<OCTANTS; ++i) {
       if  (group->geom_stat   &  testbit) {
          // look at contributions of individual triangle colors
          Blend(group, i, tri_list, color);
          ushort3   &coord  = group->node[i].coord;
          queueVoxel(color, coord);
          StoreColor(color, group->node[i].color);
       }
       testbit  <<= 1;
    }
}

void Display::displayVoxel (NodeGroup *group, const Level &level)
{

    if  (level.eval   <   context.terminal_level || context.ID != 0)
       return;

    if  (g_antialias)
       AntiAlias(group);
    else
       BlendTop(group);
}

// quick and dirty way to display false positives
// takes the original group, not the copy.
void Display::displayVoxelFP (NodeGroup *group, const Level &level)
{
    unsigned   char  testbit = 0x01;
    int  i;
    float3   color;

    // false positive in RED, per convention
    color.x  = 1.0;
    color.y  = 0.0;
    color.z  = 0.0;

    // display original octants in RED
    for  (i = 0; i  <   OCTANTS; ++i) {
       if  (group->geom_stat   &  testbit) {
          ushort3   &coord  = group->node[i].coord;
          queueVoxel(color, coord);
          StoreColor(color, group->node[i].color);
       }
       testbit  <<= 1;
    }
```

```
}

// Note that level comes in as 0, but eval level is level + 1 = 1,
// so we get the first subdivision of the unit cube.
void Display::MakeMeshData (NodeGroup *ng_ptr, int octant, int level)

{

    if (!context.buffer_display_data)
       return;

    // get N for terminal level
    int Nt = context.geom_w.NewN(context.terminal_level);
    int N = context.geom_w.NewN(level + 1);

    // if terminal level is 4, and current level is 1, we have:
    // level 1 = 2 ; level 4 = 16, so: 16 / 2 = 8.
    // 0 * 8 = 0 ; 1 * 8 = 8; [0 - 1] = 0 to 8; [1 - 2] = 8 to 16.
    int scale = Nt / N;

   MeshData * md = new MeshData;
   md->length = scale;

    ushort3 &coord = ng_ptr->node[octant].coord;

    // get XYZ offset for current group, but scaled to terminal level N
    md->p1.x = coord.x * scale;
    md->p1.y = coord.y * scale;
    md->p1.z = coord.z * scale;

    my_stat_thread.EnqueueM(md);
}

void Display::MakeRayData (ReducedRay *ray)
{
    if (!context.buffer_display_data)
       return;
    my_stat_thread.EnqueueR(ray);
}

// put the context check here: allows color to be computed.
void Display::queueVoxel (const float3 &color, const ushort3 &coord) [private]
{
    int x, y, z;

    if (!context.buffer_display_data)
       return;

   x = coord.x;
```

```
   y = coord.y;
   z = coord.z;

    VoxelData  *vd =  new   VoxelData(x, y, z);
   vd->r  = color.x;
   vd->g  = color.y;
   vd->b  = color.z;

    my_stat_thread.Enqueue(vd);
}

void Display::StoreColor (float3 &color, uchar3 &ncolor) [private]
{
   ncolor.x  = (unsigned  char)lroundf(color.x  * 255.0);
   ncolor.y  = (unsigned  char)lroundf(color.y  * 255.0);
   ncolor.z  = (unsigned  char)lroundf(color.z  * 255.0);
}

// caller knows enough to get n levels
void Display::terminateLevel ()
{

    if  (!context.buffer_display_data)
       return;

    ReducedRay  *ray =  new   ReducedRay;
    ray->level  = -1;
    // no count, no list
    my_stat_thread.EnqueueR(ray);
}

void Display::terminateMesh ()
{
    int   x,  y,  z;

    if  (!context.buffer_display_data)
       return;

   x = y = z = -1;
   MeshData  *md =  new   MeshData;
   md->p1.x  =  x;
   md->p1.y  =  y;
   md->p1.z  =  z;

    my_stat_thread.EnqueueM(md);
}

// do this even if display is off, to release the caller!
```

```
// octree works in positive coordinates:
// send negative coords to terminate transfer
void Display::terminateTransfer ()
{
    int   x,  y,  z;

    // this is a kluge to avoid adding an extra terminator during
    // false positive processing, which has an ID of 1.
    if  (context.ID  != 0)
       return;

    x = y = z = -1;
    VoxelData  *vd =  new   VoxelData(x, y, z);
    my_stat_thread.Enqueue(vd);
}
```

The documentation for this class was generated from the following files:
- Display.h
- Display.cpp

FPUtil Class Reference

Public Member Functions

FPUtil ()
~FPUtil ()

:: precision should typically be 1.0e-10
bool equalBounds (double lhs, double rhs, double precision)

bool equalBoundsf (float lhs, float rhs, float precision)
bool greaterEqualBounds (double lhs, double rhs, double precision)
bool greaterEqualBoundsf (float lhs, float rhs, float precision)
bool greaterBounds (double lhs, double rhs, double precision)
bool greaterBoundsf (float lhs, float rhs, float precision)
bool lessThanBounds (double lhs, double rhs, double precision)
bool lessThanBoundsf (float lhs, float rhs, float precision)
bool lessEqualBounds (double lhs, double rhs, double precision)
bool lessEqualBoundsf (float lhs, float rhs, float precision)

:: floor will return flakey values: check them!
double checkfloor (double value)
float checkfloorf (float value)

double max (double v1, double v2)

Detailed Description

Floating point utility for geometry comparisons.

Constructor & Destructor Documentation

FPUtil::FPUtil () [inline]
{}

FPUtil::~FPUtil () [inline]
{}

Member Function Documentation

```
// floor will return flakey values: check them!
double FPUtil::checkfloor (double value)
{
```

```
    double  checkval, near_one;

    // assume value comes up short by a hair's breadth (5.9999 for 6)
    checkval = floor(value);
    near_one =  value  - checkval;
    // - 6.00001 ->  - 7 : near_one = 0.99999
    // 3.9999 ->  3 : near_one = 0.99999
    if  (equalBounds(near_one, 1.0,  PRECISION))
        return  checkval + 1.0;
    return  checkval;
}

float FPUtil::checkfloorf (float value)
{
    float  checkval, near_one;

    // assume value comes up short by a hair's breadth (5.9999 for 6)
    checkval = floorf(value);
    near_one =  value  - checkval;
    // - 6.00001 ->  - 7 : near_one = 0.99999
    // 3.9999 ->  3 : near_one = 0.99999
    if  (equalBoundsf(near_one, 1.0,  PRECISION))
        return  checkval + 1.0;
    return  checkval;
}

// precision should typically be 1.0e-10
bool FPUtil::equalBounds (double lhs, double rhs, double precision)
{
    double  diff;

    diff = fabs(lhs - rhs);
    if  (diff  <  precision)
       return   true;
    return   false;
}

bool FPUtil::equalBoundsf (float lhs, float rhs, float precision)
{
    float  diff;

    diff = fabsf(lhs - rhs);
    if  (diff  <  precision)
       return   true;
    return   false;
}

bool FPUtil::greaterBounds (double lhs, double rhs, double precision)
{
```

```
    double  diff;

    if  (equalBounds(lhs, rhs, precision))
       return   false;

    diff = lhs - rhs;
    if  (diff  >  0.0)
       return   true;
    return   false;
}

bool FPUtil::greaterBoundsf (float lhs, float rhs, float precision)
{
    float  diff;

    if  (equalBoundsf(lhs, rhs, precision))
       return   false;

    diff = lhs - rhs;
    if  (diff  >  0.0)
       return   true;
    return   false;
}

bool FPUtil::greaterEqualBounds (double lhs, double rhs, double precision)
{
    double  diff;

    if  (equalBounds(lhs, rhs, precision))
       return   true;

    diff = lhs - rhs;
    if  (diff  >  0.0)
       return   true;
    return   false;
}

bool FPUtil::greaterEqualBoundsf (float lhs, float rhs, float precision)
{
    float  diff;

    if  (equalBoundsf(lhs, rhs, precision))
       return   true;

    diff = lhs - rhs;
    if  (diff  >  0.0)
       return   true;
    return   false;
}
```

```
bool FPUtil::lessEqualBounds (double lhs, double rhs, double precision)
{
   double  diff;

   if  (equalBounds(lhs, rhs, precision))
      return  true;

   diff = lhs - rhs;
   if  (diff  <  0.0)
      return  true;
   return  false;
}

bool FPUtil::lessEqualBoundsf (float lhs, float rhs, float precision)
{
   float  diff;

   if  (equalBoundsf(lhs, rhs, precision))
      return  true;

   diff = lhs - rhs;
   if  (diff  <  0.0)
      return  true;
   return  false;
}

bool FPUtil::lessThanBounds (double lhs, double rhs, double precision)
{
   double  diff;

   if  (equalBounds(lhs, rhs, precision))
      return  false;

   diff = lhs - rhs;
   if  (diff  <  0.0)
      return  true;
   return  false;
}

bool FPUtil::lessThanBoundsf (float lhs, float rhs, float precision)
{
   float  diff;

   if  (equalBoundsf(lhs, rhs, precision))
      return  false;

   diff = lhs - rhs;
   if  (diff  <  0.0)
      return  true;
```

```
   return   false;
}

double FPUtil::max (double v1, double v2)
{
   if  (v1   >   v2)
      return   v1;
   return   v2;
}
```

Local Data

```
static const double PRECISION = 1.0e-10;
static const float PRECISIONf = 1.0e-5;
```

The documentation for this class was generated from the following files:
- FPUtil.h
- FPUtil.cpp

GeomUtil Class Reference

Public Member Functions

GeomUtil ()
~GeomUtil ()
GeomUtil operator= (GeomUtil rhs)

::)First thing to do at every level switch (LevelWorker.cpp)
int NewN (int level, int terminal_level, bool is_terminal)

int getN (int level)
voidSetBBoxDeltas ()

:: cascaded from GeomWorker
unsigned int setRaster (const unsigned int value)

unsigned int getRaster ()

:: Master bbox (to be scaled at all levels)
void BoundingBox (float3 &tri_bbox0, float3 &tri_bbox1, float3 &v0, float3 &v1, float3 &v2)

void ScaleTriangleBBox (float3 &tri_bbox0, float3 &tri_bbox1, Triangle *tri)

:: compute integer bbox
void ComputeIntegerBBox (int3 &tri_bbox0i, int3 &tri_bbox1i, const float3 &tri_bbox0, const float3 &tri_bbox1)

void makeSpheres (Triangle *tri)
void makeHaloes (Triangle *tri)

:: only need to init these once per level
void InitPlaneTestVars (const float3 &n, const float3 &v0, Triangle *tri)

:: coord is the voxel base coordinate (integer space)
bool PlaneTest (const ushort3 &coord, const float3 &n, Triangle *tri)

:: These top routines deal with the triangle's dominant axis.
bool RasterizeTop (const ushort3 &coord, Triangle *tri)

bool Rasterize_26sepTop (const ushort3 &coord, Triangle *tri)
void swap (float4 &a, float4 &b)
float3 min3 (const float4 a, const float4 b, const float4 c)
float3 max3 (const float4 a, const float4 b, const float4 c)
float3 cross (const float3 &op1, const float3 &op2)
float3 anti_cross (const float3 &op1, const float3 &op2)
int min (int a, int b)

int max (int a, int b)
void copy_float3 (const float3 &source, float3 &dest)
void copy_float4 (const float4 &source, float4 &dest)

:: perform triangle setup : this is VoxelPipe math for 26-sep,
:: but is slightly modified (as a numeric bugfix) to match the
:: Schwarz & Seidel math for "conservative" (26-sep).
template<int32 AXIS>void triangle_setup (Triangle *tri, float3 &n_delta_u, float3 &n_delta_v, float3 &a)

:: perform triangle setup 6 separating case
template<int32 AXIS>void triangle_setup_6sep (Triangle *tri, FineVars &fine, short select)

:: perform plane setup
template<int32 AXIS>void plane_setup (const float3 &v0, const float3 &n, float4 &plane_eq)
template<int32 AXIS>void plane_setup_6sep (const float3 &v0, const float3 &n, float4 &plane_eq)

Private Member Functions

:: called by constructor
void Init ()

void MakeBBoxDelta (float3 &delta)
void MakeInvBBoxDelta (float3 &delta)
bool centerTest (const float3 coord, const float3 center, float radius)
void EdgeTests (const ushort3 &coord, Triangle *tri, short &facecount)
bool StraightToSphere (const float3 vox_center, const float3 center, float radius, float &dist)
bool TrivertSpheres (Triangle *tri, const float3 vox_center)
bool OneOfSixToSphere (const float3 vox_center, const float3 center, float radius, int dom_axis)
bool OneOfSixToEmbeddingPlane (const float3 vox_center, Triangle *tri, int dom_axis, float range_max, float3 &rangelist)
bool EmbeddedNormal (const float3 vox_center, Triangle *tri, int dom_axis)
bool LookAheadChildrenToEmbedding (const float3 vox_center, Triangle *tri, int dom_axis, float last_range, float max_range, short cur_level, short deep)
bool OneOfSixToTriIntersect (const float3 vox_center, Triangle *tri, int dom_axis)
void AlphaBetaIntersection (Triangle *tri, unsigned short select, const float2 alpha_beta, float3 &P)
bool EmbeddingPlaneIntersection (const float3 vox_center, Triangle *tri, const float3 D, float num, float3 &V)
void getOrder (int *order, int dom_axis)
bool checkRange (const float3 rangelist, float last_range)
bool Intersects (Triangle *tri, float2 &v_p0, float2 &v_p1, unsigned short select)
int pointPos (float2 &p1, float2 &p2, float2 &v_p0, float2 &v_p1)
bool Inside (Triangle *tri, const float2 vox_center, const float2 direction, unsigned short select, float2 &alpha_beta, bool use_halo, unsigned char &checks)
void makeBigSphere (const float3 v0, const float3 v1, const float3 v2, float3 &center, float &radius)
void makeLittleSphere (const float3 v0, const float3 v1, const float3 v2, float3 &center, float &radius)
void makeHalo (const float2 c0, const float2 c1, const float2 c2, Triangle *tri, int select)
void opposingDistance (const float2 midp, float2 &reach, const float2 v0, const float2 v1, const

float2 opp)
bool strainTestX (const float2 v0, const float2 v1, const float2 reach, const float2 midp, const float2 prime, const float2 opp)
bool strainTestY (const float2 v0, const float2 v1, const float2 reach, const float2 midp, const float2 prime, const float2 opp)
void maxAwayFromEdge (const float2 reach, const float2 v0, const float2 v1, const float2 midp, float2 &ortho)
void findParallel (const float2 ortho, const float2 v0, const float2 v1, float3 &coeff)
void intersectPair (const float3 coeff1, const float3 coeff2, float2 &hp)
bool getSlopeIntercept (float2 p1, float2 p2, float &m, float &b, float3 &coeff)
void getWorkingRadius (const float2 p1, const float2 p2, const float2 p3, float2 center, float &radius)
void Bisector (const float2 p1, const float2 p2, const float2 p3, float &la1, float &lb1, float &lc1)
void getOriginAndSides (const float3 v0, const float3 v1, const float3 v2, UVPack &uvpack)
void makeOrigin (UVPack &uvpack)
void makeDirectionCosines (UVPack &uvpack)
void length3 (const float3 v0, const float3 v1, float &len01)
void length3 (const double3 v0, const double3 v1, double &len01)
short dominantCoord (const float3 v0, const float3 v1)
void Bbox (const float2 c0, const float2 c1, const float2 c2, float2 &min, float2 &max)
void getP1P3 (const float3 v0, const float3 v1, float3 &p1, float3 &p3)

:: 26-separating raster using basic VoxelPipe code and triangle setup
template<int32 AXIS>bool rasterize (const ushort3 &coord, Triangle *tri)

:: 6-separating "thin" raster
template<int32 AXIS>bool rasterize_6sep (const ushort3 &coord, Triangle *tri)

:: 26-separating raster (Schwarz & Seidel 3 overlap tests)
template<int32 AXIS>boolrasterize_26sep (const ushort3&coord, Triangle *tri)

template<int32 AXIS>bool IntersectsTop (const ushort3 &coord, Triangle *tri)

Private Attributes

int N
short g_level
short g_terminal_level
bool terminal
unsigned int raster
float3 bbox0
float3 bbox1
float3 bbox_delta
float3 inv_bbox_delta
FPUtil fp_math

Detailed Description

Geometry utilities for rasterization of triangles

Constructor & Destructor Documentation

```
GeomUtil::GeomUtil () [inline]
{
  Init();
}

GeomUtil::~GeomUtil () [inline]
{}
```

Member Function Documentation

```
void GeomUtil::AlphaBetaIntersection (Triangle *tri, unsigned short select, const float2 alpha_beta,
float3 &P) [private]
{
    float3  lefthand, righthand;
    float   alpha, beta;

    // using alpha and beta to get point-intersect from which
    // to compute the orthogonal  "range"...
    float3  v0  =  make_float3(tri->fine.c0[select].x,
                     tri->fine.c0[select].y,
                     tri->fine.cw[select].x);     // v0.w
    float3  v1  =  make_float3(tri->fine.c1[select].x,
                     tri->fine.c1[select].y,
                     tri->fine.cw[select].y);     // v1.w
    float3  v2  =  make_float3(tri->fine.c2[select].x,
                     tri->fine.c2[select].y,
                     tri->fine.cw[select].z);     // v2.w
    // are we within range?
   alpha = alpha_beta.x;
   beta = alpha_beta.y;

    // actual intersection (Graphics Gems, Eq. 4 p.391)
   lefthand.x  = alpha * (v1.x  - v0.x);
   lefthand.y  = alpha * (v1.y  - v0.y);
   lefthand.z  = alpha * (v1.z  - v0.z);
   righthand.x  = beta * (v2.x  - v0.x);
   righthand.y  = beta * (v2.y  - v0.y);
   righthand.z  = beta * (v2.z  - v0.z);

   P.x  = (lefthand.x  + righthand.x) + v0.x;
   P.y  = (lefthand.y  + righthand.y) + v0.y;
   P.z  = (lefthand.z  + righthand.z) + v0.z;
}
```

float3 GeomUtil::anti_cross (const float3 &op1, const float3 &op2)

```
{
    return  make_float3(
          op1.z*op2.y  - op1.y*op2.z,
          op1.x*op2.z  - op1.z*op2.x,
          op1.y*op2.x  - op1.x*op2.y  );
}
```

void GeomUtil::Bbox (const float2 c0, const float2 c1, const float2 c2, float2 &min, float2 &max) [private]

```
{
   min.x  = c0.x;
   min.y  = c0.y;

   min.x  = fminf( c1.x, min.x  );
   min.y  = fminf( c1.y, min.y  );

   min.x  = fminf( c2.x, min.x  );
   min.y  = fminf( c2.y, min.y  );

   max.x  = c0.x;
   max.y  = c0.y;

   max.x  = fmaxf( c1.x, max.x  );
   max.y  = fmaxf( c1.y, max.y  );

   max.x  = fmaxf( c2.x, max.x  );
   max.y  = fmaxf( c2.y, max.y  );
}
```

void GeomUtil::Bisector (const float2 p1, const float2 p2, const float2 p3, float &la1, float &lb1, float &lc1) [private]

```
{
    float  m1, m2, b1, b2, d1, d2;
    float  k1, k2;
    float3  coeff1, coeff2;
    bool  vertical1, vertical2, choose_b1;

   vertical1 =  getSlopeIntercept(p1, p2, m1, b1, coeff1);
   vertical2 =  getSlopeIntercept(p2, p3, m2, b2, coeff2);

    // first get bisector for sides 1/2 and 2/3
    short  negative = 0;
    if  (m1  <  0.0f)
       ++negative;
    if  (m2  <  0.0f)
       ++negative;

    // get opposite point: p3
```

```
// don't need to permute signs if using original m
if (m1 < 0.0f)
  d1 = -(coeff1.x * p3.x + coeff1.y * p3.y + coeff1.z);
else
  d1 = (coeff1.x * p3.x + coeff1.y * p3.y + coeff1.z);
if (d1 < 0.0f)
  ++negative;

// for other side, opposite point is p1
if (m2 < 0.0f)
  d2 = -(coeff2.x * p1.x + coeff2.y * p1.y + coeff2.z);
else
  d2 = (coeff2.x * p1.x + coeff2.y * p1.y + coeff2.z);
if (d2 < 0.0f)
  ++negative;

choose_b1 = false;
if (negative == 1 || negative == 3) // odd
   choose_b1 = true;

if (vertical1 || vertical2) {
   // I think these are redundant in terms of the numerics,
   // but the logic is different for verticals, so keep
   // the redundant equations with the special logic.
   if (vertical1) {
      // k1 is a no-go
      k2 = sqrt(coeff2.x * coeff2.x + coeff2.y * coeff2.y);
      if (p1.y < p2.y) {
        la1 = coeff2.x + k2;
        lc1 = coeff2.z + coeff1.z * k2;
      } else {
        la1 = coeff2.x - k2;
        lc1 = coeff2.z - coeff1.z * k2;
      }
      lb1 = coeff2.y;
   } else {
      // k2 is a no go
      k1 = sqrt(coeff1.x * coeff1.x + coeff1.y * coeff1.y);
      if (p2.y < p3.y) {
        la1 = coeff1.x + k1;
        lc1 = coeff1.z + coeff2.z * k1;
      } else {
        la1 = coeff1.x - k1;
        lc1 = coeff1.z - coeff2.z * k1;
      }
      lb1 = coeff1.y;
   }
} else {
   k1 = sqrt(coeff1.x * coeff1.x + coeff1.y * coeff1.y);
```

```
      k2 = sqrt(coeff2.x  * coeff2.x  + coeff2.y  * coeff2.y);
       if  (choose_b1) {
         la1 = coeff1.x  * k2 + coeff2.x  * k1;
         lb1 = coeff1.y  * k2 + coeff2.y  * k1;
         lc1 = coeff1.z  * k2 + coeff2.z  * k1;
      } else {
         la1 = coeff1.x  * k2 - coeff2.x  * k1;
         lb1 = coeff1.y  * k2 - coeff2.y  * k1;
         lc1 = coeff1.z  * k2 - coeff2.z  * k1;
      }
   }
}

// Master bbox (to be scaled at all levels)
void GeomUtil::BoundingBox (float3 &tri_bbox0, float3 &tri_bbox1, float3 &v0, float3 &v1, float3 &v2)
{
   tri_bbox0.x  = v0.x  -  bbox0.x;
   tri_bbox0.y  = v0.y  -  bbox0.y;
   tri_bbox0.z  = v0.z  -  bbox0.z;
   tri_bbox0.x  = fminf( v1.x  -  bbox0.x, tri_bbox0.x  );
   tri_bbox0.y  = fminf( v1.y  -  bbox0.y, tri_bbox0.y  );
   tri_bbox0.z  = fminf( v1.z  -  bbox0.z, tri_bbox0.z  );
   tri_bbox0.x  = fminf( v2.x  -  bbox0.x, tri_bbox0.x  );
   tri_bbox0.y  = fminf( v2.y  -  bbox0.y, tri_bbox0.y  );
   tri_bbox0.z  = fminf( v2.z  -  bbox0.z, tri_bbox0.z  );

   tri_bbox1.x  = v0.x  -  bbox0.x;
   tri_bbox1.y  = v0.y  -  bbox0.y;
   tri_bbox1.z  = v0.z  -  bbox0.z;
   tri_bbox1.x  = fmaxf( v1.x  -  bbox0.x, tri_bbox1.x  );
   tri_bbox1.y  = fmaxf( v1.y  -  bbox0.y, tri_bbox1.y  );
   tri_bbox1.z  = fmaxf( v1.z  -  bbox0.z, tri_bbox1.z  );
   tri_bbox1.x  = fmaxf( v2.x  -  bbox0.x, tri_bbox1.x  );
   tri_bbox1.y  = fmaxf( v2.y  -  bbox0.y, tri_bbox1.y  );
   tri_bbox1.z  = fmaxf( v2.z  -  bbox0.z, tri_bbox1.z  );
}

bool GeomUtil::centerTest (const float3 coord, const float3 center, float radius) [private]
{
    float  dx, dy, dz, dist;

   dx = vox_center.x - center.x;
   dy = vox_center.y - center.y;
   dz = vox_center.z - center.z;

   dist = dx * dx + dy * dy + dz * dz;
    return  (dist  <= radius * radius);
}
```

```
bool GeomUtil::checkRange (const float3 rangelist, float last_range) [private]
{
    // These are axes, not a coordinates
    if (rangelist.x   <= last_range)
       return   true;
    if (rangelist.y   <= last_range)
       return   true;
    if (rangelist.z   <= last_range)
       return   true;
    return   false;
}

// compute integer bbox
void GeomUtil::ComputeIntegerBBox (int3 &tri_bbox0i, int3 &tri_bbox1i, const float3 &tri_bbox0,
const float3 &tri_bbox1)
{
   tri_bbox0i.x  =  min(  max(  int( tri_bbox0.x  ), 0 ),  N  );
   tri_bbox0i.y  =  min(  max(  int( tri_bbox0.y  ), 0 ),  N  );
   tri_bbox0i.z  =  min(  max(  int( tri_bbox0.z  ), 0 ),  N  );

   tri_bbox1i.x  =  min(  max(  int( ceilf( tri_bbox1.x  ) ), 0 ),  N  );
   tri_bbox1i.y  =  min(  max(  int( ceilf( tri_bbox1.y  ) ), 0 ),  N  );
   tri_bbox1i.z  =  min(  max(  int( ceilf( tri_bbox1.z  ) ), 0 ),  N  );
}

void GeomUtil::copy_float3 (const float3 &source, float3 &dest)
{
   dest.x  = source.x;
   dest.y  = source.y;
   dest.z  = source.z;
}

void GeomUtil::copy_float4 (const float4 &source, float4 &dest)
{
   dest.x  = source.x;
   dest.y  = source.y;
   dest.z  = source.z;
   dest.w  = source.w;
}

float3 GeomUtil::cross (const float3 &op1, const float3 &op2)
{
    return   make_float3(
          op1.y*op2.z  - op1.z*op2.y,
          op1.z*op2.x  - op1.x*op2.z,
          op1.x*op2.y  - op1.y*op2.x  );
}

short GeomUtil::dominantCoord (const float3 v0, const float3 v1) [private]
```

```
{
    float  diff1, diff2, diff3;

   diff1 = fabs(v0.x  - v1.x);
   diff2 = fabs(v0.y  - v1.y);
   diff3 = fabs(v0.z  - v1.z);

    if  (diff1  >= diff2  &&  diff1  >= diff3)
       return  0;
    if  (diff2  >= diff1  &&  diff2  >= diff3)
       return  1;
    return  2;
}

void GeomUtil::EdgeTests (const ushort3 &coord, Triangle *tri, short &facecount) [private]
{
    bool  planetest[3];
    short  i;

   planetest[0] = IntersectsTop<X>(coord, tri);
   planetest[1] = IntersectsTop<Y>(coord, tri);
   planetest[2] = IntersectsTop<Z>(coord, tri);

   facecount = 0;
    for  (i = 0; i  <  3; ++i) {
       if  (planetest[i])
          ++facecount;
    }
}

bool GeomUtil::EmbeddedNormal (const float3 vox_center, Triangle *tri, int dom_axis) [private]
{
    int  order[6];
    float3  D, V;
    float   num, denom,  t,  range, dx, dy, dz;

    getOrder(order, dom_axis);   // this is a pointer

    // tri->d is the same as d0 etc. for the conservative
    // rasterization: see triangle_setup_6sep in GeomUtil.h
    num = tri->d  + (
         tri->n.x  * vox_center.x  +
         tri->n.y  * vox_center.y  +
         tri->n.z  * vox_center.z);

    // Graphics Gems, p.390
    // tri_v = EO . V
    // get ray direction V
    // get same answer if using negative normal or positive
```

```
D.x  = tri->n.x;
D.y  = tri->n.y;
D.z  = tri->n.z;

 // get magnitude ray scalar t
denom = tri->n.x  * D.x  +
        tri->n.y  * D.y  +
       tri->n.z  * D.z;
 if  (fp_math.equalBoundsf(denom, 0.0f,  PRECISIONf))
    return   false;  // parallel, will never happen with normal
 t = -num / denom;

 // intersect to plane
V.x  = vox_center.x  + D.x  *  t;
V.y  = vox_center.y  + D.y  *  t;
V.z  = vox_center.z  + D.z  *  t;

dx = (V.x  - vox_center.x);
dy = (V.y  - vox_center.y);
dz = (V.z  - vox_center.z);

range = sqrt(dx * dx + dy * dy + dz * dz);

 // if == will be picked up by next voxel over.
 // but need to do some association to make this work:
 // if even, is a negative direction: use  <=
 // if odd, is positive direction: use  <
 // for normals, just compare vox_center with
 // the intersection in the dominant axis coord
 // to set the direction.
 if  (dom_axis ==  X) {
    if  (V.x   <= vox_center.x) {
       if  (range  <= 0.5f)
          return   true;
   }  else  {
       if  (range  <  0.5f)
          return   true;
   }
}  else   if  (dom_axis ==  Y) {
    if  (V.y   <= vox_center.y) {
       if  (range  <= 0.5f)
          return   true;
   }  else  {
       if  (range  <  0.5f)
          return   true;
   }
}  else  {  // Z
    if  (V.z   <= vox_center.z) {
       if  (range  <= 0.5f)
```

```
            return  true;
        } else {
            if (range < 0.5f)
                return  true;
        }
    }
    return  false;
}

bool GeomUtil::EmbeddingPlaneIntersection (const float3 vox_center, Triangle *tri, const float3 D,
float num, float3 &V) [private]
{
    float  t, denom;

    // get magnitude ray scalar t
    denom = tri->n.x  * D.x  +
         tri->n.y  * D.y  +
         tri->n.z  * D.z;
    if (fp_math.equalBoundsf(denom, 0.0f,  PRECISIONf))
       return  false; // parallel
    t = -num  / denom;

    // intersect to plane
    V.x  = vox_center.x  + D.x  *  t;
    V.y  = vox_center.y  + D.y  *  t;
    V.z  = vox_center.z  + D.z  *  t;
    return  true;
}

void GeomUtil::findParallel (const float2 ortho, const float2 v0, const float2 v1, float3 &coeff)
[private]
{
    float  m,  b, newb;
    float3  coeffb;  // baseline
    bool  vertical;

    // get line coeffs for original triangle edge
    vertical =  getSlopeIntercept(v0, v1, m, b, coeffb);
    if  (vertical) {
      newb = ortho.x;
      coeff.x  = coeffb.x;   // 1
      coeff.y  = coeffb.y;   // 0
      coeff.z  = -newb;      // standard form
      return;
    }

    // slope is -A / B, can reform standard into
    // mx - y + b = 0; plug in point for new b, use m
    newb = -(m * ortho.x  - ortho.y);
```

```
    // rearranging gives:
    newb = newb * -coeffb.y;   // e.g. C * -B

    // so the new line is:
   coeff.x  = coeffb.x;
   coeff.y  = coeffb.y;
   coeff.z  = newb;
}

int GeomUtil::getN (int level)
{
    return  (int) lroundf(powf(2.0, (float)level));
}

void GeomUtil::getOrder (int *order, int dom_axis) [private]
{
    switch  (dom_axis) {
    case  0:
      order[0] = 0;
      order[1] = 1;
      order[2] = 2;    // xx...
      order[3] = 3;
      order[4] = 4;
      order[5] = 5;
       break;
    case  1:
      order[0] = 2;
      order[1] = 3;
      order[2] = 4;    // xx...
      order[3] = 5;
      order[4] = 0;
      order[5] = 1;
       break;
    case  2:
      order[0] = 4;
      order[1] = 5;
      order[2] = 0;    // xx...
      order[3] = 1;
      order[4] = 2;
      order[5] = 3;
       break;
    }
}

void GeomUtil::getOriginAndSides (const float3 v0, const float3 v1, const float3 v2, UVPack
&uvpack) [private]
{
    float  len01, len02, len03;
```

```
    // first get the side lengths, use longest for origin
    // this might flip things around, but it will all be
    // flipped back.
    length3(v0, v1, len01);
    length3(v1, v2, len02);
    length3(v2, v0, len03);
    if (len01 >= len02 && len01 >= len03) {
      // len01
      getP1P3(v0, v1, uvpack.p1, uvpack.p3);
      uvpack.p2.x = v2.x;
      uvpack.p2.y = v2.y;
      uvpack.p2.z = v2.z;
    } else if (len02 >= len01 && len02 >= len03) {
      // len02
      getP1P3(v1, v2, uvpack.p1, uvpack.p3);
      uvpack.p2.x = v0.x;
      uvpack.p2.y = v0.y;
      uvpack.p2.z = v0.z;
    } else {
      // len03
      getP1P3(v2, v0, uvpack.p1, uvpack.p3);
      uvpack.p2.x = v1.x;
      uvpack.p2.y = v1.y;
      uvpack.p2.z = v1.z;
    }
    makeOrigin(uvpack);
    makeDirectionCosines(uvpack);
}

void GeomUtil::getP1P3 (const float3 v0, const float3 v1, float3 &p1, float3 &p3) [private]
{
    short dominant, assign;

    dominant = dominantCoord(v0, v1);
    if (dominant == 0) {
      // X
      assign = 1;
      if (v0.x <= v1.x)
        assign = 0;
    } else if (dominant == 1) {
      // Y
      assign = 1;
      if (v0.y <= v1.y)
        assign = 0;
    } else {
      // Z
      assign = 1;
      if (v0.z <= v1.z)
        assign = 0;
```

```
    }
    if  (assign == 0) {
        p1.x  = v0.x;
        p1.y  = v0.y;
        p1.z  = v0.z;
        p3.x  = v1.x;
        p3.y  = v1.y;
        p3.z  = v1.z;
    } else  {
        p1.x  = v1.x;
        p1.y  = v1.y;
        p1.z  = v1.z;
        p3.x  = v0.x;
        p3.y  = v0.y;
        p3.z  = v0.z;
    }
}

unsigned int GeomUtil::getRaster ()
{
    return   raster;
}

bool GeomUtil::getSlopeIntercept (float2 p1, float2 p2, float &m, float &b, float3 &coeff) [private]
{
    if  (fp_math.equalBoundsf(p2.x, p1.x,  PRECISIONf)) {
        m = 1.0f;    // undefined but set to anything, unused
        coeff.x  = 1.0f;
        coeff.y  = 0.0f;   // y term will vanish
        b  = p1.x;
        coeff.z  = -b;
        return   true;
    }

    // Note that slope-intercept form, y = mx + b, has m = A/B
    // But the conversion to  "standard form"  has -A/B in front of X,
    // so a negative sign is added below for  "standard"  use.
    // However, this reflects the actual slope of A/B on the RHS.
    coeff.x  = (p2.y  - p1.y);
    coeff.y  = (p2.x  - p1.x);
    m = coeff.x  / coeff.y;

    // and correct for Lefthand Side
    coeff.x  = -coeff.x;

    // b in standard form gets multiplied by B after being
    // shifted to the LHS (negated).
    b  = (p1.y  - m * p1.x);
    coeff.z  = -b  * coeff.y;
```

```
    return  false;
}

void GeomUtil::getWorkingRadius (const float2 p1, const float2 p2, const float2 p3, float2 center,
float &radius) [private]
{
    float m, b;
    float3 coeff;

    if (fp_math.equalBoundsf(p2.x, p1.x, PRECISIONf)) {
        // only 1 line can be vertical: use another
        getSlopeIntercept(p2, p3, m, b, coeff);
    } else {
        getSlopeIntercept(p1, p2, m, b, coeff);
    }
    // note that the full solution is for r^2, hence take fabs
    // (Chasen, Appendix B)
    radius = fabs(coeff.x * center.x + coeff.y * center.y + coeff.z) /
         sqrt(coeff.x * coeff.x + coeff.y * coeff.y);
}

// called by constructor
void GeomUtil::Init () [private]
{
    bbox0 = make_float3( -1.1f, -1.1f, -1.1f );
    bbox1 = make_float3( 1.1f, 1.1f, 1.1f );

    // MAX_DEEP heuristic tracks g_terminal to make
    // sure recursion for look ahead is adequate
    MAX_DEEP = g_terminal / 2 + 1;

    double  start = 0.5f;
    float entry;
    for (short i = 0; i < MAX_DEEP; ++i) {
       entry = start + sqrt(start); // ortho dist to max-45 plane
       ray_dist[i] = entry;
    }
}

// only need to init these once per level
void GeomUtil::InitPlaneTestVars (const float3 &n, const float3 &v0, Triangle *tri)
{
    // compute the bbox´s critical point
    const  float3  c = make_float3(
         n.x > 0 ? bbox_delta.x : 0.0f,
         n.y > 0 ? bbox_delta.y : 0.0f,
         n.z > 0 ? bbox_delta.z : 0.0f);

    // precompute discriminants for the bbox/triangle plane test
```

```
   tri->r1  =
          n.x  * (c.x  - v0.x) +
          n.y  * (c.y  - v0.y) +
          n.z  * (c.z  - v0.z);

   tri->r2  =
          n.x  * (bbox_delta.x  - c.x  - v0.x) +
          n.y  * (bbox_delta.y  - c.y  - v0.y) +
          n.z  * (bbox_delta.z  - c.z  - v0.z);
}
```

bool GeomUtil::Inside (Triangle *tri, const float2 vox_center, const float2 direction, unsigned short select, float2 &alpha_beta, bool use_halo, unsigned char &checks) [private]

```
{

    // this is just the transformed triangle v0
    // always use w direction as defined by select
    // f.e: w for 0 (X axis) gives uv for YZ plane.
    // f.e: w for 2 (Z axis) gives uv for XY plane.
    // w_c0 really means c0.x = c0.u; c0.y = c0.v
    float2  *c0;
    float2  *c1;
    float2  *c2;

    if  (use_halo) {
       // is polygon orthogonal to principal plane?
       unsigned   char  selbit = 0x01  <<  select;
       if  (!(tri->fine.planebits   &  selbit))
          return   false;

       c0 =  &(tri->fine.h0[select]);
       c1 =  &(tri->fine.h1[select]);
       c2 =  &(tri->fine.h2[select]);
       checks = 0x00;  // initialize
    }  else  {
       c0 =  &(tri->fine.c0[select]);
       c1 =  &(tri->fine.c1[select]);
       c2 =  &(tri->fine.c2[select]);
    }
    const   float2   &w_c0 = *c0;
    const   float2   &w_c1 = *c1;
    const   float2   &w_c2 = *c2;

    float2  w_uv1, w_uv2;
    w_uv1.x  = w_c1.x  - w_c0.x;
    w_uv1.y  = w_c1.y  - w_c0.y;
    w_uv2.x  = w_c2.x  - w_c0.x;
    w_uv2.y  = w_c2.y  - w_c0.y;
```

```
// ray direction is along the AXIS of dominant axis
// always work from voxel origin (as the ray origin)
// O = (u + 0.5f, v + 0.5f, w + 0.5f)
// D = (0.0, 0.0. 1.0) [for example]
// P = O + Dt
// P = (u + 0.5f, v + 0.5f, w + 0.5f + 1)
float2  P =  make_float2(
      vox_center.x  + direction.x,
      vox_center.y  + direction.y);

// P.z would be the dominant axis: the projection can
// be on the origin plane face or on origin + 1 face,
// doesn't matter. But actual intersection point +
// direction.z *will* matter for range test.
// in (uvw) coordinates, ray direction = w = 1.0f.
// Ray magnitude (t) doesn't matter, leave it at implicit 1.0.
float2  w_uv0 =  make_float2(
         P.x  - w_c0.x,
         P.y  - w_c0.y);

float   alpha, beta;
alpha = beta = -1.0f;   // neg means default out of bounds
if  (fp_math.equalBoundsf(w_uv1.x, 0.0f,  PRECISIONf)) {
   beta = w_uv0.x  / w_uv2.x;
    if  (use_halo  &&  beta  >= 0.0f   &&  beta  <= 1.0f)
      checks |=  BETA_IN_01;

    if  (checks  &   BETA_IN_01)
      alpha = (w_uv0.y  - beta * w_uv2.y) / w_uv1.y;
} else  {
    // compute the determinant as in Graphics Gems,
    // Glassner, Vol 1, p. 393
    beta = (w_uv0.y  * w_uv1.x  - w_uv0.x  * w_uv1.y) /
        (w_uv2.y  * w_uv1.x  - w_uv2.x  * w_uv1.y);
    if  (use_halo  &&  beta  >= 0.0f   &&  beta  <= 1.0f)
      checks |=  BETA_IN_01;

    if  (checks  &   BETA_IN_01)
      alpha = (w_uv0.x  - beta * w_uv2.x) / w_uv1.x;
}
alpha_beta.x  =  alpha;
alpha_beta.y  = beta;

// beta conditions determine alpha, don't need to retest beta
// only care about this for halo; status for original triangle
// as calculated below (on second call) is ignored.
bool  inside = (alpha  >= 0.0f)  &&  ((alpha + beta)  <= 1.0f);

// here we put an indiscriminate return for  "just
```

```
    // being inside"  without any range tests. The caller
    // is responsible for using alpha and beta to check
    // the range.
    return  inside;
}

void GeomUtil::intersectPair (const float3 coeff1, const float3 coeff2, float2 &hp) [private]
{
    float  lla1, llc1, lla2, llc2, diffla, difflc;

    // solve simultaneously : A = x, B = y, C = z
    if  (fp_math.equalBoundsf(coeff1.y, 0.0f,  PRECISIONf)) {
       // solve first equation for y
       hp.x  = -coeff1.z  / coeff1.x;   // may be 0 if vertical
       hp.y  = (-coeff2.z  - hp.x  * coeff2.x) / coeff2.y;
   }  else   if  (fp_math.equalBoundsf(coeff2.y, 0.0f,  PRECISIONf)) {
       // solve second equation for y
       hp.x  = -coeff2.z  / coeff2.x;
       hp.y  = (-coeff1.z  - hp.x  * coeff1.x) / coeff1.y;
   }  else  {
       lla1 = coeff1.x  * coeff2.y;
       llc1 = coeff1.z  * coeff2.y;
       lla2 = coeff2.x  * coeff1.y;
       llc2 = coeff2.z  * coeff1.y;

       diffla = lla1 - lla2;
       difflc = llc1 - llc2;
        // diffla should never be 0.0f?

        // get new point:
        hp.x  = -difflc / diffla;
        // solve for y
        hp.y  = ((coeff1.x  * hp.x) + coeff1.z) / (-coeff1.y);
    }
}

bool GeomUtil::Intersects (Triangle *tri, float2 &v_p0, float2 &v_p1, unsigned short select) [private]
{

    float2  t_p0, t_p1;  // t = triangle, v = voxel
    // transformed triangle vertices, 2D
    const   float2   &c0 = tri->fine.c0[select];
    const   float2   &c1 = tri->fine.c1[select];
    const   float2   &c2 = tri->fine.c2[select];
    const   short  COINCIDE = 1;
    const   short  PARALLEL = 2;
    const   short  CROSS = 3;
    const   short  NO_CROSS = 4;
    short   type;
```

```
float  a, b, c, s, x, y;

// for triangle edges
for (int i = 0; i < 3; ++i) {
  switch (i) {
  case 0:
    t_p0.x = c0.x; t_p0.y = c0.y;
    t_p1.x = c1.x; t_p1.y = c1.y;
     break;
  case 1:
    t_p0.x = c1.x; t_p0.y = c1.y;
    t_p1.x = c2.x; t_p1.y = c2.y;
     break;
  case 2:
    t_p0.x = c2.x; t_p0.y = c2.y;
    t_p1.x = c0.x; t_p1.y = c0.y;
     break;
  }
  a = (t_p1.y - t_p0.y) * (v_p1.x - v_p0.x) -
    (t_p1.x - t_p0.x) * (v_p1.y - v_p0.y);
  b = (t_p0.x - v_p0.x) * (v_p1.y - v_p0.y) -
    (t_p0.y - v_p0.y) * (v_p1.x - v_p0.x);
  c = (t_p0.x - v_p0.x) * (t_p1.y - t_p0.y) -
    (t_p0.y - v_p0.y) * (t_p1.x - t_p0.x);

  if (fp_math.equalBoundsf(a, 0.0f, PRECISIONf)) {
    if (fp_math.equalBoundsf(b, 0.0f, PRECISIONf))
      type = COINCIDE;
    else
      type = PARALLEL;
  } else {
    if (a > 0.0f) {
      if ((b >= 0.0f && b <= a) &&
         (c >= 0.0f && c <= a))
        type = CROSS;
      else
        type = NO_CROSS;
    } else {
      if ((b <= 0.0f && b >= a) &&
         (c <= 0.0f && c >= a))
        type = CROSS;
      else
        type = NO_CROSS;
    }
  }
  // determine if there's a crossing
  switch (type) {
  case NO_CROSS:
  case PARALLEL:
```

```
      case COINCIDE:
         break;
      case CROSS:
         // c == 0 is intersect of tri edge with vox endpoint: reject
         // b == 0 is tri endpoint on vox faceline: accept
         if (fp_math.equalBoundsf(b, a, PRECISIONf) ||
            fp_math.equalBoundsf(c, a, PRECISIONf) ||
            fp_math.equalBoundsf(c, 0.0f, PRECISIONf))
            break;
/*
         s = b / a;
         if (fp_math.equalBoundsf(v_p0.x, v_p1.x, PRECISIONf))
            x = v_p0.x;
         else
            x = t_p0.x + s * (t_p1.x - t_p0.x);

         if (fp_math.equalBoundsf(v_p0.y, v_p1.y, PRECISIONf))
            y = v_p0.y;
         else
            y = t_p0.y + s * (t_p1.y - t_p0.y);
*/
         return true;
      }
      // try next edge    }
   return false;
}

template<int32 AXIS>
bool GeomUtil::IntersectsTop (const ushort3 &coord, Triangle *tri) [private]
{
   bool plane_status;
   float2 v_p0, v_p1;   // voxel points
   unsigned short p0_off, p1_off, edge, select;

   // X:0=YZ; Y:1=XZ; Z:2=XY
   typedef uvw<AXIS> sel;
   select = AXIS;

   for (edge = 0; edge < 4; ++edge) {
      p0_off = (select << 2) + edge;
      p1_off = (select << 2) + (edge + 1)%4;
      float3 p0 = make_float3(
            faces[p0_off][0],
            faces[p0_off][1],
            faces[p0_off][2]);
      float3 p1 = make_float3(
            faces[p1_off][0],
            faces[p1_off][1],
            faces[p1_off][2]);
```

```
      v_p0.x  = sel::u(coord) + sel::u(p0);
      v_p0.y  =  sel::v(coord) +  sel::v(p0);
      v_p1.x  = sel::u(coord) + sel::u(p1);
      v_p1.y  =  sel::v(coord) +  sel::v(p1);

      plane_status =  Intersects(tri, v_p0, v_p1, select);
      // any intersection counts as TRUE for voxel face.
      if  (plane_status)
         return   true;
   }
   return   false;
}

void GeomUtil::length3 (const double3 v0, const double3 v1, double &len01) [private]
{
   len01 = sqrt( (v1.x  - v0.x) * (v1.x  - v0.x) +
              (v1.y  - v0.y) * (v1.y  - v0.y) +
              (v1.z  - v0.z) * (v1.z  - v0.z));
}

void GeomUtil::length3 (const float3 v0, const float3 v1, float &len01) [private]
{
   len01 = sqrt( (v1.x  - v0.x) * (v1.x  - v0.x) +
              (v1.y  - v0.y) * (v1.y  - v0.y) +
              (v1.z  - v0.z) * (v1.z  - v0.z));
}

bool GeomUtil::LookAheadChildrenToEmbedding (const float3 vox_center, Triangle *tri, int
dom_axis, float last_range, float max_range, short cur_level, short deep) [private]
{

   // do a local subdivision without scaling, and pass
   // to OneOfSixToEmbeddingPlane
   float3   coord, child_center, ranges;
   float  last_off = last_range;
   float  cur_off = max_range;
   float  next_range = max_range / 2.0f;
   bool  in_range;

   // recursion terminal condition is terminal level!
   if  (cur_level ==  g_terminal_level  || deep ==  MAX_DEEP)
      return   false;

   // reassign last_range to reflect max-45 ray distance
   last_range =  ray_dist[deep];

   coord.x  = vox_center.x  - last_off;
   coord.y  = vox_center.y  - last_off;
   coord.z  = vox_center.z  - last_off;
```

```
child_center.x  = coord.x  + cur_off;
child_center.y  = coord.y  + cur_off;
child_center.z  = coord.z  + cur_off;
 if  (OneOfSixToEmbeddingPlane(child_center, tri, dom_axis, max_range, ranges))
    return   true;

 if  (checkRange(ranges, last_range)) {
    in_range =  LookAheadChildrenToEmbedding(child_center, tri, dom_axis,
          max_range, next_range, cur_level + 1, deep + 1);
    if  (in_range)
       return   true;
}

child_center.x  = coord.x  + cur_off;
child_center.y  = coord.y  + cur_off;
child_center.z  = coord.z  + last_off + cur_off;
 if  (OneOfSixToEmbeddingPlane(child_center, tri, dom_axis, max_range, ranges))
    return   true;

 if  (checkRange(ranges, last_range)) {
    in_range =  LookAheadChildrenToEmbedding(child_center, tri, dom_axis,
          max_range, next_range, cur_level + 1, deep + 1);
    if  (in_range)
       return   true;
}

child_center.x  = coord.x  + last_off + cur_off;
child_center.y  = coord.y  + cur_off;
child_center.z  = coord.z  + last_off + cur_off;
 if  (OneOfSixToEmbeddingPlane(child_center, tri, dom_axis, max_range, ranges))
    return   true;

 if  (checkRange(ranges, last_range)) {
    in_range =  LookAheadChildrenToEmbedding(child_center, tri, dom_axis,
          max_range, next_range, cur_level + 1, deep + 1);
    if  (in_range)
       return   true;
}

child_center.x  = coord.x  + last_off + cur_off;
child_center.y  = coord.y  + cur_off;
child_center.z  = coord.z  + cur_off;
 if  (OneOfSixToEmbeddingPlane(child_center, tri, dom_axis, max_range, ranges))
    return   true;

 if  (checkRange(ranges, last_range)) {
    in_range =  LookAheadChildrenToEmbedding(child_center, tri, dom_axis,
          max_range, next_range, cur_level + 1, deep + 1);
```

```
    if (in_range)
        return true;
}

//
child_center.x = coord.x + cur_off;
child_center.y = coord.y + last_off + cur_off;
child_center.z = coord.z + cur_off;
 if (OneOfSixToEmbeddingPlane(child_center, tri, dom_axis, max_range, ranges))
    return true;

 if (checkRange(ranges, last_range)) {
    in_range = LookAheadChildrenToEmbedding(child_center, tri, dom_axis,
         max_range, next_range, cur_level + 1, deep + 1);
    if (in_range)
        return true;
}

child_center.x = coord.x + cur_off;
child_center.y = coord.y + last_off + cur_off;
child_center.z = coord.z + last_off + cur_off;
 if (OneOfSixToEmbeddingPlane(child_center, tri, dom_axis, max_range, ranges))
    return true;

 if (checkRange(ranges, last_range)) {
    in_range = LookAheadChildrenToEmbedding(child_center, tri, dom_axis,
         max_range, next_range, cur_level + 1, deep + 1);
    if (in_range)
        return true;
}

child_center.x = coord.x + last_off + cur_off;
child_center.y = coord.y + last_off + cur_off;
child_center.z = coord.z + last_off + cur_off;
 if (OneOfSixToEmbeddingPlane(child_center, tri, dom_axis, max_range, ranges))
    return true;

 if (checkRange(ranges, last_range)) {
    in_range = LookAheadChildrenToEmbedding(child_center, tri, dom_axis,
         max_range, next_range, cur_level + 1, deep + 1);
    if (in_range)
        return true;
}

child_center.x = coord.x + last_off + cur_off;
child_center.y = coord.y + last_off + cur_off;
child_center.z = coord.z + cur_off;
 if (OneOfSixToEmbeddingPlane(child_center, tri, dom_axis, max_range, ranges))
    return true;
```

```
    if (checkRange(ranges, last_range)) {
        in_range = LookAheadChildrenToEmbedding(child_center, tri, dom_axis,
            max_range, next_range, cur_level + 1, deep + 1);
        if (in_range)
            return true;
    }

    return false;
}

void GeomUtil::MakeBBoxDelta (float3 &delta) [private]
{
    delta.x = (bbox1.x - bbox0.x) / float(N);
    delta.y = (bbox1.y - bbox0.y) / float(N);
    delta.z = (bbox1.z - bbox0.z) / float(N);
}

void GeomUtil::makeBigSphere (const float3 v0, const float3 v1, const float3 v2, float3 &center,
float &radius) [private]
{
    float a1, a2, a3, ka, b1, b2, b3, kb;
    float c1, c2, c3, d1, d2, d3, numx, numy, numz, denom;
    float3 baseC;

    // First work in XY plane, then in XZ
    if (fp_math.equalBoundsf(v1.x, v0.x, PRECISIONf)) {
        // vertical: use 3:1 and 3:2 instead of 1:2 and 1:3
        // transpose the system to the origin
        // a = A - C
        a1 = v0.x - v2.x;
        a2 = v0.y - v2.y;
        a3 = v0.z - v2.z;
        baseC.x = v2.x;
        baseC.y = v2.y;
        baseC.z = v2.z;

        // find the barycenter
        ka = (a1 * a1 + a2 * a2 + a3 * a3);

        // b = B - C
        b1 = v1.x - v2.x;
        b2 = v1.y - v2.y;
        b3 = v1.z - v2.z;
        kb = (b1 * b1 + b2 * b2 + b3 * b3);
    } else {
        // a = A - C
        a1 = v1.x - v0.x;
        a2 = v1.y - v0.y;
```

```
        a3 = v1.z  - v0.z;

        baseC.x  = v0.x;
        baseC.y  = v0.y;
        baseC.z  = v0.z;

        ka = (a1 * a1 + a2 * a2 + a3 * a3);

         // b = B - C
        b1 = v2.x  - v0.x;
        b2 = v2.y  - v0.y;
        b3 = v2.z  - v0.z;
        kb = (b1 * b1 + b2 * b2 + b3 * b3);
    }
     // length / cross-product in 3D
     // length: a and b are swapped
     // (||a||^2 * b - ||b||^2 * a) x (a x b)
     // numerator
    c1 = (ka * b1 - kb * a1);
    c2 = (ka * b2 - kb * a2);
    c3 = (ka * b3 - kb * a3);

     // a x b
    d1 = a2 * b3 - a3 * b2;
    d2 = -(a1 * b3 - a3 * b1);
    d3 = a1 * b2 - a2 * b1;
    numx = c2 * d3 - c3 * d2;
    numy = -(c1 * d3 - c3 * d1);
    numz = c1 * d2 - c2 * d1;

    denom = 2.0 * (d1 * d1 + d2 * d2 + d3 * d3);

    center.x  = numx / denom + baseC.x;
    center.y  = numy / denom + baseC.y;
    center.z  = numz / denom + baseC.z;

     // finally, compute radius (expensive!)
     // (could also leave it as radius squared)
    numx = (a1 * a1 + a2 * a2 + a3 * a3) *
          (b1 * b1 + b2 * b2 + b3 * b3) *
          ((a1 - b1) * (a1 - b1) +
           (a2 - b2) * (a2 - b2) +
           (a3 - b3) * (a3 - b3));
    radius = sqrt(numx / (4.0 * (d1 * d1 + d2 * d2 + d3 * d3)));
}

void GeomUtil::makeDirectionCosines (UVPack &uvpack) [private]
{
     double3  p1, p2, p4;
```

```
    double  d1, d1ct, d1st;

    p1.x  = (double)uvpack.p1.x;
    p1.y  = (double)uvpack.p1.y;
    p1.z  = (double)uvpack.p1.z;
    p2.x  = (double)uvpack.p2.x;
    p2.y  = (double)uvpack.p2.y;
    p2.z  = (double)uvpack.p2.z;
    p4.x  = uvpack.p4.x;
    p4.y  = uvpack.p4.y;
    p4.z  = uvpack.p4.z;

    d1 = uvpack.p1p2;
    d1ct = d1 * uvpack.cos_theta;

    uvpack.cos_alpha.x  = (p4.x  - p1.x) / d1ct;
    uvpack.cos_alpha.y  = (p4.y  - p1.y) / d1ct;
    uvpack.cos_alpha.z  = (p4.z  - p1.z) / d1ct;

    d1st = d1 * uvpack.sin_theta;

    uvpack.cos_beta.x  = (p2.x  - p4.x) / d1st;
    uvpack.cos_beta.y  = (p2.y  - p4.y) / d1st;
    uvpack.cos_beta.z  = (p2.z  - p4.z) / d1st;
}

void GeomUtil::makeHalo (const float2 c0, const float2 c1, const float2 c2, Triangle *tri, int select)
[private]
{
    int  i;
    float2  mid01, mid12, mid20;
    float2  reach01, reach12, reach20;
    float2  ortho01, ortho12, ortho20;
    float3  coeff01, coeff12, coeff20;

    // take the midpoints of each triangle edge
    mid01.x  = c0.x  + (c1.x  - c0.x) / 2.0f;
    mid01.y  = c0.y  + (c1.y  - c0.y) / 2.0f;
    mid12.x  = c1.x  + (c2.x  - c1.x) / 2.0f;
    mid12.y  = c1.y  + (c2.y  - c1.y) / 2.0f;
    mid20.x  = c2.x  + (c0.x  - c2.x) / 2.0f;
    mid20.y  = c2.y  + (c0.y  - c2.y) / 2.0f;

    // for each edge of triangle projection
    for  (i = 0; i  <  3; ++i) {
       switch  (i) {
       case  0:
          opposingDistance(mid01, reach01, c0, c1, c2);
          maxAwayFromEdge(reach01, c0, c1, mid01, ortho01);
```

```
            break;
        case 1:
            opposingDistance(mid12, reach12, c1, c2, c0);
            maxAwayFromEdge(reach12, c1, c2, mid12, ortho12);
            break;
        case 2:
            opposingDistance(mid20, reach20, c2, c0, c1);
            maxAwayFromEdge(reach20, c2, c0, mid20, ortho20);
            break;
        }
    }
    // Now we have all the off-triangle points
    // Next, make lines for the original edges
    // for lines parallel to those edges through
    // the off-triangle points.
    findParallel(ortho01, c0, c1, coeff01);
    findParallel(ortho12, c1, c2, coeff12);
    findParallel(ortho20, c2, c0, coeff20);

    // intersect line pairs for new (halo) triangle points
    // Make sure the h's are in the same corners as the c's
    intersectPair(coeff20, coeff01, tri->fine.h0[select]);
    intersectPair(coeff01, coeff12, tri->fine.h1[select]);
    intersectPair(coeff12, coeff20, tri->fine.h2[select]);
}

void GeomUtil::makeHaloes (Triangle *tri)
{
    int i, select;
    float2  min, max;
    unsigned  char or_bit;

    // This won't be possible for orthogonal triangles:
    // they'll be excluded for principal planes that
    // degenerate to a line.

    // for all projection planes: YZ, XZ, XY
    tri->fine.planebits = 0x00;

    for (i = 0; i < 3; ++i) {
      select = i;

        // get the transformed coordinates created
        // in a previous step (GeomWorker.cpp) for
        // the current principal plane.
        float2  &c0 = tri->fine.c0[select];
        float2  &c1 = tri->fine.c1[select];
        float2  &c2 = tri->fine.c2[select];
```

```
        Bbox(c0, c1, c2, min, max);
        if (fp_math.equalBoundsf(min.x, max.x,  PRECISIONf))
           continue;
        if (fp_math.equalBoundsf(min.y, max.y,  PRECISIONf))
           continue;

        // this says:  "there's a halo available"
        or_bit = 0x01  <<  select;
        tri->fine.planebits  |= or_bit;

        makeHalo(c0, c1, c2, tri, select);
   }
}

void GeomUtil::MakeInvBBoxDelta (float3 &delta) [private]
{
   delta.x  = float(N) / (bbox1.x  -  bbox0.x);
   delta.y  = float(N) / (bbox1.y  -  bbox0.y);
   delta.z  = float(N) / (bbox1.z  -  bbox0.z);
}

void GeomUtil::makeLittleSphere (const float3 v0, const float3 v1, const float3 v2, float3 &center,
float &radius) [private]
{
    float2  p1, p2, p3,  c;
    float  la1, lb1, lc1, la2, lb2, lc2;
    float  lla1, llc1, lla2, llc2;
    float  diffla, difflc;
    double  cu, cv;

    UVPack  uvpack;
    // here we transform the triangle to (u, v) space,
    // inscribe a circle, then transform the center back
    // to 3D space.

    // do the transform
    getOriginAndSides(v0, v1, v2, uvpack);

    // now we have enough info to recast the triangle
    // as a (u, v) coordinate system in 2D.
    p1.x  = float(-uvpack.p1p4);
    p1.y  = 0.0f;
    p2.x  = 0.0f;
    p2.y  = float(uvpack.p4p2);
    p3.x  = float(uvpack.p1p3  - uvpack.p1p4);
    p3.y  = 0.0f;

 /*
    // arbitrary 2D test case from passed 3D coords
```

```
    p1.x = v0.x;
    p1.y = v0.y;
    p2.x = v1.x;
    p2.y = v1.y;
    p3.x = v2.x;
    p3.y = v2.y;

    // vertical test cases
    p1.x = 0.0f;
    p1.y = 0.0f;
    p2.x = 1.0f;
    p2.y = 0.0f;
    p3.x = 1.0f;
    p3.y = 1.0f;

    p1.x = 1.0f;
    p1.y = 0.0f;
    p2.x = 1.0f;
    p2.y = 1.0f;
    p3.x = 0.0f;
    p3.y = 0.0f;
*/
    // the l's are the linear coefficients
    Bisector(p1, p2, p3, la1, lb1, lc1);

    // now do everything with k1 and k3 (instead of k2)
    Bisector(p1, p3, p2, la2, lb2, lc2);

    // solve simultaneously :
    if (fp_math.equalBoundsf(lb1, 0.0f, PRECISIONf)) {
       // solve first equation for y
       c.x = -lc1 / la1;  // may be 0 if bisector is vertical
       c.y = (-lc2 - c.x * la2) / lb2;
    } else if (fp_math.equalBoundsf(lb2, 0.0f, PRECISIONf)) {
       // solve second equation for y
       c.x = -lc2 / la2;
       c.y = (-lc1 - c.x * la1) / lb1;
    } else {
       lla1 = la1 * lb2;
       llc1 = lc1 * lb2;
       lla2 = la2 * lb1;
       llc2 = lc2 * lb1;

       diffla = lla1 - lla2;
       difflc = llc1 - llc2;
       // with all the sign checks, diffla should never be 0.0f?

       // get circle center:
       c.x = -difflc / diffla;
```

```
        // solve for y
        c.y  = ((la1 * c.x) + lc1) / (-lb1);
    }

    // Sylvan Chasen does not make this easy.
    getWorkingRadius(p1, p2, p3, c, radius);

    // finally, xform back to (xyz) space.
    cu = (double)c.x;
    cv = (double)c.y;

    center.x  = (float)(cu * uvpack.cos_alpha.x  +
                 cv * uvpack.cos_beta.x  + uvpack.p4.x);
    center.y  = (float)(cu * uvpack.cos_alpha.y  +
                 cv * uvpack.cos_beta.y  + uvpack.p4.y);
    center.z  = (float)(cu * uvpack.cos_alpha.z  +
                 cv * uvpack.cos_beta.z  + uvpack.p4.z);

}

void GeomUtil::makeOrigin (UVPack &uvpack) [private]
{
    double  d1, d3, d4, cos_theta, sin_theta;
    double3  p1, p2, p3, p4,  t, pp4;

    p1.x  = (double)uvpack.p1.x;
    p1.y  = (double)uvpack.p1.y;
    p1.z  = (double)uvpack.p1.z;
    p2.x  = (double)uvpack.p2.x;
    p2.y  = (double)uvpack.p2.y;
    p2.z  = (double)uvpack.p2.z;
    p3.x  = (double)uvpack.p3.x;
    p3.y  = (double)uvpack.p3.y;
    p3.z  = (double)uvpack.p3.z;

    // first find P4 (according to Chasen, p. 142)
    length3(p1, p2, d1);
    length3(p1, p3, d3);

    cos_theta = (
        (p2.x  - p1.x) * (p3.x  - p1.x) +
        (p2.y  - p1.y) * (p3.y  - p1.y) +
        (p2.z  - p1.z) * (p3.z  - p1.z)) / (d1 * d3);

    // origin : d4 is dist ratio between p1/p4
    d4 = ((d1 * cos_theta) / d3);
    p4.x  = p1.x  + d4 * (p3.x  - p1.x);
    p4.y  = p1.y  + d4 * (p3.y  - p1.y);
    p4.z  = p1.z  + d4 * (p3.z  - p1.z);
```

```
    // sine theta is orthogonal to cos in the vector world.
    // t is translation vector     t.x  = p4.x  - p1.x;
   t.y  = p4.y  - p1.y;
   t.z  = p4.z  - p1.z;

    // translated p4/p2 to p1: call it p4'  (prime)
   pp4.x  = p2.x  - t.x;
   pp4.y  = p2.y  - t.y;
   pp4.z  = p2.z  - t.z;

    length3(p4, p2, d4);   // p2 to p4 (same as len pp4)
    sin_theta = (
         (pp4.x  - p1.x) * (p2.x  - p1.x) +
         (pp4.y  - p1.y) * (p2.y  - p1.y) +
         (pp4.z  - p1.z) * (p2.z  - p1.z)) / (d1 * d4);

   uvpack.p1p3  = d3;
   uvpack.p1p2  = d1;
   uvpack.p1p4  = d1 * cos_theta;
   uvpack.p4p2  = d4;
   uvpack.cos_theta  = cos_theta;
   uvpack.sin_theta  = sin_theta;
   uvpack.p4.x  = p4.x;
   uvpack.p4.y  = p4.y;
   uvpack.p4.z  = p4.z;
}

void GeomUtil::makeSpheres (Triangle *tri)
{
    // Get the transformed coordinates of the triangle
    // irrespective of uv specialization
    const  float3  v0  =  make_float3(
            (tri->v0.x  -  bbox0.x) *  inv_bbox_delta.x,
            (tri->v0.y  -  bbox0.y) *  inv_bbox_delta.y,
            (tri->v0.z  -  bbox0.z) *  inv_bbox_delta.z);
    const  float3  v1  =  make_float3(
            (tri->v1.x  -  bbox0.x) *  inv_bbox_delta.x,
            (tri->v1.y  -  bbox0.y) *  inv_bbox_delta.y,
            (tri->v1.z  -  bbox0.z) *  inv_bbox_delta.z);
    const  float3  v2  =  make_float3(
            (tri->v2.x  -  bbox0.x) *  inv_bbox_delta.x,
            (tri->v2.y  -  bbox0.y) *  inv_bbox_delta.y,
            (tri->v2.z  -  bbox0.z) *  inv_bbox_delta.z);

    makeBigSphere(v0, v1, v2, tri->big_center, tri->big_radius);
    makeLittleSphere(v0, v1, v2, tri->little_center, tri->little_radius);
}
```

```
int GeomUtil::max (int a, int b)
{
   if (a > b)
      return a;
   return b;
}

float3 GeomUtil::max3 (const float4 a, const float4 b, const float4 c)
{
   return make_float3(
        fmax( a.x, fmaxf( b.x, c.x ) ),
        fmax( a.y, fmaxf( b.y, c.y ) ),
        fmax( a.z, fmaxf( b.z, c.z ) ) );
}

void GeomUtil::maxAwayFromEdge (const float2 reach, const float2 v0, const float2 v1, const float2
midp, float2 &ortho) [private]
{
    double dx, dy, distx, disty;
    float m, b, perpm, perpb;
    float3 coeff, pcoeff;
    float2 x_perp_on_edge, y_perp_on_edge;

    // vertical and horizontal are simply points on
    // the original edge (and will always have shorter
    // chords than their orthogonal counterpart)
    if (fp_math.equalBoundsf(reach.x, midp.x, PRECISIONf)) {
       ortho.x = midp.x;
       ortho.y = reach.y;
       return;
    }
    if (fp_math.equalBoundsf(reach.y, midp.y, PRECISIONf)) {
       ortho.x = reach.x;
       ortho.y = midp.y;
       return;
    }

    // drop a perpendicular: only way to do it.
    // get line equation of original edge
    // checks above guarantee line isn't vertical
    getSlopeIntercept(v0, v1, m, b, coeff);

    // first outward point: reach.x
    // perpendicular slope is B/A eg .y/.x
    perpm = coeff.y / coeff.x;
    perpb = -(perpm * reach.x - midp.y);
    pcoeff.x = perpm;
    pcoeff.y = -1.0f;
    pcoeff.z = perpb;
```

```
    intersectPair(coeff, pcoeff, x_perp_on_edge);

    // second outward point: reach.y
   perpb = -(perpm * midp.x  - reach.y);
   pcoeff.z  = perpb;
    intersectPair(coeff, pcoeff, y_perp_on_edge);

    // get perp distance to reach.x
   dx = reach.x  - x_perp_on_edge.x;
   dy = midp.y  - x_perp_on_edge.y;
   distx = dx * dx + dy * dy;

    // get perp distance to reach.y
   dx = midp.x  - y_perp_on_edge.x;
   dy = reach.y  - y_perp_on_edge.y;
   disty = dx * dx + dy * dy;

    if  (disty  >  distx) {
       ortho.x  = midp.x;
       ortho.y  = reach.y;   // this pair is higher
    }  else  {
       ortho.x  = reach.x;
       ortho.y  = midp.y;    // else this one is
    }
}

int GeomUtil::min (inta, intb)
{
    if  (a   <   b)
        return   a;
    return   b;
}

float3 GeomUtil::min3 (const float4a, const float4b, const float4c)
{
    return   make_float3(
          fminf( a.x, fminf( b.x, c.x  ) ),
          fminf( a.y, fminf( b.y, c.y  ) ),
          fminf( a.z, fminf( b.z, c.z  ) ) );
}

// First thing to do at every level switch (LevelWorker.cpp)
int GeomUtil::NewN (int level, int terminal_level, bool is_terminal)
{
    g_level  = (short)level;
    g_terminal_level  = (short)terminal_level;
    terminal  = is_terminal;
    return   N  = (int) lroundf(powf(2.0, (float)level));
}
```

```
bool GeomUtil::OneOfSixToEmbeddingPlane (const float3 vox_center, Triangle *tri, int dom_axis,
float range_max, float3 &rangelist) [private]
{
    int  i, j;
    int  order[6];
    float3  D, V;
    float   num,  range;
    unsigned   short  axis;

    getOrder(order, dom_axis);   // this is a pointer

    // tri->d is the same as d0 etc. for the conservative
    // rasterization: see triangle_setup_6sep in GeomUtil.h
    num = tri->d  + (
         tri->n.x  * vox_center.x  +
         tri->n.y  * vox_center.y  +
         tri->n.z  * vox_center.z);

    // Graphics Gems, p.390
     for  (i = 0; i  <  6; ++i) {
       // tri_v = EO . V
       // get ray direction V
       D.x  =  ray6[order[i]][0];
       D.y  =  ray6[order[i]][1];
       D.z  =  ray6[order[i]][2];

       if  (!EmbeddingPlaneIntersection(vox_center, tri, D, num, V))
          continue;

       // look at ray direction coord as coord of interest
       j = order[i]  &  0x01;
       if  (order[i]  <  2) {
          // 0: negative direction
          if  (j == 0)
             range = (vox_center.x  - V.x);
          else    // 1: positive
             range = (V.x  - vox_center.x);
          if  (range  <  0.0f)
             continue;
       } else   if  (order[i]  <  4) {
          if  (j == 0)
             range = (vox_center.y  - V.y);
          else
             range = (V.y  - vox_center.y);
          if  (range  <  0.0f)
             continue;
       } else  {
          if  (j == 0)
             range = (vox_center.z  - V.z);
```

```
        else
            range = (V.z  - vox_center.z);
        if (range  <  0.0f)
            continue;
    }
    axis = (order[i])>>1;

    // if == will be picked up by next voxel over.
    // but need to do some association to make this work:
    // if even, is a negative direction: use  <=
    // if odd, is positive direction: use  <
    if  (j == 0) {
        if  (range  <= range_max)
            return   true;
        // skip redundant calc
        ++i;
    } else  {
        if  (range  <  range_max)
            return   true;
    }
    // store for look ahead check
    if  (axis == 0)
        rangelist.x  =  range;
    else   if  (axis == 1)
        rangelist.y  =  range;
    else
        rangelist.z  =  range;

    // try next direction
  }
  return   false;
}

bool GeomUtil::OneOfSixToSphere (const float3 vox_center, const float3 center, float radius, int
dom_axis) [private]
{
  float3  V, P;
  float  eox, eoy, eoz, tri_v, disc, d,  scale;
  float  vsx, vsy, vsz,  range;
  int  i;
  int  order[6];

  getOrder(order, dom_axis);   // this is a pointer

  // Graphics Gems, p.388
  for  (i = 0; i  <  6; ++i) {
    // tri_v = EO . V
    // get ray direction V
    V.x  =  ray6[order[i]][0];
```

```
      V.y  =  ray6[order[i]][1];
      V.z  =  ray6[order[i]][2];

      // O is sphere center (origin)
      // E is voxel center (passed in)
      // store this since it's used twice
      eox = center.x  - vox_center.x;
      eoy = center.y  - vox_center.y;
      eoz = center.z  - vox_center.z;

      // tri_v = triangle side
      tri_v = eox * V.x  + eoy * V.y  + eoz * V.z;

      // disc = r^2 - ((EO . EO) - tri_v^2)
      disc = radius * radius -
         ((eox * eox + eoy * eoy + eoz * eoz) -
          tri_v * tri_v);
      if  (disc  <  0.0f)
         continue;   // no intersection, try next of 6
      d = sqrt(disc);

      // P = E + (tri_v - d)V
      scale = tri_v  - d;
      vsx = scale * V.x;
      vsy = scale * V.y;
      vsz = scale * V.z;

      // here's the intersection point on the sphere:
      P.x  = vox_center.x  + vsx;
      P.y  = vox_center.y  + vsy;
      P.z  = vox_center.z  + vsz;

      // look at ray direction coord as coord of interest
      if  (order[i]  <  2)
         range = fabs(P.x  - vox_center.x);
      else   if  (order[i]  <  4)
         range = fabs(P.y  - vox_center.y);
      else
         range = fabs(P.z  - vox_center.z);

      //  <= should be okay for this outside test.
      if  (range  <= 0.5f)
         return   true;
   }
   return   false;
}
```

bool GeomUtil::OneOfSixToTriIntersect (const float3 vox_center, Triangle *tri, int dom_axis) [private]

```
{
```

```
int  i, j;
int  order[6];
float3  D, P;
float2  selcoord, direction, alpha_beta;
float   num,  range;
bool  use_halo;
unsigned   char  checks;

getOrder(order, dom_axis);   // this is a pointer

// Graphics Gems, p.390
// Since the intersection formula doesn't care about
// parallel planes (the resulting projection will be
// the same for either), then we don't need to iterate
// on 6 ray directions: instead just iterate on the 3
// principal planes.

// tri->d is the same as d0 etc. for the conservative
// rasterization: see triangle_setup_6sep in GeomUtil.h
num = tri->d  + (
      tri->n.x  * vox_center.x  +
      tri->n.y  * vox_center.y  +
      tri->n.z  * vox_center.z);

// no visible difference when enabling non-dominant axes
// so just loop over first (dominant) pair.
for  (i = 0; i  <  1; ++i) {
   // get ray direction D (but only use u and v);
   // only change between i  &  i+1 is dom axis dir,
   // which is being assumed and ignored.
  D.x  =  ray6[order[i<<1]][0];
  D.y  =  ray6[order[i<<1]][1];
  D.z  =  ray6[order[i<<1]][2];

   // it's possible to match the selected (u,v)
   // dimensions with the plane-face that ends
   // up having edge overlaps in UV. That can be
   // done by checking the planetest returns as
   // in EdgeTests(). But generally you start
   // with the dominant axis plane and go from
   // there: e.g. the ordering of this loop.
   unsigned   short  select;
   j = (order[i<<1])>>1;   // 4 ->  2; 2 ->  1; 0 ->  0
   switch  (j) {
   case   X:
     selcoord.x  = vox_center.y;
     selcoord.y  = vox_center.z;
     direction.x  = D.y;
     direction.y  = D.z;
```

```
      select =  X;
       break;
    case  Y:
      selcoord.x  = vox_center.x;
      selcoord.y  = vox_center.z;
      direction.x  = D.x;
      direction.y  = D.z;
      select =  Y;
       break;
    case  Z:
      selcoord.x  = vox_center.x;
      selcoord.y  = vox_center.y;
      direction.x  = D.x;
      direction.y  = D.y;
      select =  Z;
       break;
   }
    // first compute with threshold perimeter, to see
    // if the extended voxel distance of 0.5 is  "in".
    // will also fail if principal plane is  "edge on"  in
    // non-dominant axis and no halo was made for that orientation.
    if  (!Inside(tri, selcoord, direction, select, alpha_beta,
          use_halo =  true, checks))
        continue;

    // if it passes the threshold, use the threshold checks
    // to compute the actual intersection (alpha and beta)
    // ** Since we're not using alpha:beta can skip this second
    // call.
/*
    Inside(tri, selcoord, direction, select, alpha_beta,
           use_halo = false, checks);
*/
    // Use status as signal that voxel position may be within
    // range. Can use an embedding plane calc, or an alpha:beta
    // calc. They both give same results, so use the faster one:
    if  (!EmbeddingPlaneIntersection(vox_center, tri, D, num, P))
        continue;

//      AlphaBetaIntersection(tri, select, alpha_beta, P);

    // we've got the intersection point on the triangle
    // but we don't know which side of vox center it's on.
    // this matters for the equality test at the end.
    for  (j = 0; j  <  2; ++j) {
       // look at ray direction coord as coord of interest
       // Important Note: for select = 0, P.z is X (e.g. w);
       // for select = 1, P.z is Y; for select = 2, P.z = Z.
       // Secondary Note: we are not using alpha:beta, which
```

```
            // has a (u,v) mapping associated with it and thus the
            // the (w) coord (P.z) is the critical intersection.
            // Instead, using generic Embedding which has no (u,v)
            // association and so we use P.x, P.y, and P.z accordingly.
            if (order[i<<1] < 2) {
                // 0: negative direction
                if (j == 0)
                    range = (vox_center.x - P.x);
                else   // 1: positive
                    range = (P.x - vox_center.x);
                if (range < 0.0f)
                    continue;
            } else if (order[i<<1] < 4) {
                if (j == 0)
                    range = (vox_center.y - P.y);
                else
                    range = (P.y - vox_center.y);
                if (range < 0.0f)
                    continue;
            } else {
                if (j == 0)
                    range = (vox_center.z - P.z);
                else
                    range = (P.z - vox_center.z);
                if (range < 0.0f)
                    continue;
            }
            // if == will be picked up by next voxel over.
            // but need to do some association to make this work:
            // if even, is a negative direction: use <=
            // if odd, is positive direction: use <
            if (j == 0) {
                if (range <= 0.5f)
                    return true;
                // skip redundant calc
                break;
            } else {
                if (range < 0.5f)
                    return true;
            }
        } // j
    } // i
    return false;
}

GeomUtil GeomUtil::operator= (GeomUtil rhs)
{
    if (this != &rhs)       // alias test
    {
```

```
        copy_float3(rhs.bbox0,  bbox0);
        copy_float3(rhs.bbox1,  bbox1);
        copy_float3(rhs.bbox_delta,  bbox_delta);
        copy_float3(rhs.inv_bbox_delta,  inv_bbox_delta);
        N  = rhs.N;
    }
    return  *this;            // return pointer to self
}
```

void GeomUtil::opposingDistance (const float2 midp, float2 &reach, const float2 v0, const float2 v1, const float2 opp) [private]

```
{
    float2  dir, prime;
    float  dx, dy, distp, disto;   // distance to prime, to original
    bool  omitx, omity, flip;

    // we are looking for outward-pointing orthogonal distances
    // corresponding to the voxel 1of 6 orthogonal axes.
    // project opposite point to opposing side
    // tack the direction vector to v0.
    dir.x  = -(opp.x  - v1.x);
    dir.y  = -(opp.y  - v1.y);
    prime.x  = v0.x  + dir.x;
    prime.y  = v0.y  + dir.y;

    reach.x  = midp.x  + 0.5f;
    reach.y  = midp.y  + 0.5f;   // defaults
    omitx = omity =  false;
    if  (fp_math.equalBoundsf(v0.y, v1.y,  PRECISIONf)) {
      reach.x  = midp.x;
      omitx =  true;
    } else   if  (fp_math.equalBoundsf(v0.x, v1.x,  PRECISIONf)) {
      reach.y  = midp.y;
      omity =  true;
    }
    // just looking for the correct orientation on the outward vector
    // work by symmetry
    // reach is really two directions, not a complete point
    if  (!omitx) {
      flip =  false;
      // be careful with roundoff: check primary values, not derived:
      if  (fp_math.equalBoundsf(prime.x, midp.x,  PRECISIONf)) {
        flip =  strainTestX(v0, v1, reach, midp, prime, opp);
      } else  {
        dx = reach.x  - prime.x;
        dy = midp.y  - prime.y;
        distp = dx * dx + dy * dy;
        dx = reach.x  - opp.x;
        dy = midp.y  - opp.y;
```

```
        disto = dx * dx + dy * dy;

         if (distp > disto)
           flip = true;
      }
       if (flip)
        reach.x = midp.x - 0.5f;    // switch directions
   }
   if (!omity) {
     flip = false;
     if (fp_math.equalBoundsf(prime.y, midp.y, PRECISIONf)) {
        flip = strainTestY(v0, v1, reach, midp, prime, opp);
     } else {
        dx = reach.y - prime.y;
        dy = midp.x - prime.x;
        distp = dx * dx + dy * dy;
        dx = reach.y - opp.y;
        dy = midp.x - opp.x;
        disto = dx * dx + dy * dy;

         if (distp > disto)
           flip = true;
     }
      if (flip)
        reach.y = midp.y - 0.5f;
   }
}

// perform plane setup
template<int32 AXIS>
void GeomUtil::plane_setup (const float3 &v0, const float3 &n, float4 &plane_eq)
{
   typedef  uvw<AXIS>  sel;

   const  float  inv_n = 1.0f / (sel::w(n));  //__frcp_rn( sel::w( n ) );
   plane_eq.x = sel::u( n ) * inv_n;
   plane_eq.y = sel::v( n ) * inv_n;
   plane_eq.z =
          plane_eq.x  * (sel::u( v0 ) - sel::u(  bbox0  ))
        + plane_eq.y  * (sel::v( v0 ) - sel::v(  bbox0  ))
        +  sel::w( v0 ) -  sel::w(  bbox0  );
  plane_eq.w = inv_n;
}

template<int32 AXIS>
void GeomUtil::plane_setup_6sep (const float3 &v0, const float3 &n, float4 &plane_eq)
{
   typedef  uvw<AXIS>  sel;
   float3  nt =  make_float3(sel::u(n),
```

```
                    sel::v(n),
                    sel::w(n));

    // homogeneous coordinates: w = 1/z, zw = z = 1
    const   float  inv_n = 1.0f / nt.z;
    plane_eq.x  = nt.x  * inv_n;
    plane_eq.y  = nt.y  * inv_n;
    plane_eq.z  =
            plane_eq.x  * (sel::u( v0 ) - sel::u(bbox_delta))
          + plane_eq.y  * (sel::v( v0 ) - sel::v(bbox_delta))
          + (sel::w( v0 ) -  sel::w(bbox_delta));  // e.g. z = 1.0
    plane_eq.w  = inv_n;
}

// coord is the voxel base coordinate (integer space)
bool GeomUtil::PlaneTest (const ushort3 &coord, const float3 &n, Triangle *tri)
{
    const   float  np =
          n.x  * (bbox0.x  +  float(coord.x) *  bbox_delta.x) +
          n.y  * (bbox0.y  +  float(coord.y) *  bbox_delta.y) +
          n.z  * (bbox0.z  +  float(coord.z) *  bbox_delta.z);

    return  ((np + tri->r1) * (np + tri->r2)  <= 0.0f);
}

int GeomUtil::pointPos (float2 &p1, float2 &p2, float2 &v_p0, float2 &v_p1) [private]
{
    float  dx = v_p1.x  - v_p0.x;
    float  dy = v_p1.y  - v_p0.y;
    float  dx1 = p1.x  - v_p0.x;
    float  dy1 = p1.y  - v_p0.y;
    float  dx2 = p2.x  - v_p1.x;
    float  dy2 = p2.y  - v_p1.y;
    float  p_1 = (dx * dy1 - dy * dx1);
    float  p_2 = (dx * dy2 - dy * dx2);
    if  (fp_math.equalBoundsf(p_1, 0.0f,  PRECISIONf) ||
         fp_math.equalBoundsf(p_2, 0.0f,  PRECISIONf))
        return  0;
    if  ((p_1  >  0.0f   &&  p_2  <  0.0f) ||
         (p_1  <  0.0f  &&  p_2  >  0.0f))
        return  -1;
    return  1;
}

// 26-separating raster using basic VoxelPipe code and triangle setup
template<int32 AXIS>
bool GeomUtil::rasterize (const ushort3 &coord, Triangle *tri) [private]
{
    typedef   uvw<AXIS>  sel;
```

```
const  float4  &plane_eq = tri->fine.plane_eq;

const  float3  &n_delta_u = tri->fine.n_delta_u[0];
const  float3  &n_delta_v = tri->fine.n_delta_v[0];
const  float3  &a  = tri->fine.a[0];

// the unit voxel is it: no iterating as in voxel-pipe
int32  u = sel::u(coord);
int32   v  =  sel::v(coord);

// translate in voxel space since post-translation in
// unit space combined with deltas won't work.
// Don't overwrite original (u, v, w) variables.
const  float  u_trans = float(u - (N   >>  1));
const  float  v_trans = float(v - (N   >>  1));

const  float3   b  =  make_float3(
        u_trans * n_delta_u.x,
        u_trans * n_delta_u.y,
        u_trans * n_delta_u.z  );

const  float3   c  =  make_float3(
        v_trans * n_delta_v.x,
        v_trans * n_delta_v.y,
        v_trans * n_delta_v.z  );

const  float  c0 = a.x  + b.x  + c.x;
const  float  c1 = a.y  + b.y  + c.y;
const  float  c2 = a.z  + b.z  + c.z;

const  bool  inside =
      (c0  >= 0.0f)  &&
      (c1  >= 0.0f)  &&
      (c2  >= 0.0f);

// next, if inside, see what the w-range is and clip.
// note: this has been tested and it DOES reject voxels
if  (inside) {
   // compute W depth
   const   float  min_uf = (u + (plane_eq.x   <  0.0f ? 1.0f : 0.0f)) * sel::u(  bbox_delta  );
   const   float  min_vf = (v + (plane_eq.y   <  0.0f ? 1.0f : 0.0f)) * sel::v(  bbox_delta  );
   const   float  min_wf = plane_eq.z  - (plane_eq.x*min_uf + plane_eq.y*min_vf);
   int32  min_w =  int32( min_wf *  sel::w(  inv_bbox_delta  ) );

   const   float  max_uf = (u + (plane_eq.x   >  0.0f ? 1.0f : 0.0f)) * sel::u(  bbox_delta  );
   const   float  max_vf = (v + (plane_eq.y   >  0.0f ? 1.0f : 0.0f)) * sel::v(  bbox_delta  );
   const   float  max_wf = plane_eq.z  - (plane_eq.x*max_uf + plane_eq.y*max_vf);
   int32  max_w =  int32( max_wf *  sel::w(  inv_bbox_delta  ) );
```

```
        if (max_w < min_w) {
            int32 tmp = min_w;
            min_w = max_w;
            max_w = tmp;
        }

        // clipping:
        // note we have another "clamp" here: max of the min, and min of the max,
        // for the "most interior" range : it will bypass loop if voxel w is
        // outside the range; else will enter loop on unit voxel.
        min_w = max( min_w, sel::w( coord ) );
        max_w = min( max_w, sel::w( coord ) );

        // VoxelPipe doesn't do the remaining two projection tests.
        // It simply accepts the clipped/clamped value.
        for (int32 w = min_w; w <= max_w; ++w) { // test
            // guaranteed that w == sel::w( coord ) from clip and entry
            return true;
        }

    } // inside
    return false;
}

// 26-separating raster (Schwarz & Seidel 3 overlap tests)
template<int32 AXIS>
bool GeomUtil::rasterize_26sep (const ushort3 &coord, Triangle *tri) [private]
{
    typedef uvw<AXIS> sel;

    // in X 0 (uvw::yzx) U: uv is wv:xz ... U is wv: u_n_delta_u, u_n_delta_v@0 = uv::xz (1)
    //                   V: uv is wu:xy ... V is wu: v_n_delta_u, v_n_delta_v@1 = uv::xy (2)
    // in Y 1 (uvw::xzy) U: uv is wv:yz ... U is wv: u_n_delta_u, u_n_delta_v@3 = uv::yz (0)
    //                   V: uv is uw:xy ... V is uw: v_n_delta_u, v_n_delta_v@4 = uv::xy (2)
    // in Z 2 (uvw::xyz) U: uv is vw:yz ... U is vw: u_n_delta_u, u_n_delta_v@6 = uv::yz (0)
    //                   V: uv is uw:xz ... V is uw: v_n_delta_u, v_n_delta_v@7 = uv::xz (1)

    const float4 &plane_eq = tri->fine.plane_eq;

    const float3 &u_n_delta_u = tri->fine.n_delta_u[0];
    const float3 &v_n_delta_u = tri->fine.n_delta_u[1];
    const float3 &w_n_delta_u = tri->fine.n_delta_u[2];

    const float3 &u_n_delta_v = tri->fine.n_delta_v[0];
    const float3 &v_n_delta_v = tri->fine.n_delta_v[1];
    const float3 &w_n_delta_v = tri->fine.n_delta_v[2];

    const float3 &u_a = tri->fine.a[0];
```

```
const  float3  &v_a = tri->fine.a[1];
const  float3  &w_a = tri->fine.a[2];

// the unit voxel is it: no iterating as in voxel-pipe
int32  u = sel::u(coord);
int32  v = sel::v(coord);

// translate in voxel space since post-translation in
// unit space combined with deltas won't work.
// Don't overwrite original (u, v, w) variables.
const  float  u_trans = float(u - (N  >>  1));
const  float  v_trans = float(v - (N  >>  1));

const  float3  w_b =  make_float3(
          u_trans * w_n_delta_u.x,
          u_trans * w_n_delta_u.y,
          u_trans * w_n_delta_u.z  );

const  float3  w_c =  make_float3(
          v_trans * w_n_delta_v.x,
          v_trans * w_n_delta_v.y,
          v_trans * w_n_delta_v.z  );

const  float  c0 = w_a.x  + w_b.x  + w_c.x;
const  float  c1 = w_a.y  + w_b.y  + w_c.y;
const  float  c2 = w_a.z  + w_b.z  + w_c.z;

const  bool  inside =
     (c0  >= 0.0f)  &&
     (c1  >= 0.0f)  &&
     (c2  >= 0.0f) ;

// This has been tested for rejection and it DOES reject voxels, so keep all this code.
if  (inside) {
   // set the bit for this column
   // Offset is 1 or 0 depending on plane equation signs:
   // compute W depth range
   const  float  min_uf = (u + (plane_eq.x  <  0.0f ? 1.0f : 0.0f)) * sel::u(  bbox_delta  );
   const  float  min_vf = (v + (plane_eq.y  <  0.0f ? 1.0f : 0.0f)) * sel::v(  bbox_delta  );
   const  float  min_wf = plane_eq.z  - (plane_eq.x*min_uf + plane_eq.y*min_vf);
   int32  min_w =  int32( min_wf *  sel::w(  inv_bbox_delta  ) );

   const  float  max_uf = (u + (plane_eq.x  >  0.0f ? 1.0f : 0.0f)) * sel::u(  bbox_delta  );
   const  float  max_vf = (v + (plane_eq.y  >  0.0f ? 1.0f : 0.0f)) * sel::v(  bbox_delta  );
   const  float  max_wf = plane_eq.z  - (plane_eq.x*max_uf + plane_eq.y*max_vf);
   int32  max_w =  int32( max_wf *  sel::w(  inv_bbox_delta  ) );

   if  (max_w  <  min_w) {
      int32  tmp = min_w;
```

```
        min_w = max_w;
        max_w = tmp;
    }

    // note we have another "clamp" here: max of the min, and min of the max,
    // for the "most interior" range : it will bypass loop if voxel w is
    // outside the range; else will enter loop on unit voxel.
    min_w = max( min_w, sel::w( coord ) );
    max_w = min( max_w, sel::w( coord ) );

    // min_w is always equal to max_w
    // do the remaining 2 projection tests for single voxel in the w-column
    // it will just iterate once, but we need it because it excludes
    for (int32 w = min_w; w <= max_w; ++w) {
        // U-axis test
        {
            const float u_u = AXIS == 2 ? float(v) : float(w);
            const float u_v = AXIS == 2 ? float(w) : float(v);

            const float u_u_trans = u_u - float(N >> 1);
            const float u_v_trans = u_v - float(N >> 1);

            // test the U-axis
            const float3 u_c = make_float3(
                u_a.x + u_u_trans * u_n_delta_u.x + u_v_trans * u_n_delta_v.x,
                u_a.y + u_u_trans * u_n_delta_u.y + u_v_trans * u_n_delta_v.y,
                u_a.z + u_u_trans * u_n_delta_u.z + u_v_trans * u_n_delta_v.z );

            if ((u_c.x < 0.0f) ||
                (u_c.y < 0.0f) ||
                (u_c.z < 0.0f))
                return false;
        } // U

        // V-axis test
        {
            const float v_u = AXIS == 0 ? float(w) : float(u);
            const float v_v = AXIS == 0 ? float(u) : float(w);

            const float v_u_trans = v_u - float(N >> 1);
            const float v_v_trans = v_v - float(N >> 1);

            // test the V-axis
            const float3 v_c = make_float3(
                v_a.x + v_u_trans * v_n_delta_u.x + v_v_trans * v_n_delta_v.x,
                v_a.y + v_u_trans * v_n_delta_u.y + v_v_trans * v_n_delta_v.y,
                v_a.z + v_u_trans * v_n_delta_u.z + v_v_trans * v_n_delta_v.z );

            if ((v_c.x < 0.0f) ||
```

```
                (v_c.y  <  0.0f) ||
                (v_c.z  <  0.0f))
               return  false;
         } // V
         // It's in the current voxel.
         return  true;
      } // w column
   } // inside
   return  false;
}

bool GeomUtil::Rasterize_26sepTop (const ushort3 &coord, Triangle *tri)
{
    if (raster ==  CONSERVATIVE_OV1) {
       // VoxelPipe or CONSERVATIVE_OV1
       if  (tri->axis  == 0)
          return  rasterize<X>(coord, tri);
       if  (tri->axis  == 1)
          return  rasterize<Y>(coord, tri);
       return  rasterize<Z>(coord, tri);
    }
    // Schwarz  &  Seidel or CONSERVATIVE_OV3
    if  (tri->axis  == 0)
       return  rasterize_26sep<X>(coord, tri);
    if  (tri->axis  == 1)
       return  rasterize_26sep<Y>(coord, tri);
    return  rasterize_26sep<Z>(coord, tri);
}

// 6-separating "thin" raster
template<int32 AXIS>
bool GeomUtil::rasterize_6sep (const ushort3 &coord, Triangle *tri) [private]
{
    typedef   uvw<AXIS>  sel;

    // you need to think in three dimensions to do this.
    // but not only that, you need to think upstream and
    // downstream, e.g. what happens at each level as
    // subdivision progresses -- you could call this the
    //  "time"  dimension. So really this is a 4D algorithm.
    float3  vox_center, ranges;
    int  dom_axis = AXIS;
    short  facecount;
    float  dist;

   vox_center.x  = coord.x  + 0.5f;
   vox_center.y  = coord.y  + 0.5f;
   vox_center.z  = coord.z  + 0.5f;
```

```
if (vox_center.x  == 35.5f  &&
     vox_center.y  == 23.5f  &&
     vox_center.z  == 25.5f)
    int   a  = 1;       // breakpoint : TestTriangle

 // first test if inside the big sphere
 if  (!centerTest(vox_center, tri->big_center, tri->big_radius)) {
     // outside: do the center-to-center ray test
     if  (!StraightToSphere(vox_center,
           tri->big_center, tri->big_radius, dist)) {
         // not in or within 0.5 of big sphere, but may
         // be close. This next test is to catch the single
         // voxels at a triangle vertex, when resolution gets
         // higher. dist comes back squared: 1^2 = 1.0f
         if  (dist  <= 1.0f) {
             if  (!TrivertSpheres(tri, vox_center))
                 return   false;
         }
     }
     // else fall through if close enough : more tests
} else   if  (terminal) {
    // inside the big sphere, now is it inside the little?
    if  (centerTest(vox_center, tri->little_center, tri->little_radius)) {
        // the little sphere entirely encompasses the triangle surface,
        // so just need to do the easy embedding plane test: guaranteed
        // triangle surface!
        return   OneOfSixToEmbeddingPlane(vox_center, tri, dom_axis,
                                  0.5f, ranges);
    }
    // else fall through to other tests; part of the
    // triangle will be outside of the little sphere
}
// we are inside of the big sphere, possibly terminal level
// or: the big sphere is close, within 0.5 of vox center.
if  (!terminal) {
    // Only run the edge tests on non-terminal levels as it's  "liberal"
    // and will otherwise introduce unwanted voxels.
    EdgeTests(coord, tri, facecount);
    if  (facecount == 3)
        return   true;
    // don't reject if facecount == 0 because there can be a
    // big  "projection hole"  at finer resolutions when a voxel
    // is in the middle of a triangle.
    if  (OneOfSixToEmbeddingPlane(vox_center, tri, dom_axis,
                             0.5f, ranges))
        return   true;

    // last_range for 0.5 is 1.0f, and 1 + sqrt(1) = 2
    if  (checkRange(ranges, 2.0f)) {
```

```
            // As a last resort (because of speed issues), look ahead.
            // Args: 0.5f last; 0.25f max
            return  LookAheadChildrenToEmbedding(vox_center, tri, dom_axis,
                0.5f, 0.25f, g_level, 0);
        }
        return  false;
    }

    // terminal and very close to acceptance: final test
    return  OneOfSixToTriIntersect(vox_center, tri, dom_axis);
}

// These top routines deal with the triangle's dominant axis.
bool GeomUtil::RasterizeTop (const ushort3 &coord, Triangle *tri)
{
    // Schwarz & Seidel, CUDA scan approach
    if (raster != THIN_OV3)
        return  false;

    if (tri->axis == 0)
        return rasterize_6sep<X>(coord, tri);
    if (tri->axis == 1)
        return rasterize_6sep<Y>(coord, tri);
    return rasterize_6sep<Z>(coord, tri);
}

void GeomUtil::ScaleTriangleBBox (float3 &tri_bbox0, float3 &tri_bbox1, Triangle *tri)
{
    tri_bbox0.x = tri->master_bbox0.x * inv_bbox_delta.x;
    tri_bbox0.y = tri->master_bbox0.y * inv_bbox_delta.y;
    tri_bbox0.z = tri->master_bbox0.z * inv_bbox_delta.z;

    tri_bbox1.x = tri->master_bbox1.x * inv_bbox_delta.x;
    tri_bbox1.y = tri->master_bbox1.y * inv_bbox_delta.y;
    tri_bbox1.z = tri->master_bbox1.z * inv_bbox_delta.z;
}

void GeomUtil::SetBBoxDeltas ()
{
    MakeBBoxDelta(bbox_delta);
    MakeInvBBoxDelta(inv_bbox_delta);
}

// cascaded from GeomWorker
unsigned int GeomUtil::setRaster (const unsigned int value)
{
    return  raster = value;
}
```

bool GeomUtil::StraightToSphere (const float3 vox_center, const float3 center, float radius, float &dist) [private]

```
{
    float3  V, P;
    float  eox, eoy, eoz, tri_v,  scale;
    float  norm, norm2, vsx, vsy, vsz,  range;

    // tri_v = EO . V
    // get ray direction V
    // it will be a vector from voxel center to sphere center
    // O is sphere center (origin)
    // E is voxel center (passed in)
    // store this since it's used twice
   eox = center.x  - vox_center.x;
   eoy = center.y  - vox_center.y;
   eoz = center.z  - vox_center.z;

   norm2 = eox * eox + eoy * eoy + eoz * eoz;
   norm = 1.0f / sqrt(norm2);

    // this is what we want for straight to center
   V.x  = eox * norm;
   V.y  = eoy * norm;
   V.z  = eoz * norm;

    // tri_v = triangle side
   tri_v = eox * V.x  + eoy * V.y  + eoz * V.z;

    // P = E + (tri_v - radius)V
   scale = tri_v  - radius;
   vsx = scale * V.x;
   vsy = scale * V.y;
   vsz = scale * V.z;

    // here's the intersection point on the sphere:
   P.x  = vox_center.x  + vsx;
   P.y  = vox_center.y  + vsy;
   P.z  = vox_center.z  + vsz;

    // how far?
   range = (P.x  - vox_center.x) * (P.x  - vox_center.x) +
           (P.y  - vox_center.y) * (P.y  - vox_center.y) +
           (P.z  - vox_center.z) * (P.z  - vox_center.z);
   dist =  range;

    // if == to boundary, next voxel over will be  "inside"
    // and will capture it. Voxel is sphere with r = 0.5.
    if  (range  <  (0.5 * 0.5))
       return   true;
```

```
    return  false;
}

bool GeomUtil::strainTestX (const float2 v0, const float2 v1, const float2 reach, const float2 midp,
const float2 prime, const float2 opp) [private]
{
    float Cy, Dy;

    if (v0.x  < v1.x) {
      Cy = v0.y;
      Dy = v1.y;
    } else {
      Cy = v1.y;
      Dy = v0.y;
    }
    if (Cy < Dy) {
       if (opp.y  < Dy && reach.x  > midp.x)
          return  true;
       if (opp.y  > Cy && reach.x  < midp.x)
          return  true;
    } else {
       if (opp.y  < Cy && reach.x  < midp.x)
          return  true;
       if (opp.y  > Dy && reach.x  > midp.x)
          return  true;
    }
    return  false;
}

bool GeomUtil::strainTestY (const float2 v0, const float2 v1, const float2 reach, const float2 midp,
const float2 prime, const float2 opp) [private]
{
    float Cx, Dx;

    if (v0.y  < v1.y) {
      Cx = v0.x;
      Dx = v1.x;
    } else {
      Cx = v1.x;
      Dx = v0.x;
    }
    if (Cx < Dx) {
       if (opp.x  < Dx && reach.y  > midp.y)
          return  true;
       if (opp.x  > Cx && reach.y  < midp.y)
          return  true;
    } else {
       if (opp.x  < Cx && reach.y  < midp.y)
```

```
            return  true;
        if (opp.x  > Dx && reach.y  > midp.y)
            return  true;
    }
    return  false;
}

void GeomUtil::swap (float4 &a, float4 &b)
{
    const  float4  tmp =  a;
    a =  b;
    b = tmp;
}

// perform triangle setup : this is VoxelPipe math for 26-sep,
// but is slightly modified (as a numeric bugfix) to match the
// Schwarz & Seidel math for "conservative" (26-sep).
template<int32 AXIS>
void GeomUtil::triangle_setup (Triangle *tri, float3 &n_delta_u, float3 &n_delta_v, float3 &a)
{
    typedef  uvw<AXIS>  sel;

    const  float3  &v0  = tri->v0;
    const  float3  &v1  = tri->v1;
    const  float3  &v2  = tri->v2;
    const  float3  &edge0 = tri->edge0;
    const  float3  &edge1 = tri->edge1;
    const  float3  &edge2 = tri->edge2;
    const  float3  &n  = tri->n;

    const  float  sgn_w = sel::ccw( n );

    const  float2  n0 =  make_float2( -sel::v( edge0 ) * sgn_w, sel::u( edge0 ) * sgn_w );
    const  float  d0 = -(n0.x  * sel::u( v0 ) + n0.y  *  sel::v( v0 )) +
         fmaxf( 0.0f, sel::u(  bbox_delta  )*n0.x  ) +
         fmaxf( 0.0f,  sel::v(  bbox_delta  )*n0.y  );

    const  float2  n1 =  make_float2( -sel::v( edge1 ) * sgn_w, sel::u( edge1 ) * sgn_w );
    const  float  d1 = -(n1.x  * sel::u( v1 ) + n1.y  *  sel::v( v1 )) +
         fmaxf( 0.0f, sel::u(  bbox_delta  )*n1.x  ) +
         fmaxf( 0.0f,  sel::v(  bbox_delta  )*n1.y  );

    const  float2  n2 =  make_float2( -sel::v( edge2 ) * sgn_w, sel::u( edge2 ) * sgn_w );
    const  float  d2 = -(n2.x  * sel::u( v2 ) + n2.y  *  sel::v( v2 )) +
         fmaxf( 0.0f, sel::u(  bbox_delta  )*n2.x  ) +
         fmaxf( 0.0f,  sel::v(  bbox_delta  )*n2.y  );

    a.x  = d0;
    a.y  = d1;
```

```
    a.z  = d2;

    n_delta_u.x  = n0.x  * sel::u(  bbox_delta  );
    n_delta_u.y  = n1.x  * sel::u(  bbox_delta  );
    n_delta_u.z  = n2.x  * sel::u(  bbox_delta  );

    n_delta_v.x  = n0.y  *  sel::v(  bbox_delta  );
    n_delta_v.y  = n1.y  *  sel::v(  bbox_delta  );
    n_delta_v.z  = n2.y  *  sel::v(  bbox_delta  );
}

// perform triangle setup 6 separating case
template<int32 AXIS>
void GeomUtil::triangle_setup_6sep (Triangle *tri, FineVars &fine, short select)
{
     typedef   uvw<AXIS>  sel;

     const   float3   &v0  = tri->v0;
     const   float3   &v1  = tri->v1;
     const   float3   &v2  = tri->v2;
     const   float3   &n  = tri->n;

     // avoid really small numbers and used scaled triangle coords
     float  u_v0 = (sel::u( v0 ) - sel::u(bbox0)) * sel::u(inv_bbox_delta);
     float  v_v0 = (sel::v( v0 ) -  sel::v(bbox0)) * sel::v(inv_bbox_delta);
     float  u_v1 = (sel::u( v1 ) - sel::u(bbox0)) * sel::u(inv_bbox_delta);
     float  v_v1 = (sel::v( v1 ) -  sel::v(bbox0)) * sel::v(inv_bbox_delta);
     float  u_v2 = (sel::u( v2 ) - sel::u(bbox0)) * sel::u(inv_bbox_delta);
     float  v_v2 = (sel::v( v2 ) -  sel::v(bbox0)) * sel::v(inv_bbox_delta);

    fine.c0[select].x  = u_v0;
    fine.c0[select].y  = v_v0;
    fine.c1[select].x  = u_v1;
    fine.c1[select].y  = v_v1;
    fine.c2[select].x  = u_v2;
    fine.c2[select].y  = v_v2;

     // and w's for 0, 1, 2: pack it in a float3
     float  w_v0 = (sel::w( v0 ) -  sel::w(bbox0)) *  sel::w(inv_bbox_delta);
     float  w_v1 = (sel::w( v1 ) -  sel::w(bbox0)) *  sel::w(inv_bbox_delta);
     float  w_v2 = (sel::w( v2 ) -  sel::w(bbox0)) *  sel::w(inv_bbox_delta);

    fine.cw[select].x  = w_v0;
    fine.cw[select].y  = w_v1;
    fine.cw[select].z  = w_v2;

     // also, the embedding plane value
     // this is irrespective of any dominant axis
     // the plane changes with each level since the triangle
```

```
    // is scaled and thereby its location...
    // first translate and scale:
    float3  v0t =  make_float3(
          (v0.x  -  bbox0.x) *  inv_bbox_delta.x,
          (v0.y  -  bbox0.y) *  inv_bbox_delta.y,
          (v0.z  -  bbox0.z) *  inv_bbox_delta.z);
   tri->d  = -v0t.x  * n.x  -v0t.y  * n.y  - v0t.z  * n.z;
}

bool GeomUtil::TrivertSpheres (Triangle *tri, const float3 vox_center) [private]
{
    float3  center;
    float  dist, radius;

    radius = 0.5f;
    // triangle-vertex sphere radius
    // for each triangle vertex and its virtual sphere r = 0.5
    for  (short  i = 0; i  <  3; ++i) {
       // use axis Z which goes uvw = xyz
       switch  (i) {
       case  0:
          center.x  = tri->fine.c0[2].x;
          center.y  = tri->fine.c0[2].y;
          center.z  = tri->fine.cw[2].x;  // v0
          break;
       case  1:
          center.x  = tri->fine.c1[2].x;
          center.y  = tri->fine.c1[2].y;
          center.z  = tri->fine.cw[2].y;  // v1
          break;
       case  2:
          center.x  = tri->fine.c2[2].x;
          center.y  = tri->fine.c2[2].y;
          center.z  = tri->fine.cw[2].z;  // v2
          break;
       }

       if  (StraightToSphere(vox_center,
                       center, radius, dist))
          return   true;

       // try next triangle vertex
    }
    return   false;
}
```

Local Data

```
// halo checks (triangle "inside" principal plane tests)
static const unsigned char BETA_IN_01 = 0x01;
static const unsigned char ALPHA_GTE0 = 0x02;

// voxel faces joining at voxel base point
static float faces[12][3] = {
	// YZ
	{0.0, 0.0, 0.0}, {0.0, 0.0, 1.0}, {0.0, 1.0, 1.0}, {0.0, 1.0, 0.0},
	// XZ
	{0.0, 0.0, 0.0}, {1.0, 0.0, 0.0}, {1.0, 0.0, 1.0}, {0.0, 0.0, 1.0},
	// XY
	{0.0, 0.0, 0.0}, {1.0, 0.0, 0.0}, {1.0, 1.0, 0.0}, {0.0, 1.0, 0.0}
};

// ray directions, in AXIS order (X:0, Y:1, Z:2)
static float ray6[6][3] = {
	{-1.0, 0.0, 0.0}, {1.0, 0.0, 0.0}, // X
	{0.0, -1.0, 0.0}, {0.0, 1.0, 0.0}, // Y
	{0.0, 0.0, -1.0}, {0.0, 0.0, 1.0}  // Z
};

// to eliminate false negatives, look ahead this many levels
// into the octree for the current voxel.
static short MAX_DEEP;
// allocate a lookup make it 12 entries for 12 max recursion
// levels which is beyond overkill...
static const short MAX_RECURSION = 12;
// lookup for 45-degree max dominant ray distance
static float ray_dist[MAX_RECURSION];
```

Associated Data Holders

```
struct UVPack {
   // xyz coordinates copied from scaled triangle
   float3 p1, p2, p3;
   double3 p4;  // origin
   // distances for (u,v) coordinate system
   double p1p3, p1p2, p1p4, p4p2;
   // direction cosines for xform
   double cos_theta, sin_theta;
   double3 cos_alpha, cos_beta;
};
```

The documentation for this class was generated from the following files:
- GeomUtil.h
- GeomUtil.cpp

GeomWorker Class Reference

Public Member Functions

GeomWorker ()
~GeomWorker ()
GeomWorker operator= (GeomWorker rhs)

:: convert basic triangles to Master list triangles
TriangleList *TriangleConvert2MasterList (Vector<BasicTriangle * > &geom)

:: For spawned node, get a copy of the parent triangles.
void transferTriangles (TriangleList *orig_list)

int NewN (int level, int terminal_level, bool is_terminal)
int getN (int level)
void SetBBoxDeltas ()

:: per level
voidDoTriangleWork ()

:: Get all triangles, since the root encloses everything
:: Note, only get the index.
void getRootTriangles (Vector< int > &tri_idx)

:: Outer loop: triangles ; inner loop: voxels per octant.
VTList *CoarseTest (Vector< int >&tri_idx, NodeGroup *group)

:: if at least one triangle overlaps the current octant,
:: then return true: the octant will spawn children.
boolFineTest (NodeGroup *group, int octant, int begin, int end)

TriangleList *getTriangleList ()
int getTriListCount ()

:: all-important, context-sensitive!
void setRaster (const unsigned int value)

unsigned intgetRaster ()

Private Member Functions

voidAddExtras (Vector<ushort3 * > &extras, int tri_idx, int level, Vector<TGPair * > &pairs)

:: scale to a bi-unit bounding box and translate to straddle the origin.

TriangleList *BiUnitScale (Vector<BasicTriangle * > &geom)

void MasterEdgesAndNormal ()
void MasterEdges (float3 &v0, float3 &v1, float3 &v2, Triangle *tri)
void MasterNormal (float3 &edge0, float3 &edge2, Triangle *tri)
void MasterTriAxis (float3 &n, Triangle *tri)

:: call after TriAxis
:: get plane coefficients for rasterize functions
void PlaneEquation (Triangle *tri)

:: do this the easy way by overwriting -1 for invalid triangles
:: This preserves the TSpan indexing.
void compactPairList (VTPair **pair, Vector< int > &compact_list)

:: do this once per level
voidTriangleSetup (Triangle *tri)

:: In C++ could have a copy operator in the Triangle structure,
:: but this would increase its size.
voidCopyMasterData (const Triangle *source, Triangle *dest)

Private Attributes

TriangleList *tri_list
GeomUtil g_u
unsigned int raster

Detailed Description

Higher level coarse and fine testing on triangle geometry.

Constructor & Destructor Documentation

```
GeomWorker::GeomWorker () [inline]
: tri_list(NULL) {}

GeomWorker::~GeomWorker (void)
{
   if (tri_list == NULL)
      return;

   int count = tri_list->count;
   for (int i = 0; i < count; ++i) {
      Triangle *tri = tri_list->list[i];
      delete tri;
   }
```

```
    delete [] tri_list->list;
    delete  tri_list;
    tri_list = NULL;
}
```

Member Function Documentation

```
// scale to a bi-unit bounding box and translate to straddle the origin.
TriangleList * GeomWorker::BiUnitScale (Vector<BasicTriangle * > &geom) [private]
{
    int i, j, size;
    float min_x, min_y, min_z;
    float max_x, max_y, max_z;
    float cur_x, cur_y, cur_z;
    float dist_x, dist_y, dist_z;
    double  scale;
    double trans_x, trans_y, trans_z;
    BasicTriangle *tri_ptr;

   size = geom.size();
   min_x = min_y = min_z = 1.0e+38;
   max_x = max_y = max_z = -1.0e+38;

    for (i=0; i<size; ++i) {
      tri_ptr = geom[i];
       for (j=0; j < TRI_VERTS; ++j) {
         cur_x = tri_ptr->vert[j].x;
         cur_y = tri_ptr->vert[j].y;
         cur_z = tri_ptr->vert[j].z;
          if (cur_x < min_x)
            min_x = cur_x;
          if (cur_y < min_y)
            min_y = cur_y;
          if (cur_z < min_z)
            min_z = cur_z;

          if (cur_x > max_x)
            max_x = cur_x;
          if (cur_y > max_y)
            max_y = cur_y;
          if (cur_z > max_z)
            max_z = cur_z;
      }
   }
   dist_x = max_x - min_x;
   dist_y = max_y - min_y;
   dist_z = max_z - min_z;
```

```
    // scale by largest dimension
    if (dist_x > dist_y && dist_x > dist_z)
      scale = dist_x;
    else if (dist_y > dist_x && dist_y > dist_z)
      scale = dist_y;
    else
      scale = dist_z;

    // As we scale, create master triangle list
    // since it's bi-unit, halve the scale factor
    scale = 2.0 / scale;

    // translate first, then scale
    trans_x = -(min_x + dist_x / 2.0);
    trans_y = -(min_y + dist_y / 2.0);
    trans_z = -(min_z + dist_z / 2.0);

    tri_list = new TriangleList;
    tri_list->count = size;

    Triangle **plist = new Triangle * [size];
    tri_list->list = plist;

    for (i=0; i<size; ++i) {
       Triangle *cur_tri = new Triangle;
       tri_list->list[i] = cur_tri;
       tri_ptr = geom[i];
       cur_tri->color = tri_ptr->color;

       // verts are made explicit for permuting
       cur_tri->v0.x = (tri_ptr->vert[0].x + trans_x) * scale;
       cur_tri->v0.y = (tri_ptr->vert[0].y + trans_y) * scale;
       cur_tri->v0.z = (tri_ptr->vert[0].z + trans_z) * scale;

       cur_tri->v1.x = (tri_ptr->vert[1].x + trans_x) * scale;
       cur_tri->v1.y = (tri_ptr->vert[1].y + trans_y) * scale;
       cur_tri->v1.z = (tri_ptr->vert[1].z + trans_z) * scale;

       cur_tri->v2.x = (tri_ptr->vert[2].x + trans_x) * scale;
       cur_tri->v2.y = (tri_ptr->vert[2].y + trans_y) * scale;
       cur_tri->v2.z = (tri_ptr->vert[2].z + trans_z) * scale;
    }
    return tri_list;
}


// Outer loop: triangles ; inner loop: voxels per octant.
VTList * GeomWorker::CoarseTest (Vector< int > &tri_idx, NodeGroup *group)
```

```
{
   int  i, j,  size;
   unsigned   short   x,  y,  z;
   Vector<VTPair *>  pairs;

   size = tri_idx.size();
   for  (i = 0; i  <   size; ++i) {
      Triangle  *tri =  tri_list->list[ tri_idx[i] ];

      for  (j=0; j<OCTANTS; ++j) {
         NodeData  voxel = group->node[j];
         x = voxel.coord.x; y = voxel.coord.y; z = voxel.coord.z;
         if  ((x  >= tri->bbox0i.x   &&   x  <= tri->bbox1i.x)  &&
             (y  >= tri->bbox0i.y   &&   y  <= tri->bbox1i.y)  &&
             (z  >= tri->bbox0i.z   &&   z  <= tri->bbox1i.z)) {
            // tri bbox volume includes (x,y,z)
            // make the voxel-triangle pair
            VTPair  *pair =  new   VTPair;
            pair->tri_idx  = tri_idx[i];
            pair->vox_idx  = j;       // reference from zero
            pairs.push_back(pair);
         }
      }  // octants
   }  // triangles     size = pairs.size();
   VTList  * vt_list =  new   VTList;
   vt_list->count  =  size;
   vt_list->list  = NULL;
   if  (size != 0) {
      VTPair  **plist =  new   VTPair  * [size];
      vt_list->list  = plist;
   }
   // copy pointers
    for  (i = 0; i  <   size; ++i) {
     vt_list->list[i] = pairs[i];
   }
   // go ahead and attach to group
   group->pairs  = vt_list;

   // pairs about to go out of scope, but not what the pointers point to
   return  vt_list;
}

// do this the easy way by overwriting -1 for invalid triangles
// This preserves the TSpan indexing.
void GeomWorker::compactPairList (VTPair **pair, Vector< int > &compact_list) [private]


{
   int  i,  size,  index;
```

```
    size = compact_list.size();
    for  (i = 0; i<   size; ++i) {
        index = compact_list[i];
        pair[index]->tri_idx  =  INVALID;  // = -1
    }
}

// In C++ could have a copy operator in the Triangle structure,
// but this would increase its size.
void GeomWorker::CopyMasterData (const Triangle *source, Triangle *dest) [private]
{
    g_u.copy_float3(source->v0, dest->v0);
    g_u.copy_float3(source->v1, dest->v1);
    g_u.copy_float3(source->v2, dest->v2);
    g_u.copy_float3(source->edge0, dest->edge0);
    g_u.copy_float3(source->edge1, dest->edge1);
    g_u.copy_float3(source->edge2, dest->edge2);
    g_u.copy_float3(source->n, dest->n);
    g_u.copy_float3(source->master_bbox0, dest->master_bbox0);
    g_u.copy_float3(source->master_bbox1, dest->master_bbox1);
    g_u.copy_float4(source->fine.plane_eq, dest->fine.plane_eq);
   dest->color.r  = source->color.r;
   dest->color.g  = source->color.g;
   dest->color.b  = source->color.b;
   dest->axis  = source->axis;
}

// per level
void GeomWorker::DoTriangleWork ()
{
    if  (tri_list  == NULL)
        return;

    int   count  =  tri_list->count;
    for  (int  i = 0; i<count; ++i) {
        Triangle  * tri =  tri_list->list[i];
        g_u.ScaleTriangleBBox(tri->bbox0, tri->bbox1, tri);
        g_u.ComputeIntegerBBox(tri->bbox0i, tri->bbox1i,
              tri->bbox0, tri->bbox1);
        g_u.InitPlaneTestVars(tri->n, tri->v0, tri);
        TriangleSetup(tri);
   }
}

// if at least one triangle overlaps the current octant,
// then return true: the octant will spawn children.
bool GeomWorker::FineTest (NodeGroup *group, int octant, int begin, int end)
{
```

```
    int  i;
    VTPair  **pair = group->pairs->list;
    Vector<int>  compact_list;
    bool  valid, tvalid;
    const   ushort3   &coord  = group->node[octant].coord;

    // for all triangles of current octant
    valid =  false;
    for  (i = begin; i  <=  end; ++i) {
       int  tri_idx = pair[i]->tri_idx;
       Triangle  *tri =  tri_list->list[tri_idx];

       //
       if  (!g_u.PlaneTest(coord, tri->n, tri)) {
          compact_list.push_back(i);
          continue;    // try another triangle
       }

       // next, call rasterize or rasterize_26sep
       if  (raster   &   CONSERVATIVE_MASK)
          tvalid =  g_u.Rasterize_26sepTop(coord, tri);
       else
          tvalid =  g_u.RasterizeTop(coord, tri);

       if  (!tvalid) {
          compact_list.push_back(i);
          continue;
       }
       // one triangle overlap is enough to validate voxel
       if  (!valid)
         valid =  true;
    }
    // whether valid or not, may need to compact pair list
    compactPairList(pair, compact_list);

    return  valid;
}

int GeomWorker::getN (int level)
{
    return   g_u.getN(level);
}

unsigned int GeomWorker::getRaster ()
{
    return   g_u.getRaster();
}

// Get all triangles, since the root encloses everything
```

```
// Note, only get the index.
void GeomWorker::getRootTriangles (Vector< int > &tri_idx)
{
   if (tri_list == NULL)
      return;

   int  count = tri_list->count;
   for (int i = 0; i <  count; ++i) {
      tri_idx.push_back(i);
   }
}

TriangleList * GeomWorker::getTriangleList ()
{
   return  tri_list;
}

int GeomWorker::getTriListCount ()
{
   return  tri_list->count;
}

void GeomWorker::MasterEdges (float3 &v0, float3 &v1, float3 &v2, Triangle *tri) [private]
{
   // compute triangle´s edges and normal
   // note that the make_float3 goes on the stack,
   // and will be copied over to the heap (edges in tri)
   tri->edge0 = make_float3( v1.x - v0.x, v1.y - v0.y, v1.z - v0.z );
   tri->edge1 = make_float3( v2.x - v1.x, v2.y - v1.y, v2.z - v1.z );
   tri->edge2 = make_float3( v0.x - v2.x, v0.y - v2.y, v0.z - v2.z );
}

void GeomWorker::MasterEdgesAndNormal () [private]
{
   if (tri_list == NULL)
      return;

   int  count = tri_list->count;
   for (int i = 0; i <  count; ++i) {
      Triangle * tri = tri_list->list[i];
      MasterEdges(tri->v0, tri->v1, tri->v2, tri);
      MasterNormal(tri->edge0, tri->edge2, tri);
      MasterTriAxis(tri->n, tri);
      PlaneEquation(tri);
      g_u.BoundingBox(tri->master_bbox0, tri->master_bbox1,
           tri->v0, tri->v1, tri->v2);
   }
}
```

```
void GeomWorker::MasterNormal (float3 &edge0, float3 &edge2, Triangle *tri) [private]
{
    // anti-cross because edge2 order is  "triangle order"
    // not  "crow's feet"  order normally used for normals.
    tri->n  =  g_u.anti_cross( edge0, edge2 );
}

void GeomWorker::MasterTriAxis (float3 &n, Triangle *tri) [private]
{
    // compute dominant axis
    const   bool  byx = fabsf( n.y  )  >  fabsf( n.x  );
    const   bool  byz = fabsf( n.y  )  >  fabsf( n.z  );
    const   bool  bzx = fabsf( n.z  )  >  fabsf( n.x  );
    tri->axis  = byx ? (byz ? 1 : 2) : (bzx ? 2 : 0);
}

int GeomWorker::NewN (intlevel, int terminal_level, bool is_terminal)
{
    return   g_u.NewN(level, terminal_level, is_terminal);
}

GeomWorker GeomWorker::operator= (GeomWorker rhs)
{
    if  (this  !=  &rhs)        // alias test
    {
       transferTriangles(rhs.tri_list);
       g_u  = rhs.g_u;
    }
    return  *this;             // return pointer to self
}

// call after TriAxis
// get plane coefficients for rasterize functions
void GeomWorker::PlaneEquation (Triangle *tri) [private]
{
    // all three for thin rasterization
    if  (raster  ==  THIN_OV3) {
        if  (tri->axis  == 0)
           g_u.plane_setup_6sep<uvw<X>::W>(tri->v0, tri->n, tri->fine.plane_eq);
        else   if  (tri->axis  == 1)
           g_u.plane_setup_6sep<uvw<Y>::W>(tri->v0, tri->n, tri->fine.plane_eq);
        else
           g_u.plane_setup_6sep<uvw<Z>::W>(tri->v0, tri->n, tri->fine.plane_eq);
        return;
    }
    if  (tri->axis  == 0) {
        if  (raster  ==  CONSERVATIVE_OV3)
           g_u.plane_setup<uvw<X>::W>(tri->v0, tri->n, tri->fine.plane_eq);
```

```
        else
            g_u.plane_setup<X>(tri->v0, tri->n, tri->fine.plane_eq);
    } else if (tri->axis == 1) {
        if (raster == CONSERVATIVE_OV3)
            g_u.plane_setup<uvw<Y>::W>(tri->v0, tri->n, tri->fine.plane_eq);
        else
            g_u.plane_setup<Y>(tri->v0, tri->n, tri->fine.plane_eq);
    } else {
        if (raster == CONSERVATIVE_OV3)
            g_u.plane_setup<uvw<Z>::W>(tri->v0, tri->n, tri->fine.plane_eq);
        else
            g_u.plane_setup<Z>(tri->v0, tri->n, tri->fine.plane_eq);
    }
}

void GeomWorker::SetBBoxDeltas ()
{
    g_u.SetBBoxDeltas();
}

// all-important, context-sensitive!
void GeomWorker::setRaster (const unsigned intvalue)
{
    raster = g_u.setRaster(value);
}

// For spawned node, get a copy of the parent triangles.
void GeomWorker::transferTriangles (TriangleList *orig_list)
{
    if (orig_list == NULL)
        return;

    int size = orig_list->count;
    if (size == 0)
        throw ItemNotFoundException("Empty Triangle List: Spawn transfer.");

    tri_list = new TriangleList;
    tri_list->count = size;

    Triangle **plist = new Triangle * [size];
    tri_list->list = plist;

    for (int i = 0; i < size; ++i) {
        Triangle *tri_s = orig_list->list[i];
        Triangle *tri_d = new Triangle;
        tri_list->list[i] = tri_d;
        CopyMasterData(tri_s, tri_d);
    }
}
```

```
// convert basic triangles to Master list triangles
TriangleList * GeomWorker::TriangleConvert2MasterList (Vector<BasicTriangle * >&geom)
{
   if (tri_list != NULL)
      return  tri_list;

   tri_list = BiUnitScale(geom);

   // compute edges, normal, dominant axis for each triangle
   MasterEdgesAndNormal();

   return  tri_list;
}

// do this once per level
void GeomWorker::TriangleSetup (Triangle *tri) [private]
{
   // all three axes for thin rasterization
   if (raster == THIN_OV3) {
      if (tri->axis == 0) {
         g_u.triangle_setup_6sep<uvw<X>::U>(tri, tri->fine, 1);
         g_u.triangle_setup_6sep<uvw<X>::V>(tri, tri->fine, 2);
         g_u.triangle_setup_6sep<uvw<X>::W>(tri, tri->fine, 0);
      } else  if (tri->axis == 1) {
         g_u.triangle_setup_6sep<uvw<Y>::U>(tri, tri->fine, 0);
         g_u.triangle_setup_6sep<uvw<Y>::V>(tri, tri->fine, 2);
         g_u.triangle_setup_6sep<uvw<Y>::W>(tri, tri->fine, 1);
      } else {
         g_u.triangle_setup_6sep<uvw<Z>::U>(tri, tri->fine, 0);
         g_u.triangle_setup_6sep<uvw<Z>::V>(tri, tri->fine, 1);
         g_u.triangle_setup_6sep<uvw<Z>::W>(tri, tri->fine, 2);
      }
      // only need to do this in the default (x,y,z) orientation
      g_u.makeSpheres(tri);
      // do this for as many principal planes as possible
      g_u.makeHaloes(tri);
      return;
   }

   if (tri->axis == 0) {
      if (raster == CONSERVATIVE_OV1) {
         g_u.triangle_setup<X>(tri, tri->fine.n_delta_u[0],
                           tri->fine.n_delta_v[0],
                           tri->fine.a[0]);
      } else {
         g_u.triangle_setup<uvw<X>::U>(tri, tri->fine.n_delta_u[0],
                           tri->fine.n_delta_v[0],
                           tri->fine.a[0]);
         g_u.triangle_setup<uvw<X>::V>(tri, tri->fine.n_delta_u[1],
```

```
                        tri->fine.n_delta_v[1],
                        tri->fine.a[1]);
        g_u.triangle_setup<uvw<X>::W>(tri, tri->fine.n_delta_u[2],
                        tri->fine.n_delta_v[2],
                        tri->fine.a[2]);
    }
  } else  if (tri->axis == 1) {
    if (raster == CONSERVATIVE_OV1) {
        g_u.triangle_setup<Y>(tri, tri->fine.n_delta_u[0],
                        tri->fine.n_delta_v[0],
                        tri->fine.a[0]);
    } else {
        g_u.triangle_setup<uvw<Y>::U>(tri, tri->fine.n_delta_u[0],
                        tri->fine.n_delta_v[0],
                        tri->fine.a[0]);
        g_u.triangle_setup<uvw<Y>::V>(tri, tri->fine.n_delta_u[1],
                        tri->fine.n_delta_v[1],
                        tri->fine.a[1]);
        g_u.triangle_setup<uvw<Y>::W>(tri, tri->fine.n_delta_u[2],
                        tri->fine.n_delta_v[2],
                        tri->fine.a[2]);
    }
  } else {
    if (raster == CONSERVATIVE_OV1) {
        g_u.triangle_setup<Z>(tri, tri->fine.n_delta_u[0],
                        tri->fine.n_delta_v[0],
                        tri->fine.a[0]);
    } else {
        g_u.triangle_setup<uvw<Z>::U>(tri, tri->fine.n_delta_u[0],
                        tri->fine.n_delta_v[0],
                        tri->fine.a[0]);
        g_u.triangle_setup<uvw<Z>::V>(tri, tri->fine.n_delta_u[1],
                        tri->fine.n_delta_v[1],
                        tri->fine.a[1]);
        g_u.triangle_setup<uvw<Z>::W>(tri, tri->fine.n_delta_u[2],
                        tri->fine.n_delta_v[2],
                        tri->fine.a[2]);
    }
  }
}
```

Local Data

```
static const int TRI_VERTS = 3;
```

The documentation for this class was generated from the following files:

- GeomWorker.h
- GeomWorker.cpp

GLWorker Class Reference

Public Member Functions

GLWorker ()

:: Called when window requires paint.
virtual void OnRender (void)

:: Called on idle. This should never be used to draw anything.
virtual void OnIdle ()

:: When OnInit is called, a render context (in this case GLUT-Window)
:: is already available!
virtual void OnInit ()

:: Called when Window is resized.
virtual void OnResize (int w, int h)

:: Called when Window is closed.
virtual void OnClose (void)

:: Called when Mouse button is pressed.
virtual void OnMouseDown (int button, int x, int y)

:: Called when Mouse button is released.
virtual void OnMouseUp (int button, int x, int y)

:: Called when mouse wheel is used.
virtual void OnMouseWheel (int nWheelNumber, int nDirection, int x, int y)

:: Called when a key is pressed on keyboard.
virtual void OnKeyDown (int nKey, char cAscii)

:: Called when a key is released on keyboard.
virtual void OnKeyUp (int nKey, char cAscii)

Protected Attributes

cwc::glShaderManager SM
cwc::glShader *shaderGL
uint ProgramObject, clock_t time0, clock_t time1
float timer010
bool bUp
float vp_ratio

Private Member Functions

:: create the octree, evaluate voxels
void PaintVoxels ()

void ShowMesh ()voidCastRays ()
void DrawMesh (MeshData &mesh)
void cleanupThread ()
void DrawAxes (double x2, double y2, double z2)
void TransformCube (double x, double y, double z)
void MakeCube ()
void MakeLocalFace (int a, int b, int c, int d)
void UpdateTimer ()

:: delay to simulate actual compute latency
void Wait ()

void DemoLight ()
void MakeTestTriangles (Vector<BasicTriangle * > &my_geom)
void MakeTriangle (BasicTriangle *t, vertex *vert, float r, float g, float b)
void PaintVoxel (VoxelData &voxel)

:: Only show filled entries here.
void DrawRay (ReducedRay *ray, DevicePack &device)

void DrawArm (ReducedRay *ray, DevicePack &device)

:: only call if voxel isn't empty
void MakeLED (ReducedRay *ray, int t, bool in_flag)

void DrawDots (ReducedRay *ray, DevicePack &device)
void DrawLED (float3&position)

:: free the model memory
void freeGeomList (Vector<BasicTriangle * > &my_geom)

:: Only need to do this once : put it in scaledv.
void TranslateScaleCube ()

void RotateAngle (float angle)
void MakeTetrahedron (Vector<BasicTriangle * > &my_geom)
void MakeHouse (Vector<BasicTriangle * > &my_geom)

Private Attributes

bool do_transx
bool do_transz
double angle
double transx

double transsz
Transform xform

Detailed Description

All of the OpenGL drawing and thread queueing and de-queueing code for the voxel application.

Constructor & Destructor Documentation

GLWorker::GLWorker () [inline]
{}

Member Function Documentation

```
void GLWorker::CastRays () [private]
{
    int i, size, level, x;
    ReducedRay *my_ptr;
    Vector<ReducedRay *> ptr_list;
    extern OctreeThread my_stat_thread;

    // compute key variables
   DevicePack device;
   device.Nt = (int)lroundf(powf(2.0, (float)g_terminal));
   device.spindle_diam = device.Nt / 16;       // spindle ratio
   device.max_level = (device.Nt - device.spindle_diam) / MAX_COURSE;
   device.helical_index = DEGREES_360 / device.max_level;
   device.total_levels = device.max_level * MAX_COURSE * T_ALPHABETA *
LEVEL_SHOW / LEVEL_BAND;

    TranslateScaleCube();

    // launch a thread for computing & displaying radial mapping
    my_stat_thread.RayStart();

    // loop over queue and get entries
    for (level = 0, x = 0; level < device.total_levels; ++level, x = 0) {
       while (x != -1) { // -1 terminates the level
          if (!my_stat_thread.IsEmptyR()) {
             my_ptr = my_stat_thread.DequeueR();
              if ((x = my_ptr->level) != -1) {
                 // add it to a list
                 ptr_list.push_back(my_ptr);
             }
          }
```

```
      }
      // delete level terminator (no embedded list)
       delete  my_ptr;

      size = ptr_list.size();
       for  (i = 0; i  <   size; ++i) {
          my_ptr = ptr_list[i];
            DrawRay(my_ptr, device);
      }
       // free the original pointers on the heap
       for  (i = 0; i  <   size; ++i) {
          my_ptr = ptr_list[i];
            delete  [] my_ptr->list;
            delete  my_ptr;
      }
       // going to reuse this so clear it
       ptr_list.clear();
   }

   my_stat_thread.RayEnd();
}

void GLWorker::cleanupThread () [private]
{
    extern   OctreeThread   my_stat_thread;

   my_stat_thread.CleanUp();
}

void GLWorker::DemoLight () [private]
{
    glEnable(GL_LIGHTING);
    glEnable(GL_LIGHT0);
    glEnable(GL_NORMALIZE);
    //glEnable(GL_BLEND);
    // Light model parameters:
    // -------------------------------------------
    // turn up the ambient light
    GLfloat  lmKa[] = {0.5, 0.5, 0.5, 1.0 };

    glLightModelfv(GL_LIGHT_MODEL_AMBIENT, lmKa);
    glLightModeli(GL_LIGHT_MODEL_LOCAL_VIEWER,  GL_FALSE);
    glLightModelf(GL_LIGHT_MODEL_TWO_SIDE, 0.0);

    // make faces two-sided
    //glLightModeli(GL_LIGHT_MODEL_TWO_SIDE, GL_TRUE);
    float  lmax = lroundf(powf(2.0, (float)g_terminal));
    if  (g_antialias)
      lmax /= 2.0;
```

```
    // ------------------------------------------
    // Spotlight Attenuation
    GLfloat  spot_direction[] = {lmax/2.0f, lmax/2.0f, lmax/2.0f};
    GLint  spot_exponent = 4;
    GLint  spot_cutoff = 180;

    glLightfv(GL_LIGHT0,  GL_SPOT_DIRECTION, spot_direction);
    glLighti(GL_LIGHT0,  GL_SPOT_EXPONENT, spot_exponent);
    glLighti(GL_LIGHT0,  GL_SPOT_CUTOFF, spot_cutoff);

    GLfloat  Kc = 1.0;
    GLfloat  Kl = 0.0;
    GLfloat  Kq = 0.0;

    glLightf(GL_LIGHT0,  GL_CONSTANT_ATTENUATION,Kc);
    glLightf(GL_LIGHT0,  GL_LINEAR_ATTENUATION, Kl);
    glLightf(GL_LIGHT0,  GL_QUADRATIC_ATTENUATION, Kq);

    // ------------------------------------------
    // Lighting parameters:
    GLfloat  light_pos[] = {lmax, lmax, lmax, 1.0f};
    GLfloat  light_Ka[]  = {0.5f, 0.5f, 0.5f, 1.0f};
    GLfloat  light_Kd[]  = {0.5f, 0.5f, 0.5f, 1.0f};
    GLfloat  light_Ks[]  = {0.5f, 0.5f, 0.5f, 1.0f};

    glLightfv(GL_LIGHT0,  GL_POSITION, light_pos);
    glLightfv(GL_LIGHT0,  GL_AMBIENT, light_Ka);
    glLightfv(GL_LIGHT0,  GL_DIFFUSE, light_Kd);
    glLightfv(GL_LIGHT0,  GL_SPECULAR, light_Ks);

    // ------------------------------------------
    // Material parameters:
    GLfloat  material_Ka[] = {0.3f, 0.3f, 0.3f, 1.0f};
    GLfloat  material_Kd[] = {0.4f, 0.4f, 0.4f, 1.0f};
    GLfloat  material_Ks[] = {0.2f, 0.2f, 0.2f, 1.0f};

    // emission gives material a  "glow"     GLfloat  material_Ke[] = {0.1f, 0.1f, 0.1f, 1.0f};
    GLfloat  material_Se = 2.0f;

    glMaterialfv(GL_FRONT,  GL_AMBIENT, material_Ka);
    glMaterialfv(GL_FRONT,  GL_DIFFUSE, material_Kd);
    glMaterialfv(GL_FRONT,  GL_SPECULAR, material_Ks);
    glMaterialfv(GL_FRONT,  GL_EMISSION, material_Ke);
    glMaterialf(GL_FRONT,  GL_SHININESS, material_Se);
}

void GLWorker::DrawArm (ReducedRay *ray, DevicePack &device) [private]
{
```

```
    float3  tD, position;

    int   length  = (device.Nt  - device.spindle_diam) / 2;

    // start point is ray origin; end point:
    xform.VectorScale(tD, ray->base_direction,  float(length));
    xform.VectorAdd(position, ray->base_origin, tD);

    glBegin(GL_LINES);

    // green      glColor4f(0.0, 1.0, 0.0, 1.0);

    glVertex3f(ray->base_origin.x,
            ray->base_origin.y,
            ray->base_origin.z);
    glVertex3f(position.x,
            position.y,
            position.z);
    glEnd();
}

void GLWorker::DrawAxes (double x2, double y2, double z2) [private]
{
    glBegin(GL_LINES);

    // red is x
    glColor4f(1.0, 0.0, 0.0, 1.0);
    glVertex3f(0.0, 0.0, 0.0);
    glVertex3f(x2, 0.0, 0.0);

    // green is y
    glColor4f(0.0, 1.0, 0.0, 1.0);
    glVertex3f(0.0, 0.0, 0.0);
    glVertex3f(0.0, y2, 0.0);

    glColor4f(0.0, 0.0, 1.0, 1.0);
    glVertex3f(0.0, 0.0, 0.0);
    glVertex3f(0.0, 0.0, z2);

    glEnd();
}

void GLWorker::DrawDots (ReducedRay *ray, DevicePack &device) [private]
{
    float3  tD, position;
    int   t;
    int   length  = (device.Nt  - device.spindle_diam) / 2;

    glBegin(GL_POINTS);
```

```
    // dim red
    glColor4f(0.2, 0.0, 0.0, 1.0);

    for (t = 0; t <= length; t += 10) {
      // dot on sweep
      xform.VectorScale(tD, ray->base_direction, float(t));
      xform.VectorAdd(position, ray->base_origin, tD);

      glVertex3f(position.x,
              position.y,
              position.z);
    }
    glEnd();
}

void GLWorker::DrawLED (float3 &position) [private]
{
    int i;
    // make the local coordinates
    for (i = 0; i < 8; ++i) {
      localv[i][0] = rotatedv[i][0] + position.x;
      localv[i][1] = rotatedv[i][1] + position.y;
      localv[i][2] = rotatedv[i][2] + position.z;
    }

    // looking from above, so draw bottom first
    // draw the top last
    for (i = 0; i < 6; ++i) {
      glNormal3f(rotatedn[i][0],
               rotatedn[i][1],
               rotatedn[i][2]);
      MakeLocalFace(face_index[i][0],
              face_index[i][1],
              face_index[i][2],
              face_index[i][3]);
    }
}

void GLWorker::DrawMesh (MeshData &mesh) [private]
{
    float base_x, base_y, base_z, off_x, off_y, off_z, len;

    glBegin(GL_LINES);

    // green
    glColor4f(0.0, 1.0, 0.0, 1.0);

   base_x = mesh.p1.x;
```

```
    base_y = mesh.p1.y;
    base_z = mesh.p1.z;
    len = mesh.length;

    off_x = base_x +  len;
    off_y = base_y +  len;
    off_z = base_z +  len;

    glVertex3f(base_x, base_y, base_z);
    glVertex3f(off_x, base_y, base_z);

    glVertex3f(base_x, base_y, base_z);
    glVertex3f(base_x, off_y, base_z);

    glVertex3f(base_x, base_y, base_z);
    glVertex3f(base_x, base_y, off_z);

    //
    glVertex3f(off_x, off_y, off_z);
    glVertex3f(base_x, off_y, off_z);

    glVertex3f(off_x, off_y, off_z);
    glVertex3f(off_x, base_y, off_z);

    glVertex3f(off_x, off_y, off_z);
    glVertex3f(off_x, off_y, base_z);

    //
    glVertex3f(base_x, off_y, base_z);
    glVertex3f(off_x, off_y, base_z);

    glVertex3f(base_x, off_y, base_z);
    glVertex3f(base_x, off_y, off_z);

    glVertex3f(off_x, base_y, off_z);
    glVertex3f(base_x, base_y, off_z);

    glVertex3f(off_x, base_y, off_z);
    glVertex3f(off_x, base_y, base_z);

    //
    glVertex3f(base_x, base_y, off_z);
    glVertex3f(base_x, off_y, off_z);

    glVertex3f(off_x, base_y, base_z);
    glVertex3f(off_x, off_y, base_z);

    glEnd();
}
```

```
// Only show filled entries here.
void GLWorker::DrawRay (ReducedRay *ray, DevicePack &device) [private]
{
    float3  color;
    float  angle;
    unsigned  char read_byte;
    int i, j, count, runlength, t;
    bool  in;

    // rotate the default cube (and normals) by the ray angle
    if (ray->interleave == T_ALPHA)
      angle = float((ray->level % device.max_level) * device.helical_index + ray->angle);
    else
      angle = float((ray->level % device.max_level) * device.helical_index + ray->angle) + 179.5;

    RotateAngle(angle);

    // draw arm: always positioned at angle == 0
/*
    if (ray->angle == 0)
       DrawArm(ray, device);
*/
/*
    else if (ray->angle % 10 == 0)
       DrawDots(ray, device);
*/

    // For LEDs on ray
   count = ray->count;
    for (i = 0, t = 0; i < count; ++i) {
      read_byte = ray->list[i];
      runlength = read_byte & (~IN_BIT);
      in = read_byte & IN_BIT;
      if (in) {
         read_byte = ray->list[++i];
         color.x = (float)read_byte / 255.0;
         read_byte = ray->list[++i];
         color.y = (float)read_byte / 255.0;
         read_byte = ray->list[++i];
         color.z = (float)read_byte / 255.0;
         glBegin(GL_QUADS);

#ifdef TWO_COLOR_INTERLEAVE
        if (ray->interleave == T_ALPHA)
           glColor4f(color.x, color.y, color.z, 1.0);
        else
           glColor4f(1.0, color.y, color.z, 1.0);
#else
```

```
        glColor4f(color.x, color.y, color.z, 1.0);
#endif
        for (j = 0; j < runlength; ++j, ++t)
            MakeLED(ray, t, in);

        glEnd();

    } else {
        for (j = 0; j < runlength; ++j, ++t)
            ; // count zero runlength        }
  }
}

// free the model memory
void GLWorker::freeGeomList (Vector<BasicTriangle * > &my_geom) [private]
{
   BasicTriangle *geom_ptr;
   int i, size;

   size = my_geom.size();
   for (i = 0; i < size; ++i) {
      geom_ptr = my_geom[i];
      delete geom_ptr;
   }
}

void GLWorker::MakeCube () [private]
{
   int i;

   // looking from above, so draw bottom first
   // draw the top last
   for (i = 0; i < 6; ++i) {
      glNormal3f(normals[i][0],
                 normals[i][1],
                 normals[i][2]);
      MakeLocalFace(face_index[i][0],
                face_index[i][1],
                face_index[i][2],
                face_index[i][3]);
   }
}

void GLWorker::MakeHouse (Vector<BasicTriangle * > &my_geom) [private]
{
   BasicTriangle *t1;
   vertex vert[3];

   // front
```

```
 t1 =  new   BasicTriangle;

vert[0].x  = 2.0;
vert[0].y  = 0.0;
vert[0].z  = 2.0;
vert[1].x  = 3.0;
vert[1].y  = 0.0;
vert[1].z  = 2.0;
vert[2].x  = 2.0;
vert[2].y  = 2.0;
vert[2].z  = 2.0;

 MakeTriangle(t1, vert, 1.0, 0.8, 0.0);
my_geom.push_back(t1);

t1 =  new   BasicTriangle;

vert[0].x  = 3.0;
vert[0].y  = 0.0;
vert[0].z  = 2.0;
vert[1].x  = 3.0;
vert[1].y  = 2.0;
vert[1].z  = 2.0;
vert[2].x  = 2.0;
vert[2].y  = 2.0;
vert[2].z  = 2.0;

 MakeTriangle(t1, vert, 1.0, 0.8, 0.0);
my_geom.push_back(t1);

t1 =  new   BasicTriangle;

vert[0].x  = 4.0;
vert[0].y  = 0.0;
vert[0].z  = 2.0;
vert[1].x  = 5.0;
vert[1].y  = 0.0;
vert[1].z  = 2.0;
vert[2].x  = 4.0;
vert[2].y  = 2.0;
vert[2].z  = 2.0;

 MakeTriangle(t1, vert, 1.0, 0.8, 0.0);
my_geom.push_back(t1);

t1 =  new   BasicTriangle;

vert[0].x  = 5.0;
vert[0].y  = 0.0;
```

```
vert[0].z  = 2.0;
vert[1].x  = 5.0;
vert[1].y  = 2.0;
vert[1].z  = 2.0;
vert[2].x  = 4.0;
vert[2].y  = 2.0;
vert[2].z  = 2.0;

 MakeTriangle(t1, vert, 1.0, 0.8, 0.0);
my_geom.push_back(t1);

 // front gable
 t1 =  new   BasicTriangle;

vert[0].x  = 5.0;
vert[0].y  = 2.0;
vert[0].z  = 2.0;
vert[1].x  = 3.5;
vert[1].y  = 4;
vert[1].z  = 2.0;
vert[2].x  = 2.0;
vert[2].y  = 2.0;
vert[2].z  = 2.0;

 MakeTriangle(t1, vert, 0.8, 0.6, 0.0);
my_geom.push_back(t1);

 // rear
 t1 =  new   BasicTriangle;

vert[0].x  = 5.0;
vert[0].y  = 0.0;
vert[0].z  = 8.0;
vert[1].x  = 2.0;
vert[1].y  = 0.0;
vert[1].z  = 8.0;
vert[2].x  = 2.0;
vert[2].y  = 2.0;
vert[2].z  = 8.0;

 MakeTriangle(t1, vert, 1.0, 1.0, 0.0);
my_geom.push_back(t1);

t1 =  new   BasicTriangle;

vert[0].x  = 5.0;
vert[0].y  = 0.0;
vert[0].z  = 8.0;
vert[1].x  = 2.0;
```

```
vert[1].y  = 2.0;
vert[1].z  = 8.0;
vert[2].x  = 5.0;
vert[2].y  = 2.0;
vert[2].z  = 8.0;

 MakeTriangle(t1, vert, 1.0, 1.0, 0.0);
my_geom.push_back(t1);

 // rear gable
 t1 =  new   BasicTriangle;

vert[0].x  = 5.0;
vert[0].y  = 2.0;
vert[0].z  = 8.0;
vert[1].x  = 2.0;
vert[1].y  = 2.0;
vert[1].z  = 8.0;
vert[2].x  = 3.5;
vert[2].y  = 4.0;
vert[2].z  = 8.0;

 MakeTriangle(t1, vert, 1.0, 1.0, 0.0);
my_geom.push_back(t1);

 // roof
 t1 =  new   BasicTriangle;

vert[0].x  = 5.0;
vert[0].y  = 2.0;
vert[0].z  = 2.0;
vert[1].x  = 5.0;
vert[1].y  = 2.0;
vert[1].z  = 8.0;
vert[2].x  = 3.5;
vert[2].y  = 4.0;
vert[2].z  = 8.0;

 MakeTriangle(t1, vert, 0.8, 0.0, 0.5);
my_geom.push_back(t1);

t1 =  new   BasicTriangle;

vert[0].x  = 3.5;
vert[0].y  = 4.0;
vert[0].z  = 8.0;
vert[1].x  = 3.5;
vert[1].y  = 4.0;
vert[1].z  = 2.0;
```

```
vert[2].x  = 5.0;
vert[2].y  = 2.0;
vert[2].z  = 2.0;

 MakeTriangle(t1, vert, 0.8, 0.0, 0.5);
my_geom.push_back(t1);

t1 =  new   BasicTriangle;

vert[0].x  = 3.5;
vert[0].y  = 4.0;
vert[0].z  = 2.0;
vert[1].x  = 3.5;
vert[1].y  = 4.0;
vert[1].z  = 8.0;
vert[2].x  = 2.0;
vert[2].y  = 2.0;
vert[2].z  = 2.0;

 MakeTriangle(t1, vert, 0.5, 0.0, 0.8);
my_geom.push_back(t1);

t1 =  new   BasicTriangle;

vert[0].x  = 2.0;
vert[0].y  = 2.0;
vert[0].z  = 2.0;
vert[1].x  = 3.5;
vert[1].y  = 4.0;
vert[1].z  = 8.0;
vert[2].x  = 2.0;
vert[2].y  = 2.0;
vert[2].z  = 8.0;

 MakeTriangle(t1, vert, 0.5, 0.0, 0.8);
my_geom.push_back(t1);

 // sides
 t1 =  new   BasicTriangle;

vert[0].x  = 5.0;
vert[0].y  = 0.0;
vert[0].z  = 2.0;
vert[1].x  = 5.0;
vert[1].y  = 2.0;
vert[1].z  = 8.0;
vert[2].x  = 5.0;
vert[2].y  = 2.0;
vert[2].z  = 2.0;
```

```
 MakeTriangle(t1, vert, 0.8, 0.8, 0.8);
my_geom.push_back(t1);

t1 = new  BasicTriangle;

vert[0].x = 5.0;
vert[0].y = 0.0;
vert[0].z = 2.0;
vert[1].x = 5.0;
vert[1].y = 0.0;
vert[1].z = 8.0;
vert[2].x = 5.0;
vert[2].y = 2.0;
vert[2].z = 8.0;

 MakeTriangle(t1, vert, 0.8, 0.8, 0.8);
my_geom.push_back(t1);

t1 = new  BasicTriangle;

vert[0].x = 2.0;
vert[0].y = 0.0;
vert[0].z = 2.0;
vert[1].x = 2.0;
vert[1].y = 2.0;
vert[1].z = 8.0;
vert[2].x = 2.0;
vert[2].y = 0.0;
vert[2].z = 8.0;

 MakeTriangle(t1, vert, 0.8, 0.8, 0.8);
my_geom.push_back(t1);

t1 = new  BasicTriangle;

vert[0].x = 2.0;
vert[0].y = 0.0;
vert[0].z = 2.0;
vert[1].x = 2.0;
vert[1].y = 2.0;
vert[1].z = 2.0;
vert[2].x = 2.0;
vert[2].y = 2.0;
vert[2].z = 8.0;

 MakeTriangle(t1, vert, 0.8, 0.8, 0.8);
my_geom.push_back(t1);
}
```

```
// only call if voxel isn't empty
void GLWorker::MakeLED (ReducedRay *ray, intt, boolin_flag) [private]
{
    float3  tD, position;

    xform.VectorScale(tD, ray->base_direction, (float)t);
    xform.VectorAdd(position, ray->base_origin, tD);

    DrawLED(position);
}

void GLWorker::MakeLocalFace (int a, int b, int c, int d) [private]
{
    glVertex3fv(localv[d]);
    glVertex3fv(localv[c]);
    glVertex3fv(localv[b]);
    glVertex3fv(localv[a]);
}

void GLWorker::MakeTestTriangles (Vector<BasicTriangle * > &my_geom) [private]
{
    BasicTriangle  *t1;
    vertex  vert[3];
 /*
   t1 = new BasicTriangle;
   vert[0].x = 0.1;
   vert[0].y = 0.0;
   vert[0].z = 0.5;
   vert[1].x = 0.7;
   vert[1].y = 0.5;
   vert[1].z = 1.0;
   vert[2].x = -1.0;
   vert[2].y = 0.25;
   vert[2].z = 0.3;
   MakeTriangle(t1, vert, 0.5, 0.5, 0.5);
   my_geom.push_back(t1);
*/
   t1 =  new   BasicTriangle;
   vert[0].x  = 1.0;
   vert[0].y  = 1.0;
   vert[0].z  = 1.0;
   vert[1].x  = -1.0;
   vert[1].y  = 1.0;
   vert[1].z  = -1.0;
   vert[2].x  = -1.0;
   vert[2].y  = -1.0;
   vert[2].z  = 1.0;
```

```
    MakeTriangle(t1, vert, 0.5, 0.5, 0.5);
   my_geom.push_back(t1);

}

void GLWorker::MakeTetrahedron (Vector<BasicTriangle * > &my_geom) [private]
{
    BasicTriangle  *t1;
    vertex  vert[3];

   t1 =  new   BasicTriangle;

   vert[0].x  = 1.0;
   vert[0].y  = 1.0;
   vert[0].z  = 1.0;
   vert[1].x  = 1.0;
   vert[1].y  = -1.0;
   vert[1].z  = -1.0;
   vert[2].x  = -1.0;
   vert[2].y  = 1.0;
   vert[2].z  = -1.0;

    MakeTriangle(t1, vert, 1.0, 0.0, 0.0);
   my_geom.push_back(t1);

   t1 =  new   BasicTriangle;

   vert[0].x  = 1.0;
   vert[0].y  = -1.0;
   vert[0].z  = -1.0;
   vert[1].x  = -1.0;
   vert[1].y  = 1.0;
   vert[1].z  = -1.0;
   vert[2].x  = -1.0;
   vert[2].y  = -1.0;
   vert[2].z  = 1.0;

    MakeTriangle(t1, vert, 0.0, 1.0, 0.0);
   my_geom.push_back(t1);

   t1 =  new   BasicTriangle;

   vert[0].x  = 1.0;
   vert[0].y  = 1.0;
   vert[0].z  = 1.0;
   vert[1].x  = 1.0;
   vert[1].y  = -1.0;
   vert[1].z  = -1.0;
   vert[2].x  = -1.0;
```

```
   vert[2].y  = -1.0;
   vert[2].z  = 1.0;

    MakeTriangle(t1, vert, 0.0, 0.0, 1.0);
   my_geom.push_back(t1);

   t1 =  new   BasicTriangle;

   vert[0].x  = 1.0;
   vert[0].y  = 1.0;
   vert[0].z  = 1.0;
   vert[1].x  = -1.0;
   vert[1].y  = 1.0;
   vert[1].z  = -1.0;
   vert[2].x  = -1.0;
   vert[2].y  = -1.0;
   vert[2].z  = 1.0;

    MakeTriangle(t1, vert, 0.0, 1.0, 1.0);
   my_geom.push_back(t1);
}

void GLWorker::MakeTriangle (BasicTriangle *t, vertex *vert, floatr, floatg, floatb) [private]
{
    int  i;

   t->color.r  =  r;
   t->color.g  =  g;
   t->color.b  =  b;

    for  (i=0; i<3; ++i) {
      t->vert[i].x  = vert[i].x;
      t->vert[i].y  = vert[i].y;
      t->vert[i].z  = vert[i].z;
   }
}

// Called when Window is closed.
// Reimplemented from cwc::glutWindow.
virtual void GLWorker::OnClose (void) [inline, virtual]
{}

// Called on idle. This should never be used to draw anything.
// Reimplemented from cwc::glutWindow.
void GLWorker::OnIdle (void) [virtual]
{
    //glRotatef(timer010*360, 1.0f, 0.0f, 0.0f);
}
```

```
// When OnInit is called, a render context (in this case GLUT-Window)
// is already available!
void GLWorker::OnInit (void) [virtual]
{
   //glEnable( GL_BLEND );
#ifdef MOVE_TEST
   //glBlendFunc(GL_SRC_ALPHA, GL_ONE);
#endif
#ifdef INTEN_TEST
   //glBlendFunc(GL_SRC_ALPHA, GL_ONE_MINUS_SRC_ALPHA);
#endif

    glutInitDisplayMode(GLUT_DEPTH);
    glEnable(GL_DEPTH_TEST);
    glClearDepth(0);
    glEnable(GL_DEPTH_FUNC);
    glDepthFunc(GL_GREATER);

    // basic black background (darkness)
    glClearColor(0.0f, 0.0f, 0.0f, 1.0f);
    glShadeModel(GL_FLAT);
    // for transparency, take out the backface cull (we want to see them)
    // This also speeds up the rendering!!
    glEnable(GL_CULL_FACE);
    glFrontFace(GL_CCW);

    const  char *vfile = "/home/daniel/raycast/raycast/Debug/vertexshader.txt";
    const  char *ffile = "/home/daniel/raycast/raycast/Debug/fragmentshader.txt";

    char * vbuf = new  char[strlen(vfile)];
    strcpy(vbuf, vfile);
    char * fbuf = new  char[strlen(ffile)];
    strcpy(fbuf, ffile);

    // load (and compile, link) from file
    shader = SM.loadfromFile(vbuf, fbuf);

    if (shader==0)
      std::cout << "Error Loading, compiling or linking shader\n";
    else
       ProgramObject = shader->GetProgramObject();

    time0 = clock();
    timer010 = 0.0f;
    bUp = true;
    do_transx = do_transz = false;

    DemoLight();
}
```

```
// Called when a key is pressed on keyboard.
// Reimplemented from cwc::glutWindow.
void GLWorker::OnKeyDown (int nKey, char cAscii) [virtual]
{
   if (cAscii == 27) { // 0x1b = ESC
      this->Close(); // Close Window!
   } else if (cAscii == 'r') {
      glRotatef(15.0, 0.0f, 1.0f, 0.0f);
   } else if (cAscii == 'b') {
      glRotatef(-10.0, 0.0f, 1.0f, 0.0f);
   } else if (cAscii == 'x') {
      glTranslatef(-3.0f, 0.0f, 0.0f);
   } else if (cAscii == 'c') {
      glTranslatef(2.0f, 0.0f, 0.0f);
   } else if (cAscii == 'a') {
      angle += 5;     // degrees
   } else if (cAscii == 't') {
      do_transx = true;
   } else if (cAscii == 'y') {
      do_transz = true;
   }
}

// Called when a key is released on keyboard.
// Reimplemented from cwc::glutWindow.
void GLWorker::OnKeyUp (int nKey, char cAscii) [virtual]
{
    if (cAscii == 's')         // s: Shader
       shader->enable();
    else if (cAscii == 'f') // f: Fixed Function
       shader->disable();
}

// Called when Mouse button is pressed.
// Reimplemented from cwc::glutWindow.
virtual void GLWorker::OnMouseDown (int button, int x, int y) [inline, virtual]
{}

// Called when Mouse button is released.
// Reimplemented from cwc::glutWindow.
virtual void GLWorker::OnMouseUp (int button, int x, int y) [inline, virtual]
{}

// Called when mouse wheel is used.
// Reimplemented from cwc::glutWindow.
virtual void GLWorker::OnMouseWheel (int nWheelNumber, int nDirection, int x, int y) [inline, virtual]
{}

// Called when window requires paint.
```

```
// Reimplemented from cwc::glutWindow.
void GLWorker::OnRender (void) [virtual]
{
    glClear(GL_COLOR_BUFFER_BIT | GL_DEPTH_BUFFER_BIT);

    //timer010 = 0.09;
    //for screenshot! (in other words, timer is static)
    //glutSolidTeapot(1.0);
    //glutSolidSphere(1.0, 10, 10);
    if (do_transx) {
        transx += 0.1;
    }
    if (do_transz) {
        transz += 0.1;
    }
    //transx = 0.5;
    //transz = 0.5;
    glPushMatrix();
    if (shader) shader->begin();

    PaintVoxels();
    //ShowMesh();
    //CastRays();
    cleanupThread();

    if (shader) shader->end();
    glutSwapBuffers();
    glPopMatrix();

    if (do_transx) {
        do_transx = false;
    }
    if (do_transz) {
        do_transz = false;
    }
    UpdateTimer();

    Repaint();
    //Wait();
}

// Called when Window is resized.
// Reimplemented from cwc::glutWindow.
void GLWorker::OnResize (int w, int h) [virtual]
{

    if(h == 0) h = 1;
    float ratio = 1.0f * (float)w / (float)h;
    vp_ratio = ratio;
```

```
    glMatrixMode(GL_PROJECTION);
    glLoadIdentity();
    glViewport(0, 0,  w, h);

    float  vp_max = lroundf(powf(2.0, (float)g_terminal));
    vp_max *= (1.0 + 1.0 / (vp_max * 0.5));
    if  (g_antialias)
      vp_max /= 2.0;

    // first quadrant
    if  (w   <= h)
       glOrtho(-2.0, vp_max, -2.0/ratio, vp_max/ratio, -vp_max, vp_max);
    else
       glOrtho(-2.0 * ratio, vp_max * ratio, -2.0, vp_max, -vp_max, vp_max);

    glMatrixMode(GL_MODELVIEW);
    glLoadIdentity();

    // camera, forward, up
    gluLookAt(0.0,0.0,14.0,
          -2.0,2.5,-5.0,
           0.0,1.0,0.0);
}

void GLWorker::PaintVoxel (VoxelData &voxel) [private]
{
    double   x,  y,  z;

    x = (double)voxel.x;
    y = (double)voxel.y;
    z = (double)voxel.z;

    // translate and store in static global
    TransformCube(x, y, z);

    // draw a bunch of cube faces
    glBegin(GL_QUADS);

    // this will be r, g, b now.
    glColor4f(voxel.r, voxel.g, voxel.b, 1.0);

    // make a cube that represents a voxel...
    MakeCube();

    glEnd();
}

// create the octree, evaluate voxels
```

```
void GLWorker::PaintVoxels () [private]
{
   int  i,  size,  x;
   VoxelData  *my_ptr;
   Vector<VoxelData>  my_list;
   Vector<VoxelData *>  ptr_list;
   extern   OctreeThread   my_stat_thread;

   DrawAxes(10.0, 5.0, 5.0);

   // specify geometry with triangle(s)
   //Vector<BasicTriangle *>  my_geom;
   //MakeTetrahedron(my_geom);
   //MakeHouse(my_geom);
   //MakeTestTriangles(my_geom);
/*
   Stellation1 shape;
   shape.Top();
   Vector<BasicTriangle *>   &  my_geom = shape.getGeomList();
*/
   Load3DS  model;
   color3  my_color;
   my_color.r  = 0.4;
   my_color.g  = 0.2;
   my_color.b  = 0.9;

   const   char  *file3ds =  "/home/daniel/raycast/raycast/Debug/Harrier.3ds";  //chesspawn.3ds
   model.LoadAndTransfer(file3ds, my_color);
   Vector<BasicTriangle *>   &  my_geom = model.getGeomList();

   // this will spawn the Octree thread
   my_stat_thread.EvalStart(my_geom);

   x = 0;

   // loop over queue and get entries
   while  (x != -1) {
      if  (!my_stat_thread.IsEmpty()) {
         my_ptr = my_stat_thread.Dequeue();
          if  ((x = my_ptr->x) != -1) {
             // add it to a list
            my_list.push_back(*my_ptr);
            ptr_list.push_back(my_ptr);
         }
      }
   }
   std::cout  <<  std::endl  <<   "Done!"   <<  std::endl;

   my_stat_thread.EvalEnd();
```

```
    // delete terminator
    delete  my_ptr;

    if  (my_list.size() == 0) {
       //freeGeomList(my_geom);
       model.freeGeomList();
       //shape.freeGeomList();
        return;
   }

    // now sort the list by -z to +z (draw order)
    quicksort(my_list);

   size = my_list.size();
   std::cout  <<  "voxels: "  <<  size  <<  std::endl;
   for  (i = 0; i  <  size; ++i) {
       VoxelData   &my_data = my_list[i];
       PaintVoxel(my_data);
   }

    // free the original pointers on the heap
   for  (i = 0; i  <  size; ++i) {
      my_ptr = ptr_list[i];
       delete  my_ptr;
   }
//  freeGeomList(my_geom);
    model.freeGeomList();
//  shape.freeGeomList();
}

void GLWorker::RotateAngle (float angle) [private]
{
    float3  temp, result;
    int  i;

    for  (i = 0; i  <  8; ++i) {
      temp.x  =  scaledv[i][0];
      temp.y  =  scaledv[i][1];
      temp.z  =  scaledv[i][2];
       xform.rotateYAxisNT(result, temp,  angle);
       rotatedv[i][0] = result.x;
       rotatedv[i][1] = result.y;
       rotatedv[i][2] = result.z;
   }

    for  (i = 0; i  <  6; ++i) {
      temp.x  =  normals[i][0];
      temp.y  =  normals[i][1];
```

```
      temp.z  =  normals[i][2];
       xform.rotateYAxisNT(result, temp,  angle);
       rotatedn[i][0] = result.x;
       rotatedn[i][1] = result.y;
       rotatedn[i][2] = result.z;
   }
}

void GLWorker::ShowMesh () [private]
{
    int  i,  size,  x;
    MeshData  *my_ptr;
    Vector<MeshData>  my_list;
    Vector<MeshData *>  ptr_list;
    extern   OctreeThread   my_stat_thread;

    // launch a second thread for displaying adaptive mesh
   my_stat_thread.MeshStart();
   x = 0;

    // loop over queue and get entries
    while  (x != -1) {
       if  (!my_stat_thread.IsEmptyM()) {
         my_ptr = my_stat_thread.DequeueM();
          if  ((x = my_ptr->p1.x) != -1) {
             // add it to a list
            my_list.push_back(*my_ptr);
            ptr_list.push_back(my_ptr);
         }
      }
   }
   my_stat_thread.MeshEnd();

    // delete terminator
    delete  my_ptr;

    // now sort the list by -z to +z (draw order)
    //quicksort(my_list);
    size = my_list.size();
    for  (i = 0; i  <   size; ++i) {
       MeshData   &my_data = my_list[i];
       DrawMesh(my_data);
   }

    // free the original pointers on the heap
    for  (i = 0; i  <   size; ++i) {
      my_ptr = ptr_list[i];
       delete  my_ptr;
   }
```

```
}

void GLWorker::TransformCube (double x, double y, double z) [private]
{
    for (int i = 0; i < 8; ++i) {
        localv[i][0] = vertices[i][0] + x;
        localv[i][1] = vertices[i][1] + y;
        localv[i][2] = vertices[i][2] + z;
    }
}

// Only need to do this once : put it in scaledv.
void GLWorker::TranslateScaleCube () [private]
{
    for (int i = 0; i < 8; ++i) {
        for (int j = 0; j < 3; ++j) {
            scaledv[i][j] = vertices[i][j] - 0.5;
            //scaledv[i][j] = scaledv[i][j] * 0.75;
        }
    }
}

void GLWorker::UpdateTimer () [private]
{
    time1 = clock();
    float delta = static_cast<float>(static_cast<double>(time1-time0)/
static_cast<double>(CLOCKS_PER_SEC));

    delta = delta / 4;
    if (delta > 0.00005f) {
        time0 = clock();
        if (bUp) {
            timer010 += delta;
            if (timer010>=1.0f) { timer010 = 1.0f; bUp = false; }
        } else {
            timer010 -= delta;
            if (timer010<=0.0f) { timer010 = 0.0f; bUp = true; }
        }
    }
}

// delay to simulate actual compute latency
void GLWorker::Wait () [private]
{
    float delta;
    clock_t time0, time1;

    time0 = clock();
    delta = 0.0;
```

```
    while (delta < 5.0f) { // 5 s
      time1 = clock();
      delta = static_cast<float>(static_cast<double>(time1-time0)/
static_cast<double>(CLOCKS_PER_SEC));
    }
}
```

Local Data

```
#define DRAW_VOXELS
#define INTEN_TEST
//#define MOVE_TEST

static GLfloat vertices[8][3] = {
        {0.0, 0.0, 0.0}, {1.0, 0.0, 0.0},
        {1.0, 1.0, 0.0}, {0.0, 1.0, 0.0}, {0.0, 0.0, 1.0},
        {1.0, 0.0, 1.0}, {1.0, 1.0, 1.0}, {0.0, 1.0, 1.0}
};

static GLfloat normals[6][3] = {
      {0.0, 1.0, 0.0}, {0.0, 0.0, -1.0},
      {1.0, 0.0, 0.0}, {-1.0, 0.0, 0.0},
      {0.0, 0.0, 1.0}, {0.0, -1.0, 0.0}
};

static int face_index[6][4] = {
      {0, 1, 5, 4}, {0, 3, 2, 1},
      {0, 4, 7, 3}, {1, 2, 6, 5},
      {4, 5, 6, 7}, {2, 3, 7, 6}
};

// take default, translate by 0.5, scale by 0.75:
static GLfloat scaledv[8][3];
// then rotate scaled coords into position:
static GLfloat rotatedv[8][3];
// normals are directly rotated, need no translation:
static GLfloat rotatedn[6][3];
// take rotated, add to current t for ray, and make faces
static GLfloat localv[8][3];
```

The documentation for this class was generated from the following files:
- GLWorker.h
- GLWorker.cpp

GroupWorker Class Reference

Public Member Functions

GroupWorker (Context &mcontext)

:: The vector will delete the array of pointers,
:: but not what the pointers point to. Do that here.
~GroupWorker ()

:: Hide details from caller.
NodeGroup *InstantiateRoot (Glassner new_ID)

:: set the geom_stat bits in the parent
:: NodeGroup (passed in)
:: instantiate new groups for set bits
voidGeomProcess (NodeGroup *group, const Level &level)

:: note: msb_pos may be zero after a return from false-pos processing.
void checkVTPairs (const Level &level)

:: public entry-point, used at end of context switch
voidDeprecate ()

void resetCurrent (NodeGroup *group)

:: get last n for parent group and return array
NodeGroupList *getNewGroups (NodeGroup *parent)

:: don't need the list anymore: pointers still valid!
void freeGroupPointers (NodeGroupList *ngl)

unsigned char getChildrenBits ()

:: for destruction
void setTreePointer (Octree<NodeGroup * > *tree_ptr)

Private Member Functions

void instantiateNewGroups (NodeGroup *group, int size)

:: instantiate NodeGroup for voxel with overlap
NodeGroup *instantiateGroup (NodeGroup *parent, Glassner new_ID)
void FillXYZ (NodeGroup *ng)
bool CoarseProcess (const Level &level)

:: Note that TSpans have been compacted from the previous level's fine tests
:: i.e., individual triangle indices marked as INVALID.
void retrieveParentTriangles (Vector< int > &tri_idx, int fetch_level)

:: Note that the worst case is storage of the entire preceding level
:: because of level-order iteration.
void DeleteVTPairs (NodeGroup *group)

:: recursive : actually deletes more than the last level if any
:: VTPairs can be found...
void LastLevelDelete (OctreeNode<NodeGroup * > *node)

:: vt_list has already been checked and sorted by caller
void MakeTriangleSpans ()

void SetDefaultTSpan (NodeGroup *ng)

:: A natural trimming of false positives: note that
:: the deprecated node will still be deleted since it's
:: in the deletion vector array.
:: Called when geom_stat = 0x00 or vt_list->count = 0.
void DeprecateNodesOnUp (NodeGroup *group)

:: follow voxel-pipe example and loop by voxel in the fine stage
void FineProcess (const Level &level)

Private Attributes

NodeGroup *currentVector<NodeGroup * >ng_list
Octree<NodeGroup * > *tree
Context &context
IDWorker id_w

Detailed Description

High-level code for NodeGroup object initialization and processing.

Constructor & Destructor Documentation

GroupWorker::GroupWorker (Context&mcontext) [inline]
: current(NULL), context(mcontext){}

// The vector will delete the array of pointers,
// but not what the pointers point to. Do that here.
GroupWorker::~GroupWorker ()

```
{
   int  i,  size;

   OctreeNode<NodeGroup *>  *root =  tree->getRoot();

   // delete VTList and VTPairs for last level
   if  (root != NULL) {
      LastLevelDelete(root);
   }

   // delete node groups (many!)
   if  ((size =  ng_list.size())  >  0) {
      for  (i = 0; i<size; ++i) {
         delete   ng_list[i];
      }
   }
   ng_list.clear();
}
```

Member Function Documentation

```
// note: msb_pos may be zero after a return from false-pos processing.
void GroupWorker::checkVTPairs (const Level&level)
{
   int  msb_pos;

   // Can't delete parent VT pairs until all subnodes have been
   // processed for that parent. We're in just one octant of
   // possibly several octants spawned from the parent.
   // Note eval_level = 1 is still working off the root NodeGroup,
   // hence no parent.
   if  (level.fetch   >=  context.start_level) {
       msb_pos =  id_w.getMostSignificantSetBit(current->parent->geom_stat);
       if  (msb_pos ==  current->node_idx) {
           // done with all subnodes of parent; delete VTPairs for parent
           DeleteVTPairs(current->parent);
       }
   }
}

bool GroupWorker::CoarseProcess (const Level &level) [private]
{
   Vector<int>  tri_idx;   // goes away when done
   QuickSort  sort;

   // for spawned object already processed
   if  (current->pairs  != NULL)
```

```
        return  false;

    // fill a vector of parent Triangle indices
    retrieveParentTriangles(tri_idx, level.fetch);

    if  (current->ID  == 12218)  // 7124
        int   a  = 1;   // break for debug

    // note: this attaches vt_list to the current group
    VTList  * vt_list =  context.geom_w.CoarseTest(tri_idx,  current);

    // with increasing resolution false positives due to
    // roundoff error from previous levels may disappear. Trim.
    if  (vt_list->count  == 0) {
        DeprecateNodesOnUp(current);
        return   false;
    }

    // sort the VTPairs for current node
    sort.quicksort(vt_list);

    // now make the Triangle spans for each octant
    MakeTriangleSpans();

    return   true;
}

// Note that the worst case is storage of the entire preceding level
// because of level-order iteration.
void GroupWorker::DeleteVTPairs (NodeGroup *group) [private]
{
    VTList  *vt_list = group->pairs;

    if  (vt_list == NULL)
        return;

    int   count  = vt_list->count;
    for  (int  i = 0; i <  count; ++i) {
        VTPair  *pair = vt_list->list[i];
        delete  pair;
    }
    delete  [] vt_list->list;
    delete  vt_list;
    group->pairs  = NULL;
}

// public entry-point, used at end of context switch
void GroupWorker::Deprecate ()
```

```
{
    DeprecateNodesOnUp(current);
}

// A natural trimming of false positives: note that
// the deprecated node will still be deleted since it's
// in the deletion vector array.
// Called when geom_stat = 0x00 or vt_list->count = 0.
void GroupWorker::DeprecateNodesOnUp (NodeGroup *group) [private]
{
    int  msb_pos;

    // check parent NULL: this can happen at level 1
    // if there's a bug in the rasterization and/or everything
    // is a false positive...
    if  (group->parent  == NULL)
        return;

    NodeGroup  *parent = group->parent;

    msb_pos =  id_w.getMostSignificantSetBit(parent->geom_stat);
    if  (msb_pos == group->node_idx) {
        DeleteVTPairs(parent);
    }

    // set geom_stat no matter what
    parent->geom_stat   &=  id_w.getCompAtNodeIdx(group->node_idx);  // complement
    if  (parent->geom_stat  == 0x00) {
        DeprecateNodesOnUp(parent);
    }
}

void GroupWorker::FillXYZ (NodeGroup *ng) [private]
{
    int  i;
    Glassner  base;

    base = ng->ID  * 10;

    for  (i=0; i<OCTANTS; ++i) {
        id_w.getXYZ((Glassner)(base + i + 1), ng->node[i].coord);
    }
}

// follow voxel-pipe example and loop by voxel in the fine stage
void GroupWorker::FineProcess (const Level &level) [private]
{
    int  i,  count, begin,  end;
    unsigned   char  setbit = 0x01;
```

```
    current->geom_stat  = 0x00;

    for  (i=0, count = 0; i<OCTANTS; ++i) {
       // get the begin-end indices
       begin =  current->span[i].begin;
       end =  current->span[i].end;
       if  (begin != -1) {
          if  (context.geom_w.FineTest(current, i, begin, end)) {
             current->geom_stat  |= setbit;
            ++count;
          }
       }
       setbit  <<= 1;
    }
    // clean up the tree
    if  (count == 0) {
       DeprecateNodesOnUp(current);
       return;
    }

    if  (level.eval   <   context.terminal_level)
       instantiateNewGroups(current, count);
}

// don't need the list anymore: pointers still valid!
void GroupWorker::freeGroupPointers (NodeGroupList *ngl)
{
    // NodeGroupList frees its own list array
    delete  ngl;
}

// set the geom_stat bits in the parent NodeGroup (passed in)
// instantiate new groups for set bits
void GroupWorker::GeomProcess (NodeGroup *group, const Level&level)
{
    // mark the parent as  "current"  during term of child processing
    current  = group;

    if  (!CoarseProcess(level))
       return;

    FineProcess(level);
}

unsigned char GroupWorker::getChildrenBits ()
{
    return   current->geom_stat;
}
```

```
// get last n for parent group and return array
// call AFTER geom_stat has been set by overlap code
// NOTE! This is paired with the free routine: caller must call free
// after copying pointers from this function (see OctreeWorker.cpp)
NodeGroupList * GroupWorker::getNewGroups (NodeGroup *parent)
{
    int i, j, size, count;

    if ((count = id_w.numSetBits(parent->geom_stat)) == 0)
        return NULL;
    if ((size = ng_list.size()) == 0)
        return NULL;

    NodeGroupList * ngl = new NodeGroupList;
    NodeGroup **plist = new NodeGroup * [count];
    j = 0;

    for (i = size - count; i < size; ++i) {
        NodeGroup *node = ng_list[i];
        plist[j++] = node;
    }
    ngl->list = plist;
    ngl->count = count;

    return ngl;
}

// instantiate NodeGroup for voxel with overlap
// parent_ID is the full Glassner ID
NodeGroup * GroupWorker::instantiateGroup (NodeGroup *parent, Glassner new_ID) [private]
{
    // the index into the octant array
    Glassner mask = (new_ID / 10) * 10;
    unsigned char pidx = new_ID - mask; // just a value
    NodeGroup *ng = new NodeGroup(parent, pidx, new_ID);
    ng_list.push_back(ng);

    // Set default -1 vals for TSpan array
    SetDefaultTSpan(ng);

    // make voxel coords
    FillXYZ(ng);

    return ng;
}

void GroupWorker::instantiateNewGroups (NodeGroup *group, int size) [private]
{
    Glassner *id_list = new Glassner [size];
```

```
    id_w.getChildIDs(id_list, group->ID, group->geom_stat);

    for (int i = 0; i < size; ++i) {
        instantiateGroup(group, id_list[i]);
    }
}

// Hide details from caller.
NodeGroup * GroupWorker::InstantiateRoot (Glassner new_ID)
{
    return instantiateGroup(NULL, new_ID);
}

// recursive : actually deletes more than the last level if any
// VTPairs can be found...
void GroupWorker::LastLevelDelete (OctreeNode<NodeGroup * > *node) [private]
{
    if (node->child_count == 0) {
        NodeGroup *ng_ptr = node->element;
        DeleteVTPairs(ng_ptr);
        return;
    }

    int count = node->child_count;
    for (int i = 0; i<count; ++i) {
        LastLevelDelete(node->child[i]);
    }
}

// vt_list has already been checked and sorted by caller
void GroupWorker::MakeTriangleSpans () [private]
{
    unsigned short vox_id, prev_id;
    int i, count;

    VTList *vt_list = current->pairs;
    count = vt_list->count;

    // init the first pair...
    VTPair *pair = vt_list->list[0];
    vox_id = pair->vox_idx;
    current->span[vox_id].begin = 0;
    current->span[vox_id].end = 0;

    prev_id = vox_id;

    // and succeeding pairs...
    for (i = 1; i < count; ++i) {
        VTPair *pair = vt_list->list[i];
```

```
        vox_id = pair->vox_idx;
        if  (vox_id != prev_id) {
            current->span[vox_id].begin  = i;
            current->span[prev_id].end  = i - 1;
            prev_id = vox_id;
        }
    }
    // final end value
    current->span[vox_id].end  = i - 1;
}

void GroupWorker::resetCurrent (NodeGroup *group)
{
    current  = group;
}

// Note that TSpans have been compacted from the previous level's fine tests
// i.e., individual triangle indices marked as INVALID.
void GroupWorker::retrieveParentTriangles (Vector< int > &tri_idx, int fetch_level) [private]
{
    int  i,  start,  end;

    try  {
        // check level == 1 to use TriangleList to make new Pairs
        // (L = 1 applies to the NodeGroup of L = 0; evaluation of that
        // group promotes the level to L = 1 in the LevelWorker switch code.)
        if  (fetch_level == 0) {
            context.geom_w.getRootTriangles(tri_idx);
        } else  {
            // else use the parent TSpan for the current octant index
            NodeGroup  *parent =  current->parent;
            int  octant_index =  current->node_idx;
            start = parent->span[octant_index - 1].begin;
            end = parent->span[octant_index - 1].end;

            // Should never happen: iterated node group is guaranteed
            // to have parent triangles, otherwise it wouldn't exist!
            if  (start == -1)
                throw   IteratorException("No parent triangles for iterated node.\n");

            for  (i = start; i  <=  end; ++i) {
                VTPair  *pair = parent->pairs->list[i];
                if  (pair->tri_idx  !=  INVALID)
                    tri_idx.push_back(pair->tri_idx);
            }
        }
    }
    catch(IteratorException   &  e) {
        std::cout  <<  e.toString();
```

```
    }
}

// -1 means empty
void GroupWorker::SetDefaultTSpan (NodeGroup *ng) [private]
{
    for (int i = 0; i < OCTANTS; ++i) {
        ng->span[i].begin = -1;
        ng->span[i].end = -1;
    }
}

// for destruction
void GroupWorker::setTreePointer (Octree<NodeGroup * > *tree_ptr)
{
    tree = tree_ptr;
}
```

The documentation for this class was generated from the following files:
- GroupWorker.h
- GroupWorker.cpp

IDWorker Class Reference

Public Member Functions

IDWorker ()
~IDWorker ()

:: return an array of Child IDs
void getChildIDs (Glassner *id_list, Glassner parent_ID, unsigned char child_bits)

void addScaledUnitOffset (ushort3 &r_coord, const ushort3 &coord, int scale, unsigned char idx)

:: returns index (1 to 8) of MSB set bit
int getMostSignificantSetBit (unsigned char geom_stat)

int TensMagnitude (Glassner ID)
int Level (Glassner ID)

:: allow for count of 0, else 10^(c-1)
Glassner TensMinusOne (int count)

:: gets the min coord of the voxel bbox for level
void getXYZ (Glassner ID, ushort3 &coord)

Glassner getNode (ushort3 &coord, int level)
unsigned char numSetBits (unsigned char geom_stat)

:: node_idx is 1 to 8
unsigned char getCompAtNodeIdx (unsigned char node_idx)

:: counts from 1 to 8
int getBitCountAtNodeIdx (unsigned char geom_stat, unsigned char node_idx)

:: node_idx passed in 1 to 8
bool checkOctantValid (unsigned char geom_stat, unsigned char node_idx)

Detailed Description

Octree node labelling and manipulation routines.

Constructor & Destructor Documentation

IDWorker::IDWorker () [inline]
{}

```
IDWorker::~IDWorker () [inline]
{}
```

Member Function Documentation

```
void IDWorker::addScaledUnitOffset (ushort3 &r_coord, const ushort3 &coord, int scale, unsigned
char idx)
{
   r_coord.x  = coord.x  * scale +  ax[idx - 1] *  scale;
   r_coord.y  = coord.y  * scale +  ay[idx - 1] *  scale;
   r_coord.z  = coord.z  * scale +  az[idx - 1] *  scale;
}

// node_idx passed in 1 to 8
bool IDWorker::checkOctantValid (unsigned char geom_stat, unsigned char node_idx)
{
    unsigned   char  testbit = 0x01;

    testbit  <<= (node_idx - 1);
    return  (geom_stat  &  testbit);
}

// counts from 1 to 8
int IDWorker::getBitCountAtNodeIdx (unsigned char geom_stat, unsigned char node_idx)
{
    unsigned   char  testbit = 0x01;
    unsigned   char   count  = 0;

    for  (int  i = 0; i  <   OCTANTS; ++i) {
       if  (geom_stat  &  testbit)
          ++count;
       if  (i == node_idx - 1)
          break;
       testbit  <<= 1;
   }
   return   count;
}

// return an array of Child IDs
// called for a parent ID AFTER the children have been geom tested
// parent ID is retrieved from the NodeGroup parent. May be 0 for root.
// EXAMPLE:
// lev1: parent_ID = 0
// lev1: NodeGroup IDs are {1, 2, 3, ... , 8}
// lev2: parent_ID = 1
// lev2: NodeGroup IDs are {11, 12, 13, ... , 18}
// VERY IMPORTANT: the id_list is filled in increasing LSB to MSB order.
```

```
// Everything hinges on this ordering!
void IDWorker::getChildIDs (Glassner *id_list, Glassner parent_ID, unsigned char child_bits)
{
    int  i, j;

    for  (i = 1, j = 0; i  <=  OCTANTS; ++i) {
        // test LSB and shift
        // 0 + 1 = 1 ; 20 + 4 = 24
        if  (child_bits  &  0x01)
            id_list[j++] = parent_ID * 10 + i;

        child_bits  >>= 1;
    }
}

// node_idx is 1 to 8
unsigned char IDWorker::getCompAtNodeIdx (unsigned char node_idx)
{
    unsigned   char  testbit = 0x01;
    testbit  <<= (node_idx - 1);
    return  (testbit ^ 0xFF);
}

// returns index (1 to 8) of MSB set bit
int IDWorker::getMostSignificantSetBit (unsigned chargeom_stat)
{
    unsigned   char  testbit = 0x80;
    unsigned   char   count  = 8;

    while  (count  >  0) {
        if  (geom_stat  &  testbit)
            break;
        --count; testbit  >>= 1;
    }
    return   count;
}

// reverse lookup returns ID from coord
Glassner IDWorker::getNode (ushort3 &coord, int level)
{
    float  x,  y,  z;
    float  xs, ys, zs;
    unsigned   short   n, m, u;
    Glassner  ID = 0;

    x = float(coord.x);
    y = float(coord.y);
    z = float(coord.z);
    float  Nt = lroundf(powf(2.0,  float(level  - 1)));
```

```
int N = 1;
n = m = u = N;
float3 center = make_float3((float)n, (float)m, (float)u);

while (level-- > 0) {
   // scale center and position at each iteration
   xs = x / Nt;
   ys = y / Nt;
   zs = z / Nt;
   Nt /= 2.0;
   center.x = (float)n;
   center.y = (float)m;
   center.z = (float)u;

    if (xs >= center.x) {
       n = n * 2 + 1;
       if (ys >= center.y) {
          m = m * 2 + 1;
          if (zs >= center.z) {
             u = u * 2 + 1;
             ID = (ID * 10) + 6;
          } else {
             ID = (ID * 10) + 8;
             u = u * 2 - 1;
          }
       } else {
          m = m * 2 - 1;
          if (zs >= center.z) {
             u = u * 2 + 1;
             ID = (ID * 10) + 2;
          } else {
             u = u * 2 - 1;
             ID = (ID * 10) + 4;
          }
       }
    } else { // xs < center.x
       n = n * 2 - 1;
       if (ys >= center.y) {
          m = m * 2 + 1;
          if (zs >= center.z) {
             u = u * 2 + 1;
             ID = (ID * 10) + 5;
          } else {
             u = u * 2 - 1;
             ID = (ID * 10) + 7;
          }
       } else {
          m = m * 2 - 1;
          if (zs >= center.z) {
```

```
                u = u * 2 + 1;
                ID = (ID * 10) + 1;
            } else {
                u = u * 2 - 1;
                ID = (ID * 10) + 3;
            }
        }
      }
   } // levels
   return ID;
}

// gets the min coord of the voxel bbox for level
void IDWorker::getXYZ (Glassner ID, ushort3 &coord)
{
    Glassner mag, tID;
    int x, y, z, count;

    count = TensMagnitude(ID);          // 412 returns 3
    mag = TensMinusOne(count);          // 3 returns 100
    x = y = z = 0;

    while (mag >= 1) {
        tID = ID / mag;
        x = (x << 1) + ax[tID - 1];
        y = (y << 1) + ay[tID - 1];
        z = (z << 1) + az[tID - 1];

        tID *= mag;
        ID -= tID;
        mag /= 10;
    }
    coord.x = x;
    coord.y = y;
    coord.z = z;
}

int IDWorker::Level (Glassner ID)
{
    return TensMagnitude(ID);
}

unsigned char IDWorker::numSetBits (unsigned char geom_stat)
{
    unsigned char testbit = 0x01;
    unsigned char count = 0;

    for (int i = 0; i < OCTANTS; ++i) {
        if (geom_stat & testbit)
```

```
      ++count;
    testbit <<= 1;
  }
  return count;
}

int IDWorker::TensMagnitude (Glassner ID)
{
  int count = 0;

  while (ID >= 1) {
    ID /= 10;
    ++count;
  }
  return count;
}

// allow for count of 0, else 10^(c-1)
Glassner IDWorker::TensMinusOne (int count)
{
  Glassner mag = 0;
  for (int i = 1; i <= count; ++i) {
    if (i == 1)
      mag = 1;
    else
      mag *= 10;
  }
  return mag;
}
```

Local Data

```
static int ax[] = {0, 1, 0, 1, 0, 1, 0, 1};
static int ay[] = {0, 0, 0, 0, 1, 1, 1, 1};
static int az[] = {1, 1, 0, 0, 1, 1, 0, 0};
```

Associated Data Holders

```
// 4 bytes
typedef unsigned long Glassner;
```

The documentation for this class was generated from the following files:
- IDWorker.h
- IDWorker.cpp

LevelOrder< Object > Class Template Reference

Public Member Functions

:: constructor for LevelOrder iterator
LevelOrder (const Octree< Object > &theTree)

~LevelOrder ()
void first ()
bool get ()
bool isEmpty ()

:: want to enqueue the OctreeNode<Object> that holds the Object,
:: not the Object itself
void put (OctreeNode< Object > **list, int count)

:: reiterate/recycle current node (passed as parent)
void put (OctreeNode< Object > *parent)

Private Attributes

QueueAr<OctreeNode< Object > * >q

Detailed Description

Iterate over queue of OctreeNode objects.
Implements TreeIterator< Object >.

Constructor & Destructor Documentation

```
// constructor for LevelOrder iterator
template<class Object >
LevelOrder< Object >::LevelOrder(const Octree< Object >&theTree)
   : TreeIterator<Object>( theTree )
{
    q.makeEmpty();
    if  (TreeIterator<Object>::root  != NULL)
       q.enqueue(  TreeIterator<Object>::root  );
}

template<class Object>
LevelOrder< Object >::~LevelOrder() [inline]
{}
```

Member Function Documentation

```
template<class Object >
void LevelOrder< Object >::first() [virtual]
{
    // currently no init ops
}

template<class Object >
bool LevelOrder< Object >::get () [virtual]
{
    if (q.isEmpty() ) {
        if (TreeIterator<Object>::current == NULL)
            throw IteratorException( "Advance past end" );
        TreeIterator<Object>::current = NULL;
        return false;
    }

    TreeIterator<Object>::current = q.getFront();
    q.dequeue();
    return true;
}

template<class Object >
bool LevelOrder< Object >::isEmpty () [virtual]
{
    if (q.isEmpty() ) {
        if (TreeIterator<Object>::current == NULL)
            throw IteratorException( "Advance past end" );
        // don't change the state: just query
        return true;
    }

    return false;
}

// want to enqueue the OctreeNode<Object> that holds the Object,
// not the Object itself
template<class Object >
void LevelOrder< Object >::put (OctreeNode< Object > **list, int count) [virtual]
{
    if (list == NULL)
        return;

    for (int i = 0; i < count; ++i)
        q.enqueue(list[i]);
}
```

```
// reiterate/recycle current node (passed as parent)
template<class Object >
void LevelOrder< Object >::put (OctreeNode< Object > *parent) [virtual]
{
    if  (parent == NULL)
        return;

    q.enqueue(parent);   // requeue
}
```

Associated Data Holders

```
template <class Object>
class TreeIterator
{
public:
   TreeIterator(const Octree<Object> & theTree )
       : root( theTree.root ), current( NULL) {}

   virtual ~TreeIterator() {}

   virtual void first() = 0;
   virtual bool get() = 0;
   virtual void put(OctreeNode<Object> **list, int count) = 0;
   virtual void put(OctreeNode<Object> *parent) = 0;
   virtual bool isEmpty() = 0;
   bool isValid() const { return current != NULL; }
   const Object & retrieve() const;
   OctreeNode<Object> * currentOctreeNode() { return current; }

protected:
   OctreeNode<Object> * root;
   OctreeNode<Object> * current;
};
```

The documentation for this class was generated from the following files:
- Iterate.h
- Iterate.tpp

LevelWorker Class Reference

Public Member Functions

LevelWorker (Context &mcontext)
~LevelWorker ()

:: See if we've switched levels via the ID.
bool LevelSwitch (Glassner ID)

:: At every level switch...
voidDoLevelWork ()

const Level& getLevel ()
bool TerminalLevel ()
void setFetchAndEvalLevels (int fetch, int eval)

Private Attributes

IDWorker id_w
Level level
Context &context
int current_eval_level
int current_fetch_level
int N

Detailed Description

Level management; moving from one level to the next; conditions, etc. The "level" refers to the current level of subdivision of the octree.

Constructor & Destructor Documentation

```
LevelWorker::LevelWorker (Context&mcontext) [inline]
                        : context(mcontext),
        current_eval_level(mcontext.start_level  - 1),
        current_fetch_level(mcontext.start_level  - 1),  N(0) {}
```

```
LevelWorker::~LevelWorker () [inline]
{}
```

Member Function Documentation

```
// At every level switch...
void LevelWorker::DoLevelWork ()
{
    N  =  context.geom_w.NewN(current_eval_level,
                        context.terminal_level,
                        TerminalLevel());
    context.geom_w.SetBBoxDeltas();
    context.geom_w.DoTriangleWork();
}

const Level& LevelWorker::getLevel ()
{
    level.eval =  current_eval_level;
    level.fetch =  current_fetch_level;
    return   level;
}

// See if we've switched levels via the ID.
// fetch_level -> from ID of what comes out of the Iterator queue
// eval_level -> fetch_level + 1
bool LevelWorker::LevelSwitch (Glassner ID)
{
    int  fetch_level =  id_w.Level(ID);
    int  eval_level = fetch_level + 1;

    if  (eval_level !=  current_eval_level) {
        current_eval_level  = eval_level;
        current_fetch_level  = fetch_level;
        return   true;
    }
    return   false;    // no level switch
}

void LevelWorker::setFetchAndEvalLevels (int fetch, int eval)
{
    current_fetch_level  = fetch;
    current_eval_level  = eval;
}

bool LevelWorker::TerminalLevel ()
{
    return  (current_eval_level  ==  context.terminal_level);
}
```

Associated Data Holders

```
struct Level {
```

```
    int eval, fetch;
};
```

The documentation for this class was generated from the following files:
- LevelWorker.h
- LevelWorker.cpp

LList< Object > Class Template Reference

Public Member Functions

:: Construct the list.
LList (const Object element)

:: Copy constructor.
LList (const LList &rhs)

:: Destructor.
virtual ~LList ()

:: Test if the list is logically empty.
bool isEmpty () const

:: Make the list logically empty.
void makeEmpty ()

:: Return an iterator representing the header node.
LListNode< Object > *zeroth () const

:: Return an iterator representing the first node in the list.
LListNode< Object > *first () const

:: Insert item x after p.
virtual void insert (const Object x, const LListItr< Object > &p)

:: Insert item x after p.
virtual LListNode< Object > *insertNext (const Object x, const LListItr< Object >&p)

:: Return iterator corresponding to the first node containing an item x.
LListNode< Object > *find (const Object x) const

:: Return iterator prior to the first node containing an item x.
LListNode< Object > *findPrevious (const Object x) const

LListNode< Object > *findNext (const Object x) const

:: Remove the first occurrence of an item x.
void remove (const Object x)

:: Deep copy of linked lists.
const LList&operator= (const LList &rhs)

Private Attributes

LListNode< Object > *header

Detailed Description

Templated linked list class and associated templated iterator class.

Constructor & Destructor Documentation

```
// Construct the list.
// constructor requires valid header element.
template<class Object >
LList< Object >::LList(const Object element)
{
    header = new LListNode<Object>(element);
}

// Copy constructor.
template<class Object >
LList< Object >::LList(const LList< Object > &rhs)
{
    header = new LListNode<Object>(rhs.header->element);
   *this = rhs;  // use operator= for copy
}

// Destructor.
template<class Object >
LList< Object >::~LList() [virtual]
{
    makeEmpty( );
    delete header;
}
```

Member Function Documentation

```
// Return iterator corresponding to the first node containing an item x.
// Iterator isPastEnd if item is not found.
template<class Object >
LListNode< Object > * LList< Object >::find (const Object x) const
{
    LListNode<Object> *p = header->next;

    while( p != NULL && p->element != x )
      p = p->next;

    return p;
```

```
}

template<class Object >
LListNode< Object > * LList< Object >::findNext (const Object x) const
{
   LListNode<Object> *p = header->next;

   while( p != NULL && p->element != x )
     p = p->next;

   if (p == NULL) throw BadIterator();

   return p->next;
}

// Return iterator prior to the first node containing an item x.
// Don't force Object to be a reference: != comparison is on Object,
// which if it's not a pointer, will need a != overload operator.
template<class Object >
LListNode< Object > * LList< Object >::findPrevious (const Object x) const
{
   LListNode<Object> *p = header;

   while( p->next != NULL && p->next->element != x )
     p = p->next;

   return p;
}

// Return an iterator representing the first node in the list.
// This operation is valid for empty lists.
template<class Object >
LListNode< Object > * LList< Object >::first() const
{
   return header->next;
}

// Insert item x after p.
// Reimplemented in SortedLList< Object, ConstObj >.
template<class Object >
void LList< Object >::insert (const Object x, const LListItr< Object > &p) [virtual]
{
   if ( p.current != NULL )
      p.current->next = new LListNode<Object>( x, p.current->next );
}

// Insert item x after p.
// Reimplemented in SortedLList< Object, ConstObj >.
template<class Object >
```

```
LListNode< Object > * LList< Object >::insertNext (const Object x, const LListItr< Object > &p)
[virtual]
{
    if ( p.current  == NULL )
       return  NULL;

   p.current->next =  new   LListNode<Object>(  x, p.current->next );
   return  p.current->next;
}

// Test if the list is logically empty.
// Return true if empty, false, otherwise.
template<class Object >
bool LList< Object >::isEmpty () const
{
    return   header->next == NULL;
}

// Make the list logically empty.
template<class Object >
void LList< Object >::makeEmpty ()
{
    while( !isEmpty( ) )
       remove(  first( )->element );
}

// Deep copy of linked lists.
template<class Object >
const LList< Object >&LList< Object >::operator= (const LList< Object > &rhs)
{
    if(  this  !=  &rhs )
    {
       makeEmpty( );

       LListItr<Object>  ritr =  LListItr<Object>(rhs.first( ));
       LListItr<Object>  itr =  LListItr<Object>(zeroth( ));
       for( ; !ritr.isPastEnd( ); ritr.advance( ), itr.advance( ) )
          insert( ritr.retrieve( ), itr );
    }
    return  *this;
}

// Remove the first occurrence of an item x.
template<class Object >
void LList< Object >::remove (const Object x)
{
    LListNode<Object>  *p  =  findPrevious(  x  );

    if( p->next  != NULL )
```

```
    {
        LListNode<Object>  *oldNode = p->next;
        p->next  = p->next->next;   // Bypass deleted node
        delete  oldNode;
    }
}

// Return an iterator representing the header node.
template<class Object >
LListNode< Object > * LList< Object >::zeroth () const
{
    return   header;
}
```

Associated Data Holders

```
template <class Object>
class LListNode
{
public:
    // require first argument, don't force it to
    // be a reference.
   LListNode( const Object theElement,
            LListNode * n = NULL )
     : element( theElement ), next( n ) { }

   Object     element;
   LListNode *next;

   friend class LList<Object>;
   friend class LListItr<Object>;
};

template <class Object>
class LListItr
{
  public:
   LListItr( ) : current( NULL ) { }
   LListItr( LListNode<Object> *theNode )
     : current( theNode ) { }
   bool isValid() const
     { return current != NULL; }
   bool isPastEnd( ) const
     { return current == NULL; }
   bool advance( ) {
       if( isPastEnd( ) ) return false;
      current = current->next; return true;
```

```
  }
  bool peekNextValid() {
      return (current->next != NULL);
  }
  // Don't force return of Object reference
  const Object retrieve( ) const
   { if( isPastEnd( ) ) throw BadIterator( );
     return current->element; }
  void reset(LListNode<Object> *theNode) {
      current = theNode;
  }

 private:
  LListNode<Object> *current;         // Current position

  friend class LList<Object>;     // Grant access to "current"
};
```

The documentation for this class was generated from the following files:
- LinkedList.h
- LinkedList.tpp

Load3DS Class Reference

Public Member Functions

Load3DS ()
~Load3DS ()
bool LoadAndTransfer (const char *p_filename, color3 &color)
Vector<BasicTriangle * > &getGeomList ()

:: user is responsible for calling this
void freeGeomList ()

Private Member Functions

bool Load (obj_3ds_ptr p_object, const char *p_filename)

Private Attributes

Vector<BasicTriangle * >my_geom

Detailed Description

Loads triangles from the 3DS Max graphics file.

Constructor & Destructor Documentation

Load3DS::Load3DS () [inline]
{}

Load3DS::~Load3DS () [inline]
{}

Member Function Documentation

```
// user is responsible for calling this
void Load3DS::freeGeomList ()
{
    int  size  =  my_geom.size();
    for  (int  i = 0; i  <   size; ++i)
        delete   my_geom[i];
}
```

```
Vector<BasicTriangle * >& Load3DS::getGeomList ()
{
   return  my_geom;
}

bool Load3DS::Load (obj_3ds_ptr p_object, const char *p_filename) [private]
{
   int i;
   FILE *l_file;

   unsigned  short  l_chunk_id;      //Chunk identifier
   unsigned  int  l_chunk_length;     //Chunk length
   unsigned  char  l_char;
   unsigned  short  l_qty;           //Number of elements in each chunk
   unsigned  short  l_face_flags;    //Flag that stores some face information

   //Open the file
   if  ((l_file=fopen (p_filename,  "rb"))== NULL)  return   false;

   //Loop to scan the whole file
   fseek(l_file, 0L, SEEK_END);
   long  filelength = ftell(l_file);
   rewind(l_file);

   // ftell (l_file)  <  filelength (fileno (l_file))
   while  (ftell (l_file)  <  filelength) {
      //Read the chunk header
      fread (&l_chunk_id, 2, 1, l_file);
      //printf("ChunkID: %x\n",l_chunk_id);
      //Read the length of the chunk
      fread (&l_chunk_length, 4, 1, l_file);
      //printf("ChunkLength: %x\n",l_chunk_length);

      switch  (l_chunk_id)
      {
         //----------------- MAIN3DS -----------------
         // Description: Main chunk, contains all the other chunks
         // Chunk ID: 4d4d
         // Chunk Length: 0 + sub chunks
         //-------------------------------------------
         case  0x4d4d:
         break;

         //----------------- EDIT3DS -----------------
         // Description: 3D Editor chunk, objects layout info
         // Chunk ID: 3d3d (hex)
         // Chunk Length: 0 + sub chunks
         //-------------------------------------------
         case  0x3d3d:
```

```
break;

//--------------- EDIT_OBJECT ---------------
// Description: Object block, info for each object
// Chunk ID: 4000 (hex)
// Chunk Length: len(object name) + sub chunks
//-------------------------------------------
case  0x4000:
   i=0;
   do  {
      fread (&l_char, 1, 1, l_file);
      p_object->name[i]=l_char;
      i++;
  } while(l_char !=  '\0'   &&  i<NAME_LEN);
  if  (i ==  NAME_LEN)
      p_object->name[i]=  '\0';
break;

//--------------- OBJ_TRIMESH ---------------
// Description: Triangular mesh, contains chunks for 3d mesh info
// Chunk ID: 4100 (hex)
// Chunk Length: 0 + sub chunks
//-------------------------------------------
case  0x4100:
break;

//--------------- TRI_VERTEXL ---------------
// Description: Vertices list
// Chunk ID: 4110 (hex)
// Chunk Length: 1 x unsigned short (number of vertices)
//            + 3 x float (vertex coordinates) x (number of vertices)
//            + sub chunks
//-------------------------------------------
case  0x4110:
  fread (&l_qty,  sizeof  (unsigned   short), 1, l_file);
  p_object->vertices_qty  = l_qty;
   //printf("Number of vertices: %d\n", l_qty);
  for  (i=0; i<l_qty; i++)
  {
      fread (&p_object->vertex[i].x,  sizeof(float), 1, l_file);
      //printf("Vertices list x: %f\n",p_object->vertex[i].x);
      fread (&p_object->vertex[i].y,  sizeof(float), 1, l_file);
      //printf("Vertices list y: %f\n",p_object->vertex[i].y);
      fread (&p_object->vertex[i].z,  sizeof(float), 1, l_file);
      //printf("Vertices list z: %f\n",p_object->vertex[i].z);
  }
   break;

//-------------- TRI_FACEL1 ---------------
```

```
        // Description: Polygons (faces) list
        // Chunk ID: 4120 (hex)
        // Chunk Length: 1 x unsigned short (number of polygons)
        //          + 3 x unsigned short (polygon points) x (number of polygons)
        //          + sub chunks
        //-------------------------------------------
        case  0x4120:
          fread (&l_qty,  sizeof  (unsigned   short), 1, l_file);
          p_object->polygons_qty  = l_qty;
           //printf("Number of polygons: %d\n",l_qty);
          for  (i=0; i<l_qty; i++)
          {
              fread (&p_object->polygon[i].a, sizeof (unsigned   short), 1, l_file);
              //printf("Polygon point a: %d\n",p_object->polygon[i].a);
              fread (&p_object->polygon[i].b, sizeof (unsigned   short), 1, l_file);
              //printf("Polygon point b: %d\n",p_object->polygon[i].b);
              fread (&p_object->polygon[i].c, sizeof (unsigned   short), 1, l_file);
              //printf("Polygon point c: %d\n",p_object->polygon[i].c);
              fread (&l_face_flags,  sizeof  (unsigned   short), 1, l_file);
              //printf("Face flags: %x\n",l_face_flags);                }
           break;

        //------------- TRI_MAPPINGCOORS ------------
        // Description: Vertices list
        // Chunk ID: 4140 (hex)
        // Chunk Length: 1 x unsigned short (number of mapping points)
        //          + 2 x float (mapping coordinates) x (number of mapping points)
        //          + sub chunks
        //-------------------------------------------
        //----------- Skip unknown chunks ------------
        // We need to skip all the chunks that currently we don't use
        // We use the chunk length information to set the file pointer
        // to the same level next chunk
        //-------------------------------------------
        default:
           fseek(l_file, l_chunk_length-6, SEEK_CUR);
      }
   }

   // Close the file stream
   fclose (l_file);

   return   true;  // OK
}

bool Load3DS::LoadAndTransfer (const char *p_filename, color3 &color)
{
   int  l_index, v_index;
   // put this baby on the stack for quick disposal
```

```
    obj_3ds  object;

    if  (!Load(&object, p_filename))
       return   false;

    for  (l_index=0; l_index<object.polygons_qty; l_index++)
   {
       BasicTriangle  *tri =  new   BasicTriangle;
       my_geom.push_back(tri);

       //----------------- FIRST VERTEX -----------------
       // Coordinates of the first vertex
       v_index =  object.polygon[l_index].a;
       tri->vert[0].x  =  object.vertex[ v_index ].x;
       tri->vert[0].y  =  object.vertex[ v_index ].y;
       tri->vert[0].z  =  object.vertex[ v_index ].z;

       //----------------- SECOND VERTEX -----------------
       // Coordinates of the second vertex
       v_index =  object.polygon[l_index].b;
       tri->vert[1].x  =  object.vertex[ v_index ].x;
       tri->vert[1].y  =  object.vertex[ v_index ].y;
       tri->vert[1].z  =  object.vertex[ v_index ].z;

       //----------------- THIRD VERTEX -----------------
       // Coordinates of the Third vertex
       v_index =  object.polygon[l_index].c;
       tri->vert[2].x  =  object.vertex[ v_index ].x;
       tri->vert[2].y  =  object.vertex[ v_index ].y;
       tri->vert[2].z  =  object.vertex[ v_index ].z;

       // color passed in
       tri->color.r  = color.r;
       tri->color.g  = color.g;
       tri->color.b  = color.b;
   }
   return   true;
}
```

Local Data

```
#define MAX_VERTICES 80000   // Max number of vertices (for each object)
#define MAX_POLYGONS 80000 // Max number of polygons (for each object)
#define NAME_LEN 20
```

Associated Data Holders

```
// vertex type

typedef struct {
   float x,y,z;
} vertex_type;

// The polygon (triangle), 3 numbers for 3 vertices

typedef struct {
   int a,b,c;
} polygon_type;

// 3DS object type

typedef struct {
   char name[NAME_LEN + 1];

   int vertices_qty;
   int polygons_qty;

   vertex_type vertex[MAX_VERTICES];
   polygon_type polygon[MAX_POLYGONS];

} obj_3ds, *obj_3ds_ptr;
```

The documentation for this class was generated from the following files:
- Load3DS.h
- Load3DS.cpp

MeshData Class Reference

Public Member Functions

MeshData ()
MeshData (float3 &mp1, float mlen)
~MeshData ()

:: copy constructor
MeshData (const MeshData&rhs)

const MeshData& operator= (const MeshData &rhs)

:: for OpenGL z draw order
bool operator< (const MeshData &rhs)

Public Attributes

float3 p1
float length

Detailed Description

Basic data structure for showing the boundary volume data
(e.g. the enclosing mesh).

Constructor & Destructor Documentation

```
MeshData::MeshData () [inline]
{}

MeshData::MeshData (float3&mp1, floatmlen) [inline]
{
        p1.x  = mp1.x;
        p1.y  = mp1.y;
        p1.z  = mp1.z;
        length  = mlen;
}

MeshData::~MeshData ()
{
}

// copy constructor
```

```
MeshData::MeshData (const MeshData &rhs)
{
    p1.x  = rhs.p1.x;
    p1.y  = rhs.p1.y;
    p1.z  = rhs.p1.z;
    length  = rhs.length;
}
```

Member Function Documentation

```
// for OpenGL z draw order
bool MeshData::operator<(const MeshData &rhs)
{
    if  (this  !=  &rhs) {
        return  (p1.z   <  rhs.p1.z);
    }
    return   false;    // equal
}

const MeshData& MeshData::operator= (const MeshData &rhs)
{
    if  (this  !=  &rhs) {  // standard alias test
        p1.x  = rhs.p1.x;
        p1.y  = rhs.p1.y;
        p1.z  = rhs.p1.z;
        length  = rhs.length;
    }
    return  *this;
}
```

The documentation for this class was generated from the following files:
- MeshData.h
- MeshData.cpp

Octree< Object > Class Template Reference

Public Member Functions

Octree ()
Octree (const Object &rootItem)
Octree (Object &rootItem)
Octree (const Octree &rhs)
~Octree ()
const Octree& operator= (const Octree &rhs)
void makeEmpty ()
bool isEmpty () const
void addRoot (Object &rootItem, OctreeNode< Object > *parent)
OctreeNode< Object > *getRoot ()
void setRootNull ()

Private Types

typedef OctreeNode< Object > Node

Private Member Functions

OctreeNode<Object> *copy_over (OctreeNode<Object> &orig) const
void makeEmpty (Node *&t)

Private Attributes

Node *root

Friends

class TreeIterator< Object >
(See listing for LevelOrder)

Detailed Description

Templated octree class and supporting OctreeNode structure.

Member Typedef Documentation

typedef OctreeNode<Object> Octree< Object >::Node [private]

Constructor & Destructor Documentation

```
template<class Object>
Octree< Object >::Octree() [inline]
:  root(NULL) {}

template<class Object>
Octree< Object >::Octree(const Object &rootItem) [inline]
:  root  (new   Node(rootItem, NULL)) {}

template<class Object>
Octree< Object >::Octree(Object &rootItem) [inline]
:  root  (new   Node(rootItem, NULL)) {}

template<class Object>
Octree< Object >::Octree(const Octree< Object > &rhs) [inline]
:  root(NULL) {*this  = rhs;}

template<class Object>
Octree< Object >::~Octree() [inline]
{  makeEmpty(); }
```

Member Function Documentation

```
template<class Object>
void Octree< Object >::addRoot (Object &rootItem, OctreeNode< Object > *parent)
{
    if  (root  != NULL)
       return;

    root  =  new   Node(rootItem, parent);
}

template<class Object>
OctreeNode<Object> *Octree< Object >::copy_over (OctreeNode<Object> &orig) const [private]
{
    OctreeNode<Object> *cur_copy = new OctreeNode<Object>( orig.element );
    if (orig.child == NULL)
        return cur_copy;

    int size = orig.child_count;
    OctreeNode<Object> **children = new OctreeNode<Object> * [size];
    cur_copy.child = children;

    for (int i = 0; i < size; ++i)
      cur_copy->child[i] = copy_over(*(orig.child[i]));
```

```
    return cur_copy;
}

template<class Object>
OctreeNode<Object>* Octree< Object >::getRoot () [inline]
{  return   root; }

template<class Object>
bool Octree< Object >::isEmpty () const [inline]
{return   root  == NULL; }

template<class Object>
void Octree< Object >::makeEmpty (Node *&t) [private]
{
    if (t != NULL) {
        int size = t->child_count;

        for (int i = 0; i < size; ++i)
            makeEmpty(t->child[i]);
        if (size > 0)
            delete [] t->child;

          delete t;
          t = NULL;
    }
}

template<class Object>
void Octree< Object >::makeEmpty () [inline]
{  makeEmpty(  root  ); }

template<class Object >
const Octree< Object >&Octree< Object >::operator= (const Octree< Object > &rhs)
{
    if  (this  !=  &rhs) {
      makeEmpty();
      if  (rhs.root  != NULL)
        root  =  copy_over(rhs.root);
    }
    return  *this;
}

template<class Object>
void Octree< Object >::setRootNull () [inline]
{root  = NULL;}
```

Associated Data Holders

```
// Node element to be managed by Octree class

template <class Object>
struct OctreeNode
{
    Object element;
    unsigned char child_bits, child_count;
    OctreeNode *parent;
    // "count" OctreeNode *'s follow, but start with default NULL.
    OctreeNode **child;

    // be strict and require the parent argument
    OctreeNode(Object & theElement, OctreeNode *mparent,
            unsigned short mcount = 0) : element(theElement),
            child_count(mcount), parent(mparent) { child = NULL;}
};
```

The documentation for this class was generated from the following files:
- Octree.h
- Octree.tpp

OctreeThread Class Reference

Public Member Functions

OctreeThread ()
virtual~OctreeThread ()

:: start the thread
voidEvalStart (Vector<BasicTriangle * >&geom)

:: join frees up thread resources and returns
voidEvalEnd ()

:: display adaptive mesh
voidMeshStart ()
voidMeshEnd ()

:: compute LED positions on armature
voidRayStart ()
voidRayEnd ()

:: Since the OctreeThread is global, explicitly call this
:: instead of putting it in the destructor.
voidCleanUp ()

VoxelData *Dequeue ()
bool IsEmpty ()
VoxelData *Enqueue (VoxelData *vp)
MeshData *DequeueM ()
bool IsEmptyM ()
MeshData *EnqueueM (MeshData *mp)
ReducedRay *DequeueR ()
bool IsEmptyR ()
ReducedRay *EnqueueR (ReducedRay *ray)

Private Member Functions

void *EvalThread (void *arg)
void *MeshThread (void *unused)

:: use existing octree (from Eval)
void *RayThread (void *unused)

Static Private Member Functions

static void *EvalThreadWrapper (void *arg)
static void *MeshThreadWrapper (void *arg)
static void *RayThreadWrapper (void *arg)

Private Attributes

ThreadData *pass_data
RenderQueue<VoxelData * > render_queue
RenderQueue<MeshData * > mesh_queue
RenderQueue<ReducedRay * > ray_queue
OctreeWorker *octree_w
RayWorker *ray_w
ContextWorker *context_w
pthread_toctree_thread
pthread_tmesh_thread
pthread_tray_thread

Detailed Description

Spawns threads into the octree processor.
There are different threads for different contexts:
for example, to compute and draw voxels;
to draw the boundary volume mesh;
or to cast rays to simulate the volumetric display device. (See ContextWorker class.)

Constructor & Destructor Documentation

```
OctreeThread::OctreeThread ()
{
}

OctreeThread::~OctreeThread () [virtual]
{
}
```

Member Function Documentation

```
// Since the OctreeThread is global, explicitly call this
// instead of putting it in the destructor.
void OctreeThread::CleanUp ()
{
   if (octree_w  != NULL)
      delete   octree_w;
   if (ray_w  != NULL)
      delete   ray_w;
   if (context_w  != NULL)
```

```
        delete   context_w;

    // clear the static vector or else stale pointers hang around
    ContextWorker::CleanUp();
}

VoxelData* OctreeThread::Dequeue () [inline]
{
        return   render_queue.dequeue();
}

MeshData* OctreeThread::DequeueM () [inline]
{
        return   mesh_queue.dequeue();
}

ReducedRay* OctreeThread::DequeueR () [inline]
{
        return   ray_queue.dequeue();
}

VoxelData* OctreeThread::Enqueue (VoxelData *vp) [inline]
{
        return   render_queue.enqueue(vp);
}

MeshData* OctreeThread::EnqueueM (MeshData *mp) [inline]
{
        return   mesh_queue.enqueue(mp);
}

ReducedRay* OctreeThread::EnqueueR (ReducedRay *ray) [inline]
{
        return   ray_queue.enqueue(ray);
}

// join frees up thread resources and returns
// Note that when this is called the queue should be empty!
// No need to explicitly empty it.
void OctreeThread::EvalEnd ()
{
    pthread_join(octree_thread, NULL);
    if  (pass_data  != NULL)
        delete   pass_data;
}

// start the thread
void OctreeThread::EvalStart (Vector<BasicTriangle * > &geom)
{
```

```
    pass_data = new ThreadData;

    pass_data->context = this;
    pass_data->geom = &geom;

    // spawn a thread for voxel computation / scene subdivision
    pthread_create(&octree_thread, NULL, &(this->EvalThreadWrapper), pass_data);
}

void * OctreeThread::EvalThread (void *arg) [private]
{
    Vector<BasicTriangle *> * geom = reinterpret_cast< Vector<BasicTriangle *> * > (arg);

    std::cout << "LAUNCHED!" << std::endl;

    // context for main iteration
    // note start level is 1, i.e., the eval_level
    context_w = new ContextWorker;
    context_w->makeContext(1, g_terminal, true, g_check_false_pos); // display true for now
    context_w->setRaster(g_raster);

    // send in basic triangle geometry
    context_w->CopyOverTriangles(*geom);
    int contextID = context_w->getContextID();

    // iterate
    octree_w = new OctreeWorker(contextID);
    octree_w->Top(context_w);

    return NULL;
}

void * OctreeThread::EvalThreadWrapper (void *arg) [static, private]
{
    ThreadData * data = reinterpret_cast< ThreadData * > (arg);
    ((OctreeThread *)data->context)->EvalThread(data->geom);
    return NULL;
}

bool OctreeThread::IsEmpty () [inline]
{
        return render_queue.isEmpty();
}

bool OctreeThread::IsEmptyM () [inline]
{
        return mesh_queue.isEmpty();
}
```

```
bool OctreeThread::IsEmptyR () [inline]
{
      return  ray_queue.isEmpty();
}

void OctreeThread::MeshEnd ()
{
   pthread_join(mesh_thread, NULL);
   if  (pass_data  != NULL)
      delete  pass_data;
}

// display adaptive mesh
void OctreeThread::MeshStart ()
{
   pass_data  =  new  ThreadData;

   pass_data->context  =  this;
   pass_data->geom  = NULL;

   // spawn a second thread to display the voxel hierarchy
   pthread_create(&mesh_thread, NULL,  &(this->MeshThreadWrapper),  pass_data);
}

void * OctreeThread::MeshThread (void *unused) [private]
{
   // reuse existing context and octree
   octree_w->MeshTop();

   return  NULL;
}

void * OctreeThread::MeshThreadWrapper (void *arg) [static, private]
{
   ThreadData *  data  =  reinterpret_cast<  ThreadData *  >  (arg);
   ((OctreeThread  *)data->context)->MeshThread(NULL);
   return  NULL;
}

void OctreeThread::RayEnd ()
{
   pthread_join(ray_thread, NULL);
   if  (pass_data  != NULL)
      delete  pass_data;
}

// compute LED positions on armature
void OctreeThread::RayStart ()
{
```

```
    pass_data = new ThreadData;

    pass_data->context = this;
    pass_data->geom = NULL;

    // spawn a second thread to display the voxel hierarchy
    pthread_create(&ray_thread, NULL, &(this->RayThreadWrapper), pass_data);
}

// use existing octree (from Eval)
void * OctreeThread::RayThread (void *unused) [private]
{
    // context for ray work, seems easier than somehow
    // reusing the octree context.
    // note start level is 1, i.e., the eval_level
    context_w = new ContextWorker;

    // we just care about g_terminal and display, since everything
    // else applies to what's already been done in Eval stage.
    context_w->makeContext(1, g_terminal, true, g_check_false_pos);
    context_w->setRaster(g_raster);

    int contextID = context_w->getContextID();

    // instantiate RayWorker
    ray_w = new RayWorker(contextID, octree_w->getTree());
    ray_w->Top();

    return NULL;
}

void * OctreeThread::RayThreadWrapper (void *arg) [static, private]
{
    ThreadData * data = reinterpret_cast< ThreadData * > (arg);
    ((OctreeThread *)data->context)->RayThread(NULL);
    return NULL;
}
```

Associated Data Holders

```
struct ThreadData {
    OctreeThread *context;
    Vector<BasicTriangle *> * geom;
};
```

The documentation for this class was generated from the following files:

- OctreeThread.h
- OctreeThread.cpp

OctreeWorker Class Reference

Public Member Functions

OctreeWorker (int my_contextID)

:: Note that GeomWorker will delete triangles when it goes out of scope
:: (When OctreeWorker goes out of scope in OctreeThread.cpp.)
:: Likewise, GroupWorker will delete all NodeGroups when it goes out of scope
:: Octree will delete itself when it goes out of scope with this class
~OctreeWorker ()

:: tree is already made; iterate through recursively
void Top (ContextWorker *context_w)

void MeshTop ()
Octree<NodeGroup * > &getTree ()

Private Member Functions

:: Weiss makes this an Object template: don't do that. Define the type explicitly.
void Iterate (TreeIterator<NodeGroup * > &itr)

:: will reuse this
void MakeFPContext ()

:: check for false positive processing
void SwitchContext (NodeGroup *group)

:: for spawn call (for false positive processing)
void TopFP (NodeGroup *ng_ptr)

:: Takes a parent arg but we set it to NULL.
void OctreeRoot (NodeGroup *ng_ptr, OctreeNode<NodeGroup * > *parent)

:: assume the root is one giant voxel that contains the geometry
NodeGroup *NodeGroupRoot (Glassner new_ID)

void IterateTop ()

:: allocate o_list, return with entries
OctreeNode<NodeGroup * > **MakeChildOctreeNodes (NodeGroup *group,
TreeIterator<NodeGroup * > &itr, int &count)

void SetChildBitsOnly (NodeGroup *group, TreeIterator<NodeGroup * > &itr)

:: how many geom_stat bits are set?
bool isFPCandidate ()

:: mirror what's just happened in the NodeGroup hierarchy
void DeprecateOctreeNodesOnUp (OctreeNode<NodeGroup * > *node)

:: recursive
void DrawMesh (OctreeNode<NodeGroup * > *node, int level)

:: delay to simulate actual compute latency
void Wait ()

Private Attributes

Context &context
ContextWorker *eval_context
int contextID
ContextWorker *fp_context
int fp_contextID
int fp_count
Octree<NodeGroup * > tree
GroupWorker group_w
LevelWorker level_w
IDWorker id_w
Display display
NodeGroup *current_group

Detailed Description

The highest level code on the octree side of the universe:
starts the iteration, returns voxels from input triangles.

Constructor & Destructor Documentation

```
OctreeWorker::OctreeWorker (int my_contextID) [inline]
                          :
      context  (ContextWorker::getContext(my_contextID)),
      contextID(my_contextID),  fp_context(NULL),  fp_contextID(INVALID),
      group_w(context),  level_w(context),  display(context) {}
```

```
// Note that GeomWorker will delete triangles when it goes out of scope
// (When OctreeWorker goes out of scope in OctreeThread.cpp.)
// Likewise, GroupWorker will delete all NodeGroups when it goes out of scope
// Octree will delete itself when it goes out of scope with this class
OctreeWorker::~OctreeWorker ()
```

```
{
   if (fp_context != NULL)
      delete  fp_context;

   // clear the static vector in calling method (in OctreeThread)
}
```

Member Function Documentation

```
// mirror what's just happened in the NodeGroup hierarchy
// Note that the current node and all parent nodes have already
// been taken out of the queue, so there's no danger of corruption.
void OctreeWorker::DeprecateOctreeNodesOnUp (OctreeNode<NodeGroup * > *node) [private]
{
   int old_index, new_index, bit_offset, child_count;

   NodeGroup  *group = node->element;
   OctreeNode<NodeGroup *>  *parent = node->parent;

   // this is more severe than NodeGroups in that we actually delete the node
   delete  node;

   // can happen on spawned octree via false-pos context
   if (parent == NULL) {
      tree.setRootNull();      // important! GroupWorker destructor checks this.
      return;
   }

   // now look at the parent of this deleted Octree Node
   // close up the list after copy
   child_count = parent->child_count;
   // returns 1 - 8
   bit_offset =  id_w.getBitCountAtNodeIdx(parent->child_bits, group->node_idx);

   if (child_count  >  1) {
      OctreeNode<NodeGroup *>  **children =
               new   OctreeNode<NodeGroup *>  * [child_count - 1];

      new_index = 0;
      for  (old_index = 0; old_index  <  child_count; ++old_index) {

         if  (old_index == bit_offset - 1)
            continue;

         children[new_index] = parent->child[old_index];
         ++new_index;
      }
```

```
        delete [] parent->child;
        parent->child = children;
    } else {
        delete [] parent->child;
        parent->child = NULL;
    }

    // now change status on the parent
    parent->child_bits &= id_w.getCompAtNodeIdx(group->node_idx); // complement
    --parent->child_count;

    if (parent->child_bits == 0) {
        DeprecateOctreeNodesOnUp(parent);
    }
}

// recursive
void OctreeWorker::DrawMesh (OctreeNode<NodeGroup * > *node, int level) [private]
{
    // this is the voxel itself, so draw nothing
    if (node->child_count == 0) {
        if (node->child_bits == 0) {
            std::cout << "FOUND ZERO CHILD COUNT" << std::endl;
            NodeGroup *ng_ptr = node->element;
            std::cout << "ID: " << ng_ptr->ID << std::endl;
        }
        return;
    }

    unsigned char testbit = 0x01;
    int count = 0;

    for (int i = 0; i<OCTANTS; ++i) {
        if (node->child_bits & testbit) {
            // reference node by number of set bits, not by octant
            DrawMesh(node->child[count], level + 1);
            ++count;
        } else {
            NodeGroup *ng_ptr = node->element;
            display.MakeMeshData(ng_ptr, i, level);
        }
        testbit <<= 1;
    }
}

Octree<NodeGroup *>& OctreeWorker::getTree () [inline]
{return tree;}

// how many geom_stat bits are set?
```

```
bool OctreeWorker::isFPCandidate () [private]
{
   // count of 1-bits
   unsigned  char  newChildren =  group_w.getChildrenBits();
   unsigned  char  child_count =  id_w.numSetBits(newChildren);

   // if it's zero it's already been culled!
   return  (child_count  >  0  &&  child_count  <=  g_false_pos_candidate_count);
}

// Weiss makes this an Object template: don't do that. Define the type explicitly.
void OctreeWorker::Iterate (TreeIterator<NodeGroup * >&itr) [private]
{
   OctreeNode<NodeGroup *>  **o_list = NULL;
   int   count  = 0;

   try  {
      //  "put"  will enqueue children
      for  (itr.first(); itr.get(); itr.put(o_list, count) ) {
         NodeGroup  *ng_ptr = itr.retrieve();

         if  (level_w.LevelSwitch(ng_ptr->ID))
            level_w.DoLevelWork();

         const   Level   &level  =  level_w.getLevel();
         group_w.GeomProcess(ng_ptr, level);

         // false-positive processing
         if  (context.check_false_pos)
            SwitchContext(ng_ptr);

         // check and delete parent VTPairs (after FP processing!)
         group_w.checkVTPairs(level);

         display.displayVoxel(ng_ptr, level);

         if  (!level_w.TerminalLevel()) {
           o_list =  MakeChildOctreeNodes(ng_ptr, itr, count);
         }  else  {
            SetChildBitsOnly(ng_ptr, itr);
            o_list = NULL;
         }
      }
      // terminate the transfer to OpenGL (if active)
      display.terminateTransfer();
   }
   catch(IteratorException   &  e) {
      std::cout  <<  e.toString();
   }
```

```
}

void OctreeWorker::IterateTop () [private]
{
   // Level Order iteration : enqueues the root
   LevelOrder<NodeGroup *>  my_iter(tree);
   Iterate(my_iter);
}

// allocate o_list, return with entries
OctreeNode<NodeGroup * > ** OctreeWorker::MakeChildOctreeNodes (NodeGroup *group,
TreeIterator<NodeGroup * > &itr, int &count) [private]
{
   OctreeNode<NodeGroup *>  * parent = itr.currentOctreeNode();

   // count of 1-bits
   unsigned   char  newChildren =  group_w.getChildrenBits();
   unsigned   char  child_count =  id_w.numSetBits(newChildren);

   // parent in the context of adding children, but really
   // the current node....
   parent->child_bits  = newChildren;
   parent->child_count  = child_count;
   count  = child_count;     // for caller
   // false positives may result in zero children
   if  (child_count == 0) {
      DeprecateOctreeNodesOnUp(parent);
      return  NULL;
   }
   // put this on the heap : keep it around for life of octree
   OctreeNode<NodeGroup *>  **children =
            new   OctreeNode<NodeGroup *>  * [child_count];
   parent->child  = children;

   // get the new NodeGroup pointers : pair with freeGroupPointers below
   NodeGroupList  * grouplist =  group_w.getNewGroups(group);

   for  (int  i = 0; i  <  child_count; ++i) {
      OctreeNode<NodeGroup *>  *current =
            new   OctreeNode<NodeGroup *>(grouplist->list[i], parent);

      // can't set children of this child until next level
      // set the parent-child pointer
      parent->child[i] = current;
   }
   // paired with getNewGroups above
   group_w.freeGroupPointers(grouplist);

   return  children;
```

```
}

// will reuse this
void OctreeWorker::MakeFPContext () [private]
{
    // second context for false positives
    // do this once to avoid copying over triangle list multiple times
    fp_context = new  ContextWorker;
    // g_terminal is the eval level to start at
    fp_context->makeContext(g_terminal, g_false_pos_level, false, false);

    // this goes directly to the GeomWorker class:
    fp_context->setRaster(g_raster);

    fp_context->CopyOverTriangles(context.geom_w);
    fp_contextID = fp_context->getContextID();
}

// tree is already made; iterate through recursively
void OctreeWorker::MeshTop ()
{
    DrawMesh(tree.getRoot(), 0);
    display.terminateMesh();
}

// assume the root is one giant voxel that contains the geometry
// Main iteration: allocate first (level L = 1) NodeGroup
// False Pos processing: will be at g_terminal level
NodeGroup * OctreeWorker::NodeGroupRoot (Glassner new_ID) [private]
{
    return  current_group = group_w.InstantiateRoot(new_ID);
}

// Takes a parent arg but we set it to NULL.
void OctreeWorker::OctreeRoot (NodeGroup *ng_ptr, OctreeNode<NodeGroup * > *parent) [private]
{
    tree.addRoot(ng_ptr, parent);
    // transfer tree pointer so GroupWorker can use tree for cleanup
    group_w.setTreePointer(&tree);
}

void OctreeWorker::SetChildBitsOnly (NodeGroup *group, TreeIterator<NodeGroup * > &itr) [private]
{
    OctreeNode<NodeGroup *>  * terminal = itr.currentOctreeNode();

    // geom_stat essentially (for  "current")
    unsigned  char  newChildren = group_w.getChildrenBits();

    // clean up the tree, even if terminal
```

```
    if (newChildren == 0x00) {
        DeprecateOctreeNodesOnUp(terminal);
        return;
    }
    // no new nodes are created, but children status is stored.
    terminal->child_bits = newChildren;
    terminal->child_count = 0;
}

// check for false positive processing
void OctreeWorker::SwitchContext (NodeGroup *group) [private]
{
    // entry conditions
    if (!level_w.TerminalLevel())
        return;

    // see if this node is a candidate
    if (!isFPCandidate())
        return;

    // iterate
   OctreeWorker  octree_w(fp_contextID);
   octree_w.TopFP(group);
}

void OctreeWorker::Top (ContextWorker *context_w)
{
    // need this to reset levels for 6sep fp
    eval_context  = context_w;

    // make the NodeGroup FIRST
    NodeGroup  *ng_ptr =  NodeGroupRoot((Glassner)0);

    // store it to the Octree as root
    OctreeRoot(ng_ptr, NULL);

    // before iterating, check false pos status
    if (context.check_false_pos)
        MakeFPContext();

    IterateTop();
}

// for spawn call (for false positive processing)
void OctreeWorker::TopFP (NodeGroup *ng_ptr) [private]
{
    // copy the node via instantiateGroup, so it will be destroyed
    NodeGroup  * ng_ptr =  NodeGroupRoot(orig_ptr->ID);
```

```
    // for getting the parent tris need to assign the parent ptr;
    // will allow sub-tree deprecate to enter the main tree, and
    // meanwhile there's no danger of parent-node deletion since
    // the parent isn't in the ng_list in GroupWorker class.
    ng_ptr->parent  = orig_ptr->parent;

    // store it in the (loosely attached) Octree as root;
    // make a new root node with NULL parent pointer to
    // stop deprecateOctreeNodesOnUp in its tracks.
    OctreeRoot(ng_ptr, NULL);

    IterateTop();

    // over-copy the original geom_stat
    if  (ng_ptr->geom_stat  == 0x00) {
      if  (context.buffer_display_data) {
        // for diagnostics, display FP in RED
        const   Level   &level  =  level_w.getLevel();
        display.displayVoxelFP(orig_ptr, level);
      }

      // copy geom stat after displaying original
      orig_ptr->geom_stat = ng_ptr->geom_stat;

      // Note that the entire spawned octree will have
      // been deleted if this is true. The original
      // octree node and its parents will be processed
      // through main iteration to follow.
      std::cout  <<   "FALSE POS!"   <<  std::endl;
    }
}

// delay to simulate actual compute latency
void OctreeWorker::Wait () [private]
{
   float  delta;
   clock_t time0, time1;

   time0 = clock();
   delta = 0.0;
   while  (delta  <  0.01f) {  // 10 ms
      time1 = clock();
      delta =  static_cast<float>(static_cast<double>(time1-time0)/
static_cast<double>(CLOCKS_PER_SEC));
   }
}
```

The documentation for this class was generated from the following files:
- OctreeWorker.h
- OctreeWorker.cpp

QueueAr< Object > Class Template Reference

Public Member Functions

QueueAr ()

:: Test if the queue is logically empty.
:: Return true if empty, false, otherwise.
boolisEmpty () const

:: Return and remove the least recently inserted item from the queue.
:: Throws UnderflowException if queue is already empty.
Object dequeue ()

:: Insert x into the queue.
Object enqueue (Object x)

:: Return the least recently inserted item in the queue
:: or throw UnderflowException if empty.
Object getFront ()

:: Make the queue logically empty.
void makeEmpty ()

Private Member Functions

:: Internal method to increment x with wraparound.
void increment (int &x) const

:: Internal method to double capacity.
void doubleQueue ()

Private Attributes

vector< Object > theArray
int currentSize
int front
int back

Detailed Description

Templated queue class, using an array rather than a linked list.

Constructor & Destructor Documentation

```
template<class Object>
QueueAr< Object >::QueueAr() [inline]
            : theArray( 1 ) {
        currentSize  = 0;
        front  = 0;
        back  =  theArray.size( ) - 1;
}
```

Member Function Documentation

```
// Return and remove the least recently inserted item from the queue.
// Throws UnderflowException if queue is already empty.
template<class Object >
Object QueueAr< Object >::dequeue ()
{
    if ( isEmpty( ) )
       throw   UnderflowException( );

    currentSize--;
    Object frontItem =  theArray[  front  ];
    increment(  front  );
    return  frontItem;
}

// Internal method to double capacity.
template<class Object >
void QueueAr< Object >::doubleQueue () [private]
{
    theArray.resize(  theArray.size( ) * 2 + 1 );
    if ( front  != 0 )
    {
       for(  int  i = 0; i  <   front; i++ )
          theArray[ i +  currentSize  ] =  theArray[ i ];
       back  +=  currentSize;
    }
}

// Insert x into the queue.
template<class Object>
Object QueueAr< Object >::enqueue (Object x)
{
    if ( currentSize  ==  theArray.size( ) )
       doubleQueue( );
    increment(  back  );
    theArray[  back  ] =  x;
    currentSize++;
```

```
    return   x;
}

// Return the least recently inserted item in the queue
// or throw UnderflowException if empty.
template<class Object >
Object QueueAr< Object >::getFront ()
{
    if ( isEmpty( ) )
        throw   UnderflowException( );
    return   theArray[  front  ];
}

// Internal method to increment x with wraparound.
template<class Object >
void QueueAr< Object >::increment (int &x) const [private]
{
    if ( ++x  ==  theArray.size( ) )
        x  = 0;
}

// Test if the queue is logically empty.
// Return true if empty, false, otherwise.
template<class Object >
bool QueueAr< Object >::isEmpty () const
{
    return   currentSize  == 0;
}

// Make the queue logically empty.
template<class Object >
void QueueAr< Object >::makeEmpty ()
{
    currentSize  = 0;
    front  = 0;
    back  =  theArray.size( ) - 1;
}
```

The documentation for this class was generated from the following files:
- QueueAr.h
- QueueAr.tpp

QuickSort Class Reference

Public Member Functions

QuickSort ()
~QuickSort ()
void quicksort (VTList *a)
void quicksort (TGList *a)
void quicksort (VTPair **a, int count)
void quicksort (TGPair **a, int count)

Private Member Functions

void insertionSort (VTList *a, int low, int high)
void quicksort (VTList *a, int low, int high)
void insertionSort (TGList *a, int low, int high)
void quicksort (TGList *a, int low, int high)
void insertionSort (VTPair **b, int low, int high)
void quicksort (VTPair **b, int low, int high)
void insertionSort (TGPair **b, int low, int high)
void quicksort (TGPair **b, int low, int high)

Detailed Description

Sorts voxel-triangle pairs by voxel index.

Constructor & Destructor Documentation

QuickSort::QuickSort () [inline]
{}

QuickSort::~QuickSort () [inline]
{}

Member Function Documentation

void QuickSort::insertionSort (VTList *a, int low, int high) [private]

```
{
   int  j,  p;
   VTPair  **b  = a->list;
   VTPair  tmp;

   for ( p = low + 1; p  <= high; p++ )
```

```
    {
        tmp.tri_idx  = b[  p  ]->tri_idx;
        tmp.vox_idx  = b[  p  ]->vox_idx;

        for ( j = p; j  >  low  &&  tmp.vox_idx   <  b[ j - 1 ]->vox_idx; j-- ) {
            b[ j ]->tri_idx  = b[ j - 1 ]->tri_idx;
            b[ j ]->vox_idx  = b[ j - 1 ]->vox_idx;
        }
        b[ j ]->tri_idx  = tmp.tri_idx;
        b[ j ]->vox_idx  = tmp.vox_idx;
    }
}

void QuickSort::insertionSort (VTPair **b, int low, int high) [private]
{
    int  j,  p;
    VTPair  tmp;

    for ( p = low + 1; p  <= high; p++ )
    {
        tmp.tri_idx  = b[  p  ]->tri_idx;
        tmp.vox_idx  = b[  p  ]->vox_idx;

        for ( j = p; j  >  low  &&  tmp.tri_idx   <  b[ j - 1 ]->tri_idx; j-- ) {
            b[ j ]->tri_idx  = b[ j - 1 ]->tri_idx;
            b[ j ]->vox_idx  = b[ j - 1 ]->vox_idx;
        }
        b[ j ]->tri_idx  = tmp.tri_idx;
        b[ j ]->vox_idx  = tmp.vox_idx;
    }
}

void QuickSort::insertionSort (TGPair **b, int low, int high) [private]
{
    int  j,  p;
    TGPair  tmp;

    for ( p = low + 1; p  <= high; p++ )
    {
        tmp.tri_idx  = b[  p  ]->tri_idx;
        tmp.vox_idx  = b[  p  ]->vox_idx;

        for ( j = p; j  >  low  &&  tmp.vox_idx   <  b[ j - 1 ]->vox_idx; j-- ) {
            b[ j ]->tri_idx  = b[ j - 1 ]->tri_idx;
            b[ j ]->vox_idx  = b[ j - 1 ]->vox_idx;
        }
        b[ j ]->tri_idx  = tmp.tri_idx;
        b[ j ]->vox_idx  = tmp.vox_idx;
    }
```

```
}

void QuickSort::insertionSort (TGList *a, int low, int high) [private]
{
   int j, p;
   TGPair **b = a->list;
   TGPair tmp;

   for ( p = low + 1; p <= high; p++ )
   {
      tmp.tri_idx = b[ p ]->tri_idx;
      tmp.vox_idx = b[ p ]->vox_idx;

      for ( j = p; j > low && tmp.tri_idx < b[ j - 1 ]->tri_idx; j-- ) {
         b[ j ]->tri_idx = b[ j - 1 ]->tri_idx;
         b[ j ]->vox_idx = b[ j - 1 ]->vox_idx;
      }
      b[ j ]->tri_idx = tmp.tri_idx;
      b[ j ]->vox_idx = tmp.vox_idx;
   }
}

void QuickSort::quicksort (TGList *a)
{
   quicksort( a, 0, a->count - 1 );
}

void QuickSort::quicksort (TGList *a, int low, int high) [private]
{
   if ( low + CUTOFF > high )
      insertionSort( a, low, high );
   else {
      TGPair **b = a->list;

      // Sort low, middle, high
      int middle = ( low + high ) / 2;
      if ( b[ middle ]->tri_idx < b[ low ]->tri_idx )
         swap( b[ low ], b[ middle ] );
      if ( b[ high ]->tri_idx < b[ low ]->tri_idx )
         swap( b[ low ], b[ high ] );
      if ( b[ high ]->tri_idx < b[ middle ]->tri_idx )
         swap( b[ middle ], b[ high ] );

      // Place pivot at position high - 1
      int pivot = b[ middle ]->tri_idx;
      swap( b[ middle ], b[ high - 1 ] );

      // Begin partitioning
      int i, j;
```

```
        for ( i = low, j = high - 1; ; )
        {
            while ( b[ ++i ]->tri_idx  <  pivot ) { }
            while ( pivot  <  b[ --j ]->tri_idx ) { }
            if ( i  <  j )
                swap( b[ i ], b[ j ] );
            else
                break;
        }
        swap( b[ i ], b[ high - 1 ] );   // Restore pivot
        quicksort( a, low, i - 1 );      // Sort small elements
        quicksort( a, i + 1, high );     // Sort large elements
    }
}

void QuickSort::quicksort (VTList *a)
{
    quicksort( a, 0, a->count  - 1 );
}

void QuickSort::quicksort (VTList *a, int low, int high) [private]
{
    if ( low +  CUTOFF   >  high )
        insertionSort( a, low, high );
    else    {
        VTPair  **b  = a->list;

        // Sort low, middle, high
        int  middle = ( low + high ) / 2;
        if ( b[ middle ]->vox_idx  <  b[ low ]->vox_idx )
            swap( b[ low ], b[ middle ] );
        if ( b[ high ]->vox_idx  <  b[ low ]->vox_idx )
            swap( b[ low ], b[ high ] );
        if ( b[ high ]->vox_idx  <  b[ middle ]->vox_idx )
            swap( b[ middle ], b[ high ] );

        // Place pivot at position high - 1
        int  pivot = b[ middle ]->vox_idx;
        swap( b[ middle ], b[ high - 1 ] );

        // Begin partitioning
        int  i, j;
        for ( i = low, j = high - 1; ; )
        {
            while ( b[ ++i ]->vox_idx  <  pivot ) { }
            while ( pivot  <  b[ --j ]->vox_idx ) { }
            if ( i  <  j )
                swap( b[ i ], b[ j ] );
            else
```

```
            break;
        }
        swap( b[ i ], b[ high - 1 ] );   // Restore pivot
        quicksort( a, low, i - 1 );      // Sort small elements
        quicksort( a, i + 1, high );     // Sort large elements
    }
}

void QuickSort::quicksort (TGPair **a, int count)
{
    quicksort( a, 0,  count  - 1 );
}

void QuickSort::quicksort (TGPair **b, int low, int high) [private]
{
    if ( low +  CUTOFF   >  high )
        insertionSort( b, low, high );
    else    {
        // Sort low, middle, high
        int  middle = ( low + high ) / 2;
        if ( b[ middle ]->vox_idx  <  b[ low ]->vox_idx )
            swap( b[ low ], b[ middle ] );
        if ( b[ high ]->vox_idx  <  b[ low ]->vox_idx )
            swap( b[ low ], b[ high ] );
        if ( b[ high ]->vox_idx  <  b[ middle ]->vox_idx )
            swap( b[ middle ], b[ high ] );

        // Place pivot at position high - 1
        Glassner  pivot = b[ middle ]->vox_idx;
        swap( b[ middle ], b[ high - 1 ] );

        // Begin partitioning
        int  i, j;
        for ( i = low, j = high - 1; ; )
        {
            while ( b[ ++i ]->vox_idx  <  pivot ) { }
            while ( pivot  <  b[ --j ]->vox_idx ) { }
            if ( i  <  j )
                swap( b[ i ], b[ j ] );
            else
                break;
        }
        swap( b[ i ], b[ high - 1 ] );   // Restore pivot
        quicksort( b, low, i - 1 );      // Sort small elements
        quicksort( b, i + 1, high );     // Sort large elements
    }
}

void QuickSort::quicksort (VTPair **a, int count)
```

```
{
    quicksort( a, 0,  count  - 1 );
}

void QuickSort::quicksort (VTPair **b, int low, int high) [private]
{
    if ( low +  CUTOFF   >  high )
        insertionSort( b, low, high );
    else    {
        // Sort low, middle, high
        int  middle = ( low + high ) / 2;
        if ( b[ middle ]->tri_idx  <  b[ low ]->tri_idx )
            swap( b[ low ], b[ middle ] );
        if ( b[ high ]->tri_idx  <  b[ low ]->tri_idx )
            swap( b[ low ], b[ high ] );
        if ( b[ high ]->tri_idx  <  b[ middle ]->tri_idx )
            swap( b[ middle ], b[ high ] );

        // Place pivot at position high - 1
        int  pivot = b[ middle ]->tri_idx;
        swap( b[ middle ], b[ high - 1 ] );

        // Begin partitioning
        int  i, j;
        for ( i = low, j = high - 1; ; )
        {
            while ( b[ ++i ]->tri_idx  <  pivot ) { }
            while ( pivot  <  b[ --j ]->tri_idx ) { }
            if ( i  <  j )
                swap( b[ i ], b[ j ] );
            else
                break;
        }
        swap( b[ i ], b[ high - 1 ] );   // Restore pivot
        quicksort( b, low, i - 1 );      // Sort small elements
        quicksort( b, i + 1, high );     // Sort large elements
    }
}
```

Local Data

```
#define CUTOFF 10
```

The documentation for this class was generated from the following files:
- QuickSort.h
- QuickSort.cpp

RayUtil Class Reference

Public Member Functions

:: constructor
RayUtil ()

~RayUtil ()
void TIntersect (Ray &ray, ushort3 &base, int voxlen)

:: same routine as in GeomUtil.cpp
int NewN (int level)

:: push into the next voxel : put coords in coord
void Push (Ray &ray, float3 &coord, TPack &tpack)

:: looks at current intersection data from Push routine, above.
bool ExitsUniverse (float3 &intersect, const float Nt)

void copy_float3 (const float3 &source, float3 &dest)
void VectorScale (float3 &tD, const float3 &D, const float t)
void VectorAdd (float3 &r, const float3 &v1, const float3 &v2)

Private Member Functions

void Init ()
void makeIntList ()
void clearIntData ()
template<int32 AXIS> void t_intersect (Ray &ray, Intersect **data, float3 &voxel_base, int len)

:: which side is the infinite parallelism on?
template<int32 AXIS> void GetInfiniteBits (const float3 &ray_origin, const float3 &A, unsigned short &bits)

template<int32 AXIS> void GetBits (const float3 &intersect, const uvw_float3 &base, int len, unsigned short &bits)
float VectorLength (const float3 &p)
void Normalize (float3 &p, float len)
float Sign (float val)

Private Attributes

FPUtil fp_u
ushort3 lt_set
ushort3 gt_set

IntersectList *int_list

Detailed Description

Ray casting utilities.
Used for emulation of display device rotating armature in terms of which voxels are illuminated based on physical arm locations. This is rudimentary ray tracing.

Constructor & Destructor Documentation

```
// constructor
RayUtil::RayUtil ()
{
    Init();
}

RayUtil::~RayUtil ()
{
    int  count = int_list->count;
    for (int i = 0; i<  count; ++i) {
        Intersect *current = int_list->list[i];
        delete current;
    }
    delete [] int_list->list;
    delete  int_list;
    int_list = NULL;
}
```

Member Function Documentation

```
void RayUtil::clearIntData () [private]
{
    for (int i = 0; i <  T_MAX; ++i) {
        Intersect *cur_int = int_list->list[i];
        cur_int->t_flag = 0;
        cur_int->t = 0.0;
        cur_int->i_bits = 0;
        cur_int->i.x = cur_int->i.y = cur_int->i.z = 0.0;
    }
}

void RayUtil::copy_float3 (const float3 &source, float3 &dest)
{
    dest.x = source.x;
    dest.y = source.y;
```

```
   dest.z  = source.z;
}

// looks at current intersection data from Push routine, above.
bool RayUtil::ExitsUniverse (float3 &intersect, const float Nt)
{
   if  (fp_u.equalBoundsf(intersect.x, 0.0,  PRECISIONf) ||
        fp_u.equalBoundsf(intersect.y, 0.0,  PRECISIONf) ||
        fp_u.equalBoundsf(intersect.z, 0.0,  PRECISIONf))
       return   true;

   if  (fp_u.equalBoundsf(intersect.x, Nt,  PRECISIONf) ||
        fp_u.equalBoundsf(intersect.y, Nt,  PRECISIONf) ||
        fp_u.equalBoundsf(intersect.z, Nt,  PRECISIONf))
       return   true;

   return   false;
}

template<int32 AXIS>
void RayUtil::GetBits (const float3 &intersect, const uvw_float3 &base, int len, unsigned short &bits)
[private]
{
   typedef   uvw<AXIS>  sel;

   // note that the lookups cycle with the template argument
   // use an epsilon!
   bits = 0;
   if  (fp_u.lessThanBoundsf(sel::u(intersect), base.u,  PRECISIONf))
     bits |= sel::u(lt_set);
   else   if  (fp_u.greaterBoundsf(sel::u(intersect), base.u  +  len,  PRECISIONf))
     bits |= sel::u(gt_set);

   if  (fp_u.lessThanBoundsf(sel::v(intersect), base.v,  PRECISIONf))
     bits |=  sel::v(lt_set);
   else   if  (fp_u.greaterBoundsf(sel::v(intersect), base.v  +  len,  PRECISIONf))
     bits |=  sel::v(gt_set);

   // w intersect is always equal to base: don't need this
   /*
   if (fp_u.lessThanBoundsf(sel::w(intersect), base.w, PRECISIONf))
      bits |= sel::w(lt_set);
   else if (fp_u.greaterBoundsf(sel::w(intersect), base.w + len, PRECISIONf))
      bits |= sel::w(gt_set);
   */
}

// which side is the infinite parallelism on?
template<int32 AXIS>
```

```
void RayUtil::GetInfiniteBits (const float3 &ray_origin, const float3 &A, unsigned short &bits) [private]
{
   typedef  uvw<AXIS>  sel;

   bits = 0;
   // default parallel and  "on"  plane; equal
   // otherwise, infinitely to one side:
   if  (fp_u.greaterBoundsf(sel::w(ray_origin),  sel::w(A),  PRECISIONf))
     bits =  sel::w(gt_set);
   else  if  (fp_u.lessThanBoundsf(sel::w(ray_origin),  sel::w(A),  PRECISIONf))
     bits =  sel::w(lt_set);
}

void RayUtil::Init () [private]
{
   lt_set.x  = 0b001000;
   lt_set.y  = 0b000010;
   lt_set.z  = 0b100000;

   gt_set.x  = 0b000100;
   gt_set.y  = 0b000001;
   gt_set.z  = 0b010000;

   // make IntersectList
   makeIntList();
}

void RayUtil::makeIntList () [private]
{
   int_list  =  new   IntersectList;
   int_list->count  =  T_MAX;

   Intersect  **plist =  new   Intersect  * [T_MAX];
   int_list->list  = plist;

   for  (int  i = 0; i  <   T_MAX; ++i) {
      Intersect  *cur_int =  new   Intersect;
      cur_int->plane  = i;
      int_list->list[i] = cur_int;
   }
}

// same routine as in GeomUtil.cpp
int RayUtil::NewN (int level)
{
   return  (int) lroundf(powf(2.0, (float)level));
}

void RayUtil::Normalize (float3&p, floatlen) [private]
```

```
{
  p.x /= len;
  p.y /= len;
  p.z /= len;
}

// push into the next voxel : put coords in coord
void RayUtil::Push (Ray &ray, float3 &coord, TPack &tpack)
{
   int i,  size, plane;
   float  max_t;
   Intersect  * current;
   Vector<Intersect *>  my_list;
   Vector<Intersect *>  top_list;
   SortByRef<Intersect *, Intersect>  my_sort;

   // fill a vector with the Intersect data
   for  (i = 0; i <  T_MAX; ++i) {
      // check infinite-zero and throw exception
      if  (int_list->list[i]->t_flag  ==  T_INFINITE_ZERO)
         throw   RayException("Infinite Zero");
      my_list.push_back(int_list->list[i]);
   }

   // sort the list
   my_sort.quicksort(my_list);

   // get the top t's (with zero ibits)
   for  (i = 0; i <  T_MAX; ++i) {
      if  (my_list[i]->i_bits == 0x00)
        top_list.push_back(my_list[i]);
   }
   // get the max t that has ibits == 0, and the intersect
   max_t = top_list[0]->t;
   copy_float3(top_list[0]->i, coord);
   // return data
   tpack.t  = max_t;
   copy_float3(coord, tpack.i);

   // go through list, look at plane vals, and push
   size = top_list.size();
   for  (i=0; i<size; ++i) {
      if  (!fp_u.equalBoundsf(top_list[i]->t, max_t,  PRECISIONf))
         break;
     current = top_list[i];
     plane = current->plane   >>  1;
     if  (plane ==  T_XY) {
        coord.z  +=  HALF_INDEX  *  Sign(ray.direction.z);
     } else   if  (plane ==  T_YZ) {
```

```
        coord.x += HALF_INDEX * Sign(ray.direction.x);
      } else { // XZ
        coord.y += HALF_INDEX * Sign(ray.direction.y);
      }
    }
}

float RayUtil::Sign (floatval) [private]
{
    return (val > 0.0 ? 1.0 : -1.0);
}

template<int32 AXIS>
void RayUtil::t_intersect (Ray &ray, Intersect **data, float3 &voxel_base, int len) [private]
{
    float3 tD, t1, t2;

    typedef uvw<AXIS> sel;
    typedef uvw_p<AXIS> put;

    uvw_float3 base;

    // everything in XY by default
    // octant planes
    base.u = sel::u(voxel_base);
    base.v = sel::v(voxel_base);
    base.w = sel::w(voxel_base);

    float3 A1, B1, C1, A2, B2, C2;

    // plane 1
    put::u(A1, base.u);
    put::v(A1, base.v + len);
    put::w(A1, base.w);

    put::u(B1, base.u);
    put::v(B1, base.v);
    put::w(B1, base.w);

    put::u(C1, base.u + len);
    put::v(C1, base.v);
    put::w(C1, base.w);

    // plane 2
    put::u(A2, sel::u(A1));
    put::v(A2, sel::v(A1));
    put::w(A2, base.w + len);

    put::u(B2, sel::u(B1));
```

```
put::v(B2,  sel::v(B1));
put::w(B2, base.w  +  len);

put::u(C2, sel::u(C1));
put::v(C2,  sel::v(C1));
put::w(C2, base.w  +  len);

// subtract for u, v
float3   v1,  v2;

put::u(v1, sel::u(C1) - sel::u(A1));
put::v(v1, sel::v(C1) -  sel::v(A1));
put::u(v2, sel::u(B1) - sel::u(A1));
put::v(v2, sel::v(B1) -  sel::v(A1));

// compute normal (un-normalized) to voxel plane
float3   n;
n.x  = n.y  = n.z  = 0.0;

float  sign = 1;
if  (AXIS ==  Y)
  sign = -1;

put::w(n, sign * (sel::u(v1) *  sel::v(v2) -  sel::v(v1) * sel::u(v2)) );

// Dot(A1, n)
float  dot_a1 =  sel::w(A1) *  sel::w(n);
// Dot(A2, n)
float  dot_a2 =  sel::w(A2) *  sel::w(n);

// Dot(ray.origin, n)
float  dot_o =  sel::w(ray.origin) *  sel::w(n);

// Dot(ray.direction, n)
float  dot_d =  sel::w(ray.direction) *  sel::w(n);

if  (fp_u.equalBoundsf(dot_d, 0.0,  PRECISIONf)) {
   // infinity
   if  (fp_u.equalBoundsf(dot_a1 - dot_o, 0.0,  PRECISIONf))
      data[0]->t_flag =  T_INFINITE_ZERO;
   else
      data[0]->t_flag  =  T_INFINITE;

   if  (fp_u.equalBoundsf(dot_a2 - dot_o, 0.0,  PRECISIONf))
      data[1]->t_flag =  T_INFINITE_ZERO;
   else
      data[1]->t_flag  =  T_INFINITE;

   GetInfiniteBits<AXIS>(ray.origin, A1, data[0]->i_bits);
```

```
        GetInfiniteBits<AXIS>(ray.origin, A2, data[1]->i_bits);

        // no intersection: caller must check t_flag
        // but make a t stand-in for the sort
        data[0]->t = data[1]->t = T_BIG_NEG;
        return;
    }

    // no parallelism
    data[0]->t = (dot_a1 - dot_o) / dot_d;
    data[1]->t = (dot_a2 - dot_o) / dot_d;
    for (int i = 0; i < T_PAIR; ++i) {
        VectorScale(tD, ray.direction, data[i]->t);
        VectorAdd(data[i]->i, ray.origin, tD);
        data[i]->t_flag = T_OKAY;
        GetBits<AXIS>(data[i]->i, base, len, data[i]->i_bits);
    }
}

void RayUtil::TIntersect (Ray &ray, ushort3 &base, int voxlen)
{
    float3 basef;
    Intersect **pair_ptr;

    // re-use the Intersect Records
    clearIntData();

    // transfer base to float coords
    basef.x = float(base.x);
    basef.y = float(base.y);
    basef.z = float(base.z);

    // XY
    pair_ptr = &int_list->list[T_XY<<1];
    t_intersect<Z>(ray, pair_ptr, basef, voxlen);
    // YZ
    pair_ptr = &int_list->list[T_YZ<<1];
    t_intersect<X>(ray, pair_ptr, basef, voxlen);
    // XZ
    pair_ptr = &int_list->list[T_XZ<<1];
    t_intersect<Y>(ray, pair_ptr, basef, voxlen);
}

void RayUtil::VectorAdd (float3 &r, const float3 &v1, const float3 &v2)
{
    r.x = v1.x + v2.x;
    r.y = v1.y + v2.y;
    r.z = v1.z + v2.z;
}
```

```
float RayUtil::VectorLength (const float3 &p) [private]
{
    return  (sqrt(p.x  * p.x  + p.y  * p.y  + p.z  * p.z));
}

void RayUtil::VectorScale (float3 &tD, const float3 &D, const float t)
{
   tD.x  = D.x  *  t;
   tD.y  = D.y  *  t;
   tD.z  = D.z  *  t;
}
```

Local Data

```
// t flags
static const int T_OKAY = 0;
static const int T_INFINITE_ZERO = 1;
static const int T_INFINITE = 2;

// plane constants
static const int T_XY = 0;
static const int T_YZ = 1;
static const int T_XZ = 2;
static const int T_PLANES = 3;
static const int T_MAX = 6;
static const int T_PAIR = 2;

// infinite T stand-in\n
// make negative so it goes at end of Intersect sorted list
static const float T_BIG_NEG = -1.0e+10;
// for the TData linked list: terminates LEDS outside of universe
static const float T_BIG_POS = 1.0e+10;

// colors
static const int T_RED = 0;
static const int T_GREEN = 1;
static const int T_BLUE = 2;
static const int T_COLORS = 3;

// other constants
static const int DEGREES_360 = 360;
static const float HALF_INDEX = 0.5;
```

Associated Data Holders

```
struct Ray {
   float3 origin, direction;
```

```
    float3 base_origin, base_direction;
    short helical_offset;  // cw from 12 o'clock (positive Z axis)
    short level, angle, interleave;
};

struct Intersect {
    int t_flag, plane;
    float t;
    unsigned short i_bits;
    float3 i;
    Intersect() : t_flag(0), t(0.0), i_bits(0) {
        i.x = i.y = i.z = 0.0;
    }
    // we're using < as a > test
    bool operator<(const Intersect & rhs) {
        if (this != &rhs) {
            // greater than
            return (rhs.t < t);
        }
        return false;     // equal
    }
};

// temporary return struct for RayWorker

struct TPack {
    float t;
    float3 i;
};

// variable-length record

struct IntersectList {
    unsigned short count;     // will always be T_MAX
    // "count" Intersect pointers follow
    Intersect **list;
};
```

The documentation for this class was generated from the following files:
- RayUtil.h
- RayUtil.cpp

RayWorker Class Reference

Public Member Functions

RayWorker (int my_contextID, Octree<NodeGroup * > &my_tree)
~RayWorker ()
void Top ()

Private Member Functions

void DoRayWork (int interleave, int course, int level, int angle)

:: Here's where the linked list comes in.
void CastRay (Ray &ray, const float3 &zero_origin)

:: pass in the TData pointer for the ray origin
:: Note: Use the relative origin and direction, not base.
void RayLoop (Ray &ray, SortedLList<TData *, TData> &td_list)

void PushRay (Ray &ray, float3 &coord, TPack &tpack)
bool RayExitsUniverse (float3 &intersect)

:: Use transformed or untransformed t values which are invariant.
:: However, make untransformed (base) positions for LEDs.
void ProcessLEDs (Ray &ray, SortedLList<TData *, TData> &td_list)

:: set "in" status for LEDs
void ScanThroughLinks (Ray &ray, SortedLList<TData *, TData> &td_list)

:: This does not merge adjacent empty voxels.
void MakeRunLengths (Ray &ray, SortedLList<TData *, TData> &td_list)

void testFindNode ()

:: See the octant numbering this follows in IDWorker.cpp
void findNode (const float3 &coord, NodePack &data)

OctreeNode<NodeGroup * > *ChildNodeForID (OctreeNode<NodeGroup * > *curnode, unsigned char octant, bool &terminal)

Private Attributes

Context &context
int contextID
Octree<NodeGroup * > &tree

RayUtil r_u
IDWorker id_w
TDataWorker tdata_w
Transform xform
Display display
int Nt
int spindle_diam
int max_level
int helical_index
float3 armature_origin

Detailed Description

Top level ray tracing code

Constructor & Destructor Documentation

```
RayWorker::RayWorker (int my_contextID, Octree<NodeGroup * > &my_tree) [inline]
:
        context  (ContextWorker::getContext(my_contextID)),
        contextID(my_contextID),  tree(my_tree),  display(context) {}

RayWorker::~RayWorker () [inline]
{}
```

Member Function Documentation

```
// Here's where the linked list comes in.
void RayWorker::CastRay (Ray &ray, const float3 &zero_origin) [private]
{
    // make a dummy TData element for the header
    TData  * td_ptr =  tdata_w.AddTDataRecord(-1.0, zero_origin);

    // Instantiate the sorted linked list
    SortedLList<TData *, TData>  td_list(td_ptr);

    // Since the ray origins will all be in some
    // voxel (either empty or filled), the linked
    // list should start out officially with a
    // t = 0 entry.
    td_ptr =  tdata_w.AddTDataRecord(0.0, ray.base_origin);

    // but we don't know the intersect status yet. Insert it
    // anyway, we can pass the base pointer to the next step.
    td_list.insert(td_ptr);
```

```
    RayLoop(ray, td_list);
    ProcessLEDs(ray, td_list);
    MakeRunLengths(ray, td_list);

    // clean up TData for finished ray
    tdata_w.DeleteTDataRecords();
}

OctreeNode<NodeGroup * > * RayWorker::ChildNodeForID (OctreeNode<NodeGroup * > *curnode,
unsigned char octant, bool &terminal) [private]
{

    // FIRST: check for empty terminal node
    if (!id_w.checkOctantValid(curnode->child_bits, octant)) {
        empty = true;
        return NULL;
    }
    // SECOND: check for terminal level
    if (curnode->child_count == 0) {
        empty = false;
        return NULL;
    }

    int bit_count = id_w.getBitCountAtNodeIdx(curnode->child_bits, octant);
    if (bit_count > curnode->child_count)
        throw ItemNotFoundException("Bit count exceeds available nodes.");

    // all is well
    empty = false;
    return curnode->child[bit_count - 1];
}

void RayWorker::DoRayWork (int interleave, int course, int level, int angle) [private]
{
    float arm_angle;
    float point5_radius, y_offset, center_coord;
    float3 twelveoclock, zero_origin, direction;

    // make angle an offset from the helical offset of the arm
    if (interleave == T_ALPHA) {
        arm_angle = float(level * helical_index + angle);
        point5_radius = float(spindle_diam + 1) / 2.0 - 0.25;
    } else {
        arm_angle = float(level * helical_index + angle) + 179.5;
        point5_radius = float(spindle_diam + 1) / 2.0 + 0.25;
    }

    center_coord = float(Nt / 2);
    armature_origin = make_float3(center_coord, center_coord, center_coord);
```

```
    zero_origin =  make_float3(0.0, 0.0, 0.0);

    // center Nt - spindle_diam on Nt / 2, i.e. add in spindle_diam / 2.
    y_offset = float(course *  max_level  +  level  +  spindle_diam  / 2 );

    // 12 o'clock in positive Z-axis direction
    twelveoclock =  make_float3(center_coord +  HALF_INDEX,
                        y_offset +  HALF_INDEX,
                        center_coord + point5_radius);

    // instantiate a ray
    Ray  ray;
    ray.helical_offset  =  level  *  helical_index;
    // accumulated level: used on OpenGL side
    ray.level  = course *  max_level  +  level;
    // note that ray.angle is only an index, not the true angle,
    // and is never used in RayUtil.cpp.
    ray.angle  = angle;
    ray.interleave  = interleave;

    // rotate by arm_angle in XZ (positive angle = ccw)
    xform.rotateYAxis(ray.base_origin, twelveoclock, arm_angle,  armature_origin);

    // make the direction vector and rotate that too.
    // (Could use NT instead of zero origin argument.)
    direction =  make_float3(0.0, 0.0, 1.0);
    xform.rotateYAxis(ray.base_direction, direction, arm_angle, zero_origin);

    // now we have the base orientation.
    // If no virtual rotation, then:
    //r_u.copy_float3(ray.base_origin, ray.origin);
    //r_u.copy_float3(ray.base_direction, ray.direction);
    // otherwise use virtual rotation (set up in Top())
    xform.rotateByMatrix(ray.origin, ray.base_origin,  armature_origin);
    xform.rotateByMatrixNT(ray.direction, ray.base_direction);

    CastRay(ray, zero_origin);
}

// See the octant numbering this follows in IDWorker.cpp
// The coord is the "pushed" ray coordinate, that we
// want to find the octree octant for.
void RayWorker::findNode (const float3 &coord, NodePack &data) [private]
{
    OctreeNode<NodeGroup *>  *curnode;
    NodeGroup  *ng_ptr;
    float  x,  y,  z;
    float3  center;
    ushort3  voxcoord;
```

```
Glassner  ID = 0;     // root
int   level,  scale, N,  Nt;
bool  empty;

OctreeNode<NodeGroup *>  *nextnode =  tree.getRoot();
x = coord.x; y = coord.y; z = coord.z;

// get N for terminal level
Nt =  r_u.NewN(context.terminal_level);
level = 0;

do  {
   curnode = nextnode;

   // get the center coordinates scaled for this level
   N =  r_u.NewN(++level);

   // if terminal level is 4, and current level is 1, we have:
   // level 1 = 2 ; level 4 = 16, so: 16 / 2 = 8.
   // 0 * 8 = 0 ; 1 * 8 = 8; [0 - 1] = 0 to 8; [1 - 2] = 8 to 16.
   scale = Nt / N;

   // get the (1,1,1) (relative) position (= center point)
   ng_ptr = curnode->element;
   voxcoord.x  = ng_ptr->node[OCTANT_EIGHT].coord.x;
   voxcoord.y  = ng_ptr->node[OCTANT_EIGHT].coord.y;
   voxcoord.z  = ng_ptr->node[OCTANT_EIGHT].coord.z;

   center.x  = float(voxcoord.x  * scale);
   center.y  = float(voxcoord.y  * scale);
   center.z  = float(voxcoord.z  * scale);

   if  (x  >  center.x) {
      if  (y  >  center.y) {
         if  (z  >  center.z)
            ID = (ID * 10) + 6;
         else
            ID = (ID * 10) + 8;
      }  else  {
         if  (z  >  center.z)
            ID = (ID * 10) + 2;
         else
            ID = (ID * 10) + 4;
      }
   }  else  {  // x  <  center.x
      if  (y  >  center.y) {
         if  (z  >  center.z)
            ID = (ID * 10) + 5;
         else
```

```
            ID = (ID * 10) + 7;
        } else {
            if (z > center.z)
                ID = (ID * 10) + 1;
            else
                ID = (ID * 10) + 3;
        }
    }
    // get child n
    nextnode = ChildNodeForID(curnode, (unsigned  char)(ID % 10L), empty);
  } while (curnode->child_count != 0 && nextnode != NULL);

  // get the (0,0,0) (relative) position (= base point)
  voxcoord.x = ng_ptr->node[OCTANT_ZERO].coord.x;
  voxcoord.y = ng_ptr->node[OCTANT_ZERO].coord.y;
  voxcoord.z = ng_ptr->node[OCTANT_ZERO].coord.z;

  // return voxel ID, offset, length, Octree Node, and empty status
  data.ID = ID;
  id_w.addScaledUnitOffset(data.coord, voxcoord, scale, (unsigned  char)(ID % 10L));
  data.length = scale;
  data.empty = empty;
  data.node = curnode;

  // get the voxel color (set in Display.cpp)
  if (!empty) {
    int  index = (int)(ID % 10L) - 1;
    data.color.x = ng_ptr->node[index].color.x;
    data.color.y = ng_ptr->node[index].color.y;
    data.color.z = ng_ptr->node[index].color.z;
  }
}

// This does not merge adjacent empty voxels.
void RayWorker::MakeRunLengths (Ray &ray, SortedLList<TData *, TData> &td_list) [private]
{
  unsigned  char write_byte;
  int i, byte_count, offset, max_led, led_count;
  TData  * current;

  LListItr<TData *> itr = LListItr<TData *>(td_list.first());

  // first count up the bytes for the run-length storage:
  // a) empty voxel is one byte (for count)
  // b) non-empty voxel is one byte (for count)    //   plus 3 bytes for the color    byte_count = 0;
  while (itr.isValid()) {
    // don't count terminator
    if (!itr.peekNextValid())
      break;
```

```
        ++byte_count;
        current = itr.retrieve();
        if (current->in)
            byte_count += 3;            // RGB
        for (i = 0; i < current->count; ++i) {
            itr.advance();
        }
        // now advance to next voxel
        itr.advance();
    } // for all entries

    // allocate ReducedRay (caller will free)
    ReducedRay *my_ray = new ReducedRay;
    r_u.copy_float3(ray.base_origin, my_ray->base_origin);
    r_u.copy_float3(ray.base_direction, my_ray->base_direction);
    my_ray->level = ray.level;
    my_ray->angle = ray.angle;
    my_ray->interleave = ray.interleave;

    my_ray->count = byte_count;

    // allocate byte list (caller will free)
    unsigned char *plist = new unsigned char[byte_count];
    my_ray->list = plist;

    // now scan through again for pertinent data
    itr.reset(td_list.first());
    offset = 0;

    // for diagnostic:
    led_count = 0;
    max_led = (Nt - spindle_diam) / 2;

    while (itr.isValid()) {
        // don't count terminator
        if (!itr.peekNextValid())
            break;

        current = itr.retrieve();
        // a diagnostic only:
        // this says: the current voxel is non-zero ("in"), but:
        // the LED count is zero. In other words, we've missed
        // a voxel because there's no LED in it. This happens when
        // the ray intersects close to a voxel corner, with a small
        // distance to the next voxel face (less than 1, the voxel
        // size).
        if (current->count == 0 && current->in && led_count < max_led) {
#ifdef DIAGNOSTIC_MSG
```

```
        std::cout <<  "SAMPLE GAP!"  << current->position.x  <<  ", "
                              << current->position.y  <<  ", "
                              << current->position.z  <<  ", T: "
                              << current->t  << std::endl;
#endif
      } else {
#ifdef DIAGNOSTIC_MSG
        std::cout <<  "no gap, count:  "  << current->count  << std::endl;
#endif
        led_count += current->count;
      }

      write_byte = current->count;
      if (current->in)
        write_byte |=  IN_BIT;

      // write count byte
      plist[offset++] = write_byte;
      if (current->in) {
        // write color bytes
        for (i = 0; i <  T_COLORS; ++i) {
          write_byte = current->color[i];
          plist[offset++] = write_byte;
        }
      }
      // skip
      for (i = 0; i < current->count; ++i) {
        itr.advance();
      }
      // now advance to next voxel
      itr.advance();
   } // for all entries
   // queue it for OpenGL display
   display.MakeRayData(my_ray);
}

// Use transformed or untransformed t values which are invariant.
// However, make untransformed (base) positions for LEDs.
void RayWorker::ProcessLEDs (Ray &ray, SortedLList<TData *, TData> &td_list) [private]
{
    int   t, max_LED;
    float  tf;
    float3  tD, LED_pos;
    TData  * td_ptr;

    // Take advantage of the fact that inserts are progressive
    // by starting insert search at previously inserted item.
    td_list.setStartNode();
```

```
    max_LED = (Nt  -  Nt  / 16) / 2;
    for  (t = 0; t  <  max_LED; ++t) {
        // use base coordinates
        tf = float(t);
        r_u.VectorScale(tD, ray.base_direction, tf);
        r_u.VectorAdd(LED_pos, ray.base_origin, tD);
        td_ptr =  tdata_w.AddTDataRecord(tf, LED_pos);
        td_ptr->LED  =  true;

        // use insertNext for speedy insertion
        td_list.insertNext(td_ptr);
    }
    ScanThroughLinks(ray, td_list);
}

void RayWorker::PushRay (Ray &ray, float3 &coord, TPack &tpack) [private]
{
    r_u.Push(ray, coord, tpack);
}

bool RayWorker::RayExitsUniverse (float3 &intersect) [private]
{
    return   r_u.ExitsUniverse(intersect,  float(Nt));
}

// pass in the TData pointer for the ray origin
// Note: Use the relative origin and direction, not base.
void RayWorker::RayLoop (Ray &ray, SortedLList<TData *, TData> &td_list) [private]
{
    TData  * current;
    TPack  tpack;
    float3   coord;
    NodePack   data;

    LListItr<TData *>  my_itr = td_list.first();
    current = my_itr.retrieve();

    // start with the ray origin
    r_u.copy_float3(ray.origin, coord);
    // set up progressive insert
    td_list.setStartNode();

    do  {
        // find the voxel node of current td_ptr
        findNode(coord, data);
        current->in  = !data.empty;
        if  (current->in) {
            current->color[T_RED] = data.color.x;
            current->color[T_GREEN] = data.color.y;
```

```
            current->color[T_BLUE] = data.color.z;
        }
        // get the intersections for this voxel
        r_u.TIntersect(ray, data.coord, data.length);

        // push the coords to the next voxel node
        PushRay(ray, coord, tpack);

        // transfer intersect to a TData record
        current =  tdata_w.AddTDataRecord(tpack.t, tpack.i);
        // progressive insert (fast)
        td_list.insertNext(current);
    }  while  (!RayExitsUniverse(tpack.i));

    // mark the last entry as a boundary (default empty)
    current->boundary  =  true;
}

// set "in" status for LEDs
void RayWorker::ScanThroughLinks (Ray &ray, SortedLList<TData *, TData> &td_list) [private]
{
    bool  found_LED;
    TData  *current, *t, *t_plus;

    LListItr<TData *>  itr =  LListItr<TData *>(td_list.first());
    current = itr.retrieve();
    if  (current->LED ==  true)
        throw   RayException("LList Does Not Start with Voxel T");

    // get successive pairs
    while  (itr.isValid()) {
        t = current;
        t_plus = NULL; found_LED =  false;
        while  (itr.advance()  &&  itr.isValid()) {
            current = itr.retrieve();
            if  (current->LED ==  false) {
                t_plus = current;
                break;
            }
            found_LED =  true;
        }
        // Note that LEDs can extend out of the universe.
        // They're all zero, but we need this info anyway.
        if  (t_plus == NULL  &&  t->boundary) {
            if  (!found_LED)
                return;
            // add a dummy terminator : will go at end of list
            TData  *td_ptr =  tdata_w.AddTDataRecord(T_BIG_POS, ray.base_origin);
            td_list.insert(td_ptr);
```

```
        itr.advance();       // point at dummy
      } else if (t_plus == NULL) {
        throw   RayException("Unpaired Voxel T in LList");
      }
      // get first LED after t
      LListItr<TData *>  LED_itr =  LListItr<TData *>(td_list.findNext(t));
      TData  *cur_LED = LED_itr.retrieve();
      // always valid because framed by voxel T
      while  (cur_LED->LED) {
        t->count++;
        cur_LED->in = t->in;
        LED_itr.advance();
        cur_LED = LED_itr.retrieve();
      }
    }
}

void RayWorker::testFindNode () [private]
{
    float3  test_coord;

    // empty (for harrier gear at N = 128, returned length = 2)
    test_coord.x  = 65.5;
    test_coord.y  = 88.5;
    test_coord.z  = 30.0;

    NodePack   data;
    findNode(test_coord, data);

    // filled (for same, returned length = 1)
    test_coord.x  = 67.5;
    test_coord.y  = 88.5;
    test_coord.z  = 32.0;
    findNode(test_coord, data);

    // empty (returned length = 64)
    test_coord.x  = 2.0;
    test_coord.y  = 1.0;
    test_coord.z  = 1.0;
    findNode(test_coord, data);
}

void RayWorker::Top ()
{
    int  interleave, course,  level, angle,  offset;

    // before doing anything, set up a virtual rotation matrix
    AnglePack  one, two, three;
```

```
    // pawn
    one.active  = two.active  =  true;
    three.active  =  false;
    one.axis  = 1;    // x
    one.angle  = -77.0;
    two.axis  = 3;    // z
    two.angle  = 12.0;

    /*
    // harrier
    one.active = two.active = true;
    three.active = false;
    one.axis = 2;   // y
    one.angle = 90.0;
    two.axis = 3;   // z
    two.angle = 80.0;
    */
    xform.setUpRotationMatrix(one, two, three);

    Nt  =  r_u.NewN(context.terminal_level);
    spindle_diam  =  Nt  / 16;
    // spindle ratio
    max_level  = (Nt  -  spindle_diam) /  MAX_COURSE;
    helical_index  =  DEGREES_360  /  max_level;

    for  (interleave = 0; interleave  <  2; ++interleave) {
       for  (course = 0; course  <   MAX_COURSE; ++course) {
          offset = 0;
          for  (level = 0; level  <   max_level; level +=  skipper[offset%4]) {
             ++offset;
             for  (angle = 0; angle  <   DEGREES_360; ++angle) {
#ifdef DIAGNOSTIC_MSG
                std::cout  <<  "ANGLE:  "  <<  angle  <<   ", LEVEL:  "  <<  level
                         <<  ", COURSE:  "  <<  course  <<  std::endl;
#endif
                DoRayWork(interleave, course, level, angle);
            }
            display.terminateLevel();
         }
      }
   }
   return;
}
```

Associated Data Holders

// stuff that gets returned from a findNode

```
struct NodePack {
    Glassner ID;      // not currently used
    ushort3 coord;      // min coord of voxel
    uchar3 color;     // color of terminal non-empty
    int length;          // size of voxel (at terminal N)
    bool empty;          // empty voxel?
    OctreeNode<NodeGroup *> *node;
};
```

The documentation for this class was generated from the following files:

- RayWorker.h
- RayWorker.cpp

RenderQueue< Object > Class Template Reference

Public Member Functions

RenderQueue ()
~RenderQueue ()
Object enqueue (Object x)
bool isEmpty ()
Object dequeue ()

Private Attributes

QueueAr< Object > q
pthread_mutex_t mutex

Detailed Description

Uses QueueAr and manipulates items in a thread-safe manner. Uses a mutex to lock accesses.

Constructor & Destructor Documentation

```
template<class Object>
RenderQueue< Object >::RenderQueue() [inline]
:  mutex(PTHREAD_MUTEX_INITIALIZER) {}

template<class Object>
RenderQueue< Object >::~RenderQueue() [inline]
{}
```

Member Function Documentation

```
template<class Object >
Object RenderQueue< Object >::dequeue ()
{
    bool  empty;
    pthread_mutex_lock(&mutex);
    empty =  q.isEmpty();
    pthread_mutex_unlock(&mutex);

    if  (empty)
       throw   UnderflowException( );

    pthread_mutex_lock(&mutex);
```

```
    Object vd =  q.dequeue();
    pthread_mutex_unlock(&mutex);
    return  vd;
}

template<class Object>
Object RenderQueue< Object >::enqueue (Object x)
{
    pthread_mutex_lock(&mutex);
    q.enqueue(x);
    pthread_mutex_unlock(&mutex);
    return   x;
}

template<class Object >
bool RenderQueue< Object >::isEmpty ()
{
    bool  empty;
    pthread_mutex_lock(&mutex);
    empty =  q.isEmpty();
    pthread_mutex_unlock(&mutex);
    return  empty;
}
```

The documentation for this class was generated from the following files:

- RenderQueue.h
- RenderQueue.tpp

SortByRef< Comparable, ConstObj > Class Template Reference

Public Member Functions

SortByRef ()
~SortByRef ()

:: Quicksort algorithm (driver).
void quicksort (Vector< Comparable > &a)

Private Member Functions

:: Internal insertion sort routine for subarrays
:: that is used by quicksort.
void insertionSort (Vector< Comparable > &a, int low, int high)

:: Internal quicksort method that makes recursive calls.
void quicksort (Vector< Comparable > &a, int low, int high)

:: Standard swap.
void swap (Comparable &obj1, Comparable &obj2)

:: This stuff is similar to Weiss' Cref wrapper class:
ConstObj get (const Comparable obj) const

bool isNull (const Comparable obj) const

Detailed Description

Dual-argument template class for sorting and returning a reference rather than pointer for the "get" routine. This is used for ray-casting and sorting the TData.

Constructor & Destructor Documentation

template<class Comparable, class ConstObj>
SortByRef< Comparable, ConstObj >::SortByRef() [inline]
{}

template<class Comparable, class ConstObj>
SortByRef< Comparable, ConstObj >::~SortByRef() [inline]
{}

Member Function Documentation

```
// This stuff is similar to Weiss' Cref wrapper class:
// We instantiate with a second template argument to
// allow a pointer to be returned as a constant version
// of that pointer. This means the instantiation is, f.e.:
// SortByRef<TData *, TData> my_sort;
template<class Comparable , class ConstObj >
ConstObj SortByRef< Comparable, ConstObj >::get (const Comparable obj) const [private]
{
   if (isNull(obj))
      throw  NullPointerException();
   return  *obj;
}

// Internal insertion sort routine for subarrays
// that is used by quicksort.
template<class Comparable , class ConstObj >
void SortByRef< Comparable, ConstObj >::insertionSort (Vector< Comparable > &a, int low, int high)
[private]
{
   for( int  p  = low + 1;  p  <= high;  p++ )
   {
      Comparable tmp = a[  p  ];
      int  j;

      for( j =  p; j  >  low  &&  get(tmp)  <  get(a[ j - 1 ]); j-- )
         a[ j ] = a[ j - 1 ];
      a[ j ] = tmp;
   }
}

template<class Comparable , class ConstObj >
bool SortByRef< Comparable, ConstObj >::isNull (const Comparable obj) const [private]
{
   return  obj  == NULL;
}

// Internal quicksort method that makes recursive calls.
template<class Comparable , class ConstObj >
void SortByRef< Comparable, ConstObj >::quicksort (Vector< Comparable > &a, int low, int high)
[private]
{
   if ( low +  CUTOFF   >  high )
      insertionSort( a, low, high );
   else    {
      // Sort low, middle, high
      int  middle = ( low + high ) / 2;
      if (  get(a[ middle ])  <   get(a[ low ]) )
```

```
            swap( a[ low ], a[ middle ] );
        if (  get(a[ high ])  <   get(a[ low ]) )
            swap( a[ low ], a[ high ] );
        if (  get(a[ high ])  <   get(a[ middle ]) )
            swap( a[ middle ], a[ high ] );

        // Place pivot at position high - 1
        // Note! Swaps pointers, so don't need  "get"
        Comparable pivot = a[ middle ];
        swap( a[ middle ], a[ high - 1 ] );

        // Begin partitioning
        int  i, j;
        for ( i = low, j = high - 1; ; )
        {
            while (  get(a[ ++i ])  <   get(pivot) ) { }
            while (  get(pivot)  <   get(a[ --j ]) ) { }
            if ( i  <  j )
                swap( a[ i ], a[ j ] );
            else
                 break;
        }
        swap( a[ i ], a[ high - 1 ] );   // Restore pivot
        quicksort( a, low, i - 1 );      // Sort small elements
        quicksort( a, i + 1, high );     // Sort large elements
    }
}

// Quicksort algorithm (driver).
template<class Comparable , class ConstObj >
void SortByRef< Comparable, ConstObj >::quicksort (Vector< Comparable > &a)
{
    quicksort( a, 0, a.size( ) - 1 );
}

// Standard swap.
// This is tricky for a pointer, because the operator[]
// for a Vector returns an Object & (reference), so we
// have a pointer reference. The pointer is still used
// to dereference the data, but the reference element
// means that the pointer values can be changed. This
// then allows the swap to work. (See Weiss, p. 648, 649)
// We are still swapping pointers, not the contents of
// the pointers!

// Note: swap will not compile if it's declared outside the class
// as an inline function (as done by Weiss).
```

```
template<class Comparable , class ConstObj >
void SortByRef< Comparable, ConstObj >::swap (Comparable &obj1, Comparable &obj2) [private]
{
   Comparable tmp = obj1;
   obj1 = obj2;
   obj2 = tmp;
}
```

Local Data

```
#define CUTOFF 10
```

The documentation for this class was generated from the following files:
- SortByRef.h
- SortByRef.tpp

SortedLList< Object, ConstObj > Class Template Reference

Public Member Functions

SortedLList (const Object element)

:: Insert item x into the list.
void insert (const Object x)

:: Insert item x after p.
void insert (const Object x, const LListItr< Object > &p)

LListNode< Object > *insertNext (const Object x)

:: Insert item x after p.
LListNode< Object > *insertNext (const Object x, const LListItr< Object > &p)

:: For quick insert when caller KNOWS that inserts are progressive.
void setStartNode ()

Private Member Functions

:: This stuff is similar to Weiss' Cref wrapper class:
ConstObj get (const Object obj) const
bool isNull (const Object obj) const

Private Attributes

LListNode< Object > *startNode

Detailed Description

Dual-argument template class for an insertion
into a linked list in sorted order. This is used for constructing
a ray during ray casting.
Inherits LinkedList, uses the LListItr (linked list iterator) in LinkedList.h.

Constructor & Destructor Documentation

template<class Object, class ConstObj>
SortedLList< Object, ConstObj >::SortedLList(const Object element) [inline]
: LList<Object>(element) {}

Member Function Documentation

```
// This stuff is similar to Weiss' Cref wrapper class:
// We instantiate with a second template argument to
// allow a pointer to be returned as a constant version
// of that pointer. This means the instantiation is, f.e.:
// SortedLList<TData *, TData> td_list(td_ptr);
template<class Object , class ConstObj >
ConstObj SortedLList< Object, ConstObj >::get (const Object obj) const [private]
{
    if  (isNull(obj))
       throw   NullPointerException();
    return  *obj;
}

// Insert item x after p.
// Reimplemented from LList< Object >.
template<class Object, class ConstObj>
void SortedLList< Object, ConstObj >::insert (const Object x, const LListItr< Object > &p) [inline,
virtual]
     {  insert(  x  ); }

// Insert item x into the list.
// comparison gets a reference to facilitate operator< overload.
template<class Object , class ConstObj >
void SortedLList< Object, ConstObj >::insert (const Object x)
{
    LListItr<Object>  prev =  LListItr<Object>(LList<Object>::zeroth( ));
    LListItr<Object>  curr =  LListItr<Object>(LList<Object>::first( ));

    while( !curr.isPastEnd( )  &&   get(curr.retrieve( ))  <   get(x) )
    {
       prev.advance( );
       curr.advance( );
    }

    LList<Object>::insert(  x, prev );
}

// Insert item x after p.
// Reimplemented from LList< Object >.
template<class Object, class ConstObj>
LListNode<Object>* SortedLList< Object, ConstObj >::insertNext (const Object x, const LListItr<
Object > &p) [inline, virtual]
     {  return   insertNext(  x  ); }

template<class Object , class ConstObj >
LListNode< Object > * SortedLList< Object, ConstObj >::insertNext (const Object x)
{
    LListItr<Object>  prev =  LListItr<Object>(startNode);
```

```
    LListItr<Object>  curr =  LListItr<Object>(startNode->next);

    while( !curr.isPastEnd( )  &&   get(curr.retrieve( ))  <   get(x) )
    {
       prev.advance( );
       curr.advance( );
    }

    return   startNode  =  LList<Object>::insertNext(  x, prev );
}

template<class Object , class ConstObj >
bool SortedLList< Object, ConstObj >::isNull (const Object obj) const [private]
{
    return   obj  == NULL;
}

// For quick insert when caller KNOWS that inserts are progressive.
template<class Object , class ConstObj >
void SortedLList< Object, ConstObj >::setStartNode ()
{
    startNode  =  LList<Object>::zeroth( );
}
```

The documentation for this class was generated from the following files:
- SortedLList.h
- SortedLList.tpp

Stellation1 Class Reference

Public Member Functions

Stellation1 ()
~Stellation1 ()
void Top ()
Vector<BasicTriangle * >& getGeomList ()

:: user is responsible for calling this
void freeGeomList ()

Private Member Functions

:: single mirrors are reversed in order;
:: double mirrors the same as reference.
:: The above holds for all others with sel:v at 0, sel:w at 0
void SetupArrays ()

void ComputeKeyVariables ()
float LengthSquared (float3 &p1, float3 &p2)

:: This is stolen from GeomUtil.cpp -- need a neutral class for this.
float3 cross (const float3 &op1, const float3 &op2)

:: Length from zero component, i.e. implicit length.
float VectorLengthSquared (float3 &vec)

:: centroid comes in already zero
void Centroid (const float3 p[], float3 &centroid)

:: stellation for principle plane (specified with template arg)
template<int32 AXIS> void FourGroup ()

:: Make triangles around centroid for reflection group.
template<int32 AXIS> void MakeStellation (const float3 p[], const float3 &centroid, const int reflection)

Private Attributes

float centroid_height
float p
float inv_p
float3 plane_pentagon [PENT_VERTS]
float3 reflection [TIMES_FOUR]

float3 color [TIMES_FOUR]
Vector<BasicTriangle * > my_geom

Detailed Description

Code to construct a stellated dodecahedron which also serves as a unit test for the multi-dimensional templated geometry code.

Constructor & Destructor Documentation

```
Stellation1::Stellation1 () [inline]
{}

Stellation1::~Stellation1 () [inline]
{}
```

Member Function Documentation

```
// centroid comes in already zero
void Stellation1::Centroid (const float3 p[], float3 &centroid) [private]
{
    int  i;

    for  (i = 0; i<PENT_VERTS; ++i) {
       centroid.x  += p[i].x;
       centroid.y  += p[i].y;
       centroid.z  += p[i].z;
    }
    centroid.x  /=  PENT_VERTSF;
    centroid.y  /=  PENT_VERTSF;
    centroid.z  /=  PENT_VERTSF;
}

void Stellation1::ComputeKeyVariables () [private]
{
    float3  centroid(0.0f, 0.0f, 0.0f);

    // choose points on any pentagonal face : choose Z rot, as above
    float3  p1 =  make_float3(-1.0f, 1.0f, -1.0f);
    float3  p2 =  make_float3(-inv_p, 0.0f, -p);

    float   c  =  LengthSquared(p1, p2);

    // find the centroid of the default group
    // note we're taking the centroid on a canted plane, but
    // we just care about the length from the centroid to
```

```
    // some vertex, which is invariant under rotation.
    Centroid(plane_pentagon, centroid);

    float   a  =  LengthSquared(p1, centroid);

    centroid_height  = sqrtf(c - a);  // c and a are squared terms
}

// This is stolen from GeomUtil.cpp -- need a neutral class for this.
float3 Stellation1::cross (const float3 &op1, const float3 &op2) [private]
{
    return   make_float3(
          op1.y*op2.z  - op1.z*op2.y,
          op1.z*op2.x  - op1.x*op2.z,
          op1.x*op2.y  - op1.y*op2.x  );
}

// stellation for principle plane (specified with template arg)
template<int32 AXIS>
void Stellation1::FourGroup () [private]
{
    int  i, j, k;
    bool  reverse;
    float3   p[PENT_VERTS];

    typedef   xyz<AXIS>  sel;

    // for all reflection groups (4)
    for  (i = 0; i  <   TIMES_FOUR; ++i) {
       // permute these in backwards order to lock onto 1-position
       float  scale_x = sel::rx(reflection[i]);
       float  scale_y = sel::ry(reflection[i]);
       float  scale_z = sel::rz(reflection[i]);

       reverse = ((i == 1 || i == 2) ?  true  :  false);
       if  (reverse)
          k =  PENT_VERTS  - 1;
       else
          k = 0;

       // get the permutation
       for  (j = 0; j  <   PENT_VERTS; ++j) {
          p[k] =  make_float3(sel::rx(plane_pentagon[j]) * scale_x,
                        sel::ry(plane_pentagon[j]) * scale_y,
                        sel::rz(plane_pentagon[j]) * scale_z);
          if  (reverse)
             --k;
          else
             ++k;
```

```
        }

        // choose first three points, translate by middle point
        float3  p1 =  make_float3(p[0].x  - p[1].x,
                          p[0].y  - p[1].y,
                          p[0].z  - p[1].z);
        float3  p2 =  make_float3(p[2].x  - p[1].x,
                          p[2].y  - p[1].y,
                          p[2].z  - p[1].z);

        // normal from cross prod
        float3   n  =  cross(p1, p2);
        float   len  = sqrtf(VectorLengthSquared(n));
        float  ratio =  centroid_height  /  len;

        // compute centroid; clear it via constructor
        float3  centroid(0.0f, 0.0f, 0.0f);
        Centroid(p, centroid);

        // translate scaled normal to centroid and voila!
        centroid.x += ratio * n.x;
        centroid.y += ratio * n.y;
        centroid.z += ratio * n.z;

        MakeStellation<AXIS>(p, centroid, i);
    }
}

// user is responsible for calling this
void Stellation1::freeGeomList ()
{
    int   size  =  my_geom.size();
    for  (int  i = 0; i  <   size; ++i)
        delete   my_geom[i];
}

Vector<BasicTriangle * >& Stellation1::getGeomList ()
{
    return   my_geom;
}

float Stellation1::LengthSquared (float3 &p1, float3 &p2) [private]
{
    float3  diff;

    diff.x  = p2.x  - p1.x;
    diff.y  = p2.y  - p1.y;
    diff.z  = p2.z  - p1.z;
```

```
    return (diff.x * diff.x + diff.y * diff.y + diff.z * diff.z);
}

// Make triangles around centroid for reflection group.
// Note that an aggregate p[] is passed by reference
template<int32 AXIS>
void Stellation1::MakeStellation (const float3 p[], const float3 &centroid, const int reflection) [private]
{
    int i, j;

    typedef xyz<AXIS> sel;

    float3 tcolor = make_float3(sel::rx(color[reflection]),
                       sel::ry(color[reflection]),
                       sel::rz(color[reflection]));

    for (i = 0; i < PENT_VERTS; ++i) {
        j = i + 1;
        if (j == PENT_VERTS)
            j = 0;      // wrap around
        BasicTriangle *tri = new BasicTriangle;
        my_geom.push_back(tri);

        // edge from i to j (ccw ordered) to centroid
        tri->vert[0].x = p[i].x;
        tri->vert[0].y = p[i].y;
        tri->vert[0].z = p[i].z;
        //
        tri->vert[1].x = p[j].x;
        tri->vert[1].y = p[j].y;
        tri->vert[1].z = p[j].z;
        //
        tri->vert[2].x = centroid.x;
        tri->vert[2].y = centroid.y;
        tri->vert[2].z = centroid.z;

        tri->color.r = tcolor.x;
        tri->color.g = tcolor.y;
        tri->color.b = tcolor.z;
    }
}

// single mirrors are reversed in order;
// double mirrors the same as reference.
// The above holds for all others with sel:v at 0, sel:w at 0
void Stellation1::SetupArrays () [private]
{
    // phi
    p = (sqrtf(5.0f) + 1.0f) / 2.0f;
```

```
    inv_p  = 1.0 /  p;

    // colors
    color[0] =  make_float3(1.0, 0.0f, 0.0f);
    color[1] =  make_float3(1.0, 0.0f, 0.5f);
    color[2] =  make_float3(1.0, 0.5f, 0.0f);
    color[3] =  make_float3(1.0, 0.5f, 0.5f);

    // reflection scalars: these are permuted
    reflection[0] =  make_float3(1.0f, 1.0f, 1.0f);
    reflection[1] =  make_float3(1.0f, -1.0f, 1.0f);
    reflection[2] =  make_float3(1.0f, 1.0f, -1.0f);
    reflection[3] =  make_float3(1.0f, -1.0f, -1.0f);

    // pentagons associated with various planes, permuted
    // default is X
    plane_pentagon[0] =  make_float3(-1.0f, 1.0f, -1.0f);
    plane_pentagon[1] =  make_float3(-inv_p, 0.0f, -p);
    plane_pentagon[2] =  make_float3(inv_p, 0.0f, -p);
    plane_pentagon[3] =  make_float3(1.0f, 1.0f, -1.0f);
    plane_pentagon[4] =  make_float3(0.0f,  p, -inv_p);
}

void Stellation1::Top ()
{
    // set up the reference polygons
    SetupArrays();

    // get the stellation variables
    ComputeKeyVariables();

    // permute calcs for each plane group
    FourGroup<X>();
    FourGroup<Y>();
    FourGroup<Z>();
}

// Length from zero component, i.e. implicit length.
float Stellation1::VectorLengthSquared (float3 &vec) [private]
{
    return  (vec.x  * vec.x  + vec.y  * vec.y  + vec.z  * vec.z);
}
```

Local Data

```
// index into the pair arrays with X, Y, or Z = {0, 1, or 2}
// always start each pentagon with a cube coordinate.
```

```
// Maintain CCW order as seen from the outside.
// index pairs and opposite sides via multiples of PENT_VERTS
// Left-handed coordinates, pos z into the screen.

// X:
// (1, 1, 1)
// (1, -1, 1)
// (1, 1, -1)
// (1, -1, -1)

static const int PENT_VERTS = 5;
static const float PENT_VERTSF = 5.0f;

static const int TIMES_FOUR = 4;
```

The documentation for this class was generated from the following files:
- Stellation1.h
- Stellation1.cpp

TDataWorker Class Reference

Public Member Functions

TDataWorker ()
~TDataWorker ()
TData *AddTDataRecord (float tval, const float3 &pos)
void DeleteTDataRecords ()

Private Member Functions

void makeEmpty ()

Private Attributes

TData *currentVector<TData * > td_list

Detailed Description

Worker class for managing TData records.
This is basically a wrapper with a
comparison function for sorting those "t" or TData values.

Constructor & Destructor Documentation

```
TDataWorker::TDataWorker () [inline]
:  current(NULL) {}

DataWorker::~TDataWorker ()
{
   makeEmpty();
}
```

Member Function Documentation

```
TData * TDataWorker::AddTDataRecord (float tval, const float3 &pos)
{
   TData  *td =  new   TData(tval, pos);
   td_list.push_back(td);
   current  = td;
   return  td;
}
```

```
void TDataWorker::DeleteTDataRecords () [inline]
{  makeEmpty(); }

void TDataWorker::makeEmpty () [private]
{
   int  i,  size;

   // delete TData records
   if  ((size =  td_list.size())  >  0) {
      for  (i = 0; i<size; ++i) {
         delete   td_list[i];
      }
   }
   td_list.clear();
}
```

Associated Data Holders

```
// The intersections of a ray with voxels occurs at various values,
// which are simply vector scalars.

class TData {
public:
   // make all of this public to emulate a struct

   float t;
   // either the intersect coord, or the LED position
   float3 position;
   // count of LED entries that follow
   short count;
   // universe boundary? ; is LED? ; leads into non-empty voxel?
   bool boundary, LED, in;
   // color of t if it's in (LED inherits this in run)
   unsigned char color[3];

   TData(float tval, const float3 &pos) {
      t = tval;
      position.x = pos.x;
      position.y = pos.y;
      position.z = pos.z;
      count = 0;
      boundary = LED = in = false;
      color[0] = color[1] = color[2] = 0;
   }

   bool operator<(const TData & rhs);
```

```
private:
    FPUtil fp_u;
};

bool TData::operator<(const TData & rhs) {
    if (this != &rhs) {
        if (fp_u.equalBoundsf(t, rhs.t, PRECISIONf) &&
                (LED == false && rhs.LED == true)) {
            return true;  // put LED AFTER voxel t
        }
        return (t < rhs.t);
    }
    return false;     // equal
}
```

The documentation for this class was generated from the following files:
- TDataWorker.h
- TDataWorker.cpp

Transform Class Reference

Public Member Functions

Transform ()
~Transform ()

:: fast single-axis transforms:
void rotateYAxis (float3 &rp, const float3 &p, const float angle, const float3 &origin)

:: angle is in degrees, no translation
void rotateYAxisNT (float3 &rp, const float3 &p, const float angle)

void VectorScale (float3 &tD, const float3 &D, const float t)
void VectorAdd (float3 &r, const float3 &v1, const float3 &v2)
void VectorSubtract (float3 &r, const float3 &a, const float3 &b)

:: set up 3 x 3 rotation matrix: order matters
:: be sure active rotations are sequential.
void setUpRotationMatrix (AnglePack &one, AnglePack &two, AnglePack &three)

:: matrix-m_vector transform
:: use previously computed R matrix
void rotateByMatrix (float3 &rp, const float3 &mp, const float3 &origin)

void rotateByMatrixNT (float3 &rp, const float3 &mp)

Private Member Functions

void getMatrix (matrix &m, double angle, short axis)
void CopyMatrix (matrix &s, matrix &d)

:: [row][col]
void MatMul (matrix &s, matrix &b, matrix &a)

:: [x y z] | |, i.e. m_vector not transposed
void VecMatMul (m_vector &r, const m_vector &v, const matrix &m)

void vectorType (m_vector &v, const float3 &t)

:: [row][col]
void getX (matrix &m, double angle)
void getY (matrix &m, double angle)
void getZ (matrix &m, double angle)

Private Attributes

matrix R

Detailed Description

Matrix and vector 3D transformation functions.

Constructor & Destructor Documentation

Transform::Transform () [inline]
{}

Transform::~Transform () [inline]
{}

Member Function Documentation

```
void Transform::CopyMatrix (matrix &s, matrix &d) [private]
{
    int i, j;
    for (i = 0; i < 3; ++i) {
        for (j = 0; j < 3; ++j)
            d[i][j] = s[i][j];
    }
}
```

```
void Transform::getMatrix (matrix &m, double angle, short axis) [private]
{
    switch(axis) {
    case 1:
        getX(m, angle);
        break;
    case 2:
        getY(m, angle);
        break;
    case 3:
        getZ(m, angle);
        break;
    default:
        break;
    }
}
```

```
// [row][col]
void Transform::getX (matrix &m, double angle) [private]
{
```

```
    m[0][0] = 1.0;
    m[0][1] = m[0][2] = 0.0;
    m[1][0] = 0.0;
    m[1][1] = cos(angle);
    m[1][2] = -sin(angle);
    m[2][0] = 0.0;
    m[2][1] = sin(angle);
    m[2][2] = cos(angle);
}

void Transform::getY (matrix &m, double angle) [private]
{
    m[0][0] = cos(angle);
    m[0][1] = 0.0;
    m[0][2] = sin(angle);
    m[1][0] = 0.0;
    m[1][1] = 1.0;
    m[1][2] = 0.0;
    m[2][0] = -sin(angle);
    m[2][1] = 0.0;
    m[2][2] = cos(angle);
}

void Transform::getZ (matrix &m, double angle) [private]
{
    m[0][0] = cos(angle);
    m[0][1] = -sin(angle);
    m[0][2] = 0.0;
    m[1][0] = sin(angle);
    m[1][1] = cos(angle);
    m[1][2] = 0.0;
    m[2][0] = 0.0;
    m[2][1] = 0.0;
    m[2][2] = 1.0;
}

// [row][col]
void Transform::MatMul (matrix &s, matrix &b, matrix &a) [private]
{
    int  i, j, k;

    for  (i = 0; i  <  3; i++) {        // row
        for  (j = 0; j  <  3; j++) {    // col
            s[i][j] = 0.0;
            for  (k = 0; k  <  3; k++)
                s[i][j] += b[i][k] * a[k][j];
        }
    }
}
```

```
// matrix-m_vector transform
// use previously computed R matrix
void Transform::rotateByMatrix (float3 &rp, const float3 &mp, const float3 &origin)
{
   float3  translated;
   m_vector   r,  p;

   VectorSubtract(translated, mp, origin);
   vectorType(p, translated);

   VecMatMul(r, p,  R);

   rp.x  = r[0] + origin.x;
   rp.y  = r[1] + origin.y;
   rp.z  = r[2] + origin.z;
}

void Transform::rotateByMatrixNT (float3 &rp, const float3 &mp)
{
   float3  translated;
   m_vector   r,  p;

   vectorType(p, mp);

   VecMatMul(r, p,  R);

   rp.x  = r[0];
   rp.y  = r[1];
   rp.z  = r[2];
}

// fast single-axis transforms:
// angle is in degrees
void Transform::rotateYAxis (float3 &rp, const float3 &p, const float angle, const float3 &origin)
{
   double  theta = angle * M_PI / 180.0;
   float3  translated;

   translated.x  = p.x  - origin.x;
   translated.z  = p.z  - origin.z;

   rp.x  = translated.x  * cos(theta) - translated.z  * sin(theta) + origin.x;
   rp.y  = p.y;
   rp.z  = translated.x  * sin(theta) + translated.z  * cos(theta) + origin.z;
}

// angle is in degrees, no translation
void Transform::rotateYAxisNT (float3 &rp, const float3 &p, const float angle)
```

```
{
    double  theta = angle * M_PI / 180.0;

    rp.x  = p.x  * cos(theta) - p.z  * sin(theta);
    rp.y  = p.y;
    rp.z  = p.x  * sin(theta) + p.z  * cos(theta);
}

// set up 3 x 3 rotation matrix: order matters
// be sure active rotations are sequential.
void Transform::setUpRotationMatrix (AnglePack &one, AnglePack &two, AnglePack &three)
{
    matrix  A, B, C, S, T;
    double  angle;

    if  (one.active) {
       angle = one.angle  * M_PI / 180.0;
       getMatrix(A, angle, one.axis);
    }
    if  (two.active) {
       angle = two.angle  * M_PI / 180.0;
       getMatrix(B, angle, two.axis);
    }
    if  (three.active) {
       angle = three.angle  * M_PI / 180.0;
       getMatrix(C, angle, three.axis);
    }
    // matmuls
    if  (three.active) {
       MatMul(S, B, A);
       MatMul(T, C, S);
       CopyMatrix(T,  R);    // save it for repeated application
    } else   if  (two.active) {
       MatMul(S, B, A);
       CopyMatrix(S,  R);
    } else
       CopyMatrix(A,  R);
}

// [x y z] |  |, i.e. m_vector not transposed
void Transform::VecMatMul (m_vector &r, const m_vector &v, const matrix &m) [private]
{
    int  i, j;
    for  (i = 0; i  <  3; i++) {
       r[i] = 0.0;
       for  (j = 0; j  <  3; j++)
          r[i] +=  v[j] * m[j][i];
    }
}
```

```
void Transform::VectorAdd (float3 &r, const float3 &v1, const float3 &v2)
{
  r.x = v1.x + v2.x;
  r.y = v1.y + v2.y;
  r.z = v1.z + v2.z;
}

void Transform::VectorScale (float3 &tD, const float3 &D, const float t)
{
  tD.x = D.x * t;
  tD.y = D.y * t;
  tD.z = D.z * t;
}

void Transform::VectorSubtract (float3 &r, const float3 &a, const float3 &b)
{
  r.x = a.x - b.x;
  r.y = a.y - b.y;
  r.z = a.z - b.z;
}

void Transform::vectorType (m_vector &v, const float3 &t) [private]
{
   v[0] = t.x;
   v[1] = t.y;
   v[2] = t.z;
}
```

Associated Data Holders

```
struct AnglePack {
   bool active;    // can send in dummy if false
   short axis;        // {1,2,3} = {x,y,z}
   float angle;    // in degrees
};

typedef double matrix[3][3];
typedef double m_vector[3];      // "vector" conflicts with other stuff
```

The documentation for this class was generated from the following files:
- Transform.h
- Transform.cpp

Vector< Object > Class Template Reference

Classes

struct VItem

Public Member Functions

Vector (int initSize=0)
Vector (Vector< Object >&rhs)
~Vector ()
Object &operator[] (int index)
const Object &operator[] (int index) const
Vector operator= (Vector rhs)
void resize (int newSize)
void reserve (int newCapacity)
void clear ()
void push_back (const Object x)
int size () const
int capacity () const

Private Attributes

int theSize
int theCapacity
VItem *objects

Detailed Description

The STL-style vector class. Inspired by Weiss (Data Structures and Problem Solving Using C++). Uses an internal array of VItems (vector items) for safest approach.

Constructor & Destructor Documentation

```
template<class Object>
Vector< Object >::Vector(int initSize = 0) [inline, explicit]
    : theSize( initSize ),  theCapacity( initSize )
    {  objects  =  new  VItem[  theCapacity  ]; }
```

```
template<class Object>
Vector< Object >::Vector(Vector< Object >&rhs) [inline]
                        : objects( NULL )
    {  operator=( rhs ); }
```

```
template<class Object>
Vector< Object >::~Vector() [inline]
    {delete  [ ]  objects; }
```

Member Function Documentation

```
template<class Object>
int Vector< Object >::capacity () const [inline]
     {  return   theCapacity; }

template<class Object >
void Vector< Object >::clear ()
{
    delete  []  objects;
    theSize  =  theCapacity  = 0;
    objects  =  new  VItem[0];
}

template<class Object >
Vector< Object > Vector< Object >::operator= (Vector< Object > rhs)
{
    if  (this  !=  &rhs)       // alias test
    {
       delete  []  objects;                    // reclaim old
       theSize  = rhs.size();                  // copy size
       theCapacity  = rhs.capacity();          // and capacity
       objects  =  new  VItem[ capacity()];    // allocate
       for  (int  k = 0; k  <  size(); k++)     // copy items
           objects[k].element = rhs.objects[k].element;
    }
    return   this;            // return pointer to self
}

template<class Object>
const Object &Vector< Object >::operator[] (int index) const [inline]
{
 #ifndef NO_CHECK
      if  (index  <  0 || index  >=  size()) {
          std::cout  <<   "INDEX:  "   <<   index   <<  std::endl;
          throw   ArrayIndexOutOfBoundsException();
      }
 #endif
      return   objects[index].element;
}

template<class Object>
Object &Vector< Object >::operator[] (int index) [inline]
```

```
{
 #ifndef NO_CHECK
      if (index < 0 || index >= size()) {
          std::cout << "INDEX: " << index << std::endl;
          throw ArrayIndexOutOfBoundsException();
      }
 #endif
       return objects[index].element;
}

template<class Object>
void Vector< Object >::push_back (const Object x)
{
   if (theSize == theCapacity)           // if no room
       reserve(2 * theCapacity + 1);     // make room
   objects[theSize++].element = x;       // add x
}

template<class Object >
void Vector< Object >::reserve (int newCapacity)
{
   VItem *oldArray = objects;            // save old
    // compute number to copy
    int numToCopy = newCapacity < theSize ? newCapacity : theSize;

    objects = new VItem[newCapacity];    // allocate new
    for (int k = 0; k < numToCopy; k++)  // copy items
       objects[k].element = oldArray[k].element;

    theSize = numToCopy;                 // set size
    theCapacity = newCapacity;           // set capacity
    delete [] oldArray;                  // reclaim old
}

template<class Object >
void Vector< Object >::resize (int newSize)
{
   if (newSize > theCapacity)            // if expanding
      reserve(newSize * 2);              // get space
   theSize = newSize;                    // set size
}

template<class Object>
int Vector< Object >::size() const [inline]
     { return theSize; }
```

Local Data

```
// vector class interface. Supports construction with initial size (default is 0),
// automatic destruction, access of the current size, array indexing via [],
// deep copy, and resizing. Index range checking is performed unless NO_CHECK is defined.
//#define NO_CHECK
```

Associated Data Holders

```
struct VItem {
    Object element;
    VItem(const Object & m_elem = Object()) : element(m_elem) {}
};
```

The documentation for this class was generated from the following files:

- Vector.h
- Vector.tpp

VoxelData Class Reference

Public Member Functions

VoxelData ()
VoxelData (int mx, int my, int mz)
~VoxelData ()
VoxelData (const VoxelData &rhs)
const VoxelData &operator= (const VoxelData &rhs)

:: for OpenGL z draw order
bool operator< (const VoxelData &rhs)

Public Attributes

int x
int y
int z
float r
float g
float b

Detailed Description

Basic voxel data that's returned to OpenGL for display.

Constructor & Destructor Documentation

```
VoxelData::VoxelData () [inline]
{}

VoxelData::VoxelData (int mx, int my, int mz) [inline]
: x(mx), y(my), z(mz) {}

VoxelData::~VoxelData ()
{}

VoxelData::VoxelData (const VoxelData &rhs)
  : x(rhs.x), y(rhs.y), z(rhs.z)
{
    r = rhs.r;
    g = rhs.g;
    b = rhs.b;
}
```

Member Function Documentation

```
// for OpenGL z draw order
bool VoxelData::operator<(const VoxelData &rhs)
{
   if (this != &rhs) {
      return (z < rhs.z);
   }
   return false;   // equal
}

const VoxelData& VoxelData::operator= (const VoxelData &rhs)
{
   if (this != &rhs) { // standard alias test
       x = rhs.x; y = rhs.y; z = rhs.z;
       r = rhs.r; g = rhs.g; b = rhs.b;
   }
   return *this;
}
```

The documentation for this class was generated from the following files:
- VoxelData.h
- VoxelData.cpp

Independent Modules

Global.h File Reference

Variables

static const unsigned int CONSERVATIVE_OV1 = 0x01
static const unsigned int CONSERVATIVE_OV3 = 0x02
static const unsigned int THIN_OV3 = 0x04

:: "and" bits for OV3 cases as a category
static const unsigned int OV3_MASK = 0x06

static const unsigned int CONSERVATIVE_MASK = 0x03

:: octree depth constant: ranges from level 2 to level 9
const int g_terminal

const int g_false_pos_level

:: rasterization type, as above (see Global.cpp)
const unsigned int g_raster

:: assume 1 level aa; eventually this can specify num levels
const bool g_antialias

const bool g_check_false_pos
const int g_false_pos_candidate_count

Detailed Description

Global variables, including initialization
of static variables in ContextWorker.

Global.cpp File Reference

#include "Global.h"
#include "ContextWorker.h"

Variables

```
:: rasterization type
:: g_raster can be set to:
:: CONSERVATIVE_OV1 (26-sep VoxelPipe) Good
:: CONSERVATIVE_OV3 (26-sep Schwarz & Seidel) Excellent
:: THIN_OV3                  (6-sep  Project V) Excellent
const unsigned int g_raster = THIN_OV3

:: assume 1 level aa; eventually this can specify num levels
const bool g_antialias = false

:: octree depth constant: ranges from level 2 to level 9
const int g_terminal = 9

const bool g_check_false_pos = true
const int g_false_pos_candidate_count = 2
const int g_false_pos_level = 10

:: this goes with each OctreeWorker instantiation
int ContextWorker::count = 0;
Vector<Context *> ContextWorker::instance;
```

Hardware.h File Reference

Data Holders

struct DevicePack

Variables

const int MAX_COURSE

:: Level constants (for diagnostic display)
const int LEVEL_SHOW
const int LEVEL_SKIP
const int skipper []
const int LEVEL_BAND

:: interleave
static const int T_ALPHA = 0
static const int T_BETA = 1
static const int T_ALPHABETA = 2

Detailed Description

Constants and utility routines for emulating
the actual volumetric display device hardware constraints.

Data Holder Definitions

```
struct DevicePack {
    int Nt;              // = (int)lroundf(powf(2.0, (float)g_terminal));
    int spindle_diam;    // = Nt / 16;        // spindle ratio
    int max_level;       // = (Nt - spindle_diam) / MAX_COURSE;
    int helical_index;   // = DEGREES_360 / max_level;
    int total_levels;    // = max_level * MAX_COURSE;
};
```

Hardware.cpp File Reference

#include "Hardware.h"

Variables

:: Constants and utility routines for emulating
:: the actual volumetric display device hardware constraints.
const int MAX_COURSE = 4

:: Level constants (for diagnostic display)
const int LEVEL_SHOW = 1
const int LEVEL_SKIP = 0
const int skipper [] = {1,1,1,1}
const int LEVEL_BAND = LEVEL_SHOW + LEVEL_SKIP

```
// int skipper[] = {1,7,1,1};
// diagnostic slicer (to see into model)
// displays 4, skips 6, with 2 at start and 2 at end
// 01      7111      7111      71
// .............................. (terminates)
// ||xxxxxx||||xxxxxx||||xxxxxx||
// 012345678901234567890123456789
// 4/10 of levels are queued (LEVEL_SHOW / LEVEL_BAND)
```

```
#ifdef DIAGNOSTIC_DISPLAY
const int LEVEL_SHOW = 4;
const int LEVEL_SKIP = 6;
const int skipper[] = {1,7,1,1};
#else
const int LEVEL_SHOW = 1;
const int LEVEL_SKIP = 0;
const int skipper[] = {1,1,1,1};              // default counter
#endif
```

NodeGroup.h File Reference

#include <cstddef>
#include "Triangle.h"
#include "IDWorker.h"

Data Holders

:: initialize the array to -1, since some voxels will have no overlap.
struct VSpan

struct TGPair
struct TGList
struct SpanList

:: can be a wrapper for any simulation data
struct NodeData

:: initialize the array to -1, since some voxels will have no overlap.
struct TSpan

struct VTPair

:: for sorting, want to put VTPairs in a Vector, then
:: reference vox_id directly in the sort routine.
:: Alternately, can reference list[i] below.
struct VTList

:: NodeGroup structure and supporting structure declarations.
struct NodeGroup

:: will go out of scope when Vector goes out of scope
struct NodeGroupList

Variables

static const int OCTANTS = 8
static const int INVALID = -1

Data Holder Definitions

```
// initialize the array to -1, since some voxels will have no overlap.
// similar to TSpan except for spans of voxels instead of triangles.
struct VSpan {
    int begin;    // many overlap possibilities
```

```
    int end;
};

// Triangle/GlassnerID pair
struct TGPair {
    int tri_idx;                // instead of Triangle *
   Glassner vox_idx;        // unique GlassnerID of voxel
};

// serves same purpose as VTList but for scanned voxels
struct TGList {
    int count;
    TGPair** list;
};

// VSpan referenced by tri_idx: mirrors TriangleList
// sorted by tri_idx, can have gaps in triangle sequence
// (relative to TriangleList indices).
struct SpanList {
    int count;
    VSpan** list;
};

// can be a wrapper for any simulation data
struct NodeData {
    ushort3 coord;
    uchar3 color;
};

// initialize the array to -1, since some voxels will have no overlap.
struct TSpan {
      int begin;     // many overlap possibilities
      int end;
};

struct VTPair {
      unsigned short vox_idx;     // voxel index, 0 - 7, reference from zero
      int tri_idx;                        // instead of Triangle *
};

// for sorting, want to put VTPairs in a Vector, then
// reference vox_id directly in the sort routine.
// Alternately, can reference list[i] below.

struct VTList {
      int count;
      VTPair **list;
};
```

```
// NodeGroup structure and supporting structure declarations.

// The NodeGroup keeps track of octants which contain some portion
// of the triangle geometry.
// There are eight octants (not all active) to a NodeGroup.

struct NodeGroup {
    NodeData node[OCTANTS];
    TSpan span[OCTANTS];
    NodeGroup *parent;           // NULL for root
    unsigned char node_idx;      // index of parent NodeData (1 - 8): 0 for root
    unsigned char geom_stat;     // overlap for nodes 1 - 8 (bit positions 0 - 7)
    unsigned char shadow_stat;   // copy of geom_stat to determine fp in 6sep
    bool geom_status;            // coarse overlap test status: only used for 6sep
    Glassner ID;                 // parent Glassner ID; make into child IDs on the fly
    VTList * pairs;

    // force parent info to be provided
    NodeGroup(NodeGroup *pnode, unsigned char pidx, Glassner mID)
         : parent(pnode), node_idx(pidx), ID(mID) {
        pairs = NULL;
        geom_stat = 0;
        geom_status = false;
    }
};

// will go out of scope when Vector goes out of scope

// Don't delete NodeGroups -- will do this in GroupWorker destructor

struct NodeGroupList {
    unsigned short count;    // number of NodeGroups
    // "count" NodeGroup pointers follow
    NodeGroup **list;
    ~NodeGroupList() {
        if (list != NULL)
            delete [] list;
    }
};
```

ReducedRay.h File Reference

Data Holders

:: Compact data structure for returning voxels on a ray
:: back to OpenGL for display. (See RayWorker.)
struct ReducedRay

Variables

static const unsigned char IN_BIT = 0x80

Data Holder Definitions

```
// Compact data structure for returning voxels on a ray\n
// back to OpenGL for display. (See RayWorker.)
struct ReducedRay {
    float3 base_origin, base_direction;
    // accumulated level; (level % max_level) * helical_index
    // + (angle = 0) determines helical offset, where max_level
    // and helical index are known.
    short level, angle, interleave;
    short count;  // bytes
    unsigned char *list;
};
```

Triangle.h File Reference

#include "vector_type.h"

Data Holders

struct color3
struct BasicTriangle

:: The indices are swizzles for (u,v) pairs per triangle dominant axis.
struct FineVars

:: uses same names as voxel-pipe
struct Triangle

:: variable-length record
struct TriangleList

Detailed Description

Triangle structures and a triangle-list structure for heap allocation.

Data Holder Definitions

```
// Triangle structures and a triangle-list structure for heap allocation.

struct color3 {
      float r, g, b;
};

struct BasicTriangle {
    float3 vert[3];
    color3 color;
};

// The indices are swizzles for (u,v) pairs per triangle dominant axis
struct FineVars {
    // master fields
   float4 plane_eq;

   // level fields
   float3 a[3];
   float3 n_delta_u[3], n_delta_v[3];
   float2 c0[3], c1[3], c2[3];         // xformed
   float2 h0[3], h1[3], h2[3];         // halo from xformed
```

```
    float3 cw[3];
    unsigned char planebits;        // valid halo planes
};

// uses same names as voxel-pipe
struct Triangle {
    // master fields
    float3 v0, v1, v2;
    float3 edge0, edge1, edge2;
    float3 n;
    float3 master_bbox0, master_bbox1;
    color3 color;
    int axis;    // dominant axis (based on normal n)

    // level fields
    int3 bbox0i, bbox1i;
    float3 bbox0, bbox1;
    float3 big_center, little_center;
    float big_radius, little_radius;

    // for plane test...
    float r1, r2;
    float d;
    // for fine test....
    FineVars fine;
};

// variable-length record
struct TriangleList {
    unsigned short status;
    int count;    // number of triangles
    // "count" Triangle pointers follow
    Triangle **list;
};
```

utils.h File Reference

```
#include <math.h>
#include "vector_type.h"
```

Data Holder Definitions

```
// Highly massaged NVidia geometry template code,
// massaged from GPU C++ to straight C++.

typedef unsigned char uint8;
typedef char int8;
typedef unsigned short uint16;
typedef short int16;
typedef unsigned int uint32;
typedef int int32;
typedef unsigned long long uint64;
typedef long long int64;

template <typename Out, typename In>
union BinaryCast
{
    In in;
    Out out;
};

template <typename Out, typename In>
Out binary_cast(const In in)
{
BinaryCast<Out,In> inout;
inout.in = in;
return inout.out;
}

#define make_ushort3(x,y,z) ushort3(x,y,z)
#define make_int3(x,y,z) int3(x,y,z)
#define make_int4(x,y,z,w) int4(x,y,z,w)
#define make_float2(x,y) float2(x,y)
#define make_float3(x,y,z) float3(x,y,z)
#define make_float4(x,y,z,w) float4(x,y,z,w)

template <int32 log_N_TILES> struct tile_id_selector { typedef uint32 type; };
template <> struct tile_id_selector<2> { typedef uint8 type; };
template <> struct tile_id_selector<3> { typedef uint16 type; };
template <> struct tile_id_selector<4> { typedef uint16 type; };
```

```
enum XYZ
{
    X = 0,
    Y = 1,
    Z = 2
};


/// templated over an arbitrary Vector type
template <typename Vec> struct base_type {};

template <> struct base_type<float2> { typedef float value_type; };
template <> struct base_type<float3> { typedef float value_type; };
template <> struct base_type<float4> { typedef float value_type; };
template <> struct base_type<int2> { typedef int value_type; };
template <> struct base_type<int3> { typedef int value_type; };
template <> struct base_type<int4> { typedef int value_type; };
template <> struct base_type<ushort3> { typedef unsigned short value_type; };

template <int32 axis>
struct xyz {};

template <>
struct xyz<0>
{
    template <typename Vec>  static typename base_type<Vec>::value_type x(const Vec a) { return a.x; }
    template <typename Vec>  static typename base_type<Vec>::value_type y(const Vec a) { return a.y; }
    template <typename Vec>  static typename base_type<Vec>::value_type z(const Vec a) { return a.z; }
    template <typename Vec>  static typename base_type<Vec>::value_type rx(const Vec a) { return a.x; }
    template <typename Vec>  static typename base_type<Vec>::value_type ry(const Vec a) { return a.y; }
    template <typename Vec>  static typename base_type<Vec>::value_type rz(const Vec a) { return a.z; }
};

template <>
struct xyz<1>
{
    template <typename Vec>  static typename base_type<Vec>::value_type x(const Vec a) { return a.y; }
    template <typename Vec>  static typename base_type<Vec>::value_type y(const Vec a) { return a.z; }
    template <typename Vec>  static typename base_type<Vec>::value_type z(const Vec a) { return a.x; }
    template <typename Vec>  static typename base_type<Vec>::value_type rx(const Vec a) { return a.z; }
    template <typename Vec>  static typename base_type<Vec>::value_type ry(const Vec a) { return a.x; }
    template <typename Vec>  static typename base_type<Vec>::value_type rz(const Vec a) { return a.y; }
};

template <>
struct xyz<2>
{
    template <typename Vec>  static typename base_type<Vec>::value_type x(const Vec a) { return a.z; }
    template <typename Vec>  static typename base_type<Vec>::value_type y(const Vec a) { return a.x; }
```

```
    template <typename Vec>  static typename base_type<Vec>::value_type z(const Vec a) { return a.y; }
    template <typename Vec>  static typename base_type<Vec>::value_type rx(const Vec a) { return a.y; }
    template <typename Vec>  static typename base_type<Vec>::value_type ry(const Vec a) { return a.z; }
    template <typename Vec>  static typename base_type<Vec>::value_type rz(const Vec a) { return a.x; }
};

template <int32 axis>
struct uvw {};

template <>
struct uvw<0>
{
    static const int32 U = 1;
    static const int32 V = 2;
    static const int32 W = 0;

    template <typename Vec>  static typename base_type<Vec>::value_type u(const Vec a) { return a.y; }
    template <typename Vec>  static typename base_type<Vec>::value_type v(const Vec a) { return a.z; }
    template <typename Vec>  static typename base_type<Vec>::value_type w(const Vec a) { return a.x; }
    template <typename Vec>  static typename base_type<Vec>::value_type x(const Vec a) { return a.z; }
    template <typename Vec>  static typename base_type<Vec>::value_type y(const Vec a) { return a.x; }
    template <typename Vec>  static typename base_type<Vec>::value_type z(const Vec a) { return a.y; }

    static int32 u_stride(const int32 T) { return T; }
    static int32 v_stride(const int32 T) { return T*T; }
    static int32 w_stride(const int32 T) { return 1; }

    static float ccw(const float3 n) { return n.x > 0.0f ? 1.0f : -1.0f; }
};

template <>
struct uvw<1>
{
    static const int32 U = 0;
    static const int32 V = 2;
    static const int32 W = 1;

    template <typename Vec>  static typename base_type<Vec>::value_type u(const Vec a) { return a.x; }
    template <typename Vec>  static typename base_type<Vec>::value_type v(const Vec a) { return a.z; }
    template <typename Vec>  static typename base_type<Vec>::value_type w(const Vec a) { return a.y; }
    template <typename Vec>  static typename base_type<Vec>::value_type x(const Vec a) { return a.x; }
    template <typename Vec>  static typename base_type<Vec>::value_type y(const Vec a) { return a.z; }
    template <typename Vec>  static typename base_type<Vec>::value_type z(const Vec a) { return a.y; }

    static int32 u_stride(const int32 T) { return 1; }
    static int32 v_stride(const int32 T) { return T*T; }
    static int32 w_stride(const int32 T) { return T; }

    static float ccw(const float3 n) { return n.y < 0.0f ? 1.0f : -1.0f; }
```

```
};

template <>
struct uvw<2>
{
    static const int32 U = 0;
    static const int32 V = 1;
    static const int32 W = 2;

    template <typename Vec>  static typename base_type<Vec>::value_type u(const Vec a) { return a.x; }
    template <typename Vec>  static typename base_type<Vec>::value_type v(const Vec a) { return a.y; }
    template <typename Vec>  static typename base_type<Vec>::value_type w(const Vec a) { return a.z; }
    template <typename Vec>  static typename base_type<Vec>::value_type x(const Vec a) { return a.x; }
    template <typename Vec>  static typename base_type<Vec>::value_type y(const Vec a) { return a.y; }
    template <typename Vec>  static typename base_type<Vec>::value_type z(const Vec a) { return a.z; }

    static int32 u_stride(const int32 T) { return 1; }
    static int32 v_stride(const int32 T) { return T; }
    static int32 w_stride(const int32 T) { return T*T; }

    static float ccw(const float3 n) { return n.z > 0.0f ? 1.0f : -1.0f; }
};

/// "put" templates

template <int32 axis>
struct uvw_p {};

template <>
struct uvw_p<0>
{
    static const int32 U = 1;
    static const int32 V = 2;
    static const int32 W = 0;

    template <typename Vec> static void u(Vec &a,
            typename base_type<Vec>::value_type val) { a.y = val; }
    template <typename Vec> static void v(Vec &a,
            typename base_type<Vec>::value_type val) { a.z = val; }
    template <typename Vec> static void w(Vec &a,
            typename base_type<Vec>::value_type val) { a.x = val; }
};

template <>
struct uvw_p<1>
{
    static const int32 U = 0;
    static const int32 V = 2;
    static const int32 W = 1;
```

```
    template <typename Vec> static void u(Vec &a,
            typename base_type<Vec>::value_type val) { a.x = val; }
    template <typename Vec> static void v(Vec &a,
            typename base_type<Vec>::value_type val) { a.z = val; }
    template <typename Vec> static void w(Vec &a,
            typename base_type<Vec>::value_type val) { a.y = val; }
};

template <>
struct uvw_p<2>
{
    static const int32 U = 0;
    static const int32 V = 1;
    static const int32 W = 2;

    template <typename Vec> static void u(Vec &a,
            typename base_type<Vec>::value_type val) { a.x = val; }
    template <typename Vec> static void v(Vec &a,
            typename base_type<Vec>::value_type val) { a.y = val; }
    template <typename Vec> static void w(Vec &a,
            typename base_type<Vec>::value_type val) { a.z = val; }
};

template <int32 AXIS>  float3 swap_coords(const float3 a) {
    return make_float3( uvw<AXIS>::u( a ), uvw<AXIS>::v( a ), uvw<AXIS>::w( a ) );
}
template <int32 AXIS>  float4 swap_coords(const float4 a) {
    return make_float4( uvw<AXIS>::u( a ), uvw<AXIS>::v( a ), uvw<AXIS>::w( a ), a.w );
}
template <int32 AXIS>  int3 swap_coords(const int3 a) {
    return make_int3( uvw<AXIS>::u( a ), uvw<AXIS>::v( a ), uvw<AXIS>::w( a ) );
}
template <int32 AXIS>  int4 swap_coords(const int4 a) {
    return make_int4( uvw<AXIS>::u( a ), uvw<AXIS>::v( a ), uvw<AXIS>::w( a ), a.w );
}
```

vector_type.h File Reference

// NVidia vector types to support utils.h.
// vector_type.h and utils.h are public domain per agreement that follows.

```
struct  char1
{
signed char x;
};
struct  uchar1
{
unsigned char x;
};
struct   char2
{
signed char x, y;
};
struct   uchar2
{
unsigned char x, y;
};
struct  char3
{
signed char x, y, z;
};
struct  uchar3
{
unsigned char x, y, z;
};
struct   char4
{
signed char x, y, z, w;
};
struct   uchar4
{
unsigned char x, y, z, w;
};
struct  short1
{
short x;
};
struct  ushort1
{
unsigned short x;
};
struct   short2
```

```
{
short x, y;
};
struct  ushort2
{
unsigned short x, y;
};
struct  short3
{
short x, y, z;
};
struct  ushort3
{
    ushort3(){}
    ushort3(int mx, int my, int mz) : x(mx), y(my), z(mz) {}
    unsigned short x, y, z;
};
struct short4
{
short x, y, z, w;
};
struct ushort4
{
unsigned short x, y, z, w;
};
struct  int1
{
int x;
};
struct  uint1
{
unsigned int x;
};
struct int2
{
int x, y;
};
struct uint2
{
unsigned int x, y;
};
struct  int3
{
    int3(){}
    int3(int mx, int my, int mz) : x(mx), y(my), z(mz) {}
    int x, y, z;
};
struct  uint3
{
```

```
unsigned int x, y, z;
};
struct  int4
{
    int4(){}
    int4(int mx, int my, int mz, int mw) : x(mx), y(my), z(mz), w(mw) {}
    int x, y, z, w;
};
struct  uint4
{
unsigned int x, y, z, w;
};
struct  long1
{
long int x;
};
struct  ulong1
{
unsigned long x;
};
struct long2
{
long int x, y;
};
struct ulong2
{
unsigned long int x, y;
};
struct  long3
{
long int x, y, z;
};
struct  ulong3
{
unsigned long int x, y, z;
};
struct  long4
{
long int x, y, z, w;
};
struct  ulong4
{
unsigned long int x, y, z, w;
};
struct  float1
{
float x;
};
struct float2
```

```
{
    float2(){}
    float2(float mx, float my) : x(mx), y(my) {}
    float x, y;
};
struct  float3
{
    float3(){}
    float3(float mx, float my, float mz) : x(mx), y(my), z(mz) {}
    float x, y, z;
};

struct uvw_float3
{
    uvw_float3(){}
    uvw_float3(float mu, float mv, float mw) : u(mu), v(mv), w(mw) {}
    float u, v, w;
};

struct float4
{
    float4(){}
    float4(float mx, float my, float mz, float mw) : x(mx), y(my), z(mz), w(mw) {}
    float x, y, z, w;
};
struct  longlong1
{
long long int x;
};
struct  ulonglong1
{
unsigned long long int x;
};
struct  longlong2
{
long long int x, y;
};
struct  ulonglong2
{
unsigned long long int x, y;
};
struct  longlong3
{
long long int x, y, z;
};
struct  ulonglong3
{
unsigned long long int x, y, z;
};
```

```
struct  longlong4
{
long long int x, y, z ,w;
};
struct  ulonglong4
{
unsigned long long int x, y, z, w;
};
struct  double1
{
double x;
};
struct  double2
{
double x, y;
};
struct  double3
{
double x, y, z;
};
struct  double4
{
double x, y, z, w;
};

/*******************************************************************************
* *
* * identifiers
* *
*******************************************************************************/
typedef  struct char1 char1;
typedef  struct uchar1 uchar1;
typedef  struct char2 char2;
typedef  struct uchar2 uchar2;
typedef  struct char3 char3;
typedef  struct uchar3 uchar3;
typedef  struct char4 char4;
typedef  struct uchar4 uchar4;
typedef  struct short1 short1;
typedef  struct ushort1 ushort1;
typedef  struct short2 short2;
typedef  struct ushort2 ushort2;
typedef  struct short3 short3;
typedef  struct ushort3 ushort3;
typedef  struct short4 short4;
typedef  struct ushort4 ushort4;
typedef  struct int1 int1;
typedef  struct uint1 uint1;
typedef  struct int2 int2;
```

```
typedef  struct uint2 uint2;
typedef  struct int3 int3;
typedef  struct uint3 uint3;
typedef  struct int4 int4;
typedef  struct uint4 uint4;
typedef  struct long1 long1;
typedef  struct ulong1 ulong1;
typedef  struct long2 long2;
typedef  struct ulong2 ulong2;
typedef  struct long3 long3;
typedef  struct ulong3 ulong3;
typedef  struct long4 long4;
typedef  struct ulong4 ulong4;
typedef  struct float1 float1;
typedef  struct float2 float2;
typedef  struct float3 float3;
typedef  struct float4 float4;
typedef  struct longlong1 longlong1;
typedef  struct ulonglong1 ulonglong1;
typedef  struct longlong2 longlong2;
typedef  struct ulonglong2 ulonglong2;
typedef  struct longlong3 longlong3;
typedef  struct ulonglong3 ulonglong3;
typedef  struct longlong4 longlong4;
typedef  struct ulonglong4 ulonglong4;
typedef  struct double1 double1;
typedef  struct double2 double2;
typedef  struct double3 double3;
typedef  struct double4 double4;
```

NVIDIA License Agreement

(for utils.h and vector_type.h)

Exception Classes

Except.h File Reference

#include <typeinfo>
#include <string>
#include <stdexcept>

Classes

class DSException
class RayException
class LevelException
class GraphException
class NullPointerException
class IndexOutOfBoundsException
class ArrayIndexOutOfBoundsException
class StringIndexOutOfBoundsException
class UnderflowException
class OverflowException
class ItemNotFoundException
class DuplicateItemException
class IteratorException
class IteratorOutOfBoundsException
class IteratorUninitializedException
class IteratorMismatchException
class BadArgumentException

Variables

static const int ADD = 0
static const int DESCEND = 1
static const int ASCEND = 2
static const int RETRIEVE = 3
static const int OPERATOR = 4
static const int ITER_DESCEND = 5
static const int ITER_ASCEND = 6
static const int EX_NULL = 0
static const int EX_ROOT = 1
static const int EX_PARENT = 2
static const int EX_CHILD = 3
static const int EX_PHASE = 4

Detailed Description

Simple exception classes.

Class Definitions

```
//
class DSException
{
  public:
    DSException( const string & msg = "" ) : message( msg )
      { }
    virtual ~DSException( )
     { }
    virtual string toString( ) const
#ifndef NO_RTTI
      { return "Exception " + string( typeid( *this ).name( ) ) + ": " + what( ); }
#else
      { return "Exception " + string( ": " ) + what( ); }
#endif
    virtual string what( ) const
      { return message; }

  private:
    string message;
};

//
class RayException : public DSException
{
public:
     RayException(const string & msg = "") : DSException( msg )
     {}
};

//
class LevelException : public DSException
{
public:
     LevelException(const string & msg = "") : DSException( msg )
     {}
};

//
class GraphException : public DSException
{
  public:
    GraphException( const string & msg = "" ) : DSException( msg )
      { }
};
```

```
//
class NullPointerException : public DSException
{
  public:
    NullPointerException( const string & msg = "" ) : DSException( msg )
      { }
};

//
class IndexOutOfBoundsException : public DSException
{
  public:
    IndexOutOfBoundsException( const string & msg = "" ) : DSException( msg )
      { }
    IndexOutOfBoundsException( int idx, int sz, const string & msg = "" )
      : DSException( msg ), index( idx ), size( sz ) { }

    int getIndex( ) const
      { return index; }
    int getSize( ) const
      { return size; }

  private:
    int index;
    int size;
};

//
class ArrayIndexOutOfBoundsException : public IndexOutOfBoundsException
{
  public:
    ArrayIndexOutOfBoundsException( const string & msg = "" )
      : IndexOutOfBoundsException ( msg ) { }
    ArrayIndexOutOfBoundsException( int idx, int sz, const string & msg = "" )
      : IndexOutOfBoundsException( idx, sz, msg ) { }
};

//
class StringIndexOutOfBoundsException : public IndexOutOfBoundsException
{
  public:
    StringIndexOutOfBoundsException( const string & msg = "" )
      : IndexOutOfBoundsException ( msg ) { }
    StringIndexOutOfBoundsException( int idx, int sz, const string & msg = "" )
      : IndexOutOfBoundsException( idx, sz, msg ) { }
};

//
class UnderflowException : public DSException
```

```
{
  public:
    UnderflowException( const string & msg = "" ) : DSException( msg )
      { }
};

//
class OverflowException : public DSException
{
  public:
    OverflowException( const string & msg = "" ) : DSException( msg )
      { }
};

//
class ItemNotFoundException : public DSException
{
  public:
    ItemNotFoundException( const string & msg = "" ) : DSException( msg )
      { }
};

//
class DuplicateItemException : public DSException
{
  public:
    DuplicateItemException( const string & msg = "" ) : DSException( msg )
      { }
};

//
class IteratorException : public DSException
{
  public:
    IteratorException( const string & msg = "" ) : DSException( msg )
      { }
};

//
class IteratorOutOfBoundsException : public IteratorException
{
  public:
    IteratorOutOfBoundsException( const string & msg = "" ) : IteratorException( msg )
      { }
};

//
class IteratorUninitializedException : public IteratorException
{
```

```
  public:
    IteratorUninitializedException( const string & msg = "" ) : IteratorException( msg )
      { }
};

//
class IteratorMismatchException : public IteratorException
{
  public:
    IteratorMismatchException( const string & msg = "" ) : IteratorException( msg )
      { }
};

//
class BadArgumentException : public DSException
{
  public:
    BadArgumentException( const string & msg = "" ) : DSException( msg )
      { }
};
```

Main.cpp and Compiler Settings

main.cpp File Reference

```
#include "glew.h"
#include <GL/freeglut.h>
#include "glApplication.h"
#include "GLWorker.h"
#include <iostream>
```

Classes

class myApplication

Functions

:: GLWorker and voxel application entry point.
int main (void)

Variables

:: The easiest way to make the queue global.... extern it where used.
OctreeThread my_stat_thread

Function Documentation

```
// GLWorker and voxel application entry point.
int main (void)
{
    myApplication*  pApp =  new   myApplication;
    GLWorker* myWin =  new   GLWorker();

    pApp->run();
    delete  pApp;
    return  0;
}
```

Compiler Settings

Eclipse: Paths and Symbols

```
GNU C
/usr/lib/gcc/x86_64-redhat-linux/4.6.0/include
/usr/local/include
/usr/include

GNU C++
/usr/include/c++/4.6.0
/usr/include/c++/4.6.0/x86_64-redhat-linux
/usr/include/c++/4.6.0/backward
/usr/lib/gcc/x86_64-redhat-linux/4.6.0/include
/usr/local/include
/usr/include

Settings
GCC C++ compiler
-O0 -g3 -Wall -c -fmessage-length=0 -std=c++0x

GCC C compiler
-O0 -g3 -Wall -c -fmessage-length=0

GCC C++ Linker
g++ -lm -lGL -lGLU -lglut -lpthread
```

Besides the std library Project V uses the math, GL, and thread libraries.

Index

2

A

B

C

D

E

F

G

H

I

K

L

M

N

O

P

R

S

T

U

V

W

Made in the USA
Monee, IL
05 November 2026

67858275R20286